# THE MANUSCRIPT JOURNAL OF THE REVEREND CHARLES WESLEY, M.A.

## VOLUME II

EDITED BY

*S T Kimbrough, Jr.*
*and*
*Kenneth G. C. Newport*

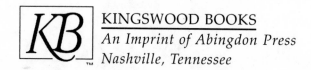
KINGSWOOD BOOKS
*An Imprint of Abingdon Press*
*Nashville, Tennessee*

THE MANUSCRIPT JOURNAL OF THE REVEREND CHARLES WESLEY, M.A.
VOLUME II

*Copyright © 2007 by Abingdon Press*

*This book is printed on acid-free paper.*

**Library of Congress Cataloging-in-Publication Data**

Wesley, Charles, 1707-1788.
  The manuscript journal of the Rev. Charles Wesley, M.A. / edited by S. T. Kimbrough, Jr. and Kenneth G. C. Newport.
    p. cm.
  ISBN 978-0-687-64604-3 (v. 1 : pbk.)—ISBN 978-0-687-64614-2 (v. 2 : pbk.)
  1. Wesley, Charles, 1707-1788—Diaries. 2. Wesley, Charles, 1707-1788—Manuscripts. 3. England—Social life and customs—18th century. 4. Oxford (England)—Social life and customs. 5. Methodist Church—Clergy—Diaries. 6. Clergy—England—Diaries. I. Kimbrough, S. T., 1936– II. Newport, Kenneth G. C. III. Title.

  BX8495.W4A34 2007
  287.092—dc22
  [B]
                                                                      2007028665

The Graeca® font used to print this work is available from Linguist's Software, Inc., PO Box 580, Edmonds, WA 98020-0580 tel (206) 775-1130.

Scripture quotations are from the King James or Authorized Version of the Bible.

08 09 10 11 12 13 14 15 16 17—10 9 8 7 6 5 4 3 2 1
MANUFACTURED IN THE UNITED STATES OF AMERICA

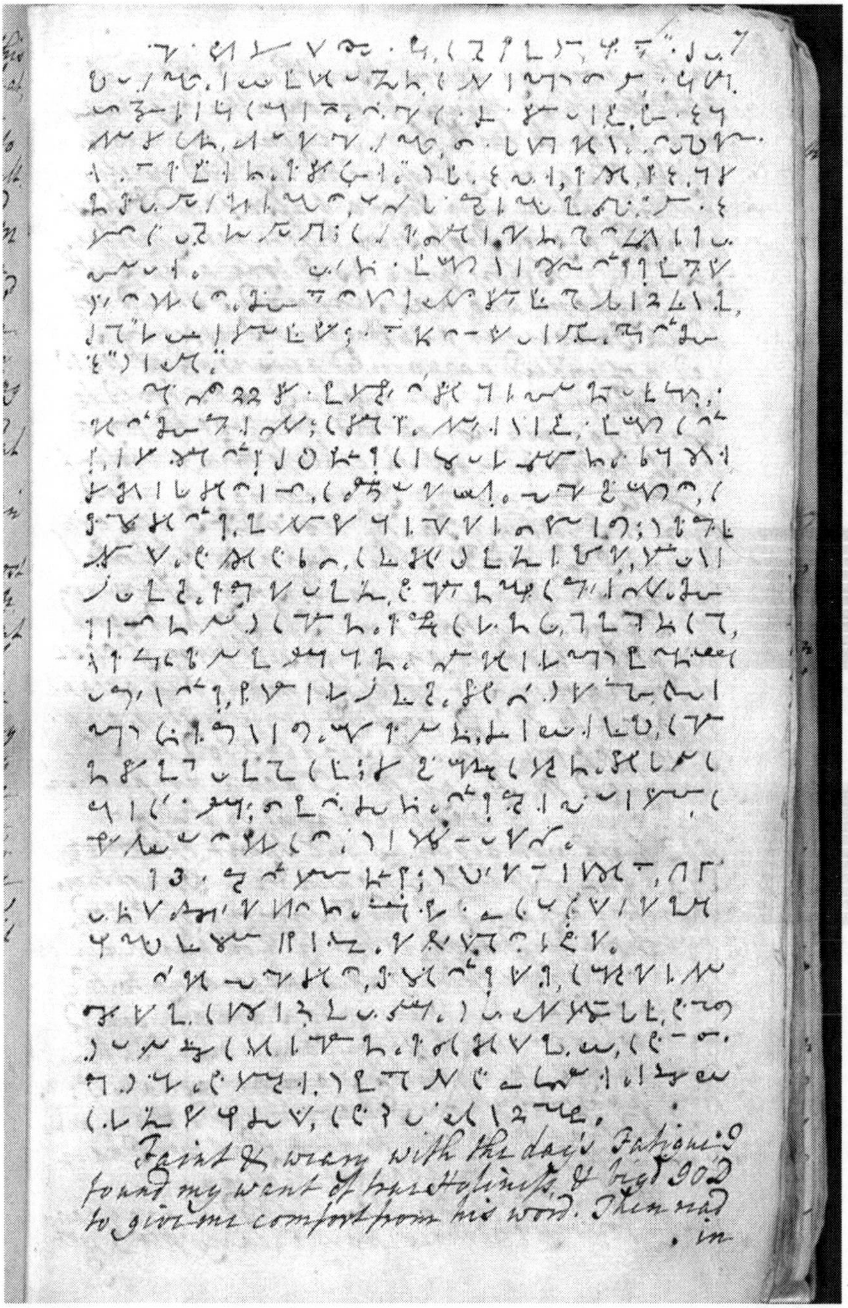
7

Faint & weary with the day's [illegible] I
found my want of [illegible], & begd God
to give me comfort from his word. Then read
in

Reproduced by courtesy of the University Librarian and Director, The John Rylands University Library, The University of Manchester.

# CHARLES WESLEY SOCIETY SERIES

The Manuscript Journal of the
Reverend Charles Wesley, M.A., Volume I

The Manuscript Journal of the
Reverend Charles Wesley, M.A., Volume II

The Journal Letters of the
Reverend Charles Wesley, M.A.

The Letters of the
Reverend Charles Wesley, M.A.

# CONTENTS

Abbreviations . . . . . . . . . . . . . . . . . . . . . . . . . . . . . . . . . . . . . . . . . . . . . . ix

Extract of Journal  . . . . . . . . . . . . . . . . . . . . . . . . . . . . . . . . . . . . . . . 337

    1743  . . . . . . . . . . . . . . . . . . . . . . . . . . . . . . . . . . . . . . . . . . . . . . 337
    1744  . . . . . . . . . . . . . . . . . . . . . . . . . . . . . . . . . . . . . . . . . . . . . . 381
    1745  . . . . . . . . . . . . . . . . . . . . . . . . . . . . . . . . . . . . . . . . . . . . . . 432
    1746  . . . . . . . . . . . . . . . . . . . . . . . . . . . . . . . . . . . . . . . . . . . . . . 453
    1747  . . . . . . . . . . . . . . . . . . . . . . . . . . . . . . . . . . . . . . . . . . . . . . 485
    1748  . . . . . . . . . . . . . . . . . . . . . . . . . . . . . . . . . . . . . . . . . . . . . . 516
    1749  . . . . . . . . . . . . . . . . . . . . . . . . . . . . . . . . . . . . . . . . . . . . . . 564
    1750  . . . . . . . . . . . . . . . . . . . . . . . . . . . . . . . . . . . . . . . . . . . . . . 587
    1751  . . . . . . . . . . . . . . . . . . . . . . . . . . . . . . . . . . . . . . . . . . . . . . 601
    1756  . . . . . . . . . . . . . . . . . . . . . . . . . . . . . . . . . . . . . . . . . . . . . . 622

Index of Persons  . . . . . . . . . . . . . . . . . . . . . . . . . . . . . . . . . . . . . . . . 651

Index of Places  . . . . . . . . . . . . . . . . . . . . . . . . . . . . . . . . . . . . . . . . . 673

Index of Topics  . . . . . . . . . . . . . . . . . . . . . . . . . . . . . . . . . . . . . . . . . 687

Index of Sermon Texts  . . . . . . . . . . . . . . . . . . . . . . . . . . . . . . . . . . . 693

Index of Scripture References and Allusions  . . . . . . . . . . . . . . . . 705

# ABBREVIATIONS

| | |
|---|---|
| AV | *Holy Bible*, Authorized Version, 1611 ("King James Version"). |
| BCP | Church of England. *Book of Common Prayer*. London, 1662. |
| *CPH* (1737) | John Wesley, ed. *A Collection of Psalms and Hymns*. Charleston: Lewis Timothy, 1737. |
| *CPH* (1738) | John Wesley, ed. *A Collection of Psalms and Hymns*. London: Bowyer for Hutton, 1738. |
| *CPH* (1741) | John Wesley, ed. *A Collection of Psalms and Hymns*. London: Strahan, 1741. |
| *CPH* (1743) | John and Charles Wesley. *A Collection of Psalms and Hymns* (2nd ed. of 1741). London: Strahan, 1743. |
| *Funeral Hymns* (1746) | [Charles Wesley.] *Funeral Hymns*. [London: Strahan, 1746.] |
| *Funeral Hymns* (1759) | [Charles Wesley.] *Funeral Hymns*. London: [Strahan,] 1759. |
| Hoole | Elijah Hoole. *Oglethorpe and the Wesleys in America*. London: R. Needham, 1863. |
| *HSP* (1739) | John and Charles Wesley. *Hymns and Sacred Poems*. London: Strahan, 1739. |

| | |
|---|---|
| *HSP* (1740) | John and Charles Wesley. *Hymns and Sacred Poems*. London: Strahan, 1740. |
| *HSP* (1749) | Charles Wesley. *Hymns and Sacred Poems*. 2 vols. Bristol: Farley, 1749. |
| Jackson | Thomas Jackson, ed. *The Journal of the Rev. Charles Wesley, M.A., . . . to which are Appended Selections from his Correspondence and Poetry*. 2 vols. London: Wesleyan Methodist Book-Room, 1849; reprinted Grand Rapids: Baker Book House, 1980. |
| MARC | The Methodist Archives Research Centre, John Rylands University Library of Manchester, England. |
| MS Journal | Charles Wesley's manuscript journal, bound in one volume, running from March 1736 through November 1756, residing in MARC (ref. DDCW 10/2). |
| *MSP* | John Wesley, ed. *A Collection of Moral and Sacred Poems from the Most Celebrated English Authors*. Bristol: Farley, 1744. |
| *OED* | *The Oxford English Dictionary*. |
| *Poetical Works* | *The Poetical Works of John and Charles Wesley*. Edited by George Osborn. 13 vols. London: Wesleyan-Methodist Conference, 1868–72. |
| *PWHS* | *Proceedings of the Wesley Historical Society*. |
| *Redemption Hymns* | [Charles Wesley.] *Hymns for those that seek, and those that have, Redemption in the Blood of Jesus Christ*. London: Strahan, 1747. |

Sermons

*The Sermons of Charles Wesley: A Critical Edition with Introduction and Notes.* Edited by Kenneth G. C. Newport. Oxford: Oxford University Press, 2001.

Telford

John Telford, ed. *The Journal of the Rev. Charles Wesley, M.A., sometime student of Christ Church, Oxford.* Vol. 1: *The Early Journal, 1736–39.* London: Robert Cully, 1910; reprinted Taylors, SC: Methodist Reprint Society, 1977.

Works

*The Works of John Wesley;* begun as "The Oxford Edition of The Works of John Wesley" (Oxford: Clarendon Press, 1975–1983); continued as "The Bicentennial Edition of The Works of John Wesley" (Nashville: Abingdon, 1984–); 16 of 35 vols. published to date.

# EXTRACT OF JOURNAL

## JANUARY 1743[1]

*Sunday, January 2.* I rode to Bexley, and discoursed in the church from Luke 1[:68], "Blessed be the Lord God of Israel, for he hath visited and redeemed his people." God gave me to speak in mild love, and some of the most rebellious began to melt into conviction.

Returned to town and expounded the barren fig tree [Luke 13:6-9] at the Foundery. Their hearts were bowed as the heart of one man.

*Monday, January 3.* Preached at Brentford, and stirred up the little Society to "look unto Jesus, the Author and Finisher of their faith" [Heb. 12:2]. A young man came and fell down very innocently on his knees to ask my blessing, because, he said, I was his spiritual Father, faith having come by hearing me one of the last times I preached here.

Rode on to Eton,[2] where I exhorted a few sincere souls to bear their Savior's cross and suffer patiently for his sake.

*Wednesday evening, January 5.* Came with George Baddiley[3] to Bristol.

---

1. The MS Journal skips the last three months of 1741 and all of 1742. There is only one journal letter (September 23–October 2, 1742) and a few other letters to help fill in this void. Several factors likely contributed to this lacuna. Significant time in early 1742 would have been devoted to preparing the sermon he preached on April 4 at Oxford ("Awake Thou that Sleepest," in *Sermons*, 211–24). Then, in June 1742, Charles suffered the death of his close friend Robert Jones, and worked through his grief by composing an extended elegy. On July 30, 1742, he lost his mother Susanna as well. Finally, it appears that while Charles continued to minister in several settings through this year, he was struggling with a debilitating health condition, as he resorted to a transcriber for his writing (as noted in his September 23, 1742, journal letter).

2. Charles spells "Eaton."

3. Likely the son of Mrs. Baddiley of London mentioned in John Wesley, *Journal* (September 19, 1747), *Works* 20:194.

*Friday, January 7.* Visited sister Edgcomb, triumphing over death and waiting every moment for full redemption.

*Saturday, January 8.* Spoke with one who thinks she has already attained. I think not. The event will show.

Met Susanna Designe's[4] band, with the three Quakers, and an extraordinary presence of God among them.

*Sunday, January 9.* Kept a Love-feast at Kingswood. As soon as we met the Spirit of prayer fell upon us, and we were filled with comfort.

*Tuesday, January 11.* Set out for London at three in the morning and reached it, God being my Helper, the next day.

*Friday, January 14.* Visited the condemned malefactors in Newgate and was locked in by the turnkey, not with them but in the yard. However, I stood upon a bench, and they climbed up to the windows of their cells, so that all could hear my exhortation and prayer.

The Lord was with us at our public intercession, from which I went to visit the sick. Was much refreshed by our dying brother Milbourne, whose whole cry was "Come, Lord Jesus, come quickly" [Rev. 22:20].

At night was comforted with all the Society by an account of our sister Pike's departure in the Lord.

*Saturday, January 15.* Went to Newgate, and was refused admittance. One Townsend thrust me away, though I showed him the sheriff's order. I was let in by another keeper, the only one who has a spark of humanity, and preached through the grates. As before, a Romish priest was there, having free egress and regress. But a clergyman of the Church of England must not hope for the like favors.

*Sunday, January 16.* Communicated at St Paul's. In going up to the table I met one who had behaved very untowardly. He said, with the look of the publican, "I repent."[5] My heart was filled with consolation and prayer for him. O that I might have the same joy in all who have grieved me by their backslidings.

---

4. Charles spells "Design."
5. Cf. Luke 18:13.

Felt an unusual weight at our Love-feast till the death of our brother Milbourne revived me. A brother related that he had caught hold on him with his convulsed hands and said, "I have neither doubt nor fear, but my spirit rejoices continually in God my Savior. He has done more for my soul than tongue can utter." The like words he had said to me, whom he kissed and could hardly part with. Was sure, he declared, that his Lord would just then receive him. Even when speechless, he showed all the tokens of happiness and died like a lamb of Jesus' fold.

*Monday, January 17.* From three till nine at night continued reading the letters, rejoicing and praying and praising God.

*Tuesday, January 18.* Buried and spake of a happy brother. It was with us as heretofore, a funeral is one of our greatest festivals.

*Saturday, January 22.* Prayed with the malefactors and felt great pity for them, especially for a poor ignorant Papist.

*Wednesday and Thursday, January 26[–27].* Reproved them for their late negligence, and on *Saturday, January 29*, saw my words had not been lost. They seemed humbled and awakened to a sense of their condition. Their lightness had been occasioned by that poor creature, the Ordinary, who is worse than no minister at all. Six times they were forced to wake him before he got through the prayers. He might just as well read them in Latin. His life and actions are worse than ever his words.

# FEBRUARY 1743

*Tuesday, February 1.* Again [Mr] Townsend refused me admittance, telling me I had forged my order from the sheriff. Another let me in with Mr Piers and Bray. Scarce were we entered the cells when the power of God fell upon us, first as a Spirit of contrition, then of strong faith and power to exhort and pray.

At night I expounded Daniel 9, and the Spirit of God burst in upon us like a flood. Surely the Lord will bring again Zion. The commandment is gone forth, and our Jerusalem shall be built.

*Friday, February 4.* Spent in examining the classes. Before we parted, the Spirit of supplication was wonderfully poured out. We asked in faith for some who still lay at the pool,[6] and they received immediately knowledge of salvation by the remission of their sins.

*Saturday, February 5.* One among the classes told my brother she had a constant sense of forgiveness and he let her pass. I could not help proving her farther, and then the justified sinner appeared full of the gall of bitterness. Said again and again of a sister present, "I do not love her, I hate her," etc. I assured her, if an angel from heaven told me she was justified, I would not believe him, for she was a murderer as such. We prayed for her and she was convinced of unbelief. I fear we have many such believers among us.

*Sunday, February 6.* Met a second time the clerk of St Luke's. In our first conference he was thoroughly convinced and has now experienced the truth. For three days together, he tells me, he has been ready to faint away through love to all mankind.

*Friday, February 11.* Three received forgiveness today, while we were praying among the classes.

*Saturday, February 12.* Showed my old order at Newgate, which was refused. Then a new one sent me by the other sheriff. Coming out, the keeper desired to see it again, and took it away from me. I wrote to the sheriff who sent me another.

*Sunday, February 13.* When I came to Newgate, the first question was as I expected, "Where is your order?" I produced my new one, which so surprised them, that they durst not refuse me admittance.

Found the poor souls turned out of the way by Mr Broughton. He told them there was no knowing our sins forgiven and if any could expect it, not such wretches as they, but the good people who had done so and so. As for his part, he had it not himself. Therefore, it was plain they could not receive it. I spoke strong words to one of them, which the Lord applied, and prayed in fervent faith. Heard the Ordinary read, prayed and preached. Then spoke with them all together in the chapel. All but one were brought back to the truth.

The God of this world was angry and sent the head jailer to ask me how I came hither. "I wonder, Sir," said I, "that you should ask me that question, when you have my order in your pocket. You did not do well in taking it away, and then forbidding my entrance. You

---

6. Cf. John 5:1-15.

have trampled upon the sheriff's authority." He answered, "If the sheriff suffers you to come here, he shall keep the jail himself." I talked to him until he was much softened. But let the world smile or frown, my work goes on. This was written to a bosom friend:

> Rather than live in all earthly comfort, I would choose just now to be cast into the sea with a millstone about my neck—but for the fear of something after death. All this day my heart has been rising in expostulation with God, have I not left all to follow him? Have I not chosen for near twenty hours to be miserable for want of him, rather than happy in the possession of all things else? For his sake I have suffered reproach, denied myself the gratification of my senses, appetites, and passion, took up my cross to suffer temptation, been afflicted, tossed with tempests, and not comforted, suffered so many things in vain, and at last to perish eternally! Who can forbear asking, wherefore then hast thou brought me forth out of the womb? O that I had given up the ghost, and no eye had seen me!
>
> His judgments are as a great deep, I am lost in them. O that I could think no more!

*Tuesday, February 22.* Weary, and through various dangers, the Lord brought me this morning to Bath.

*Wednesday, February 23.* Preached morning and night at the Society. In the evening at the lodgings of a sick friend, to several of the rich. They heard me patiently while I showed, "They that be whole have no need of a physician, but they that be sick" [Matt. 9:12].

*Thursday, February 24.* Met Mrs Carr, a daughter of affliction, and found in prayer for her that the Lifter up of her head is near.

*Sunday, February 27.* Gave the Sacrament to our colliers. The love of Christ was shed abroad in many of their hearts.

Expounded the Pool of Bethesda [John 5:1-15] at Bath. Mr Carr, and the rest of the gentry, were very attentive.

## MAY 1743[7]

*Tuesday, May 17.* Set out for the north with Mr Gurney. In the evening walked from our Brother Wynn's to Painswick. Stood in

---

7. There is another lacuna in the MS Journal for March–April 1743. It is likely that Charles

the street and invited sinners to the gospel-feast in, "Come, for all things are now ready" [Luke 14:17]. Some, even of these dead souls, received the word with joy.

**Wednesday, May 18.** Admitted a dozen new members into the Society, who brought a blessing with them. Walked to Stroud and delivered my message at the marketplace to a quiet audience. Made up a difference between two of the brethren, and carried them with me to Evesham.

Here the storm of persecution is a little blown over. He that letteth[8] at present is a Quaker. The mayor likewise keeps off the song of violence.

**Thursday, May 19.** Read prayers in Quinton church,[9] and exhorted several wild, staring people to repent and believe the gospel [Mark 1:15]. I could not refuse their pressing invitation to preach again. God gave me great plainness of speech. Some of the fiercest opposers were brought over. Mrs Taylor was fully convinced of unbelief.

Hastened back to Evesham and enforced the comprehensive promise, "Whatsoever you shall ask in my name, that will I do" [John 14:13]. Our Lord himself applied his own words.

The Society walk as becometh the gospel.[10] One only person I reproved; not suffering her any longer, notwithstanding her great gifts, to speak in the church or usurp authority over the men.[11]

**Friday, May 20.** Got once more to our dear colliers of Wednesbury.[12] Here the seed has taken root and many are added to the church. A Society of above 300 are seeking full redemption in the all-cleansing blood. The enemy rages exceedingly and preaches against them. A few have returned railing for railing, but the generality have behaved as the followers of Christ Jesus.

Preached in a garden in the first words I met, 1 Cor. 2:1, "And I, brethren, when I came unto you," etc. While I spake of his sufferings

---

was physically indisposed during this period, as he again resorted to a transcriber for his letter of April 27, 1743, to the Society at Grimsby.

8. In the BCP and the AV, "letteth" is used in the sense of "hindering" or "preventing." Cf. 2 Thess. 2:7.

9. Rev. Samuel Taylor (1711–1772), the vicar at Quinton, was a Methodist sympathizer.

10. Cf. Phil. 1:27.

11. Cf. 1 Tim. 2:12.

12. Charles spells "Wensbury."

he looked upon us, and made us look upon him and mourn. Many wept, as one that mourneth for his first-born. Exhorted and instructed the Society very lively. Surely among these prophets I have not run or laboured in vain.[13]

**Saturday, May 21.** At five commended the Woman of Canaan [Matt. 15:22-28] as an example of prevalent importunity. A young man, who had been generally vexed by the devil, was now set at liberty. Spent the morning in conference with several who have received the atonement under my brother, and saw a piece of ground given us by a Dissenter to build a preaching-house upon, and consecrated it with a hymn.

Walked with many of the brethren to Walsall and were received with the old complaint, "Behold, they that turn the world upside down are come here also" [Acts 17:6]. Walked through the town amidst the noisy greetings of our enemies and stood on the steps of the market-house. A host of men was laid against us. The floods lifted up their voice and raged horribly.[14] I opened the book on the first-presented words, Acts 20:24, "But none of these things move me. Neither count I my life dear unto myself, so that I might finish my course with joy, and the ministry which I have received of the Lord Jesus, to justify the gospel of the grace of God."

The street was full of fierce Ephesian beasts[15] (the principal man setting them on), who roared and shouted, and threw stones incessantly. Many struck without hurting me. I besought them in calm love to be reconciled to God in Christ. While I was departing, a stream of ruffians was suffered to bear me from the steps. I rose, and having given the blessing was brought down again. So the third time, when we had returned, thanks to the God of our salvation. I then, from the steps, bade them depart in peace, and walked quietly back through the thickest rioters. They mocked us, but had no commission to touch an hair of our heads.

**Sunday, May 22.** Preached to between one and two thousand peaceable people at Birmingham. Heard a miserable sermon to disprove the promise of the Father, by confining it to the Apostles. After the Sacrament, I called on many, "Repent, and be converted

---

13. Cf. Phil. 2:16.
14. Cf. Ps. 93:3.
15. Cf. 1 Cor. 15:32.

[. . .] for the promise is unto you."[16] And several gentlemen stood in the crowd with signs of deep attention.

Preached on the same words at Wednesbury, and the Spirit proved them with his own demonstration.

*Monday, May 23.* Took my leave in those words, Acts 14:22, "Confirming the souls of the disciples, and exhorting them to continue in the faith, and that we must through much tribulation enter into the kingdom of heaven." With many tears and blessings they sent me away, commended to the graces of God.

Preached at Melbourne to several, who seemed ready for it.

*Tuesday, May 24.* Again I preached the gospel to the poor at Coleorton, who heard it with great eagerness.

Rode to Donington[17] and asked, "Have ye received the Holy Ghost since ye believed?" [Acts 19:2].

At two I proclaimed the Savior of all men [1 Tim. 4:9-10] at Nottingham Cross; and in the evening, at their request, expounded to Mr [John] How's Society.

*Wednesday, May 25.* At the Cross again, pressed all to receive that faithful saying. There was no breath of opposition, but a storm must follow this calm. One gave me a kind caution, for which I sincerely thanked him: "Mr Rogers did run well, and preached the truth as you do here, but what a sad end has he made of it! Take care you don't leave the church like him!"

In the afternoon I came to the flock in Sheffield, who are as sheep in the midst of wolves, the ministers having so stirred up the people that they are ready to tear them in pieces. Most of them have passed through the fire of stillness, which came to try them as soon as they tasted the grace of the Lord.

At six went to the Society house next door to our brother [Edward] Bennet's. Hell from beneath was moved to oppose us. As soon as I was in the desk with David Taylor, the floods began to lift up their voice. An officer (Ensign Garden) contradicted and blasphemed. I took no notice of him, and sang on. The stones flew thick hitting the desk and people. To save them and the house I gave notice I should preach out, and look the enemy in the face.

---

16. A combination of Acts 3:19 and Acts 2:39.

17. Castle Donington, Leicestershire; or, more likely, the nearby home of Lady Huntingdon: Donington Park (though she was not in residence at the moment).

The whole army of aliens followed me. The Captain laid hold on me and began reviling. I gave him for answer *A Word in Season, or Advice to a Soldier*,[18] then prayed, particularly for His Majesty King George, and preached the gospel with much contention. The stones often struck me in the face. After sermon, I prayed for sinners as servants of their master, the devil, upon which Captain ran at me with great fury, threatening revenge for my abusing, as he called it, "The king his master." He forced his way through the brethren, drew his sword, and presented it to my breast. My breast was immediately steeled. I threw it open, and fixing mine eye on his, smiled in his face, and calmly said, "I fear God and honor the king." His countenance fell in a moment, he fetched a deep sigh, put up his sword, and quietly left the place.

To one of the company, who afterwards informed me, he had said, "You shall see, if I do but hold my sword to his breast, he will faint away." So perhaps I should, had I had only his principles to trust to. But if at that time I was not afraid, no thanks to my natural courage.

We returned to our brother Bennet's, and gave ourselves unto prayer. The rioters followed and exceeded in their outrage all I have seen before. Those of Moorfields, Cardiff, and Walsall were lambs to these. As there is no king in Israel (no magistrate I mean in Sheffield) every man does as seems good in his own eyes.[19] Satan now put it into their hearts to pull down the Society-house, and they set to their work while we were praying and praising God. It was a glorious time with us. Every word of exhortation sunk deep, every prayer was sealed, and many found the Spirit of glory resting on them.

One sent for the constable, who came up and desired me to leave the town, "since I was the occasion of all this disturbance." I thanked him for his advice, with all assuring him that I should not go a moment the sooner for this uproar—was sorry for *their* sakes, that they had no law or justice among them. As for myself, I had my protection, and I knew my business, as I supposed he did his. In proof whereof he went from us and encouraged the mob.

They pressed hard to break open the door. I would have gone out to them, but the brethren would not suffer me. They laboured all

---

18. This tract had just been published by John Wesley (Newcastle: Gooding, 1743).
19. Cf. 2 Kings 10:5.

night for their Master and by morning had pulled down one end of the house. I could compare them to nothing but the men of Sodom,[20] or those coming out of the tombs exceeding fierce.[21] Their outcries often waked me in the night, yet I believe I got more sleep than any of my neighbors.

*Thursday, May 26.* At five expounded the Pool of Bethesda [John 5:1-15], and stayed conversing with the Society till eight. Breakfasted with several of the brethren from Yorkshire, Derbyshire, Lancashire, and Cheshire. Met a daughter of affliction, who had long mourned in Zion.[22] God gave me immediate faith for her, which I made proof of in prayer, and in that instant she received *the comfort.*

It being agreed that I should preach in the heart of the town, I went forth nothing doubting. We heard our enemies shouting from afar. I stood in the midst of them and read the first words offered. "If God be for us, who can be against us? He that spared," etc. [Rom. 8:31-32], God made bare his arm[23] in the sight of the heathen, and so repaired the fierceness of many that not one lifted up hand or voice against us.

I took David Taylor and walked through the open street to our brother Bennet's with the multitude at my heels. We passed by the spot where the house stood. They had not left one stone upon another. Nevertheless the foundation standeth sure, as I told one of them, and our house not made with hands eternal in the heavens.[24] The mob attended me to my lodgings with great civility, but as soon as I entered the house, they renewed their threatenings to pull it down. The windows were masked in an instant and my poor host so frightened that he was ready to give up his shield.

He had been for a warrant to Mr Buck, a justice of peace in Rotherham, who refused it him unless he would promise to forsake this way.

The house was now on the point of being taken by storm. I was writing within, when the cry of my poor friend and his family, I thought, called me out to those sons of Belial.[25] In the midst of the

---

20. Cf. Gen. 13:12-13.
21. I.e., the demon-possessed; cf. Matt. 8:28.
22. Cf. Isa. 61:3.
23. Cf. Isa. 52:10.
24. Cf. 2 Cor. 5:1.
25. Cf. 1 Sam. 2:12.

rabble I found a friend of Edward's with the Riot Act.[26] At their desire I took and read it and made a suitable exhortation. One of the sturdiest rebels our constable seized, and carried away captive into the house. I marveled at the patience of his companions, but the Lord overawed them. What was done with the prisoner, I know not, for in five minutes I was fast asleep in the room they had dismantled. I feared no cold, but dropped asleep with that word "Scatter thou the people that delight in war" [Ps. 68:30]. I afterwards heard that within the hour they had all quitted the place.

*Friday, May 27.* At five took leave of the Society in those comfortable words, "Confirming the souls," etc. [Acts 14:22]. Had the extraordinary blessing I expected. Our hearts were knit together and greatly comforted. We rejoiced in hope of the glorious appearing of the great God, who had now delivered us out of the mouth of the lions.

David Taylor informed me that the people of Thorpe,[27] through which we should pass, were exceeding mad against us. So we found them as we approached the place, and were turning down the lane to Barley Hall.[28] The ambush rose and assaulted us with stones, eggs, and dirt. My horse flew from side to side, till he forced his way through them. David Taylor they wounded in his forehead, which bled much. His hat he lost in the fray. I returned and asked what was the reason a clergyman could not pass without such treatment. At first the rioters scattered, but their captain rallying answered with horrible imprecations and stones that would have killed both man and beast had they not been turned aside by an hand unseen. My horse took fright and hurried away with me down a steep hill, till we came to a lane which I turned up and took a circuit to find our brother Johnson's. The enemy spied me from afar and followed shouting. Blessed be God, I got no hurt, but only the eggs and dirt. My clothes indeed abhorred me and my arm pained me a little by a blow I received at Sheffield. David Taylor had got just before me to Barley Hall with the sisters, whom God had hid in the palm of his hand.

26. The "Riot Act" was passed by Parliament in 1715, in the context of fears of a Jacobite uprising and corresponding mob attacks on dissenting groups. It required groups of more than twelve persons to disperse within an hour of a magistrate reading the text of the act to them.
27. Thorpe Hesley, Yorkshire.
28. Barley Hall was a farmhouse near Thorpe Hesley. Cf. John Wesley, *Journal* (June 15, 1742), *Works* 19:278.

Met many sincere souls assembled to hear the word of God. Nevertheless I have known a greater power of love. All were drowned in tears, yet very happy. The Scripture I met was "Blessed be the Lord God of Israel, for he hath visited and redeemed his people" [Luke 1:68]. We rejoiced in the God of our salvation, who hath compassed us about with songs of deliverance.

By four we came to a land of rest. For the brethren of Birstall[29] have stopped the mouth of gainsayers and fairly overcome evil with good. At present peace is in all their borders. The little foxes that spoil the vineyard, or rather the wild boars out of the wood that root it up, hath no more place among them. Only the Germans still prowl about the fences to pick up stragglers.

My mouth was opened to declare God who spared not his own Son, etc. [Rom. 8:32]. The great multitude were bowed down by the victorious power of his love. It was a time much to be remembered, for the gracious rain wherewith our God refreshed us.

*Saturday, May 28.* Preached in the morning and at noon with great enlargement to the childlike people; then at Armley[30] in my way to Leeds.

*Sunday, May 29.* Not a year ago I walked to and fro in these streets and could not find a man,[31] but a spark is at last lit[32] on this place also, and a great fire it will kindle.

Met the infant Society, about fifty in number, most of them justified, and exhorted them to talk circumspectly, since so much depended on the first witnesses.

At seven stood before William Shent's door and cried to thousands, "Ho everyone that thirsteth, come to the waters!" [Isa. 55:1]. The word took place. They gave diligent heed to it, and seemed a people ready prepared for the Lord.

I went to the great church and was showed to the minister's pew. Their whole behavior said, "Friend, go up higher."[33] Five clergymen were there who confounded me by making me take place of my elders and betters. They made me help administer the Sacrament. Would not let me steal into a corner but placed me at a

---

29. Charles spells "Birstal."
30. Charles spells "Armsly."
31. Cf. Jer. 5:1.
32. Charles said "light."
33. Cf. Luke 14:10.

table opposite to him that consecrated. I assisted with eight more ministers, for whom my soul was much drawn out in prayer. But I dreaded their favour more than the stones in Sheffield.

At two found a vast multitude waiting for the word. I strongly exhorted them to repent and believe that their sins might be blotted out [Acts 3:19].

At Birstall called the poor and maimed, and halt and blind to the Great Supper [Luke 14:15-24]. My Lord disposed many hearts, I doubt not, to accept the invitation. He shows me several witnesses of the truth, which they have even now received in the love of it. Had a blessed parting with the Society.

*Monday, May 30.* Near Ripley my horse threw and fell upon me. My companion thought I had broke my neck, but my leg only was bruised, my hand sprained, and my head stunned, which spoiled my making hymns, or thinking at all, till the next day, when the Lord brought us to Newcastle.

At seven went to the room, which contained above 2,000. It was filled from end to end. My subject was, "He that spared not his own," etc. [Rom. 8:32] and God gave testimony to the word of his grace. We rejoiced for the consolation of our mutual faith.

# JUNE 1743

*Wednesday, June 1.* Preached at Pelton to a people, who seem as ignorant almost as the beasts that perish. But if the Lord hath given them a desire to know him, he can of these stones raise up children unto Abraham.[34]

*Friday, June 3.* Our room was crowded at the watch-night. Several gentry from the races stood with great attention while I set forth Christ crucified.[35] It was a season both of guilt and love.

*Saturday, June 4.* Went on at five expounding the Acts. Some stumbling blocks, with the help of God, I have removed, particularly the fits. Many no doubt were at our first preaching struck down, both soul and body, into the depth of distress. Their *outward affections* were easy to be imitated. Many counterfeits I have already

---

34. Cf. Matt. 3:9.
35. Cf. the note for the September 3–4, 1741, entry above.

detected. Today one, who came from the alehouse drunk, was pleased to fall into a fit for my entertainment and beat himself heartily. I thought it a pity to hinder him, so instead of singing over him, as had been often done, we left him to recover at his leisure. Another girl, as she began her cry, I ordered to be carried out. Her convulsion was so violent as to take away the use of her limbs till they laid and left her without the door. Then immediately she found her legs and walked off. Some very unstill sisters, who always took care to stand near me and tried which should cry loudest, since I had them removed out of my sight, have been as quiet as lambs. The first night I preached here half my words were lost through their outcries. Last night before I began I gave public notice that whosoever cried so as to drown my voice should, without any man hurting or judging them, be gently carried to the farthest corner of the room. But my porters had no employment the whole night. Yet the Lord was with us, mightily convincing of sin and of righteousness.

*Sunday, June 5.* My soul was revived by the poor people at Chowdene, and yet more at Tanfield, where I called to great numbers, "Behold the Lamb of God," etc. [John 1:29]. To the Society I spoke words not my own. At Newcastle one just come from the Sacrament received the seal of forgiveness among us.

I preached in the crowded square, chiefly to the backsliders, whom I besought with tears to be reconciled to God. Surely Jesus looked upon some of them as he looked upon Peter.[36]

Wrestled in prayer at the Society, and found it is for their sake principally that God hath brought me hither.

*Monday, June 6.* Had the great comfort of recovering some of those that had drawn back. They came confessing their sin. I trust we shall receive them again forever.

*Wednesday, June 8.* Spake to the bands severally and tried if their faith could bear shaking. We have certainly been too rash and easy in allowing persons for believers on their own testimony; nay, and even persuading them into a false opinion of themselves. Some souls 'tis doubtless necessary to encourage, but it should be done with the utmost caution. To tell one in darkness he has faith is to

---

36. Cf. Luke 22:61.

keep him in darkness still, or to make him trust in a false light, a faith that stands in the words of men, not in the power of God.

*Saturday, June 11.* Passed an hour with the keelmen[37] at the hospital. Eight of our brethren there have been gathered into the garner since our parting. The love of the rest is not waxen cold.

*Sunday, June 12.* Preached at five in the Room; at seven to the poor people in Chowdene; at nine in Tanfield; after church in the hospital square to the usual congregation, whom I warmly pressed to the great Supper [Luke 14:15-24].

*Monday, June 13.* Wrote thus to a son in the gospel,

Be not over sure that so many are justified. "By their fruits you shall know them" [Matt. 7:20]. You will see reason to be more deliberate in the judgment you pass on souls. Wait for their conversation. I don't know whether we can infallibly pronounce *at the time* that anyone is justified. I once thought several in that state who, I am now convinced, were only under the drawings of the Father. Try the spirits therefore, least you should lay the stumbling block of pride in their way; and by allowing them to have faith too soon, keep them out of it for ever.

*Tuesday, June 14.* Preached at South Biddick[38] to a multitude of earnest souls, who lamented my leaving them as soon as I found them.

*Wednesday, June 15.* Dined at Stotes Hall[39] with Mr Williams and rode in the bitter weather to Plessy. Here my labour has not been in vain. They even devoured the word while I showed them what they must do to be saved.

Observed at Newcastle that many more of the gentry come now [that] the stumbling block of their fits is taken out of their way, and I am more and more convinced it was a device of Satan to stop the course of the gospel. Since I have preached it (if I can discern anything), it never had greater success than at this time. Yet, we have

---

37. The "keelmen" were skilled boatmen who used small boats (keels) to carry coal from shore out to waiting ships in Newcastle.

38. Biddick, County Durham. Charles spells "Biddicks," and drops "South" after this occurrence.

39. A large house that stood in what is now the Jesmond Dene neighborhood of Newcastle Upon Tyne.

no fits among us and I have done nothing to prevent them, only declared that I do not think the better of anyone for crying out or interrupting my work.

*Thursday, June 16.* Set out for Sunderland with strong aversion to preaching. But I am more and more convinced that *the freedom of heart* which the Moravians and Quakers so much talk of, is a rule of the devil's inventing to supersede the written word. Dragged myself to about a 1,000 wild people and cried, "O Israel, thou hast destroyed thyself, but in me is thy help" [Hos. 13:9]. Never have I seen greater attention in any at their first hearing.

We rode on to Shields.[40] Went to church and the people flocked in crowds after me. The minister could not be heard in reading prayers, but I heard him loud enough afterwards calling for the church warden to quiet the disturbance, which none but himself raised. I fancy he thought I should preach there like some of the first Quakers. The clerk came to me bawling out it was consecrated ground, and I had no business to preach on it—was no minister. And when he had cried himself out of breath, I whispered him in the ear that I had no intention to preach there, and he stumbled upon a good saying, "Then, if you have any word of exhortation for the people, speak it to them without."

I did so at my leisure, an huge multitude waiting in the church-yard, many of them fierce and threatening—to drown me, and what not. I walked quickly through the midst of them and discoursed in strong awakening words on the jailer's question, "What must I do to be saved?" [Acts 16:30]. The churchwardens and others laboured in vain to interrupt by throwing dirt, hay, and money among the people. Having delivered my message, I rode to the ferry, crossed, and met as rough friends on the other side. The mob of North Shields waited to salute me, with the minister at their head. He had got a man with an horn instead of a trumpet, and bade him blow, and his companions shout. Others were almost as violent in their approbation. We went through honor and dishonor (but neither of them hurt us), and by six, with God's blessing, came safe to Newcastle.

*Saturday, June 18.* A woman told me she had received a great measure of the love of God in her heart and thought it forgiveness.

---

40. I.e., South Shields, County Durham.

I thought so too, especially as it was an immediate answer to our prayer. Upon my warning her against pride, she very innocently told me she "was never proud in all her life." Now what madness to tell this soul so utterly ignorant of herself if she is justified. She may be so, for what I know, but for me positively to determine it would be the way, I think, to stop the work in its beginning. Several have come with the same report since I have been here. I neither reject nor receive their saying, but require their fruits and bid them go on.

*Sunday, June 19.* Asked the multitudes in the square "Will ye also go away?" [John 6:67] and the word prospered in the thing whereunto it was sent, namely, the bringing back the wanderers. Concluded the day with our first Love-feast. Jesus was with his disciples.

Took my leave in those words, "What ye have already, hold fast till I come" [Rev. 2:25]. It was a hard parting with the Society. Their hearts were all as melting wax, and will, I trust, retain the impression made then by every word spoken. Some cried aloud, others knelt down for my blessing, most laid hold on me as I passed. All wept and made lamentation.

Preached at Swalwell. Never were people better disposed or more eager of instruction. And their love was such that they would, if possible, pluck out their eyes and give them [to] me.[41]

*Tuesday, June 21.* Set out between three and four. Met by several parties of the Society, who had walked before some miles to watch my passing. I travelled but slowly through them, blessing and being blessed.

Rode to Sandhutton. The poor people filled the house where I was. I showed them the way of salvation in the Creditor and Two Debtors [Luke 7:41-43]. They returned me many thanks.

*Wednesday, June 22.* Set out at three. Was met and turned back. When I had gone a mile out of my way, thought how could the loss be repaired and immediately it was suggested that I should pray till I got into the right road. The Spirit helped my infirmity, and I continued instant in prayer for some hours, believing that I shall after all escape safe to land.[42] I prayed on, till at ten a sailor overtook

---

41. Cf. Gal. 4:15.
42. Cf. Acts 27:44.

us. I set upon him, and he rejoiced in my welcome saying. God found me more work at Selby. Dined in a mixed company, where one asked me if there was any good in confirmation. I answered, "No, nor in baptism, nor in the Lord's Supper, or any outward thing, unless you are in Christ a new creature." I confounded all my hearers by relating my own experience under the law. Left them some books and went on my way rejoicing. Still the Spirit was upon me and I felt stronger faith *for myself* than I ever did before.

By six came to Epworth,[43] my native place. All who met saluted me with hearty joy. At eight preached in Edward Smith's yard. "He that spared not his own Son" [Rom. 8:32] and many were present and much affected. Laid me down in peace, after one of the happiest days I have ever known.

**Thursday, June 23.** Waking I found the Lord with me, even my strong Helper, the God of whom cometh salvation. Preached on "Ask and it shall be given you, seek," etc. [Matt. 7:7]. Guarded some new converts against spiritual pride, that only hindrance to the work of God. Warned another against the *poor sinners*. One of them (Parker) had frankly told her he did not understand what we meant by talking of holiness after forgiveness—that he has all he can have, and looks for no more.

Visited Mrs Bernard, a widow in affliction, whose husband is just dead suddenly; yet called at the eleventh hour. Went thence to Mr [John] Maw's, who received me gladly; being again stirred up and resolved to seek till he finds.

Passed the afternoon with our brethren from Grimsby, in mutual encouragement. At seven went out into the streets to call those that were bidden and cried from the cross: "Come, for all things are now ready" [Luke 14:17]. The minister[44] heard me at a distance.

Provoked the Society to love and good works. Warned them, without intending it, against those that seduce them and insisted with all earnestness on my constant counsel, that none of them should leave the ship till all came safe to land.

---

43. Epworth, Lincolnshire, the parish served by Samuel Wesley, Sr., and Charles's birthplace.

44. Rev. John Romley (1711–1751), who began as curate under Samuel Wesley, Sr., and was now vicar.

*Friday, June 24.* Met them again at three, and parted with the blessing and peace of God.

Rode to Nottingham with the *best company* that earth or heaven could furnish. Found my brother in the market place, calling lost sinners to Him that justifieth the ungodly. He gave notice of my preaching in the evening.

From him I had the first account of our brethren's persecution at Wednesbury.[45] Their unhappy minister[46] was the contriver of all.

The Lord opened my mouth at seven. Many thousands attended in deep silence. Surely the Lord hath much people in this place.[47] We began a Society of nine members.

*Saturday, June 25.* Came to Birmingham with the night.

*Sunday, June 26.* Several of our persecuted brethren from Wednesbury came to me, whom I endeavoured to comfort. Preached at eight and one, no men forbidding me. After evening service I expounded the Prodigal Son [Luke 15:11-32] to several thousand and many of whom (I observed by their tears) were pricked at the heart and ready to say, "I will arise and will go to my Father" [15:18].

In the name of the Lord Jesus I began our Society. The number at present is thirteen.

*Monday, June 27.* Left our brother [James] Jones to look after the little flock, and set out for London. By six in the evening came safe to Oxford. The Society is in a flourishing condition, chiefly by means of a discreet sister from London, but poor, languid, dead Mr Robson. I have trusted in this child of man, therefore is he to me as *waters* that fail.[48]

*Tuesday night, June 28.* Slept at the Foundery.

*Thursday, June 30.* Buried our sister Soane, a mother in Israel[49] she *was*, but she *is* a saint in paradise. We found the blessing which she has left behind.

---

45. John Wesley eventually published an account of this persecution in *Modern Christianity: Exemplified in Wednesbury* . . . (Newcastle: Gooding, 1745).
46. Rev. Edward Egginton (c. 1693–1743), vicar of Wednesbury (1719–1743).
47. Cf. Acts 18:10.
48. Cf. Jer. 15:18.
49. Cf. Judg. 5:7.

# JULY 1743

*Sunday, July 3.* Mr [Westley] Hall, poor Moravianized Mr Hall, met us at the chapel. I did him honor before the people. Expounded the gospel, as usual, and strongly avowed my inviolable attachment to the Church of England. Mr Meriton[50] and [Charles] Graves assisted me at the Sacrament.

It was our women's Love-feast, but I turned it into mourning by setting before them the things some of them had done and spoken in a lying spirit against their ministers. I challenged them "Which of you convinceth us of sin?" and showed at large their ingratitude to God and man. Great lamentation was among them. The stumbling block will, I trust, be soon entirely removed.

*Monday, July 4.* On our thanksgiving day we received power to wrestle with God for a blessing on all the church and especially our persecuted brethren.

*Tuesday, July 5.* Mr Hall came and spoke large in vindication of the Germans. As for their denying the ordinances, that was all an invention of my brother's, etc. I plainly told him we could have no confidence in him while he clave to them.[51]

*Wednesday, July 6.* Showed from Rom. 5 the marks of justification and overturned the confidence of several. Strongly warned them against seducers. Found my heart knit to this people.

*Friday, July 8.* John Bray came to persuade me not to preach till the bishops should bid me. They have not yet forbid me. But by the grace of God, I shall preach the word in season, out of season, though they, and all men forbade me.[52]

*Saturday, July 9.* Read my testimony to the Society (the letter in verse, "My more than friend, accept the warning lay," etc.[53]). Cautioned them against Mr Hall, and rejoiced that I had confidence of them in all things.

---

50. Rev. John Meriton (c. 1698–1753). See Charles's hymn on his death in *Funeral Hymns* (1759), 28–29 (*Poetical Works*, 6:244–46).

51. The entry of July 5 is omitted in Jackson.

52. Cf. 2 Tim. 4:2.

53. The poetic epistle can be found in S T Kimbrough Jr. and Oliver A. Beckerlegge, eds., *The Unpublished Poetry of Charles Wesley* (Nashville: Kingswood Books, 1988), 1:171–87.

*Sunday, July 10.* At our chapel, the galleries were filled with strangers. Many are daily added to the church.

Preached once more at the Foundery and earnestly exhorted the Society to continue in the faith.

*Monday, July 11.* Set out at two in hard rain which lashed all day. Yet I reached Hungerford by night, and Bristol the next day.

Both my preaching and exhortation was to convince them of unbelief. I left them examining themselves whether they be in the faith.

*Wednesday, July 13.* A brother accompanied me to Exeter, and twenty miles farther.

On *Friday, July 15,* set out alone, and by wandering made it threescore miles to Bodmin. Both horse and rider were worked down so that I slept till five next morning without once waking. It cost me four hours to reach Mitchell. My cholic made them seem four days. When I came in, I could not stand. Lay down and rose with fresh strength, which carried me to Redruth. I left it at four, and wandered toward St Ives. Passed the River Hall just before the sea came in. Two tinners met me first and wished me good luck in the name of the Lord. My next greeting was from the devil's children, who shouted as I passed, and pursued me like the men out of the tombs.[54] Met Thomas Williams. And then Mr [William] Shepherd, and rejoiced in the Lord our strength and our Redeemer.

Between seven and eight entered St Ives. The boys and others continued their rough salutes, for some time, at brother [John] Nance's, but I was too weary to regard them.

*Sunday, July 17.* I rose and forgot I had traveled from Newcastle. Spoke with some of this loving, simple people, who are as sheep in the midst of wolves. The priests stir up the people and make their minds evil affected toward the brethren.

Yet the sons of violence are much checked by the mayor,[55] an honest Presbyterian, whom the Lord hath raised up.

Preached in the room at eight on "Thou shalt call his name Jesus; for he shall," etc. [Matt. 1:21]. Found his presence sensibly among us. So did the opposers themselves.

54. Cf. Mark 5:2.
55. The mayor of St Ives in 1743 was a John Stephens.

Heard the rector preach from Matthew 5:20, "Except your righteousness exceed the righteousness of the Scribes and the Pharisees," etc. His application was downright railing at the new sect, as he calls us, those enemies to the Church, seducers, troublers, scribes and pharisees, hypocrites, etc. I had prayed for a quiet heart, and a steady countenance, and my prayer was answered. My calmness was succeeded with strong consolation.

Rode to Towednack[56] with almost all the brethren. Mr [William] Hoblyn,[57] the curate, entertained us with a curious discourse on "Beware of false prophets" [Matt. 7:15]. I stood up over against him without two yards of the pulpit, and heard such a hodge-podge of railing, foolish lies as Satan himself might have been ashamed of. I had asked that my countenance might not alter, and was kept in perfect peace. The poor people behaved very decently, and all followed me to hear the true word of God.

I stayed and mildly told the preacher he had been misinformed. "No," he answered, "it was all the truth." "Sir," said I, "if you believe what you preach, you believe a lie." "You are a liar," he replied, and I put him in mind of the great day, testified my good will, and left him for the congregation.

God opened a door of utterance to preach the gospel of Christ Jesus. I know they found the difference between the chaff and the wheat.

Returned to St Ives and met the Society. The enemies of the Lord melt away like wax, more and more being convinced that we speak as the oracles of God.

*Monday, July 18.* Went forth toward the market-house. When we came to the place of battle, the enemy was ready, set in array against us. I began the 100th Psalm, and they beating their drum and shouting. I stood still and silent for some time, finding they would not receive my testimony. Then offered to speak to some of the most violent, but they stopped their ears, and ran upon me crying I should not preach there, and catching at me to pull me down. They had no power to touch me. My soul was calm and fearless. I shook off the dust of my feet,[58] and walked leisurely through the

---

56. Charles calls it "Wednock," a slight misspelling of a common shortened version of the town name.
57. Charles spells "Hoblin."
58. Cf. Matt. 10:14.

thickest of them, who followed like ramping and roaring lions—but their mouth was shut.[59]

Met the mayor, who saluted me and threatened the rioters. Rejoiced at my lodgings in our Almighty Jesus.

Preached on Kenneggy Downs[60] to near a thousand tinners, who received the seed into honest and good hearts. While I pointed them to the Lamb of God [John 1:29], many wept, and particularly the captain, general of the sinners, a man famous in his generation for acts of valour and violence, and his usual challenge to fight any six men with his club. He is known through the west by the title of the Destroyer. This leopard will soon, I trust, lie down with the lamb.[61]

Expounded Blind Bartimeus [Mark 10:46-52] at St Ives. The power of the Lord overshadowed us, so that many of the opposers humbled and some wept.

*Tuesday, July 19.* From, "Surely shall one say, in the Lord I have righteousness and strength" [Isa. 45:24], I showed that the two inseparable marks of justification are peace, and power over all sin.

Preached at Poole, in the heart of the tinners. A drunkard got within two or three yards, designing, I suppose, to push me down the hill. I was forced to break off my prayer, and warn him to take care of himself. He attempted to lay hold on me, upon which a sinner cried, "Down with him!" In a moment the Philistines were upon him.[62] I strove to rescue him and besought them not to hurt him, otherwise I should go away and not preach at all. They were entreated for him, and, taking him by the legs and arms, quietly handed him down from one to another, till they had put him without the congregation, and he was heard no more.

I published the faithful, acceptable saying, and their hearts seemed all bowed and opened to receive it. God, I nothing doubt, will call these a people who were not a people.[63] Our prayers for the opposers also began to be answered, for the fiercest of them came in the evening to the room, and behaved with great decency.

---

59. Cf. Dan. 6:22.
60. Flat chalky plains about six miles west of Helston, five miles south of St Ives. Charles spells "Cannegy Downs."
61. Cf. Isa. 11:6.
62. Cf. Judg. 16:9.
63. Cf. Hos. 2:23.

*Wednesday, July 20.* Spake with more of the Society, most of whom have the first knowledge of salvation, as their lives show.

A. G. tells me that faith (as he thinks), came by hearing yesterday morning. He has been a sinner above other sinners till, within this fortnight, God called, and made him equal with those who have bourne the heat and burden of the day.[64]

Went to church, and heard the terrible chapter, Jeremiah 7; enough, one would think, to make even this hardened people tremble. Never were words more applicable than those:

Stand in the gate of the Lord's house, and proclaim there this word, and say, Hear ye the word of the Lord, all ye of Judah, that enter into these gates to worship the Lord. Thus saith the Lord God of hosts, the God of Israel, Amend your ways and your doings, and I will cause you to dwell in this place. Trust ye not in lying words, saying, The temple of the Lord, The temple of the Lord, The temple of the Lord, are these! [ . . . ] Behold, ye trust in lying words that cannot profit. Will ye steal, murder, commit adultery, and swear falsely, [ . . . ] and come and stand before me in this place, [ . . . truth is cut off from] their mouth" [Jer. 7:2-28].

The second lesson, John 8, was as remarkable, showing the servants' treatment in that of the Master.

Preached at Zennor,[65] one of Mr Symonds's[66] four parishes, which is come in, to a man, at the joyful news. Some hundreds of the poor people, with sincerity in their faces, received me saying, "The kingdom of heaven is at hand, repent ye, and believe the gospel" [Mark 1:15].

Began at eight expounding the Good Samaritan [Luke 10:29-37], but could not proceed for pity to the poor mockers. Many of them were present, but their mocking was over. I urged and besought, and with tears even compelled, them to come in. The Spirit made intercession for them, that God might grant them repentance unto life.

*Friday, July 22.* Rode in the rain to Morvah,[67] a settlement of tinners, to whom I could preach nothing but gospel.

---

64. Cf. Matt. 20:12.

65. Charles spells "Zunnor."

66. Rev. William Symonds (c. 1684–1776) was also vicar of St Ives and Towednack, where much of the persecution that follows takes place. He was assisted in these parishes by his curate, Rev. William Hoblyn (1723–1759).

67. Charles spells "Morva."

I had just named my text at St Ives, "Comfort ye, comfort ye my people, saith your God" [Isa. 40:1], when an army of rebels broke in upon us, like those at Sheffield or Wednesbury. They began in a most outrageous manner, threatening to murder the people if they did not go out that moment. They broke the sconces, dashed the windows in pieces, tore away the shutters, benches, poor box, and all but the stone walls. I stood silently looking on, but my eyes were unto the Lord. They swore bitterly that I should not preach there again; which I disproved, by immediately telling them Christ died for them all. Several times they lifted up their hands and clubs to strike me, but a stronger arm restrained them. They beat and dragged the women about, particularly one of a great age, and trampled on them without mercy. The longer they stayed, and the more they raged, the more power I found from above. I bade the people stand still and see the salvation of God,[68] resolving to continue with them, and see the end. In about an hour the word came, "Hitherto shalt thou come, and no farther" [Job 38:11]. The ruffians fell to quarreling among themselves, broke the town clerk's (their captain's) head, and drove one another out of the room.

Having kept the field, we gave thanks for the victory, and in prayer the Spirit of glory rested upon us. Going home we met the mayor, with another justice, and went back to show him the havoc which the gentlemen and their mob had made. He commended our people as the most quiet, inoffensive subjects; encouraged us to sue for justice; said he was no more secure from lawless violence than we; wished us success, and left us rejoicing in our strong Helper.

*Saturday, July 23.* I cannot find one of this people who fears those that can kill the body only.[69] It was next to a miracle that no more mischief was done last night. The gentlemen had resolved to destroy all within doors. They came upon us like roaring lions, headed by the mayor's son. He struck out the candles with his cane, and began courageously beating the women. I laid my hand upon him and said, "Sir, you appear like a gentleman. I desire you would show it, by restraining these of the baser sort. Let them strike the men, or me, if they please, but not hurt poor helpless women and children." He was turned into a friend immediately, and laboured the whole time to quiet his associates. Some not of

---

68. Cf. Exod. 14:13.
69. Cf. Luke 12:4.

the Society were likewise provoked to stand up for us, and put themselves between. Others held the ruffians, and made use of an art of flesh. Some of our bitterest enemies were brought over by the meekness of the sufferers, and malice of the persecutors. They had sworn to drive us all out, and then take possession of our house, but their commission did not go so far. One was overheard saying to his companions as they were going off, "I think the desk was insured. We could not touch it, or come near it."

I proved the devil a liar by preaching in the room at five. The words I first met were Isaiah 54[:3-17], "For thou shalt break forth on the right hand and on the left. [ ... ] Fear not; for thou shalt not be ashamed. Neither be thou confounded, for thou shalt not be put to shame. [ ... ] Behold, I have created the smith [ ... ] and [ ... ] the waster to destroy. No weapon that is formed against thee shall prosper," etc.

Preached at Gwennap[70] to near 2,000 hungry souls, who devoured the word of reconciliation. Half my audience were tinners from about Redruth, which, I hear, is *taken*. God has given us their hearts. If any man speak against us, say they, he deserves to be stoned. Again expounded in the room at St Ives, and advised the Society to possess their souls in patience, not threatening, or even mentioning the late uproar, but suffering all things for the sake of Jesus Christ.

*Sunday, July 24.* At Towednack many listened to my description of our Lord's sufferings from Isaiah 53. After evening service I would have finished my discourse, but the minister's mob fell upon us, threatening and striking all they came near. They swore horribly they would be revenged on us, *for our making such a disturbance on the Sabbath-day*, our taking the people from the church, and doing so much mischief continually. They assaulted us with sticks and stones, and endeavoured to pull me down. I bade them strike me, and spare the people. Many lifted up their hands and weapons, but were not permitted to touch me. My time is not yet come.[71]

We were now encompassed with an host of men bent on mischief, with no visible way of escape. But the Lord hath many ways.

---

70. The site of Gwennap Pit, where the Wesleys engaged in open-air preaching to large crowds.

71. Cf. John 7:6.

He touched the heart of one of our persecutors, who came up to me, took me by the hand, and besought me to depart in peace, assuring me he would preserve me from all violence. Another gentleman said the same. I thanked and told them I had an unseen Protector, but as I saw there was no door, I should not attempt preaching at this season.

I stayed some time to make my observation. Ten cowardly ruffians I saw upon one unarmed man, beating him with their clubs till they felled him to the ground. Another escaped by the swiftness of his horse. My convoy they set upon for dissuading them, and forced him to fly for his life.

I walked on slowly with all the rabble behind. One of the brethren attended me. The Lord hid us in the hollow of his hand. The pillar came between the Egyptians and us.[72] About six we rested at brother Nance's. The enemy still pursued. I went out and looked them in the face, and they pulled off their hats and slunk away. The right hand of the Lord hath the pre-eminence, and therewith hath he got himself the victory.[73]

The Society came. Our hearts danced for joy, and in our song did we praise him. We all longed for his last glorious appearing, and with an eye of faith saw the Son of Man as coming in the clouds of heaven, to confess us before his Father and the holy angels.

*Monday, July 25.* The mayor told us that the ministers[74] were the principal authors of all this evil, by continually representing us in their sermons as popish emissaries, and urging the enraged multitude to take all manner of ways to stop us. Their whole preaching is cursing and lies. Yet they modestly say my fellow-labourer and I are the cause of all the disturbance. It is always the lamb that troubles the water.

Yesterday we were stoned as popish incendiaries. Today it is our turn to have favour with the people.

I preached on Kenneggy Downs to a multitude of simple-hearted tinners: "Who is this that cometh from Edom, with dyed garments from Bozrah?" [Isa. 63:1]. They received the word with gladness and gratitude; wondered at the St Ives people that could endeavour to hurt us for telling them such blessed truths. At St Ives

---

72. Cf. Exod. 14:24-25.
73. Cf. Ps. 118:16.
74. I.e., William Symonds and William Hoblyn.

I had warning of an approaching trial, and was led to pray that the fierceness of men might be at this time restrained. I had scarce begun at the room when news was brought that all the gentlemen were coming to pull it down. We looked for them every moment. About half a dozen came first, and threw eggs in at the windows. Others cast great stones to break what remained of the shutters. Others struck the women, and swore they would have the house down. I prayed and dismissed our people. John Nance was gone to the mayor. I followed to stop him, and met the mayor at the head of his posse. At first hearing of the tumult, he had started up, charged all he met to assist him, and was coming to the room, when I desired him to save himself the trouble of a walk in the rain. He behaved with great civility and resolution, declaring before all that none should hurt us. This disappointed and scattered our adversaries, and I met the Society without molestation.

Glory be to God, that we are once more delivered out of mouth of these lions. They were sure of accomplishing their design this night. But the Lord beheld their threatenings, and stilled the raging of the sea, the noise of its waves, and the madness of the people.

*Tuesday, July 26.* Showed my brethren their calling from Matthew 10:22, "Ye shall be hated of all men for my name's sake. But he that endureth to the end, the same shall be saved."

At the Pool one stopped and demanded my letters of orders. I marvelled at Mr Churchwarden's ignorance, gave him my Oxford sermon,[75] and rode on. He followed me with another gentleman, and vowed I would not preach in *his parish.* When I began, he shouted and hallooed, and put his hat to my mouth. We went to another place. He followed us like Shimei.[76] I told him I should surely deliver my message, unless his master was stronger than mine. After much contention I walked away, with near two thousand people, most part tinners, to the next parish, as my wise Churchwarden supposed. He followed us another mile, and a warm walk he had of it, but left us on the borders of the neighboring parish. However, to take my leave of it, I preached in what he called *his.* In spite of Satan, the poor had the gospel preached to

---

75. Charles Wesley, *A Sermon Preached on April 4, 1742 before the University of Oxford* (London: Strahan, 1742). This is the sermon "Awake Thou that Sleepest" in *Sermons*, 211–24.
76. Cf. 2 Sam. 16:5-6.

them, and heard it joyfully. Great was their zeal and affection toward me. I marvel not that Satan should fight for his kingdom—it begins to shake in this place.

All was quiet at St Ives, the mayor having declared his resolution to swear twenty new constables and suppress the rioters by force of arms. Their drum he has sent and seized. All the time I was preaching he stood at a little distance, to awe the rebels. He has set the whole town against him, by not giving us up to their fury. But he plainly told Mr Hoblyn, the fire-and-faggot minister, that he would not be perjured to gratify any man's malice. Us he informed that he had often heard Mr Hoblyn say, "They ought to drive us away by blows, not arguments."

**Wednesday, July 27.** We could say from our hearts in the morning psalms, "If the Lord himself had not been on our side, when men rose up against us, they had swallowed us up quick, when they were so wrathfully displeased at us. But, praised be the Lord, who hath not given us over for a prey into their teeth, our soul is escaped," etc. [Ps. 124:5-6, BCP]. The words also of the lesson gave us great comfort, but we wondered Mr Symonds could read them: "If the world hate you, ye know it hated me before it hated you. [ . . . ] Remember the word that I said unto you, The servant is not greater than his Lord. If they have persecuted me, they will also persecute you," etc. [John 15:18-20].

**Thursday, July 28.** Dined at our brother Mitchel's, a confessor of the faith which once he persecuted. Rode on to St Hilary Downs.[77] Here the careless hearers were kept away by the enemy's threatenings. But near a thousand well-disposed tinners listened to the joyful tidings: "Comfort ye, comfort ye my people," etc. [Isa. 40:1]. That word of grace, "Thine iniquity is pardoned" [Isa. 6:7], quite melted them down into tears, on all sides.

Began explaining the Beatitudes[78] at St Ives. None interrupted. I don't despair but some of our persecutors themselves may yet, before we depart, receive that *damnable popish doctrine*, as Mr Hoblyn calls it, of justification by faith only.

---

77. An open chalk upland near St Hilary, Cornwall.
78. Charles clearly used the Matthew account (5:1-12) in March 1740, and it is probably that text that is in focus here too. However, the Luke account (6:20-23) is possible.

*Friday, July 29.* Rode to Morvah, and invited the whole nation of tinners to Christ. I took the names of several who were desirous of joining in a Society. The adversaries have laboured with all their might to hinder this good work, but we doubt not our seeing a glorious church in this place.

*Saturday, July 30.* Believed a door would be opened this day, and, in the strength of the Lord, set out for St Just, a town of tinners, four miles from Morvah, twelve from St Ives. My text was, "The poor have the gospel preached unto them" [Matt. 11:5]. I showed, the sum thereof is, "Thine iniquity is pardoned. [ . . . ] God, for Christ's sake, hath forgiven thee."[79] The hearts of thousands seemed moved as the trees of the forest, by that wind which bloweth as it listeth.[80] The door stood wide open, and a multitude are just entering in. Here it is that I expect the largest harvest.

Rode four miles farther, to Sennen,[81] and took up our lodging at an hospitable farmer's.

Walked with our brother Shepherd to the Land's End, and sang, on the extremest point of the rocks,

> Come, Divine Immanuel, come,
> Take possession of thy home;
> Now thy mercy's wings expand,
> Stretch throughout the happy land.[82]

Rode back to St Just and went from the evening service to a plain by the town, *made* for field-preaching. I stood on a green bank, and cried, "All we like sheep have gone astray. We have turned every one to his own way," etc. [Isa. 53:6]. About 2,000, mostly tinners, attended, no one offering to stir or move an hand or tongue. The fields are white unto harvest.[83] Lord, send forth labourers!

Returned to our host at Sennen. He is just entering the kingdom with the harlots and publicans.[84] Went early to bed, having lost most of my senses through the constant fog, in which we have laboured to breathe this fortnight.

---

79. Isa. 6:7; then, Eph. 4:32.
80. Cf. John 3:8.
81. Charles spells "Zunning."
82. "Written at the Land's End," st. 1, *HSP* (1749), 1:329 (*Poetical Works*, 5:133–34).
83. Cf. John 4:34.
84. Cf. Matt. 21:31-32.

# AUGUST 1743

*Monday, August 1.* Saw a strange light, the sun shining in Cornwall.

Expounded at nine the Song of Simeon [Luke 2:25-32]. Several very aged people were present, whom I left waiting for the consolation of Israel [2:25].

Took my leave of Kenneggy Downs in, "The blind receive their sight, and the lame walk," etc. [Matt. 11:5]. Returned to St Ives in peace. Showed the blessedness of persecution. Then exhorted the Society to pray without ceasing for humility, the grace which draws all others after it.

*Tuesday, August 2.* Carried my tinners from the Pool to the next parish. It was a glorious sight, the widespread multitude walking up the hill eager for the word of life, hungry and thirsty after righteousness! I met with that in St Matthew, "A certain man had two sons," etc. [Matt. 21:28-31]. These publicans know the time of their visitation, and bring forth fruit meet for repentance.[85]

An elderly man pressed us to turn into his house, near Camborne. It was a large old country seat, and looked like the picture of English hospitality. When he could not prevail on us to stay longer, he would ride two or three miles on our way with us, and listened all the while to the word of reconciliation.

*Wednesday, August 3.* Took my leave of the dear people of Zennor in our Lord's words, "Be thou faithful unto death, and I will give thee a crown of life" [Rev. 2:10]. With many tears they besought us to come again, and evidently showed that our labour has not been in vain in the Lord.

*Friday, August 5.* Preached my farewell sermon to our sorrowful brethren in Morvah. Many from St Just increased the lamentation. I shall think it long till I see them again, but my comfort is that I leave them following after God.

Took our leave of the friendly mayor, whom we acknowledged, under God, our deliverer from the hands of the unrighteous and cruel men. He expressed the same affection for us as from the beginning; listened to our report, for which our Lord gave us a fair

---

85. Cf. Rom. 7:4.

opportunity; ordered his servant to light us home; in a word, received and sent away the messengers in peace.

*Saturday, August 6.* Rode to Gwennap, and with many words exhorted them to save themselves from this untoward generation.[86] They were exceedingly moved, and very urgent with me to know when I should return; when my brother or any other would come. Surely they are a people ready prepared for the Lord.

Began at St Ives, before the usual time, "And now brethren, I commend you to God," etc. [Acts 20:32]. Had no thought at the rioters, though the mayor had informed us they were so imprudent as to tell him to his face they would have a parting blow at us. As soon as we were met in Society at brother Nance's, they came to the room, ready to pull it down. The drunken town-clerk led his drunken army to our lodgings. But an invisible power held them from breaking in, or hurting our brother Nance, who went out to them and stood in the midst, till our King scattered the evil with his eyes,[87] and turned them back by the way that they came.

The great power of God was, meantime, among us, overturning all before it, and melting our hearts into contrite, joyful love.

*Sunday, August 7.* At four took my leave of the Society, with that apostolical prayer: "And the very God of peace sanctify you wholly," etc. [1 Thess. 5:23]. Great peace was upon them all. Their prayers and tears of love I shall never forget. I nothing doubt, if I follow their faith, that I shall meet them in the new Jerusalem.

At six we left the lion's den, with about twenty horses. Some would have us take a back way, but I would not go forth with haste or by flight, and therefore rode through the largest street, in the face of our enemies.

At eight preached faith in Christ to many listening souls in Velling-Varine.[88] They received the word with surprising readiness. Their tears, and hearty expressions of love, convince me there is a work begun in their hearts.

Rode on rejoicing to Gwennap. As soon as I went forth, I *saw* the end of my coming to Cornwall, and of Satan's opposition. Such a

---

86. Cf. Acts 2:40.
87. Cf. Prov. 20:8.
88. Verine is a family name in Cornwall, and "vellan" is used here to mean "mill." Thus this may have been the name of a local mill, or a small hamlet surrounding such a mill. But no record of such has been found.

company assembled as I have not seen, excepting some few times at Kennington. By their looks I perceived they all heard, while I lifted up my voice like a trumpet and testified, "God sent his Son to be the Savior of the world." The convincing Spirit was in the midst as I have seldom, if ever, known. Most of the gentry from Redruth were just before me, and so hemmed in that they could not escape. For an hour my voice was heard by all, and reached farther than their outward ears. I am inclined to think that most present were convinced of righteousness or of sin. God hath now set before us an open door, and who shall be able to shut it?[89]

At four we rode on to Mitchell, my brother having summoned me to London, to confer with the heads of the Moravians and predestinarians. We had near 300 miles to ride in five days. I was willing to undertake this labour for peace, though the journey was too great for us and our weary beasts, which we have used almost every day for these three months.

*Monday, August 8.* Took horse with brother Shepherd at four, and rode as far as Okehampton.

*Tuesday, August 9.* Breakfasted twelve miles short of Exeter, at an house where the maid and landlady's daughter were convinced by a few words spoken that they were lost unbelievers.

At Exeter I met Felix Farley. Called to about 1,000 sinners, mostly gentlemen and ladies, with some clergy, "Behold the Lamb of God which taketh away the sin of the world" [John 1:29]. God gave me favour in their eyes, although I did not prophesy smooth things.[90] I found, as soon as I began to speak, that the fear of the Lord was upon them. Many followed me to my inn to take their leave, and wished me good luck in the name of the Lord. I left one behind to keep up the awakening and pursued my journey alone to London.

*Wednesday, August 10.* Missed my way, and thereby met at Bridport a poor creature, ready for the gospel. It was glad news indeed to her. When I said, "God sent me to you," she cried, "And did he, indeed?" and fell trembling and weeping. We prayed together, and she seemed not far from the kingdom of God. She

---

89. Cf. Rev. 3:8.
90. Cf. Isa. 30:10.

innocently asked me what church she should be of. I showed her the excellency of our own, and got to Blanford[91] by night.

**Thursday, August 11.** My landlord was greatly moved by my discourse, and owned he had never seen a Christian in his life. I trust he will obey the call at his eleventh hour.[92]

From ten to two got with my sister Hall in Salisbury. She stands alone.[93] Every soul of his society has forsaken the ordinances of God, for which reason she refuses to belong to it. Gathered up a few more scattered sheep between this and London, not one of whom had ever before in their lives been spoken to by any man concerning their souls. God's people perish for lack of knowledge.[94] How can any one be so devilish as to forbid our speaking to such outcasts, that they may be saved?

**Friday, August 12.** By nine at night hardly reached the Foundery. Here I heard the Moravians would not be present at the conference. Spangenberg indeed *said* he would, but immediately left England. My brother was come from Newcastle, John Nelson from Yorkshire, and I from the Land's End, to good purpose.

**Sunday, August 14.** At the chapel I expounded the Pharisee and Publican [Luke 18:9-14].[95] The two-edged sword slew some,[96] I am persuaded. Mr Garden[97] helped administer the Sacrament.

**Saturday, August 20.** Preached for the first time at the new chapel in Snowsfields.[98]

**Sunday, August 21.** My brother set out for Cornwall. I received supernatural strength to expound, after a restless night of pain.

**Tuesday, August 23.** The Spirit sealed those words on our hearts, while I expounded at Deptford, "The Spirit and the Bride say, Come"

---

91. I.e., Blandford Forum, Dorset.

92. Cf. Matt. 20:6.

93. Westley Hall at this point had left his most recent Anglican parish in London and was setting up an independent society in Salisbury. Patty remained loyal to the Church.

94. Cf. Prov. 20:15.

95. A sermon on this text has survived, though it is not certain it is the sermon preached on this occasion. See *Sermons*, 268–76.

96. Cf. Heb. 4:12.

97. Rev. James Garden (d. 1772?), rector of Slingsby, Yorkshire, and curate of Hovingham; cf. John Wesley, *Journal* (August 14, 1743), *Works* 19:330.

98. A chapel run by Sayer Rudd, in the Snowsfields, just south of London Bridge.

[Rev. 22:17]. Rode to Bexley and found my friend on a sickbed, but full of peace and comfort.

**Wednesday, August 24.** While I was exhorting them at the Foundery to constant prayer, several bore witness of the great benefit they had found therein since our last meeting.

**Thursday, August 25.** Sent for to Mr Piers, who lay a-dying in convulsions. Prayed for him first with a friend, who said, "If he is not dead already, he will not die now." Got to Bexley by three. My brother had recovered his senses about the time we were praying for him. I was much comforted by his calm resignation, and in prayer saw, as it were, heaven opened, having seldom had greater freedom of access.

Hastened back to the Foundery, and preached without any natural strength. One testified his then receiving forgiveness.

**Friday, August 26.** Met Mr Robson, who is now quite removed from the hope of the gospel, denying both justification and sanctification.

The Lord answered for himself at the chapel, while I spake on the threefold office of the Spirit.[99] His power overshadowed the Society also, and applied my exhortation to many hearts.

**Saturday, August 27.** Found the blessedness of mourning with them that mourn, even the penitents, whom we met this evening at the Foundery.

**Sunday, August 28.** At the chapel I discoursed on the Good Samaritan [Luke 10:29-37], and we felt his oil and wine poured in. To many more he was made known in the breaking of bread. Honest Howell Harris was partaker of our joy.

At the Foundery preached Christ, our prophet, priest, and king, in his own words, "The Spirit of the Lord God is upon me" etc. [Luke 4:18]. Strong words of consolation were given me now, and at the following Love-feast.

# SEPTEMBER 1743

**Friday, September 2.** Visited our brother Parker near death (as was supposed), but triumphing over it, through Him that giveth us the victory.

---

99. Possibly using John 16:5-15; on the Spirit's office to convict, convince, and guide.

News was brought me again that Mr Piers was dying. Next morning I found him more than conqueror in a mighty conflict he had for eight hours with all the powers of darkness. "Now," he told me, "I shall not die, but live, and declare the works of the Lord."

**Sunday, September 4.** Baptized a woman at the chapel, before the service. She was in the spirit of heaviness, but God magnified his ordinance, and she was therein enlightened to see her sins forgiven.

**Wednesday, September 7.** Visited one struck down on Sunday night, both soul and body, but now rejoicing in the sense of God's pardoning love.

Delivered my own soul by speaking my mind to a reviler and hater of God in his children.

Rejoiced to hear of Miss Cowper's[100] release, and found my soul mounting up after her, all this and the following day.

**Saturday, September 10.** Went to the house of our late-translated sister, and rejoiced over the breathless temple of the Holy Ghost.[101]

**Sunday, September 11.** Met one of the Tabernacle, thoroughly convinced of the necessity of holiness. Many more shall follow, if we tarry the Lord's leisure.

**Tuesday, September 13.** At Mr Watkins's I told his pharisaical sister that she was then in a lost estate, and took my leave till she feels the wrath of God abiding on her.

**Friday, September 16.** Received great power to invite poor sinners at the chapel, while enforcing, "Come now, and let us reason together, saith the Lord" [Isa. 1:18].

**Saturday, September 24.** Reproved one for swearing, among an army of porters and carmen. Spoke to them for some time, till all were overpowered. Carried two away with me to the Foundery. They received my saying and books, and departed with their eyes full of tears, and their hearts of good desires.

---

100. This appears to be Anne Cowper, whose death Charles memorialized in a poem published the next year in *MSP* 3:285–88 (*Poetical Works*, 3:177–80), though the title of the poem refers to "Mrs" Cowper.

101. Cf. 1 Cor. 6.19.

*Wednesday, September 28.* At the chapel preached "through this man forgiveness of sins" [Acts 13:38]; never with greater demonstration of the Spirit.

# OCTOBER 1743

*Saturday, October 1.* Rode out of town to Friend Hiam's country house, and had much useful conversation with him.

*Wednesday, October 5.* Described the Laodicean spirit [Rev. 3:14-22], with great convincing power.

*Thursday, October 6.* Expounded Wrestling Jacob [Gen. 32:24-31] at the Foundery, and promised the Society an extraordinary blessing if they would seek the Lord early the next morning.

*Friday, October 7.* The Foundery was full, and God confirmed the word of his servant, while I explained, "All power is given unto me" [Matt. 28:18]. Some received the *blessing* of the gospel, or forgiveness, and no one, I believe, was sent empty away. At intercession a great awe of God fell upon us, and we trembled before the presence of the Lord, before the presence of the Lord of the whole earth.

*Sunday, October 9.* Still He meets us in the place which he has chosen to record his name. John Bray was one of my joyful congregation. It was a Passover indeed.

*Friday, October 14.* A mighty awakening power was with the word, "The blind receive their sight" [Matt. 11:5].

*Saturday, October 15.* At Short's Gardens[102] I preached, "It is of thy mercy only that we are not consumed" [Lam. 3:22]; and we were all melted down by the sense of His infinite patience and long-suffering.

*Sunday, October 16.* Administered the Sacrament, and found after it the usual power in prayer.

*Monday, October 17.* Set out to meet my brother at Nottingham.

*Wednesday, October 19.* Preached twice in Markfield church, and was much comforted with my brother Ellis, and his little increasing

---

102. A neighborhood near Covent Garden, just north of central London.

flock. Talked with several, and took knowledge of them, that they have been with Jesus. One received the atonement after my word.

**Thursday, October 20.** Preached at Nottingham Cross, and met the Society we began half a year ago, increased from eleven to fifty. They have been sifted like wheat by their two potent enemies—stillness and predestination. One simple soul I was enabled to rescue. I discerned her at first sight by her form of humility and meekness. Her tone and posture spoke her a poor sinner. She confessed that the Germans had taken great pains to wean her from her bigotry to the Church and ordinances; that they laughed at her reading the Scriptures, at her praying, and fasting, and mourning after Christ. When she quoted any Scripture-proof, they set it aside with, "O, that you must not mind. That is all head-knowledge." When she said she could not rest with such an evil heart, they answered, "O, you are not willing to be a poor sinner." They were always happy, they told her, always easy; without trouble, care, or temptation of any kind. But all her sorrow and poverty, and hunger, and heaviness through manifold temptations, was bondage, and the law, and works, and because she would not be a poor sinner.

I prayed over her in faith, and scales fell from her eyes. She saw through them in a moment, and all their pretences to humility, liberty, and faith. The tempter left her for a season, and the angels came and ministered unto her.[103]

This people, I think, are faster asleep than ever, through their having been once awakened. Satan could not have gained a greater advantage than by Mr Rogers's misconduct. How is the shepherd smitten, and the flock scattered! Woe unto the man who does not continue in the ship! They only shall prosper that love Jerusalem.[104]

**Friday, October 21.** My brother came, delivered out of the mouth of the lion! He *looked* like a soldier of Christ. His clothes were torn to tatters. The mob of Wednesbury, Darlaston, and Walsall were permitted to take him by night out of the Society-house and carry him about several hours, with a full purpose to murder him. But his work is not finished, or he had now been with the souls under the altar.[105]

---

103. Cf. Matt. 4:11.
104. Cf. Ps. 122:6.
105. Cf. Rev. 6:9.

*Saturday, October 22.* The spirit of prayer was given at the Society, so that every soul was in some measure sensible of it.

*Sunday, October 23.* Went to church with Mr How (for they cannot yet wean him of that bigotry), and found a great spirit of mourning for the captive daughter of Sion.[106]

Met at the Cross the largest concourse of people (they told me) that had ever been seen there. They were more concerned than I had before observed them, and listened for an hour in fixed attention.

*Monday, October 24.* Had a blessing at parting from the Society. I set out at five, and by night came weary and wet to Birmingham.

*Tuesday, October 25.* Much encouraged by the faith and patience of our brethren from Wednesbury, who gave me some particulars of the late persecution. My brother, they told me, had been dragged about for three hours by the mob of three towns. Those of Wednesbury and Darlaston were disarmed by a few words he spoke, and thenceforward laboured to screen him from their old allies of Walsall; till they were overpowered themselves, and most of them knocked down. Three of the brethren, and one young woman, kept near him all the time, striving to intercept the blows. Sometimes he was almost borne upon their shoulders through the violence of the multitude, who struck at him continually that he might fall. And, if he had once been down, he would have rose no more. Many blows he escaped through his lowness of stature, and his enemies were struck down by them. His feet never once slipped, for in their hands the angels bore him up.[107]

The ruffians ran about asking, "Which is the minister?" and lost, and found, and lost him again. That Hand, which struck the men of Sodom and the Syrians blind, withheld or turned them aside. Some cried, "Drown him! throw him into a pit!" Some, "Hang him up upon the next tree!" Others, "Away with him! away with him!" and some did him the infinite honor to cry, in express terms, "Crucify him!" One and all said, "Kill him!" But they were not agreed what death to put him to. In Walsall several said, "Carry him out of the town. Don't kill him here. Don't bring his blood upon us!"

---

106. Cf. Isa. 52:2.
107. Cf. Matt. 4:6.

To some who cried, "Strip him, tear off his clothes!" he mildly answered, "That you need not do. I will give you my clothes, if you want them." In the intervals of tumult, he spoke, the brethren assured me, with as much composure and correctness as he used to do in their Societies. The Spirit of glory rested on him. As many as he spoke to, or but laid his hand on, he turned into friends. He did not wonder (as he himself told me) that the martyrs should feel no pain in the flames, for none of their blows hurt him, although one was so violent as to make his nose and mouth gush out with blood.

At the first justice's whither they carried him, one of his poor accusers mentioned the only crime alleged against him: "Sir, it is a downright shame. He makes people rise at five in the morning to sing psalms." Another said, "To be plain, Sir, if I must speak the truth, all the fault I find with him is that he preaches better than our parsons." Mr Justice did not care to meddle with him, or with those who were murdering an innocent man at his Worship's door. A second justice in like manner remanded him to the mob. The mayor of Walsall refused him protection when entering his house, for fear the mob should pull it down. Just as he was within another door, one fastened his hand in his hair, and drew him backward, almost to the ground. A brother, with the peril of his life, fell on the man's hand, and bit it, which forced him to loose his hold.

The instrument of his deliverance at last was the ringleader of the mob, the greatest profligate in the country. He carried him through the river upon his shoulders. A sister they threw into it. Another's arm they broke. No further hurt was done our people, but many of our enemies were sadly wounded.

The minister of Darlaston[108] sent my brother word he would join with him in any measures to punish the rioters; that the meek behaviour of our people, and their constancy in suffering, convinced him the counsel was of God; and he wished all his parish Methodists.

They pressed me to come and preach to them in the midst of the town. This was the sign agreed on betwixt my brother and me. If they asked me, I was to go. Accordingly, we set out in the dark, and came to Francis Ward's, whence my brother had been carried last Thursday night. Found the brethren assembled, standing fast in one mind and spirit, in nothing terrified by their adversaries. The

---

108. Rev. John Rowley.

word given me for them was, "Watch ye, stand fast in the faith, quit yourselves like men, be strong" [1 Cor. 16:13]. Jesus was in the midst, and covered us with a covering of his Spirit. Never was I before in so primitive an assembly. We sang praises lustily, and with a good courage, and could all set to our seal to the truth of our Lord's saying, "Blessed are they that are persecuted for righteousness' sake" [Matt. 5:10].

We laid us down and slept, and rose up again, for the Lord sustained us. Assembled before day to sing hymns to Christ as God. As soon as it was light, walked down the town and preached boldly on Rev. 2:10: "Fear none of those things which thou shalt suffer. Behold, the devil shall cast some of you into prison, that ye may be tried; and ye shall have tribulation ten days. Be thou faithful unto death, and I will give thee a crown of life." It was a most glorious time. Our souls were satisfied as with marrow and fatness,[109] and we longed for our Lord's coming to confess us before his Father and his holy angels.

We now understood what it was to receive the word in much affliction, and yet with joy in the Holy Ghost.[110]

Took several new members into the Society; and among them, the young man whose arm was broke, and (upon trial) Munchin, the late captain of the mob. He has been constantly under the word since he rescued my brother. I asked him what he thought of him. "Think of him!" said he: "That he is a man of God, and God was on his side when so many of us could not kill one man."

We rode through the town, unmolested, to Birmingham, where I preached, and one received faith. Rode on to Evesham, and found John Nelson preaching. Confirmed his word, and prayed in the Spirit.

*Thursday, October 27.* Preached at five; then read prayers, and preached twice at Quinton; and the fourth time in Evesham, with much life and liberty.

*Friday, October 28.* Called on the eager, loving souls at Gotherington,[111] "Behold the Lamb of God, who taketh away the sin of the world!" [John 1:29]. Again at Cirencester, and slept at a well-disposed widow's.

---

109. Cf. Ps. 63:5.
110. Cf. 1 Thess. 1:6.
111. Charles spells "Gutherton."

*Saturday, October 29.* Came once more to Bristol, where I have spent but one day these six months.

*Sunday, October 30.* Rejoiced among our colliers, who received the word as at the beginning, "with power, and the Holy Ghost, and in much assurance" [1 Thess. 1:5].

Preached in the Horsefair on "The Spirit and the bride say, Come" [Rev. 22:17]; and gave the Society an account of the late persecution. God sent a gracious rain upon his inheritance, and refreshed our weary souls.

*Monday, October 31.* Set out at five for Wales, commended to the grace of God. Preached in the way at farmer Whitchurch's. When we came to the Passage, the boatmen refused to venture over in such a storm. We waited till four, then committed ourselves to him whom the winds and seas obey, and embarked with Mr Ashton and faithful Felix Farley. The rest of the passengers stayed on the safe side.

The waves of the sea were mighty, and raged horribly. When, with much toiling, we were come near the opposite shore, the storm caught the vessel. Our sails were backed, and we driving full on the Black Rock, where thirty-two persons lost their lives a few weeks since. But the answer of prayer, after much fatigue, brought us to the haven. O that men would therefore praise the Lord for his goodness, and declare the wonders which he doeth for the children of men![112]

It was dark when we landed. However, we had a good Guide (the devil is no darkness to him) who conducted us through the heavy rain, to the rock and fountain. I spoke a word in season to the poor, young women servants, who dwell as in the confines of hell, and in the midst of human devils.

# NOVEMBER 1743

*Tuesday, November 1.* Took horse some hours before day, and by ten reached Cardiff. The gentlemen had threatened great things if I ever came here again. I called in the midst of them, "Is it nothing to you, all ye that pass by?" etc. [Lam. 1:12]. The love of Christ con-

---

112. Cf. Isa. 8:18.

strained me to speak and then to hear. The word was irresistible. After it, one of our most violent opposers took me by the hand and pressed me to come to see him. The rest were equally civil all the time I stayed. Only one drunkard made some disturbance, but, when sober, sent to ask my pardon.

The voice of praise and thanksgiving was in the Society. Many are grown in grace, and in the knowledge of our Lord Jesus.

Passed an hour with the wife and daughter of the chief bailiff, who are waiting as little children for the kingdom of God.

*Wednesday, November 2.* Declared in the castle yard, "The Son of man is come to seek and to save that which was lost" [Luke 19:10]. At noon my commission was still, "Comfort ye, comfort ye my people" [Isa. 40:1]. I find the truth of Mr [John] Hodges's observation, "The gospel makes way for the law."

*Thursday, November 3.* Read prayers and preached at Wenvoe, then in our old chapel at the castle, and rejoiced with my dear friends in sure and steadfast hope of the glory of God.

*Friday, November 4.* Prayed with the Society at five. Preached at seven. Rode back to Cardiff and joined in fervent intercession. Preached faith in the blood of Christ to the poor weeping prisoners. Made a collection for them, and distributed books. Besought them at the room to be reconciled to God [2 Cor. 5:20], and the power of the Lord bore all before it.

*Saturday, November 5.* Took a sweet leave of the brethren. Got to the Passage by ten, but the boatman, notwithstanding our entreaties, could not be persuaded to pass in that weather.

*Sunday, November 6.* Took boat at nine, nothing doubting. The floods lifted up their voice,[113] but faith saw Jesus walking on the water, and heard his voice, "It is I, be not afraid."[114] In eight minutes were brought safe to land by him who rides the whirlwind.

At two preached to the colliers from, "Said I not unto thee, If thou wouldst believe, thou shouldst see the glory of God?" [John 11:40]. Their spirit bore me up, as on eagles' wings.[115] We all rejoiced in our strong salvation.

---

113. Cf. Ps. 93:3.
114. Matt. 14:27; Mark 6:50; John 6:20.
115. Cf. Isa. 40:31.

*Sunday, November 13.* In the word, and Sacrament, and Love-feast, the Lord showed that the efficacy of his ministration doth not depend on the life or holiness of the minister.

*Wednesday, November 16.* Preached in Bath on my way to Cirencester. There the Lord gave testimony to his word, "I have blotted out as a thick cloud thy transgressions" [Isa. 44:22]. Preached at Gotherington, Evesham, Quinton, Oxford; and on *Thursday, November 24,* at the Foundery.

*Sunday, November 26.* Gave the Sacrament to about 1,000 of the Society, and poured out our souls in prayer.

*Wednesday, November 29.* Was greatly assisted to declare, "The Son of man came to seek and to save that which was lost" [Luke 19:10].

# DECEMBER 1743

*Thursday, December 8.* Called on Mr Witham, given over by his physicians, trembling at the approach of the king of terrors,[116] and catching at every word that might flatter his hopes of life.

*Friday, December 9.* Prayed with him again, and found him somewhat more resigned.

*Monday, December 19.* Mostly employed for some days past in comforting an afflicted friend, whose son lay dying of the smallpox.

*Tuesday, December 20.* Prayed in great faith for Mr Witham, the time of whose departure draws nigher and nigher.

*Friday, December 23.* At half-hour past seven in the evening he broke out, "Now I am delivered! I have found the thing I sought. I know what the blood of sprinkling means!" He called his family and friends to rejoice with him. Some of his last words, " 'Why tarry the wheels of his chariots' [Judg. 5:28]. 'I know that my Redeemer liveth' [Job 19:25]. Just at twelve this night my spirit will

---

116. Cf. Job 18:14.

return to him." While the clock was striking twelve, he died like a lamb with that word, "Come, Lord Jesus!" [Rev. 22:20].

*Saturday, December 24.* Called on Friend Keen's son, just as his wife had told her dream that I should come that morning. They both seem truly simple of heart. Our meeting was not in vain. Rode in the afternoon to Bexley.

*Christmas Day.* Heard that one of our fiercest persecutors, who had cut his throat, and lay for dead for some hours, was miraculously revived, as a monument of divine mercy. Many of his companions have been hurried into eternity, while fighting against God. He is now seeking him whom once he persecuted.[117] Was confounded at the sight of me, much more by my comfortable words, and a small alms. He could only thank me with his tears.

Read prayers and preached, "Glory be to God in the highest" [Luke 2:14], to a people who now have ears to hear.

*Monday, December 26.* Spent four days between Wilmington, Welling, and Bexley, preaching the gospel.

*Friday, December 30.* Called on a friend, near death yet unprepared for it, and faithfully, not fashionably, told him his condition.

*Saturday, December 31.* Visited, at his desire, an opposer of the truth, till softened by the approach of death, and showed him his want of a Savior. He now expresses incredible eagerness for redemption in the blood of Jesus.

# JANUARY 1744

*Sunday, January 1, 1744.* Rode to Bexley and expounded the character of wisdom, Proverbs 3. God, as it seems, is turning the heart of this people back again. A surprising change I find in walking the streets. Nothing but kind salutations, instead of my usual reception with stones and curses.

*Tuesday, January 3.* Triumphed with an old disciple of fourscore, dying in the faith.

---

117. Cf. Gal. 1:23.

*Thursday, January 5.* I finished H.'s account of the iniquitous Synod of Dort;[1] iniquitous even in the judgment of a predestinarian. God deliver me from their tender mercies!

*Sunday, January 8.* At the chapel explained and applied the barren fig-tree [Luke 13:6-9]. The convincing Spirit was present. A company of players roared mightily for their master, but could not stop the course of the word.

*Sunday, January 15.* My text was, "Rejoice O daughter of Sion, behold thy King cometh" [Zech. 9:9]. His near approach did gladden our hearts, and in the Sacrament our joy was increased.

*Saturday, January 21.* Preached the gospel in Snowsfields, with much contention, and continued in prayer and thanksgiving till our enemies quitted the field.

*Sunday, January 22.* Expounded the Parable of the Sower [Matt. 13:3-23], God applying his own word. Exhorted the bands to join in the great work which God is working in our days.

*Sunday, January 29.* Assisted my brother and Mr Garden in administering the Sacrament to almost our whole Society of above 2000.

*Monday, January 30.* Set out with our brother [John] Webb for Newcastle commended to the grace of God by all the brethren. By Wednesday afternoon we found our brother [James] Jones at Birmingham.

# FEBRUARY 1744

*Wednesday, February 1.* A great door is opened in this country, but there are many adversaries. At Dudley our preacher was cruelly abused by a mob of Papists and Dissenters (the latter stirred up by Mr Whitting, their minister). Probably he would have been murdered, but for an honest Quaker who helped him to escape disguised with his broad hat and coat. Staffordshire at present seems the seat of war.

---

1. Charles was almost certainly reading John Hales's (unsympathetic) letters describing the sessions of the Synod of Dort, which were published posthumously as *Golden Remains of the ever Memorable Mr John Hales* (London: T. Garthwait, 1659).

*Thursday, February 2.* Set out with brother Webb for Wednesbury, the ~~least of~~[2] field of battle. Met with variety of greetings on the road. I cried in the street, "Behold the Lamb of God which taketh away the sin of the world" [John 1:29]. Several of our persecutors stood at a distance, but none offered to make the least disturbance.

Walked through the blessings and curses of the people (but the blessings exceeded) to visit Mr [Edward] Egginton's widow. Never have I observed such bitterness as in these opposers, yet they had no power to touch us.

*Friday, February 3.* Preached and prayed with the Society and beat down the fiery self-avenging spirit of resistance which was rising in some to disgrace, if not destroy, the work of God.

Preached unmolested within sight of Dudley. Many Shimeis[3] *called* after me, and that was all. Waited on the friendly Captain Dudley who has stood in the gap at Tipton Green[4] and kept off persecution, while it raged all around. Returned in peace through the enemy's country.

On Tuesday next (they have given it out) that they will come with all the rabble of the country, and pull down the houses and destroy all the goods of our poor brethren. One would think there was no King in Israel.[5] There is certainly no magistrate who will put them to shame in anything. Mr Constable offered to make oath of their lives being in danger, but the justice refused it, saying he could do nothing. Others of our complaining brethren met with the same redress, being driven away with revilings. The magistrates do not themselves tear off their clothes, and beat them; they only stand by, and see others do it. One of them told Mr Jones it was the best thing the mob ever did, so to treat the Methodists, and he would himself give £5 to drive them out of the country. Another, when our brother Ward begged his protection, himself delivered him up to the mercy of the mob (who had half murdered him before) threw his hat round his head, and cried "Hussa, boys! Well done! Stand up for the Church!"

No wonder that the mob, so encouraged, should say and believe that there is no law for Methodists. Accordingly like outlaws they

---

2. The struck out word "least" is unclear in the MS.
3. Cf. 2 Sam. 16:5-6.
4. Charles spells "Tippen."
5. Cf. Judg. 17:6.

treat them, breaking their houses, and taking away their goods at pleasure, extorting money from those that have it, and cruelly beating those that have not.

The poor people from Darliston are the greatest sufferers. The rioters lately summoned them by proclamation of the crier to come to such a public house and set to their hands that they would never hear the Methodist preachers, if or they should have their houses pulled down. About one hundred they compelled by blows. Notwithstanding which, both then and at other times, they have broken into their houses, robbing and destroying. And still, if they hear any of them singing or reading the Scripture, they force open their doors by day and by night and spoil and beat them with all impunity. They watch their houses, that none may go to Wednesbury; and scarce a man or woman but has been knocked down in attempting it.

Their enemies are the basest of the people, who will not work themselves, but live, more to their inclination, on the labours of others. I wonder the gentlemen who set them on are so shortsighted as not to see that the little all of our poor colliers will soon be devoured, and then these sons of rapine will turn upon their foolish masters who have raised a devil they cannot lay.

*Saturday, February 4.* Discoursed from Isaiah 54:17, "No weapon that is formed against thee shall prosper." This promise shall be fulfilled in our day. Spoke with those of our brethren who have this world's goods, and found them entirely resigned to the will of God. All thoughts of resistance are over, blessed be the Lord, and the chief of them said unto me, "Naked came I into the world, and I can but go naked out of it" [Job 1:21]. They are resolved by the grace of God to follow my advice and suffer all things. Only I would have had them go round again to the justices, and make information of their danger. Mr Constable said he had just been with one of them, who redressed him with bitter reproaches, that the rest are of the same mind, and cannot plead ignorance of the intended riot, because the rioters have had the boldness to set up papers in the towns (particularly Walsall) inviting all the *country to rise with them, and destroy the Methodists.*

At noon returned to Birmingham having continued two days in the lion's den unhurt.

*Sunday, February 5.* Preached in the bull-ring, close to the church, when they rang the bells, threw dirt and stones all the time. None struck me till I had finished my discourse. Then I got several blows from the mob that followed me, till we took shelter at a sister's. Received much strength and comfort with the Sacrament.

Preached again in Wednesbury, to a large congregation, many of whom come to hear the word at the peril of their lives. I encouraged them from Isa. 51[:9], "Awake, awake put on strength, O arm of the Lord" etc. Here, and in the Society, our Captain, we found, doth not send us a warfare at our own charge.

*Monday, February 6.* We commended each other to the divine protection and at five I set out for Nottingham. Our way lay through Walsall, the enemy's head-quarters. I would rather have gone a mile another way. Entering the place, we heard one hallooing with might and main, and a great noise followed, as if the town had taken the alarm. I cannot say the sound was very musical in my ears, but I looked up and rode onward. The noise was made by a gentleman huntsman, a bitter enemy of ours. We fell in with him and his dogs, it being just day-break, and passed for very good sportsmen. Brother Webb would needs ride through the market-place, to see the flag and paper our enemies had set up—and to show his courage. Had he returned with a broken head, I should not have greatly pitied him. By six our Lord brought us safe to Nottingham.

Met the Society, on whom He laid the burden of our persecuted brethren.

Here also the storm is begun. Our brethren are violently driven from their place of meeting, pelted in the streets, etc., and mocked with vain promises of justice by the very men who underhand encourage the rioters. An honest Quaker has hardly restrained some of the brethren from resisting evil. But henceforth, I hope, they will meekly turn the other cheek.[6]

*Shrove-Tuesday, February 7.* Waked in great heaviness, which continued all day for our poor suffering brethren; yet with strong confidence that the Lord will appear in their behalf. Joined the Society at five in fervent intercession for them, and in preaching both administered and received comfort. Sent my humble thanks to the mayor for his *offer* of assistance. He pities our brethren, and

---

6. Cf. Matt. 5:39-40.

*would* defend them, but who dares do justice to a Christian? We are content to wait for it till the great day of retribution.

At church, the psalms began, "Plead thou my cause, O Lord, with them that strive with me and fight thou against them that fight against me. Lay hand upon the shield and buckler and stand up to help me. Bring forth the spear and stop the way against them that persecute me. Say unto my soul, I am thy salvation" [Ps. 35:1-3, BCP].

We continued in this prayer with the Society, and had great fellowship with the sufferers.

At the brethren's desire I began preaching in the market-place. The holiday folk broke in among the hearers. I gave notice I should preach at the Cross just by the mayor's. In the way the mob assaulted us with dirt and stones, making us as the filth and offscouring of all things. My soul was caught up, and kept in calm ~~resignation~~ recollection. I knocked at the mayor's door. He let me in himself, gave us good words, threatened the rabble, and led me to his fore-door, where the people were waiting. I walked up to the Cross, and called them to repent. They would not receive my testimony; were very outrageous, yet not permitted to hurt me. The mayor at the same time passed by us laughing. Just such protection I expected!

After fighting with wild beasts for near half-an-hour, I went down into the thickest of them, who started back, and left an open way for me to the mayor's house. Mrs Mayoress led us through her house with great courtesy and compassion. The mob pursued us with stones as before. John Webb and I were strangers to the town, but went straight forward, and entered an house prepared for us. The woman received us, and shut the door, and spoke with authority to the mob, so that they began to melt away. There the brethren found, and conducted us to our friendly Quaker's. We betook ourselves to prayer for our fellow-sufferers in Staffordshire, who have not been out of our thoughts the whole day. I expounded the Beatitudes,[7] and dwelt upon the last. Never have I been more assisted. I rejoiced with our brethren in the fires.

**Wednesday, February 8.** I cannot help observing from what passed yesterday that we ought to wait upon God for direction when

---

7. Charles clearly used the Matthew account (5:1-12) in March 1740, and likely also here, though the Luke account (6:20-23) is possible.

and where to preach, much more than we do. A false courage, which is fear of shame, may otherwise betray us into unnecessary dangers. Farther we may learn not to lean on that broken reed, human protection. To seek redress by law, unless we are very sure of obtaining it, is only to discover our own weakness and irritate our opposers. What justice can be expected from the chief men of this place if, as I am informed, they are mostly Arian Presbyterians?

I exhorted the brethren to continue in the faith, and through much persecution, to enter the kingdom.[8] Four were missing; the rest strengthened by their sufferings.

Called at brother Sant's and found him just brought home for dead. The mob had knocked him down and would probably have murdered him, but for a little child, who being shut out of doors, alarmed the family by his cries.

It was some time before he came to himself, having been struck on the temples by a large log of wood. We gave thanks to God for his deliverance, and continued in prayer and conference till midnight.

*Thursday, February 9.* Our messenger returned from Lichfield with such an account as I looked for. He had met our brother Ward, fled thither for refuge. The enemy had gone to the length of his chain. All the rabble of the county was gathered together yesterday, and laid waste all before them. A note I received from two of the sufferers whose loss amounts to about £200. My heart rejoiced in the great grace which was given them—for not one resisted evil, but they took joyfully the spoiling of their goods. We gave God the glory that Satan was not suffered to touch their lives. They have lost all besides, and rejoice with joy unspeakable.

By five in the evening we came to Sheffield. I marvelled what was come to them, that we had not one stone in riding through all the town. Peace was in all their borders and has been for some time. The brethren are not slack during this rest, but walk in the fear of God. I preached on "We are come to Mount Sion" [Heb. 12:22]. The power of the Lord was remarkably present, but the power of the adversary quite restrained.

At nine passed through Thorpe. Asked my companion, "Where are the pretty wild creatures that were for braining me and my horse the last time I came this way?" He told me they had lost their spirit with their captain, a woman, the bitterest of them all, who died

---

8. Cf. Acts 14:22.

lately in horrible despair. This quite terrified our enemies. ~~His~~ Her daughter is now a believer, and several others in the place. Nay, they have even got a Society among them.

Preached at Barley Hall, and found the great power and blessing of God with the church in that house. One of my host's sons attended me to Birstall.

**Saturday, February 11.** Preached at five from "I am come that they might have life, and that they might have it more abundantly" [John 10:10]. We were greatly comforted by our mutual faith. The little flock increases both in grace and number. The Lord fights for Israel this day against the deceitful workers.[9] I was glad to hear of one of our English brethren, lately brought back by a little child— who told his father something, came and disturbed him, so that he could not sleep at nights, since they left off family-prayer.

Preached at Adwalton, on our Lord's final coming. It was a glorious season of rejoicing and love. In the afternoon preached at Armley. Arthur Bates of Wakefield, who showed me the way, informed me that his minister, Mr Arnet,[10] repelled him from the Sacrament and said he had orders from the Archbishop so to treat all that are called Methodists. The time, we know, will come when they shall put us out of their synagogues,[11] but I much suspect Mr Arnet has slandered the good Archbishop. In Leeds also, some begin to abuse their authority and to exclude the true (yea the *truest*) members of the Church from her communion.

**Sunday, February 12.** Preached at Leeds to many serious hearers, "Fear not, little flock, for it is" etc. [Luke 12:32]. Went to Mr M.'s church,[12] and heard him explain away the promise of the Father. But he stopped at the application to the Methodists; perhaps out of tenderness for me, whom he may still have some hopes of.

Called on a larger, and equally quiet congregation, "Is it no thing to you, all ye that pass by" etc.? [Lam. 1:12]. It was a blessed season. Many looked upon him whom they have pierced.[13]

---

9. Cf. 2 Cor. 11:13.

10. Rev. George Arnet (d. 1750), was vicar of Wakefield, 1729–1750. Charles spells "Arnett."

11. Cf. John 16:2.

12. This is almost certainly Rev. John Murgatroyd (c. 1703–1768), curate of St. John's chapel in Leeds, who became increasingly critical of Methodism (cf. the August 12, 1751, entry below).

13. Cf. Zech. 12:10 (Rev. 1:7).

I found John Nelson's hill quite covered with hearers. In the midst of my discourse a gentleman came riding up, and almost over the people. Speaking of temperance and judgment to come, I turned and applied to him, "Thou art the man" [2 Sam. 12:7]. His countenance fell, and he fled before the sword of the Spirit.[14] The power of God burst forth, and a cry was heard throughout the congregation. Continued my discourse, or rather prayer, till night.

*Monday, February 13.* Preached in the evening at Sykehouse[15] to the hearts of many.

*Tuesday, February 14.* Rode to Epworth and dined at Mr [John] Maw's, whose disputing is quite over, and he is ~~willing~~ waiting to receive the kingdom as a little child. The Lord gave his blessing to my word in the Cross. At the Society the Spirit came down as in the ancient days. My voice was lost in the mournings and rejoicings on every side. All present, I believe, were either comforted or wounded.

*Wednesday, February 15.* Explained the new covenant in the market-place, and many seemed desirous to enter into it.

*Thursday, February 16.* Rode to Selby.

*Friday, February 17.*[16] The next day at Darlington. My horse fell with me from an high causeway, and threw me unhurt into deep mud.

*Saturday, February 18.* Got to Newcastle by two. Preached at night from 1 Thess. 1:5, "For our gospel came not unto you in word only, but also in power, and in the Holy Ghost, and in much assurance." The people received me with that joy and love which the world knoweth not of.

*Sunday, February 19.* Sent away John Heally,[17] that he might not be torn to pieces by the mob, some of whom he has struck. It was so at Nottingham where they brought persecution upon themselves, a little sooner than needed, by striking a butcher. The man who struck him was the first that fell away. Not that all their meekness and wisdom could have kept it off long.

---

14. Cf. Eph. 6:17.
15. Charles spells "Sikehouse."
16. The date has been moved from the end of the entry, where Charles added it after apparently noticing that it was missing.
17. Charles spells "Healey."

Breakfasted at Mr Watson's, who now professes the faith which he persecuted in his daughters.[18] Heard of a remarkable providence. A poor drunkard, who has left us for some time, was moved this morning to rise and come to the preaching, by which he escaped being crushed to death by the fall of his house. He had no sooner left it than it was blown down, the greatest part of it. Just before it fell, his wife took one with her to the window to sing a hymn, and so escaped. A sister was overwhelmed with the ruins. Yet the rafters fell endways, and a cavity was made archwise over her head. She stayed there some hours before they could dig her out, rejoicing in God her Savior.

Told a huge multitude in the square, "Ye shall be hated of all men for my name's sake" [Mark 13:13]. Stood at the door of the orphanhouse, and took in many of the disturbers, to whom I then preached without opposition; and exhorted the brethren to prepare for the fiery trial.

*Monday, February 20.* Heard, without any surprise, the news of the French invasion,[19] which only quickened us in our prayers, especially for his Majesty, King George. In the evening expounded what the Spirit saith to the church of Ephesus [Rev. 2:1-7], and received extraordinary power to warn them of the sword that is coming,[20] and to wrestle with God in prayer for the King.

*Sunday, February 26.* Preached at Tanfield on Luke 21:34,[21] "And take heed to yourselves, lest at any time your hearts be overcharged with surfeiting and drunkenness and the cares of this life, and so that day come upon you unawares" etc. My mouth and heart were opened to this people, who seem now to have got the start of those at Newcastle.

Called at the square with greater utterance than ever, "Wash ye, make you clean," etc. [Isa. 1:16]. I urged them earnestly to repent; to fear God, and honor the King; and had the clearest testimony of my own conscience that I had now delivered my own soul.

---

18. These are apparently Ann and Margaret Watson, whom John Wesley wrote on May 28, 1745 (see *Works* 26:137).

19. This was an invasion of the Netherlands by a French army, not of England. But it did come in the context of France declaring war on England. The planned Franco-Spanish invasion of England came to nothing.

20. Cf. Ezek. 33:6.

21. Charles wrote "Luke 22:34," which is incorrect.

Found a great mob about our house, and bestowed an hour in taming them. An hundred or more I admitted into the room, and when I had got them together, for two hours exhorted them to repent, in the power of love. The rocks were melted on every side, and the very ringleaders of the rebels declared they would make a disturbance no[22] more.

*Monday, February 27.* Warned them at Horsley also, from Luke 21:34, to prepare for suffering times.

*Tuesday, February 28.* Rode in the high wind to Biddick, and preached to many unawakened sinners, "Wash ye, make you clean. Put away the evil of your doings," etc. [Isa. 1:16]. All seemed affected, especially our host (a poor drunkard that was) and his wife, a virtuous Pharisee. Both are now willing to be found in Christ, not having their own righteousness.[23]

It was as much as I could do, in returning, to sit my horse, the storm was so violent. At the Room I preached "The word of God— quick and powerful and sharper than any two-edged sword" [Heb. 4:12].

*Wednesday, February 29.* Rode with much difficulty to Plessy, and preached the gospel to a poor people ready prepared for the Lord.

# MARCH 1744

*Thursday, March 1.* Preached at Spen[24] to a weeping audience.

*Friday, March 2.* Visited a brother on his death-bed, who soon after departed in the Lord.

Preached at Whickham[25] on "He that endureth to the end, the same shall be saved" [Matt. 10:22]. We had sweet fellowship with our Lord in his word.

*Sunday, March 4.* The people of Newcastle were in an uproar through their expectation of a victory. They got their candles ready and gave thanks—that is, got drunk—beforehand, and then came

22. The word "no" has been written above the line in what appears to be a hand other than that of Charles; however, the sense clearly requires "no" at this point.
23. Cf. Rom. 10:3; Phil. 3:9.
24. I.e., High Spen, County Durham.
25. Charles spells "Wickham."

down to make a riot among us. Some of the brethren they struck, and threatened to pull down the desk. We were sensible that the powers of darkness were abroad, and prayed, in faith, against them. God heard and scattered the armies of the aliens here. Afterwards news came that at this very hour they were pulling down the house in St Ives.

*Monday, March 5.* Crossed the water, and preached at the glass-houses on "The One Thing Needful" [Luke 10:42]. In our return one at the head of a mob railed and cursed us so bitterly, that I concluded he must be a Roman Catholic. Found upon inquiry that he was son to a neighboring squire, a zealous Papist.

Passed an hour with Mr Watson, one of the town-sergeants, and lately the greatest swearer in Newcastle. Now God has touched his heart. Both his fellows, and his masters, the aldermen, are set against him, as one man. The mayor he tells me asked him publicly, "What, Mr Watson, do you go to hear these men?" He answered, "Yes, at every proper opportunity, and I wish you would hear them too." One of the aldermen expressed his impatience by cursing "that fellow Watson! We can neither make him drink nor swear."

*Tuesday, March 6.* Wrote to my brother: "My objection to your address in the name of the Methodists[26] is that it would constitute us a sect. At least it would *seem to allow* that we are a body distinct from the national Church, whereas we are only a sound part of that Church. Guard against this; and ~~address~~ in the name of the Lord, address tomorrow!"

*Thursday, March 8.* The Society at parting were all in tears. Lodged that night at Darlington.

*Saturday, March 10.* Came with John Downes to Epworth. On the common Thomas Westell[27] overtook us, being driven out of Nottingham by the mob and mayor. Called on Mrs Maw, and found her in a sweet waiting way. Her sickness has been a great blessing.

Preached at the Cross on "Enter into the rock and hide yourselves," ~~in~~ etc. [Isa. 2:10], to a people willing to take warning.

---

26. Charles is referring to a short address that John wrote on March 5 to King George II affirming the loyalty of Methodists to King George and the Church of England in the context of growing concern about a French invasion in support of Prince Charles Edward Stuart (the "Young Pretender") and Roman Catholicism; cf. John Wesley, *Works* 26:104–6.
27. Charles spells "Westal."

Took John Heally's account of their treatment at Nottingham. The mayor sent for Thomas Westell. John went with him. Thomas desired time to read the oath which they offered him, upon which Mr Mayor threatened to send him to prison. While he was making his mittimus,[28] John Heally asked, "Does not the law allow a man three hours to consider of it?" This checked their haste, and they permitted him to hear first what he should swear to. He said it was all very good, and what he had often heard Mr Wesleys say—that King George was our rightful King, and no other—and he would take this oath with all his heart.

They had first asked John Heally if he would take the oaths. He answered, "I will take them now. But I would not before I heard Mr Wesleys [sic], for I was a Jacobite till they convinced me of the truth, and of His Majesty's right." "See the old Jesuit," cries one of the venerable aldermen. "He has all his paces, I warrant you!" Another, on Thomas Westell's holding his hand to his eyes, cried, "See, see! He is confessing his sins!" They treated them like Faithful and Christian at Vanity-fair,[29] only they did not burn them yet, or even put them in the cage. They demanded their horses for the King's service, and would not believe them that they had none till they sent and searched.

Not finding any cause to punish they were forced to dismiss them. But soon after the mayor sent for Thomas Westell, and commanded him to depart the town. He answered he should obey his orders, and accordingly came to Epworth. Here he told me he had found out who the Pretender was, for ~~many~~ Mr Gurney told him many years ago there was one King James, who was turned out, and one King William taken in his place and that then the Parliament made a law that no Papist should ever be King, by which law King James's son, whom he had now discovered to be the Pretender, was justly kept out.

*Sunday, March 11.* Warned the people at the Cross, and then our children, to meet God in the way of his judgments [Isa. 26:8]. Rode the next day to Birstall.

*Tuesday, March 13.* Spent the day in visiting the brethren from house to house.

---

28. A legal document for sending someone to jail.
29. An allusion to the portrayal of persecution of two Christians by the hostile culture in John Bunyan, *The Pilgrim's Progress from this World to that which is to Come* (London: Nathaniel Ponder, 1672), 125ff.

*Wednesday, March 14.* Setting out for John Bennet's[30] Societies, one told me there was a constable with a warrant in which my name was mentioned. I sent for him, and he showed it me. It was "to summon witnesses to some treasonable words said to be spoken by one Westley." The poor man trembled, said he had no business with me, and was right glad to get out of my hands. He was afterwards of my audience, and wept, as did most. I was then taking horse, but found such a bar or burden crossing me that I could not proceed. At the same time, the brethren besought me to stay, lest the enemies should say I durst not stand trial. I knew not how to determine, but by a lot. We prayed, and the lot came for my stay.

It was much upon my mind that I should be called to bear my testimony, and vindicate the loyalty of God's people. By the order of providence, several justices are now at Wakefield. A woman stands to it that she heard me talk treason, but there is an overruling providence. I found it hard not to pre-meditate or think of tomorrow.

Met the brethren at Leeds, and many others in an old upper-room. After singing, I shifted my place to draw them to the upper end. One desired me to come nearer the door, that they might hear without. I removed again, and drew the weight of the people after me. In that instant the floor sunk. I lost my senses, but recovered them in a moment, and was filled with power from above. I lifted up my head first, and saw the people under me heaps upon heaps. I cried out, "Fear not. The Lord is with us. Our lives are all safe!" and then, "Praise God, from whom all blessings flow."[31] Lifted up the fallen as fast as I could, and perceived by their countenances which were our children; several of whom were hurt, but none killed.

We found, when the dust and tumult was a little settled, that the rafters had broke off short, close to the main beam. A woman lay dangerously ill in the room below on the opposite side, and a child in the cradle just under the ruins. But the sick woman calling the nurse a minute before, she carried the child with her to the standing side, and all three were preserved.

---

30. John Bennet (1715–1759), had been converted by David Taylor and involved in itinerant ministry in Derbyshire, Lancashire, and Cheshire before making contact with the Wesleys. From 1744–1750 he worked closely with the Wesleys, even through the tensions of his marriage to Grace Murray (whose other suitor was John Wesley). But growing discomfort with their doctrine and discipline (as too "popish") led to a break in 1752, and some competition of ministries.

31. See the hymn Wesley wrote on this event: "After a Deliverance from Death by the Fall of a House," *HSP* (1749), 2:237–38 (*Poetical Works*, 5:381–82).

Another of the Society was moved, she knew not why, to go out with her child, just before the room fell. Above one hundred lay with me among the wounded. Though I did not properly fall, but slid softly down, and light on my feet. My hand was bruised, and part of the skin rubbed off my head. One sister had her arm broke, and set immediately, rejoicing with joy unspeakable. Another, strong in faith, was so crushed that she expected instant death. I asked her, when got to bed, whether she was not afraid to die. She answered that she was without fear, even when she thought her soul was departing, and only said in calm faith, "Jesus, receive my spirit!" Her body continueds full of pain, and her soul of love.

A boy of eighteen was taken up roaring, "I will be good, I will be good." They got his leg set, which was broke in two places. He had come, as usual, to make a disturbance, and struck several of the women going in, till one took him up stairs for providence to teach him better.

After the hurry I opened my book on those remarkable words, "Therefore this iniquity shall be to you as a breach ready to fall, swelling out in a high wall, whose breaking cometh suddenly at an instant" [Isa. 30:13].

The news was soon spread through the town, and drew many to the place, who expressed their compassion by wishing all our necks had been broke. I preached out of the town, in weariness and painfulness. The Lord was our strong consolation. Never did I more clearly see that not a hair of our head can fall to the ground, without our heavenly Father.[32]

*Thursday, March 15.* Baptized a Quaker, who received forgiveness in that hour.

Rode to Wakefield, and at eleven waited upon Justice Burton at his inn, with two other justices, Sir Rowland Wynn, and the Reverend Mr Zouch.[33] Told him, I had seen a warrant of his to summon witnesses to some treasonable words, "said to be spoken by one Westley"; that I had put off my journey to London to wait upon him, and answer whatever should be laid to my charge.[34]

---

32. Cf. 1 Sam. 14:45; Matt. 10:30.
33. Rev. Charles Zouch (d. 1754), vicar of Sandal.
34. Note the hymn that Charles wrote as he prepared for this interview at Wakefield, in *HSP* (1749), 2:239 (*Poetical Works*, 5:382–83).

He answered he had nothing to say against me, and I might depart. I replied that was not sufficient, without clearing my character, and that of many innocent people, whom their enemies were pleased to call Methodists. "Vindicate them!" said my brother clergyman, "that you will find a very hard task." I answered, "As hard as you may think it, I will engage to prove, that they all, to a man, are true members of the Church of England, and loyal subjects of His Majesty King George." I then desired they would administer to me the oaths, and added, "If it was not too much trouble, I could wish, gentlemen, you would send for every Methodist in England, and give them the same opportunity you do me of declaring ~~his~~ their loyalty upon oath."

Justice Burton said he was informed that we constantly prayed for the Pretender in all our Societies, or *nocturnal meetings*, as Mr Zouch called them. I answered, "The very reverse is true. We constantly pray for His Majesty King George by name. These are such hymns as we sing in our Societies, a sermon I preached before the University,[35] another my brother preached there,[36] his *Appeals*,[37] and a few more treatises, containing our principles and practice." Here I gave them our books, and was bold to say, "I am as true a Church of England man, and as loyal a subject, as any man in the kingdom." "That is impossible," they cried all. But as it was not my business to dispute, and as I could not answer till the witnesses appeared, I withdrew without farther reply.

While I waited at a neighboring house, one of the brethren brought me the constable of Birstall, whose heart God hath touched. He told me he had summoned the principal witnesses, Mary Castle, on whose information the warrant was granted, and who was setting out on horseback when the news came to Birstall that I was not gone forward to London, as they expected, but round to Wakefield. Hearing this, she turned back, and declared to him that she did not hear the treasonable words herself, but another woman told her so. Three more witnesses, who were to swear to my words, retracted likewise, and knew nothing of the matter. The fifth, good Mr Woods, the ale-house keeper, is forthcoming, it seems, in the afternoon.

---

35. Charles Wesley, *A Sermon Preached on April 4, 1742 before the University of Oxford* (London: Strahan, 1742); cf. *Sermons*, 211–24.

36. This was likely *Salvation by Faith* (London: Hutton, 1738).

37. It is unclear why Charles makes this a plural. At this point John had published only *An Earnest Appeal to Men of Reason and Religion* (Newcastle: Gooding, 1743).

Now I plainly see the consequence of my not appearing here to look my enemies in the face. Had I gone on my journey, here would have been witnesses enough, and oaths enough, to stir up a persecution against the Methodists. I took the witnesses' names: Mary Castle, W. Walker, Lionel Knowls, Arthur Furth, Joseph Woods; and a copy of the warrant, as follows:

West Riding of Yorkshire.

To the Constable of Birstall, in the said Riding, or Deputy

These are, in His Majesty's name, to require and command you to summon Mary Castle of Birstall aforesaid, and all other such persons as you are informed can give any information ~~concerning~~ against one Westley, or any other of the Methodist speakers, for speaking any treasonable words or exhortations, as praying for the banished, or for the Pretender, etc., to appear before me, and other His Majesty's Justices of the Peace for the said Riding, at the White Hart in Wakefield, on the 15th of March instant, by ten of the clock in the forenoon to be examined, and to declare the truth of what they, and each of them know, touching the premises; and that you likewise make a return hereof before us on the same day. Fail not. Given under my hand the 10th of March, 1743.[38]

E. Burton

Between two and three, honest Mr Woods came, and started back at sight of me, as if he had trod upon a serpent. One of our brothers took hold on him, and told me he trembled every joint of him. The justice's clerk had bid the constable bring him to him as soon as ever he came. But notwithstanding all the clerk's instructions, Woods frankly confessed now he was come, he had nothing to say; and would not have come at all, had they not forced him.

I waited at the door where the justices were examining the disaffected till seven. I took public notice of Mr Ockershausen,[39] the Moravian teacher, but not of Mr [William] Kendrick.[40] When all their

---

38. I.e., 1744 (Burton is using Old Style dating, where the new year begins March 25).

39. John Ockershausen, of German ancestry, had joined the Moravians in London in 1739 and was now active in Yorkshire. Charles, who did not know him well, spells "Oberhausen."

40. This is William Kendrick, who had attached to the Moravians after Charles expelled him from the Foundery Society in 1741 (which is why Charles pays him no public notice here). Charles spells "Kindrick."

business was over, and I had been insulted at their door from eleven in the morning till seven at night, I was sent for and asked, "What would Mr Wesley desire?"

[*Wesley:*] "I desire nothing, but to know what is alleged against me."

[*Justice Burton:*] "What hope of truth from him? He is another of them." Then addressing to me, "Here are two of your brethren. One so silly, it is a shame he should ever set up for a teacher. And the other has told us a thousand lies and equivocations upon oath. He has not wit enough, or he would make a complete Jesuit."

[*Wesley:*] I looked round, and said, "I see none of my brethren here, but this gentleman," pointing to the Reverend Justice, who looked as if he did not thank me for claiming him.

[*Burton:*] "Why, do you not know this man?" (showing me Kendrick).

[*Wesley:*] "Yes, Sir, very well; for two years ago I expelled him [from] our Society in London, for setting up for a preacher." To this poor Kendrick assented, which put a stop to farther reflections on the Methodists.

[*Justice Burton:*] "I might depart, for they had nothing against me."

[*Wesley:*] "Sir that is not sufficient. I cannot depart till my character is fully cleared. It is no trifling matter. Even my life is concerned in the charge."

[*Burton:*] "I did not summon you to appear."

[*Wesley:*] "I was the person meant by 'one Westley,' and my supposed words were the occasion of that order, which I read, signed with your name."

[*Burton:*] "I will not deny my order. I did send to summon the witnesses."

[*Wesley:*] "Yes, and I took down their names from the constable's paper. The principal witness, Mary Castle, was setting out, but, hearing I was here, she turned back, and declared to the constable she only heard another say that I spoke treason. Three more of the witnesses recanted for the same reason. And Mr Woods, who is here, says he has nothing to say, and should not have come neither, had he not been forced by the minister. Had I not been here he would have had enough to say. And you would have had witnesses and oaths enough. But I suppose my coming has prevented theirs."

One of the justices added, "I suppose so too." They all seemed fully satisfied, and would have had me so too. But I insisted on their hearing Mr Woods.

[*Burton:*] "Do you desire he may be called as an evidence for you?"

[*Wesley:*] "I desire he may be heard as an evidence against me, if he has ought to lay to my charge."

Then Mr Zouch asked Woods what he had to say. What were the words I spoke? Woods was as backward to speak as they to hear him, but was at last compelled to say,

[*Woods:*] "I have nothing to say against the gentleman. I only heard him pray that the Lord would call home his banished."

[*Zouch:*] "But were there no words before or after, which pointed to these troublesome times?"

[*Woods:*] "No, none at all."

[*Wesley:*] "It was on February 12, before the earliest news of the invasion. But if folly and malice may be interpreters, any words which any of you gentlemen speak may be construed into treason."

[*Zouch:*] "It is very true."

[*Wesley:*] "Now, gentlemen, give me leave to explain my own words. I had no thoughts of praying for the Pretender, but for those that confess themselves strangers and pilgrims upon earth, who seek a country, knowing this is not their place. The Scriptures, you Sir, know (to the clergyman), speak of us as captive exiles, who are absent from the Lord while in the body. We are not at home till we are in heaven."

[*Zouch:*] "I thought you would so explain the words, and it is a fair interpretation."

I asked if they were all satisfied. They said they were, and cleared me as fully as I desired. I then asked them again to administer to me the oaths. Mr Zouch looked on my sermon, asked who ordained me (the Archbishop and Bishop of London the same week), and said with the rest, it was quite unnecessary, since I was a clergyman, and student of Christ-church, and had preached before the University, and taken the oaths before.[41] Yet I motioned it again, till they acknowledged in explicit terms "my loyalty unquestionable."

---

41. The Oath of Allegiance and Supremacy signed by Charles on June 13, 1726, is still extant, held in MARC (ref. DDCW 6/83).

I then presented Sir Rowland and Mr Zouch with the appeal, and took my leave.[42]

Half hour after seven we set out for Birstall, and a joyful journey we had. Our brethren met us on the road, and we gathered together on the hill, and sang praises lustily, with a good courage. Their enemies were rising at Birstall, full of that Wednesbury devil on presumption of my not finding justice at Wakefield, wherein they were more confirmed by my delay. They had begun pulling down John Nelson's house, when our singing damped and put them to flight. Now I see if I had not gone to confront my enemies, or had been evil intreated at Wakefield, it might have occasioned a general persecution here, which the Lord hath now crushed in the birth. No weapon that is formed against us shall prosper, and every tongue that shall arise against us in judgment we shall condemn.

*Friday, March 16.* Set out for Derby. Preached at a Society of David Taylor's, whose immoderate warnings against us has made them ten times more eager to hear us. A plain proof that his *poor sinners* are still under the law.

*Saturday, March 17.* Preached at Woodhouse at noon, and in the evening a little beyond Stopport.[43] I observed some go out upon my recommending prayer, but did not wonder when I heard they were *still*.

*Sunday, March 18.* Was much assisted to explain our Lord's words concerning himself to a great multitude, "The Spirit of the Lord God is upon me," etc. [Luke 4:18]. Preached at John Bennet's father's.[44] One only woman I saw remarkably unconcerned, who was wife to a *still* speaker.

Invited a much larger company in the evening to draw nigh with a true heart, in full assurance of faith. Bestowed two hours more in warning the Society against the devices of the *still* devil.

*Monday, March 19.* Cried, in the heart of the Peak,[45] "Ho, every one that thirsteth, come ye to the waters" [Isa. 55:1]. In the evening

---

42. See the hymn "Afterwards," that Charles wrote upon completing this interrogation at Wakefield, in *HSP* (1749), 2:240 (*Poetical Works*, 5:383–84).
43. Charles appears to mean Stockport, Derbyshire (within 5 miles of Chinley).
44. In Chinley, Derbyshire.
45. A forest area in Derbyshire, between Sheffield and Manchester.

I preached at Sheffield and read the Society the account of our brethren's sufferings which seemed to quicken them much.

At Barley Hall expounded Luke 21:34 and were all broken down by the power of love. Received fresh strength to pursue my journey. While passing Rotherham, where I had never been before, the mob rose upon us, but could not keep pace with our horses.

By night we came to Nottingham, and well for us that it was night. The mob are come to a great height through the encouragement of the mayor. We knew not the way to brother Sant's, and could not inquire, but our horses carried us straight to his door. The house was immediately beset as usual. I was troubled for these few sheep in the wilderness. The wolf has made havoc of them, the magistrates being the persecutors not only refusing them justice, but cruelly abusing them as rioters. They presented a petition to Judge Abdey as he passed through the town. He spake kindly to them, and bade them, if they were farther molested, present the corporation. He chid[ed] the mayor, and made him send his officers through the town forbidding any one to injure the Methodists. Told him, "if you will begin, why don't you put down the assemblies contrary to law? Instead of that, if there be one religious society, you must set upon that, to destroy it."

As soon as the judge was out of the town, they returned to persecute the Methodists more than ever. And when they complained to the mayor he insulted them, "Why don't you go to my Lord Judge?" He threatens when the press warrants[46] come out, to take Daniel Sant, an industrious founder with four children, whose crime is that he suffers the poor people to pray in his house.

*Wednesday, March 21.* Exhorted the few remaining sheep to keep together, and rode to Northampton, and the next day to the Foundery. The Society helped me to give hearty thanks to God for the multitude of his mercies.

*Monday, March 26.* My brother set out for Cornwall, where persecution rages. Rode to see Mrs Sparrow, of Lewisham, a martyr to worldly civility.

*Tuesday, March 27.* Called at the Foundery, "Wash ye, make you clean," etc. [Isa. 1:16]. The word had great effect. Met the leaders in the solemn presence of God.

---

46. Warrants to press men into military service.

*Thursday, March 29.* My mouth was opened to denounce judgments against this nation, except they repent.

*Friday, March 30.* At the time of intercession, we were enabled to wrestle for the nation with strong cries and tears. At the chapel the Spirit of supplication fell upon us more abundantly still.

# APRIL 1744

*Sunday, April 1.* Expounded part of Isaiah 1, and had power given me to warn them of God's approaching judgments. Our hearts were filled with joy in the evening.

*Wednesday, April 4.* In speaking on "The whole creation groaneth," etc. [Rom. 8:22], we felt the truth, and joined in the universal travail.

*Wednesday, April 11.* The Foundery was filled by four with those who came to keep the national fast. I preached at the chapel in great weakness both of soul and body. In the midst of my discourse, the floor began to sink, with our people on it. But none of them cried out, or made the least disturbance, while they got off it.

*Saturday, April 14.* We were alarmed by news of a second invasion. The French, we hear, are now in the Channel. Yet this infatuated people will not believe there is any danger till they are swallowed up by it. But he that taketh warning shall deliver his soul.[47]

*Thursday, April 19.* Sent Thomas Butts to Wednesbury, with £60, which I have collected for the sufferers.

*Wednesday, April 25.* Prevented a weak brother of Wednesbury making affidavit against the justices, and wrote to the brethren to suffer all things. At night I declared, "He that endureth to the end, the same shall be saved" [Matt. 10:22].

*Friday, April 27.* Preached on "Who is a God like unto thee, that pardoneth iniquity?" [Mic. 7:18]. All our hearts were enlarged and comforted. It was a time much to be remembered.

---

47. Cf. Ezek. 33:5.

*Sunday, April 29.* The whole congregation was in tears under the word. Old Mr Erskine,[48] in particular, was quite broken down. The same, or greater, utterance I had in the afternoon.

*Monday, April 30.* Overtook in the street by a well-dressed person, and found an unusual desire to look back upon her. However, I walked on, till she called me by my name. I turned back, and found it to be an old intimate friend, delivered to me, that I might make her a first and last offer of the gospel.

# MAY 1744

*Wednesday, May 2.* Passing through the Mews,[49] an heap of stones was cast down within a quarter of a yard of me, which, had they fallen upon me, must have dashed my brains out.

Mr [Thomas] Williams told me he had been with the Archbishop for orders; and, upon my blaming his hastiness, flew out of the house, as possessed by Legion.[50]

Overtook my old friend [Peter] Appee, in a ragged red waistcoat. He would not answer to his name, but followed and spoke with me. He has been a soldier some time, having run through the last stages of sin and misery.

*Thursday, May 3.* Set out for Bristol, and reached it the next day. I left London with an heavy heart, quite weighted down by poor Williams's burden. He answers the character one of his intimates gave me of him: "I never thought him more than a mere speaker. I can see no grace he has. His conversation is quite contrary to the gospel, all light and vain. He is haughty, revengeful, headlong, and unmanageable."

*Sunday, May 6.* At Kingswood I expounded the Good Samaritan [Luke 10:29-37], and saw their tears with joy.

*Tuesday, May 8.* Gave the Sacrament to our brother Jones, a dying believer, therefore above all fear, or doubt, or desire. Sarah

---

48. James Erskine (1679–1754) served as Lord Justice Clerk of the Court of Session 1710–1734, then resigned to enter parliament. He was a frequent source of legal advice for Charles in the years covered by the MS Journal.

49. The royal stables, near Charing Cross in London.

50. Cf. Mark 5:9.

Perrin was one of the communicants, and found the Lord in what she had been taught to call a carnal ordinance.

*Wednesday, May 9.* Preached at Bath, and saw them fall under the word, broken or melted. Miss H., in particular, was as the woman in tears at the feet of Jesus.[51]

Returned to Bristol, and finished my discourse on Simon and the woman that was a sinner [Luke 7:36-50]. A general cry was heard throughout the congregation. We knew not how to part, being so closely united in the love that never faileth.

*Thursday, May 10.* Dined at Felix Farley's with Mr Meriton, longing to escape to us out of the hands of Calvin.

*Friday, May 11.* Took horse at three, and got to London by one the next day.

*Saturday, May 12.* My brother gave me a melancholy account of Mr Williams. Disappointed of orders, he rages and rails on us as Papists, tyrants, enemies of the Church, etc. Declares he has found us out, and runs about scattering firebrands and vowing revenge.

*Whitsunday, May 13.* The root of bitterness is sprung up,[52] and thereby many are defiled. Offences abound, mostly among the young women, who are ready to tear me to pieces for "my cruelty to poor dear Mr Williams, and hindering him from getting orders."

Exhorted the Society to peace and charity, while my strength lasted.

*[Monday],*[53] *May 14.* Could not sleep last night for thinking of the young man, Absalom.[54]

We prayed mightily for our dear brother Nelson, pressed for a soldier, and a prisoner in York.

*Tuesday, May [15].*[55] Enforced the example of the Woman of Canaan [Matt. 15:22-28], and many cried after him who was come into their coasts.

Spoke with all kindness to Thomas Williams, but could not in any measure humble him.

---

51. Cf. Luke 7:44.
52. Cf. Heb. 12:15.
53. MS has "Sunday," which is in error.
54. Charles is comparing Thomas Williams to King David's power-hungry son; cf. 2 Sam. 14–15.
55. MS has "May 16," which is in error.

*Saturday, May 19.* Was waked this morning by the horrid blasphemies of one who did run well, and *was* plainly justified, but, through the spirit of offence, left the Society, then fell from one wickedness to another, such as drunkenness [and] adultery, and was now come to defy the living God. Him that thinketh he standeth, let him take heed lest he fall.[56] In vain hath God forgiven the whole debt, if the evil and wicked servant will not have mercy on his fellow-servant.[57]

Once more I besought poor Thomas Williams to return, and recover himself out of the snare of the devil. The Lord touched his proud heart. He burst into tears, and confessed the devil's devices to separate him from his best and only friends, and promised obedience for the time to come. I wept over him, and felt that, with all my heart, I could both forgive and forget.

*Wednesday, May 23.* Took up my cross, to oblige my brother, and began examining the classes, after earnest prayer for meekness and discernment. This day I only left out one, an incorrigible, unconvincible, bitter scold.

*Tuesday, May 29.* We have not had so great blessing in the word for a long time as while I was explaining, "I will allure her, and bring her into the wilderness, and speak comfortably unto her" [Hos. 2:14].

# JUNE 1744

*Saturday, June 2.* Mr [Samuel] Larwood discovered to me Mr Williams's real intention, "to set up for himself." Above five hundred of the Society, he told Larwood, would follow him.

*Wednesday, June 6.* Visited poor Appee, in the Tower,[58] ready for transportation.

Toward the end of my discourse at the chapel, Mr Erskine was *sent* to receive a soldier brought by William Shent, to redeem John Nelson. He immediately took him to Lord Stair's,[59] and got a

---

56. Cf. 1 Cor. 12:10.
57. Cf. Matt. 18:32-33.
58. The Tower of London, where deportees were held prior to their expulsion.
59. John Dalrymple (1673–1747), 2nd Earl of Stair, and current field marshal of the British troops.

discharge for John Nelson. Our brother Downes also we received out of the mouth of the lion. Our prayers return thick upon us.

*Friday, June 8.* Took my last leave of my old friend Appee, who embarks today for America. I gave him books and advice, which perhaps may not be finally lost upon him.

*Tuesday, June 12.* Preached on Wrestling Jacob [Gen. 32:24-31], and a glorious time it was. Many wept with the angel, and made supplication, and were encouraged to wait upon the Lord continually.

*Friday, June 15.* Grieved to hear more and more of Williams's ingratitude. A lying spirit seems to have taken full possession of him. There is nothing so gross or improbable which he does not say.

*Monday, June 18.* Wrote to a friend, "Be not you weary of well-doing, or overcome of evil. You see your calling, to suffer all things. Pray for me, that I also may endure unto the end, for a thousand times I cry out, 'The burden of this people is more than I am able to bear.' O my good friend, you do not know them. Such depth of ingratitude I did not think was in the devils of hell."

At night I was informed that a friend had entertained the deepest prejudice against me, on supposition that I meant her in a late discourse. Lord, what is man! What is friendship!

*Wednesday, June [20].*[60] By losing my way, found, at a wavering brother's house, five stray sheep, whom I received back into the fold.

*Sunday, June 24.* Our brethren, [John] Hodges, [Samuel] Taylor, and Meriton, assisted us at the Sacrament. Received it with the whole Society, to our mutual comfort. At our Love-feast we were six ordained ministers.[61]

*Monday, June 25.* We opened our Conference[62] with solemn prayer, and the divine blessing. I preached with much assistance, and baptized Samuel Holloway, who felt in that moment the great burden taken off. Continued in Conference the rest of the week, settling our doctrines, practice, and discipline, with great love and unanimity.

---

60. MS has "June 19," which is in error.
61. The sixth (in addition to the two Wesley brothers) was Henry Piers.
62. This was the first of what became Annual Conferences for the ordained and lay preachers in the Wesleyan Methodist movement.

# JULY 1744

*Monday, July 2.* At night I was drawn out in prayer, with strong cryings and tears. Received my poor prodigal Williams with open arms.

*Sunday, July 8.* Preached on our Lord's multiplying the loaves; neither did he send us empty away.[63] Exhorted a large audience at the Foundery to take to them the whole armour of God, and continued my discourse for two hours, the Lord comforting us on every side.

*Monday, July 9.* Took horse at two, with my friend and companion Meriton, and acknowledged the next day in Bristol, "Hitherto the Lord hath helped us" [1 Sam. 7:12].

I was strengthened to preach on "Let not your hearts be troubled" [John 14:27], and the Lord made me a son of consolation. A cry of distress first, and then of joy, ran through the congregation. Miss Barr, with many others, received the word into their hearts, and sorrow and sighing fled away before it.[64]

*Wednesday, July 11.* That I might ascribe nothing to my speaking, before I opened my mouth this morning my heart was constrained, and filled with godly fear. I then expounded, "If any man sin, we have an Advocate with the Father" [1 John 2:1] and many found the benefit of his intercession.

Passed two hours in Christian conference and prayer with Dr Middleton, and the church in his house.

*Thursday, July 12.* Enforced our Lord's most seasonable saying, "He that endureth to the end, the same shall be saved" [Matt. 10:22], and set out with Mr Meriton for Cornwall.

At Middlezoy[65] called the weary and heavy-laden to Christ [Matt. 11:28]. He gave testimony to the word of his grace, and bowed the hearts of all present. It was a sweet mourning indeed!

*Friday, July 13.* Set out with our guide, John Slocombe,[66] a poor baker's boy, whom God has raised up to help these sincere souls,

---

63. With this emphasis, Charles was focusing on the Feeding of the Four Thousand; Matt. 15:29-39, Mark 8:1-10.
64. Cf. Isa. 35:10.
65. Charles spells "Middlesea."
66. Charles spells "Slocum."

and not only to labour, but also to suffer, for them. When the press-warrants came out, the world would not lose the opportunity of oppressing the Christians. He was taken, and, by his own uncle, dragged away to prison. They kept him a week, and then brought him before the commissioners, who could find no cause to punish or detain him—being of Zaccheus's stature, and nothing terrified by his adversaries. They were obliged at last, notwithstanding all their threatenings, to let him go.

Called on Hannah Bidgood, at Sticklepath, and some others, mostly Quakers. My heart was drawn out toward them in prayer and love, and I felt, "He that doeth the will of my Father, the same is my brother and my sister and my mother" [Mark 3:35].

Met an aged clergyman,[67] whom Mr Thomson[68] had sent to meet us, and found in conversing that he had been an acquaintance and contemporary with my father. Upon Mr Thomson's preaching salvation by faith, he had received the kingdom as a little child, and has ever since owned the truth and its followers. He conducted us to his house near Trewint.[69]

*Sunday, July 15.* He carried us to St Gennys, where our loving host and brother Thomson received us with open arms. I made proof of my ministry in his church from, "Comfort ye, comfort ye my people," etc. [Isa. 40:1]; and again, from Blind Bartimeus [Mark 10:46-52]. The word took place in some hearts, I cannot doubt, though I am nothing.

*Monday, July 16.* He read prayers in Mr Bennet's church.[70] I preached on "Fear not, little flock, it is your" etc. [Luke 12:32].

*Tuesday, July 17.* Came, by nine at night, with Mr Bennet and Meriton, through the pits and shafts, to our host near Gwennap.

Here a little one is become a thousand. What an amazing work hath God done in one year! The whole country is alarmed, and gone forth after the sound of the gospel. In vain do the pulpits ring of "Popery, madness, enthusiasm." Our preachers are daily pressed to new places, and enabled to preach five or six times a day. Perse-

---

67. Rev. John Bennet (c. 1670–1750), curate of the churches in Laneast, Tresmeer, and North Tamerton.

68. Rev. George Thomson (1698–1782), vicar of St Gennys. Charles fluctuates in spelling the name "Tomson" or "Tompson."

69. Bennet lived in Tresmeer, Cornwall, which is four miles north of Trewint.

70. Almost certainly the Tresmeer church.

cution is kept off till the seed takes root. Societies are springing up everywhere, and still the cry from all sides is "Come and help us."

Preached near Gwennap to about a thousand followers of Christ on "Fear not, little flock" [Luke 12:32]. Great love and joy appeared in their faces, such as the world knoweth not of.

When I came to meet the Society, I found almost the whole congregation waiting quietly without the door, longing to be admitted with the rest. Stood at the window, so as to be heard of all. I felt what manner of spirit they were of, and had sweet fellowship with them, and strong consolation.

*Thursday, July 19.* Found the same congregation at five, and pointed them to the Son of man lifted up as the serpent in the wilderness [John 3:14]. Spake to each of the Society, as their state required.

Breakfasted with one who was a fierce persecutor when I was last in the country, but is now a witness of the truth she so bitterly opposed.

Preached at Crowan, to between one and two thousand sinners, who seemed started out of the earth. Several hid their faces, and mourned inwardly, being too deeply affected to cry out. I concluded with a strong exhortation to continue in the ship—the shattered sinking Church of England—and my brother Meriton, whose heart I spake, seconded and confirmed my saying. The poor people were ready to eat us up, and sent us away with many an hearty blessing.

We then set our faces against the world, and rode to St Ives. Here the mob and ministers together have pulled down the preaching-house, and but a fortnight ago went round in the dead of the night and broke the windows of all that were only suspected of Christianity.

We entered John Nance's house without molestation. Four of our sisters there, on sight of me, sunk down, unable to utter a word through joy and love. But they welcomed me with their tears. It was a solemn, silent meeting. In some time we recovered our speech for prayer and thanksgiving.——[71] Got an hour by myself in the garden, and was suffered to feel my own great weakness. Without were fightings, within fears. But my fears were all scattered by the sight of my dear brethren and children. I rejoiced over

---

71. At this point in the MS an extended dash appears.

them with singing, but their joy and love exceeded. We all rejoiced in hope of meeting him in the air.[72] The Spirit of glory rested on the sufferers for Christ's sake. My brother Meriton added a few words to mine, and their hearts clave to him. Such a feast I have not had for many months. Even our Father's hired servants had at this time bread enough and to spare.[73]

We laid us down in peace, and took our rest, for the Lord only made us dwell in safety.[74]

*Friday, July 20.* While I applied our Lord's most comfortable words, John 14:1, we were all dissolved in tears of joy, desire, love; and seemed on the wing to our heavenly Father's house.

Walked through the town to church with Mr Meriton. Our warm friend the curate[75] saluted us courteously, and none opened their mouth against us. Mr Meriton's stature and band kept them in awe. Or rather the fear of God was upon them, restraining them, though they knew it not.

Met at one, in obedience to our Church, and lifted up our voice for the remnant that is left. We tasted the blessedness of mourning, and doubt not, however God may deal with this sinful nation, but our prayers for Jerusalem will one day be answered.

*Saturday, July 21.* While we were walking near the key[76] our friend the mob set up a shout against us, and gave plain marks of their Cainish disposition, if permitted. Only one stone was cast at us. We passed through the midst of them, and set out for St Just.

I preached on the plain, and brother Meriton after me. Our Lord rides on triumphant through this place. Upward of two hundred are settled in classes, most of whom have tasted the pardoning grace of God.

*Sunday, July 22.* At nine I cried in the street, "Ho, every one that thirsteth, come ye to the waters!" [Isa. 55:1]. The word ran very swiftly. When God gives it, who can hinder its course? Had an opportunity of communicating with a sick brother; whence we all went to church. It was crowded with these schismatical Methodists,

---

72. Cf. 1 Thess. 4:17.
73. Cf. Luke 15:17.
74. Cf. Ps. 4:8, BCP.
75. William Hoblyn.
76. I.e., "quay."

who have not all, it seems, left it through our means. The curate is looked upon by his brethren as half a Methodist, only because he does not rail at us like them.

Preached at Morvah, without, since I might not within, the church-walls. I told a man who contradicted me that I would talk with him by and by. A visible blessing confirmed the word. Afterwards I took my rough friend by the hand, carried him to the house, and begged him to accept of a book. He was won, excused his rudeness, and left me hugely pleased.

Preached at Zennor, where very few hold out against the truth, notwithstanding the minister's[77] pains to pervert the ways of the Lord. None are of his, but who are evidently on Satan's side, even his drunken companions, whom he secures against the Methodists, and warns at the alehouse not to forsake the Church. Hastened back to Morvah, and rejoiced over many who were lost and are found.[78] One hundred and fifty are joined in Society, and continue steadfastly in the Apostles' doctrine, and in fellowship, and in breaking of bread, and in prayers.[79]

*Monday, July 23.* I breakfasted at Mr L.'s, a poor slave of Satan, till, at the sound of the gospel, his chains fell off, and left him waiting for the seal of his pardon. I pointed many sinners to the Lamb of God which taketh away the sin of the world [John 1:29]. All were in tears at the remembrance of His sufferings.

*Tuesday, July 24.* Preached near Penzance, to the little flock encompassed by ravening wolves. Their minister rages above measure against this new sect, who are spread throughout his four livings. His reverend brethren follow his example. The grossest lies which are brought them they swallow without examination, and retail the following Sunday. One of the Society (James Dale) went lately to the Worshipful and Reverend Dr Borlase[80] for justice against a rioter, who had broke open his house and stole his goods. The Doctor's answer was, "Thou conceited fellow, art thou too turned religious? They may burn thy house if they will. Thou shalt have no justice." With these words he drove him from the judgment-seat.

---

77. William Symonds.
78. Cf. Luke 15:32.
79. Cf. Acts 2:42.
80. Rev. Walter Borlase (1694–1776), LLD, rector of Ludgvan and vicar of St Just and Madron, was also the magistrate of this region in Cornwall.

Preached at St Just to the largest company that had ever been seen there, and strongly warned the Society against spiritual pride.

*Wednesday, July 25.* Enforced that most seasonable caution, "Him that thinketh he standeth, let him take heed lest he fall" [1 Cor. 10:12]. Two hours after, expounded the Pool of Bethesda [John 5:1-15], and dwelt upon our Lord's admonition to every justified sinner, "Go, and sin no more, lest a worse thing happen unto thee" [John 8:11].

Found the brethren at Morvah beginning to build a Society-house. We knelt down upon the place, and prayed for a blessing.

Before preaching at St Ives I was so weighed down that I would gladly have sunk into the earth or sea to escape my own burden. But God lifted me up by the word I preached, and filled us all with an hope full of immortality. We looked through the veil of things temporal, to things eternal, and the mount of God, where we trust shortly to stand before the Lamb. Every soul did then, I believe, taste the powers of the world to come,[81] in some measure, and longed for the appearing of Jesus Christ.

One of our sisters complained to the mayor of some who had thrown into her house stones of many pounds' weight, which fell on the pillow within a few inches of her sucking child. The magistrate damned her, and said, "You shall have no justice here. You see there is none for you at London, or you would have got it before now." With this saying he drove her out of his house.

*Friday, July 27.* Preached at Gulval, and admitted some new members, particularly one who had been the greatest persecutor in all this country.

*Saturday, July 28.* The last midnight assault upon our brethren, I am now informed, was made by the townsmen, and a crew that are here fitting out for privateers who thought it prudent to make the first proof of their courage upon their own unarmed countrymen. They made their regular approaches with beat of drum, to take the poor people's houses by storm. But they were only permitted to batter them with stones, and endanger the lives of a few women and children. Woe be to the first French or Spaniards, who fall into the hands of men so flushed with victory! They only want

---

81. Cf. Heb. 6:5.

the captain who drew upon me to head them, and then they would carry the world before them!

*Sunday, July 29.* Expounded Isa. 35 at St Just, and many hands that hung down were lifted up. From church I hasted to Morvah, and preached to a vast congregation, on "Blessed are they that hear the word of God, and keep it" [Luke 11:28]. At Zennor explained the Parable of the Sower [Matt. 13:3-23]. My brother Meriton added a few words, much to the purpose. I concluded with exhorting them to meet God in the way of his judgments.

We had our first Love-feast at St Ives. The cloud stayed the whole time on the assembly. Several were so overpowered with love and joy that the vessel was ready to break. I endeavoured to moderate their joy by speaking of the sufferings which shall follow; and they who were then with Him as on Mount Tabor[82] appeared all ready to follow Him to Mount Calvary.

*Monday, July 30.* Cried to a mixed multitude of wakened and unawakened sinners near Penzance, "Is it nothing to you, all ye that pass by?" [Lam. 1:12]. Prayed with the still-increasing flock, whose greatest persecutor is their minister.[83] He and the clergy of these parts are much enraged at our people's being so ready in the Scriptures. One fairly told Jonathan Reeves he wished the Bible were in Latin only, that none of the vulgar might be able to read it. Yet these are the men that rail at us as Papists!

*Tuesday, July 31.* Expounded the Woman of Canaan [Matt. 15:22-28] to an house-full of sincere souls, who had sat up all night to hear the word in the morning. Spake with some who have tasted the good word of grace, though they live in Penzance, where Satan keeps his seat.[84]

I visited a second time a poor dying sinner, who now gives up his own filthy rags for the best robe.[85] His daughter, upon her request, I admitted into the Society.

Rode to St Just. Climbed up and down Cape Cornwall[86] with my brother Meriton, to the needless hazard of our necks. Preached in

---

82. The scene of Christ's glorious transfiguration.
83. Penzance was part of the parish of Madron at this point, so Charles likely has Walter Borlase in mind here.
84. Cf. Rev. 2:13.
85. A conflation of Isa. 64:6 and Luke 15:22.
86. Cape Cornwall, on the west coast, is north of Land's End.

the afternoon to a larger congregation than ever, and continued my discourse till night, from Luke 21:34. The Spirit of love was poured out abundantly, and great grace was upon all. Walked to the Society. Stood upon the hill, and sang, and prayed, and rejoiced with exceeding great joy. Concluded the day and month as I would wish to conclude my life.

# AUGUST 1744

*Wednesday, August 1.* Preached in a new place, to near 2000 listening strangers, "Jesus Christ, the same yesterday, to day, and for ever" [Heb. 13:8].

I returned to St Ives, and found our beloved brother [George] Thomson, who was come to see us and the children whom God had given us. Our enemies were alarmed by his coming, and the brethren strengthened. At night I set before them the example of the first Christians, who "continued steadfast in the Apostles' doctrine" etc. [Acts 2:42]. For two hours we rejoiced as men that divide the spoil.

*Thursday, August 2.* Rode with Mr Thomson and Meriton to a large gentleman's seat near Penryn. We saw the people come pouring in from Falmouth and all parts. The court-yard which might contain 2000, was quickly full. I stood in a gallery above the people, and called, "Wash ye, make you clean," etc. [Isa. 1:16]. They eagerly listened to the word of life—even the gentlemen and ladies listened—while I preached repentance towards God, and faith in Jesus Christ [Acts 20:21]. I exhorted them in many words to attend all the ordinances of the Church, to submit to every ordinance of man for the Lord's sake, to stop the mouth of gainsayers by fearing God and honoring the King, and to prevent the judgments hanging over our heads by a general reformation.

*Saturday, August 4.* Preached at Gwennap, where the awakening is general. Very many who have not courage to enter into the Society have yet broke off their sins by repentance, and are waiting for forgiveness. The whole county is sensible of the change. For last assizes there was a gaol-delivery—not one felon to be found in their prisons, which has not been known before in the memory of man. At their last revel, they had not men enough to make a wrestling match, all the Gwennap men being struck off the devil's list, and found wrestling against him, not for him.

*Sunday, August 5.* Preached my farewell sermon at Gwennap, to an innumerable multitude. They stood mostly on the green plain before me, and on the hill that surrounded it. Many scoffers from Redruth placed themselves on the opposite hill, which looked like Mount Ebal.[87] O that none of them may be found among the goats in that day![88] I warned and invited all by threatenings and promises. The adversary was wonderfully restrained, and I hope disturbed in many of his children. My Father's children were comforted on every side. They hung upon the word of life, and they shall find it able to save their souls. Spoke on for two hours. Yet knew not how to let them go. Such sorrow and love as they then expressed, the world will not believe, though a man declare it unto them. My brother Thomson was astonished, and confessed he had never seen the like among Germans, predestinarians, or any others. With great difficulty we got through them at last, and set out on our journey. Several men and women kept pace with our horses for two or three miles, then parted, in body, not in spirit. We lodged three miles short of Mitchell.

*Monday, August 6.* Between five and six in the evening got to Mr Bennet's, and preached in his church on "Repent, and be converted" [Acts 3:19]. Upon my speaking against their drunken revels, one contradicted and blasphemed. I asked, "Who is he that pleads for the devil?" and one answered in those very words, "I am he that pleads for the devil." I took occasion from hence to show the revellers their champion, and the whole congregation their state by nature. Much good I saw immediately brought out of Satan's evil. Then I set myself against his avowed advocate, and drove him out of the Christian assembly. Concluded with earnest prayer for him.

*Tuesday, August 7.* In the afternoon Mr Meriton read prayers in Tresmeer church,[89] and I expounded the Good Samaritan [Luke 10:29-37] to a thronged audience. Some gentry were come eighteen

---

87. Charles probably has Josh. 8:30 in mind here.
88. Cf. Matt. 25:32-33.
89. Charles spells "Tresmere."

miles to hear the word, and received it with joy.[90] We have not had a more gracious season since we came into the country.

**Wednesday, August 8.** Read prayers and preached at St Gennys. One of my audience was a neighboring clergyman, my contemporary at Christ-Church, who came in much love to invite me to his house.

It should not be forgot the concurrent testimony which my brethren bore with me last Monday night in Mr Bennet's church against harmless diversions. On my declaring that I was by them kept dead to God, asleep in the devil's arms, secure in a state of damnation for eighteen years: Mr Meriton added aloud "And I for twenty-five"; "And I," cried Mr Thomson "for thirty-five"; "And I" said Mr Bennet "for above seventy."

**Thursday, August 9.** Rode by Brinsworthy, Mr Thomson's house near Barnstaple, to Minehead; where I besought near 1000 sinners to repent, and believe the gospel [Mark 1:15]. I found it possible to preach the law in its rigour, with such apparent good-will as shall convince without exasperating. But not unto me, O Lord, not unto me![91]

**Saturday, August 11.** At six set sail in a sloop our sister [Mary] Jones had sent to fetch me to Fonmon. Had a delightful passage. Landed at noon near Aberthaw, and were received by our dear friend, and three of her little ones, with some sisters from Cardiff. Went on our way singing and rejoicing to the castle.

Here I received the melancholy news of the miscarriage of one, whom I loved as my own soul.[92] I was sensibly wounded by his ingratitude. He has verified all my warnings and fears. But that he should attempt to justify himself by blackening me, was beyond all that I could have imagined. Lord, humble him; but do him good in his latter end.

At night I met many faithful children whom the Lord hath given us, and discoursed to them on my favourite subject. "These are they that came out of great tribulation," etc. [Rev. 7:14]. The God of all consolation was mightily with us, even the God who comforteth us in all our temptations. O how delightfully did we mourn after

---

90. Cf. Matt. 13:20 and Luke 8:13.
91. Cf. Ps. 115:1, "Not unto us, O Lord, not to us, but to your name give glory."
92. That is, Thomas Williams.

him whom our soul loveth—not with the noisy turbulent sorrow of newly-awakened souls which most times passes away as a morning-cloud, but with the deep contrition of love. All the congregation was in tears, in silent tears of desire or joy. This is the mourning wherewith I pray the Lord to bless me, till he wipes away all tears from my eyes.[93]

*Sunday, August 12.* Mr Hodges read prayers at Wenvoe. I preached convincing words and, after the Sacrament, prayed—the Spirit sealing the answer on our hearts.

Preached in the castle-yard at Cardiff. "Enter into the rock, and into the clefts of the rock" [Isa. 2:21]. Visited two sick brethren, one waiting for the salvation of God, the other in good measure possessed of it.

*Monday, August 13.* I called on the brethren again, assembled in their room, "Be not slothful, but followers of them" etc. [Heb. 6:12]. I was much revived by our dying brother, who is now ready to be offered up. I asked him whether he had rather die or live. He answered, "To depart and to be with Christ is far better."[94] He has been, both before and since his illness, a pattern for all Christian graces. Was the first in this place who received the gospel of full salvation. Now he only waits that most welcome word, "Come up hither."[95]

Prayed with him again some hours after, and rejoiced over him with strong triumphant faith. He said there was something near him which would make him doubt, but could not, for he knew his Savior stood ready to receive his spirit. I desired his prayers, kissed him, and took my last leave. He looked up, like my Hannah Richardson, and broke out, "Lord Jesus, give him a double portion of thy Spirit." We were all in tears. Mine, I fear, flowed from envy and impatience of life—where briars and thorns are with me, and I dwell in the midst of scorpions.[96] I felt throughout my soul that I would rather be in his condition than enjoy the whole of created good.

Enlarged in the castle on our Lord's lamentation over Jerusalem, and many wept, because they knew the time of *their* visitation. In

93. Cf. Rev. 7:17; 21:4.
94. Cf. Phil. 1:23.
95. Cf. Rev. 4:1.
96. Cf. Ezek. 2:6.

the Society I was borne as on eagles' wings.[97] All were partakers of my faith and joy. We wrestled in prayer for my son Absalom[98] (surely all their prayers and tears will not be lost), for the flock in London, and for the whole church.

I now experienced the truth of a strange saying I once heard from a servant of Christ, that she could know when any were speaking evil of her, by the Spirit of God then especially resting upon her. I could not help telling it [to] the brethren, yet with a fear lest they should think of me above what they ought to think. 'Tis far, far better to be thought and spoke evil of. We continued rejoicing before God with reverence, and such deep solid comfort as I have rarely felt before. How then shall we triumph, when we are made the filth and offscouring of all things![99]

*Tuesday, August 14.* We had prayed last night with joy full of glory for our departing brother, just while he gave up his spirit— as I pray God I may give up mine. This morning I expounded that last best triumph of faith, "I have fought a good fight," etc. [2 Tim. 4:7]. The Lord administered strong consolation to those that love his appearing. We sang a song of victory for our deceased friend, then went to the house and rejoiced, and gave thanks, and rejoiced again with singing over him. The Spirit, at its departure, had left marks of its happiness on the clay. No sight upon earth in my eyes is half so lovely.

*Wednesday, August 15.* Preached near Cowbridge to many awakening sinners; and again in the castle-yard on those solemn words, "The Spirit and the Bride say, Come!" [Rev. 22:17].

*Thursday, August 16.* Preached to the prisoners, with the greatest presence of my Master that I have known in Wales. Yet afterwards in the room, confessed he had kept the greatest blessing till the last.

*Friday, August 17.* Took horse at three, crossed the water in a quarter of an hour, and at two gave thanks in Bristol for our success in all things.

Wrote to Thomas Butts as follows:

---

97. Cf. Isa. 40:31.
98. Cf. the May 14, 1744, entry above.
99. Cf. 1 Cor. 4:13.

The things which have happened I know shall be for the furtherance of the gospel. But can a mother forget her sucking child?[100] My love to those that hate me passeth the love of nature. Would to God I had died for thee, O Absalom, my son, my son![101]

O Tommy! could you be to me what he is? Indeed you could. Such is the nature of man, although at present you and I should say "Is thy servant a dog that he should do this?" I am persuaded God will never so abandon us; but we are capable of such ingratitude. Indeed my brother we are, therefore ought not to be angry at poor Thomas Williams. O that his name and sin may be buried in oblivion, or that all would think of him as I do!

*Sunday, August 19.* Heard one of our sons in the gospel at Kingswood. He spake sound words which could not be reproved.

My brother Meriton assisted me to administer the Sacrament to our whole Society. The Spirit helped our infirmity. I asked in an accepted time life for my poor rebellious son if he has not sinned the sin unto death.[102]

Related in the Society all that has lately passed at London. They received the mournful account as they ought, with tenderest pity and just abhorrence. Could they help lamenting over one who so often ministered grace to their souls? No more than they could help cleaving to their old shepherds, who first brought them the glad tidings, and cherished them since as a nurse her children. "Though many teachers, yet not many fathers" [1 Cor. 4:15]. This their hearts and tears abundantly confessed. Great confidence I had in them that if not only one,[103] but all, our preachers forsook us, they should draw no disciples after them.

*Tuesday, August 21.* Preached at Cirencester, and the next day found my brother with a large company of our friends at Oxford.

*Thursday, August 23.* Went to Christ Church prayers with several of the brethren, who thought it strange to see men in surplices talking, laughing, and pointing, as in a play-house, the whole time of service.

---

100. Cf. Isa. 49:15.
101. Cf. 2 Sam. 18:13.
102. Cf. 1 John 5:16.
103. The word "one" replaces an original word, which by scoring out has been rendered illegible. The change does not appear to be in Charles's hand.

Got two or three hours conference with my brother and found the spirit which had drawn us formerly in this place. Preached to a multitude of the brethren, gownsmen, and gentry from the races, who filled our inn and yard. The strangers that intermeddled not with our joy, seemed struck and astonished with it, while we admonished one another in psalms and hymns, etc.[104] O that all the world had a taste for *our* diversion!

*Friday, August 24.* Joined my brother in stirring up the Society. They did run well, till the Moravians turned them out of the way of God's ordinances. The Lord rebuke those grand hinderers of his work, and suffer them to proceed no farther.

At ten walked with my brother and Mr Piers and Meriton to St Mary's where my brother bore his testimony before a crowded audience,[105] much increased by the racers. Never have I seen a more attentive congregation. They did not let a word slip them. Some of the Heads stood up the whole time, and fixed their eyes on him. If they can endure sound doctrine like his, he will surely leave a blessing behind him.

The Vice-Chancellor[106] sent after him and desired his notes, which he sealed up and sent immediately.

We walked back in form, the little band of us four, for of the rest does none join himself to us. I was a little diverted at the coyness of an old friend, Mr [Christopher] Wells, who sat just before me but took great care to turn his back upon me all the time, which did not hinder my seeing through him.

At noon my brother set out for London and I for Bristol.

*Sunday, August 26.* Gave the Sacrament at Kingswood. In the afternoon expounded the Woman of Canaan [Matt. 15:22-28]. Great was the cry after Jesus. Many a soul fell at his feet and said, "Lord, help me" [15:25].

*Monday, August 27.* I administered the Sacrament to our sister B. triumphing over death. We were all partakers of her joy.

---

104. Cf. Col. 3:16.

105. This was John's last sermon before the university; cf. Sermon 4, "Scriptural Christianity," *Works* 1:159–80.

106. This was likely Walter Hodges, who served as Vice-Chancellor of Oxford 1741–1744; unless the transition had already taken place to Euseby Isham, who served 1744–1747.

Comforted with three of our brethren from Wednesbury, who brought us news that God has given them rest from all their enemies round about them. When it is most for His glory, and their good, they shall be tried again by persecution, and again praise God in the fires.

*Friday, August 31.* Passed a blessed hour in intercession for the Church of England. Surely they that mourn for her, shall rejoice with her, when the Lord doth bring again Sion.[107]

Rode to Bath, and preached Jesus Christ to our own Society, and many strangers. For two hours after, I was comforted with our children and found how good a thing it is for brethren to dwell together in unity.[108]

# SEPTEMBER 1744

*Sunday, September 2.* Received the Sacrament at the college. Met the Society, and Jesus in the midst. Scarce a soul among us but was moved, as their tears or rejoicings witnessed. Many could truly say, "Our fellowship is with the Father, and with the Son" [1 John 1:3].

*Tuesday, September 4.* Waited most of the day at the passage for our sister [Mary] Jones, and her little ones. They reached our side at last, through perils of water.

*Sunday, September 9.* Rode, in heavy rain, to Churchill, with Mr Shepherd. The justice threatened him with terrible things in case I preached. Many poor people ventured to hear, while I cried, "Behold the Lamb of God, that taketh" etc. [John 1:29]. Out of the abundance of my heart my mouth spake. When I had ended, Mr Justice called out, and bade them pull me down. He had stood at a distance, striving to raise a mob. But not a man would stir at his bidding. Only one behind struck me with a stone. While I was in my prayer, he cried again, "Pull him down." I told him I had nothing now to do but to pray for him. He answered, "I have nothing to do with prayer." "So I suppose, Sir," said I. "But we have." He came up and laid hold on my gown, but I stepped down, to save him trouble. He told me he was a justice of peace. "Then, Sir," said I, "I reverence you for your office's sake. But must not neglect my

107. Cf. Isa. 52:8.
108. Cf. Ps. 133:1.

421

own, which is to preach the gospel." "I say," said the justice and captain, "it is an unlawful assembly." "Be so good, then," I replied, "as to name the law or act of parliament we break." He answered (unhappily enough), "The Waltham Act."[109] "How so, Sir?" I asked. "I am in my proper habit, and you see none here in disguise." He insisted I should not preach there. I told him I had licence to preach throughout England and Ireland, by virtue of my Master's degree. "That I know, Sir," said he, "and am sorry for it. I think you are Fellow of a college, too." "Yes, Sir," I answered, "and a gentleman too, and as such should be glad to wait upon you, and to have a little conversation with you yourself." He answered he should be glad of it too, for I had behaved more like a gentleman than any of them. I had charged the people to say nothing, but go quietly home. So Mr Justice and I parted tolerable friends.

I rode three miles farther to Mr Star's,[110] where I preached the next morning to many listening sinners, who pressed me much to come again.

*Thursday, September 13.* Rejoiced to hear of the triumphant death of our sister [Elizabeth] Marsh, in London, whose last breath was spent in prayer for me.[111] None of our children die without leaving us a legacy. I received it this evening in the answer of her prayer. The word was as a fire, and as a hammer. The rocks were broken in pieces,[112] particularly an hardened sinner, who withstood me some time before he was struck down. Many were melted down. Some testified their then receiving the atonement.

*Sunday, September 16.* Displayed, from Isaiah 35, to our colliers, the glorious privileges of the gospel; and the wilderness and solitary place was glad for them. My brother Thomson assisted in administering and was, as he expressed it, on the highest round of Jacob's ladder. I preached again at Churchill, and called to above 2000 souls, "Ho, every one that thirsteth, come ye to the waters" [Isa. 55:1]. They expressed much satisfaction in the joyful tidings of a Savior *from* sin.

---

109. The "Waltham Black Act," passed in 1723, was directed against poaching and related offenses. It detailed a list of property offenses which, if committed while armed or disguised (as with blackened faces), could carry the death penalty. The Act was often interpreted to mean that being disguised could be considered a crime in itself.

110. Mr Star lived in Way Wick, Somerset (cf. John Wesley, *Works* 20:142).

111. Cf. John Wesley's account of her death in his *Journal* (Sept. 6, 1744), *Works* 20:38.

112. Cf. Jer. 23:29.

*Monday, September 17.* It being our thanksgiving-day, I read John Nelson's case,[113] a plain accomplishment of the promise, "I will give you a mouth and wisdom, which none of your adversaries shall be able to resist" [Luke 21:15].

*Friday, September 21.* I read the Society my brother's account of poor Mr [Thomas] Williams, and the Lord was much among us, humbling and comforting our hearts.

*Sunday, September 23.* Preached at five in the Horsefair. Gave the Sacrament at Kingswood. Baptized a child of Felix Farley's. Preached again in the Wood. Rode and preached in Bristol. Returned to our Love-feast among the colliers. And, near midnight, slept with my brother Thomson in the Horsefair.

*Monday, September 24.* Set out for London. Blundered in the dark night to a little village beyond Malmesbury. It was no great inconvenience that we found neither bed nor victuals.

*Tuesday, September 25.* I preached at Whickham, and the next day at our chapel by the Seven Dials.[114] The first Scripture I met was Jeremiah 20:7-10, etc., and never have I more felt the power of God's word. Prayer is made for me by my friends, I know and feel, for I have not enjoyed so great liberty for years past. This is to prepare me for farther work, and farther sufferings.

Talked with a serious brother, who desired my answer to the many horrid scandals Thomas Williams has raised on me, e.g. my keeping 20 mistresses only in London, etc. I simply denied them all, which was all the satisfaction I could give him till that day, and he desired no more.

Preached to a thronged audience on "These are they that came out of great tribulation" [Rev. 7:14]. The Lord greatly comforted our hearts. And again at the Society, where I forbore mentioning Mr Williams, but appointed all who had been troubled by any reports concerning me or my brother to call on me the next day.

*Friday, September 28.* Expounded Paul's shipwreck [Acts 27], and had great faith that the Lord will give us all that sail in the ship with us.

---

113. Nelson was a Methodist lay preacher impressed to military service against his will (see May 14, 1744, entry above). Charles is reading the summary that Nelson was preparing for publication, which appeared as: *The Case of John Nelson* (London: Strahan, 1745).

114. This is the West Street chapel, at the intersection of West Street and St Martin's Lane in London, just south of the "Seven Dials" intersection.

Gave the Sacrament to several sick.

At the time of conference, among others, a poor backsliding child came to me, who had been led away by the lies of Thomas Williams. She fell at my feet, asking pardon of God and me. O how easy and delightful is it to forgive one that says, "I repent!" Lord, grant me power as freely to forgive them who persist to injure me!

*Saturday, September 29.* I administered the Sacrament to our sick but happy sister Burnet, with great envy of her condition.

*Sunday, September 30.* Assisted my brother in giving it to the whole Society. Gathered another stray sheep.

# OCTOBER 1744

*Wednesday, October 10.* Took horse with N. Salthouse,[115] and came with the next night to Markfield, half dead through pain and fatigue.

*Friday, October 12.* Preached in the church, convincingly, as I afterwards heard; and rode in great pain to Donington. Met my old friend Dr [John] Byrom,[116] and lost an hour in dispute about his sacred mystics. Lay down at eleven in my clothes, as usual, but could not rest.

Talked with a friend[117] concerning the conspiracy hatching against me at London, who advised me to keep silence, and leave the matter to God. My pain (through the piles) increasing, I asked Dr Harding's advice, who forbad my riding onward tomorrow under pain of a massification.

*Monday, October 15.* Proclaimed liberty to the captives, and deeply offended some pleaders for German, instead of Christian, liberty. But whether they will hear, or whether they will forbear, I have spoken the truth. I have paid my debt, and delivered my own soul. A woman confessed she then received the sense of her pardon.

---

115. Salthouse's first name was likely "Nicholas," and he traveled with Charles as a servant, not a fellow itinerant preacher.

116. Byrom was at Donington Park visiting Lady Huntingdon, and notes this meeting with Charles Wesley in a letter to his wife; *Private Journal and Literary Remains of John Byrom*, ed. by Richard Parkinson (Manchester: Chetham Society, 1854–1857), 2:384.

117. Likely Lady Huntingdon, whom Charles was addressing in contemporaneous letters as "my only friend."

*Wednesday, October 17.* Hardly held out to Nottingham, and the next day to Sheffield. I lay down for an hour, and recovered strength to preach, "That I may know him, and the power of his resurrection" [Phil. 3:10]. The word was not bound [Cf. 2 Tim. 2:9], or weak, like me.

*Friday, October 19.* Had a woeful journey to Epworth.

*Sunday, October 21.* Met the Society twice, and preached thrice, in spite of my body.

*Monday, October 22.* Preached at Ferry[118] in the room whence John Downes had been dragged away for a soldier. I found a great blessing in the cluster there. Lodged at Sykehouse, and the next day, *Tuesday, October 23*, rejoiced among my brethren in Birstall. Here they have been sifted like wheat by Mr Viney.[119] They received him upon my brother's recommendation (whose unhappiness it is still to set the wolf to keep the sheep), and he has served them a German trick—bringing them off their *animal love* for their pastors, their prayers, fastings, works, holiness. He had well-nigh destroyed the work of God, when John Nelson returned from his captivity.

*Wednesday, October 24.* Preached at Leeds, from, "As for thee, by the blood of thy covenant I have sent up thy prisoners out of the pit" [Zech. 9:11]. Here the great blessing is. One, as far as can yet be discerned, received forgiveness. All were comforted or convinced.

*Thursday, October 25.* Preached at Bradford,[120] on "This is he that came by water and by blood" [1 John 5:6]. The whole congregation was in a flame. Surely God hath a great work to do among this people.

Met the Birstall Society, whom Mr Viney had almost quite perverted, so that they laughed at all fasting, and self-denial, and family prayer, and such-like works of the law. They were so alienated by that cunning supplanter, that they took no notice of John Nelson when he came back—for all that, Viney taught them, was "animal love."

---

118. Owston Ferry, Lincolnshire, two miles southeast of Epworth.

119. Richard Viney, the first English member of the Moravian Church, and Warden of its Yorkshire congregation, had been excluded from the Moravians for disaffection and briefly attached himself to John Wesley.

120. Bradford, Yorkshire.

*Sunday, October 28.* Preached in the street at Leeds, no man disturbing me, on "He that endureth to the end, the same shall be saved" [Matt. 24:13].

Preached on Birstall hill to a great multitude, "Watch ye, stand fast in the faith, quit yourselves like men, be strong" [1 Cor. 16:13]. Rebuked them sharply who had walked contrary, and the spirit of contrition fell upon them. It was a blessed mourning, and continued at the Society. Then first my heart was enlarged, and my faith returned for these poor shattered sheep. They confessed their sin, and God showed himself faithful and just. Our Love-feast began with sorrow, but ended with joy. The Lord received our petitions, and assured us in prayer that the plague was stayed.

*Monday, October 29.* Took leave in those words, "Finally, brethren, farewell; be perfect," etc. [2 Cor. 13:11].

*Tuesday, October 30.* After much wandering, came by night half starved to our inn; and the next day to Newcastle.

# NOVEMBER 1744

*Tuesday, November 6.* Expounded Acts 3 at Biddick, and found much life among this poor people. Many of them have received forgiveness, chiefly under the prayer of one of the brethren raised up to serve them.

Rebuked the Society at Newcastle for their slackness, and offences of various kinds. Gave notice that I should begin next morning to examine them, and put out every disorderly walker.

*Thursday evening, November [8].*[121] Took my leave of Tanfield in Rev 7[:14], "These are they that came out of," etc., and the Lord was greatly with us. I could not finish my discourse in less than two hours.

*Friday, November 9.* Proceeded with the classes. It was high time to purge them. Through their own negligence, and that of their late teachers, many were turning back into Egypt.

Spent the night in watching and prayer. Found the Lord returning to his people.

---

121. MS has "November 7," which is in error.

Retired to read my letters from London. Offered up myself to the divine disposal. Met with Psalm 144, then with Balak's hiring Balaam to curse Israel [Num. 22]. I went down to the congregation, where the Lord answered for himself. Sent an account to the brethren at London:

My dearest Brethren,

Last night I was informed that the Philistines shouted against me, and the Spirit of the Lord came mightily upon us.[122] To Him give all the glory, that I find my heart so enlarged toward you, as never before. Now I can truly say, "Ye are not straitened in me" [2 Cor. 6:12]. All my pining desires after rest are vanished, and I am at last content to do what is more than dying for you, even to live for you, and suffer out my time. Here, then, I give up myself your servant for Christ's sake, to wait upon you till all are gathered home. Where ye go I will go; and where ye lodge I will lodge; where ye die will I die, and there will I be buried. Neither shall death itself part you and me.[123]

Such a night of consolation as the last I have seldom known. Our souls were filled with faith and prayer, and knit to yours in love unchangeable. Lift up holy hands, that I may approve myself a true minister of Jesus Christ in all things.

*Sunday, November 11.* This evening I heard of poor Mr Broughton's zeal.[124] But shall not prosecute, after his example.

*Monday, November 12.* Preached, "The Lord hath said unto my Lord, Sit down on my right hand" [Ps. 110:1; Acts 2:34]—and triumphed in his kingly power. At Whickham spake of the length, and breadth, and depth, and height of the love of Christ which passes knowledge [Eph. 3:18-19]. He extended peace to us as a river. The word was with equal power at Newcastle.

*Thursday, November 15.* Passed an hour with my dear keelmen at the hospital, who are cruelly treated by their masters for the gospel's sake.

---

122. Cf. Judg. 15:14.
123. Cf. Ruth 1:16-17.
124. When Thomas Williams began making accusations against Wesley (see September 25, 1744, entry), it led two women who had become disaffected with the Wesleyan wing of the Methodist movement to swear oaths alleging sexual misconduct by Charles. Thomas Broughton brought these affidavits to the attention of the bishops (surely with a sense of how their roles were now reversed; cf. March 8–24, 1739, above). Broughton's role is noted by Howell Harris in a letter to George Whitefield (January 11, 1745), in *Selected Trevecka Letters* (1742–1747), edited by G. M. Roberts (Caernarvon: Calvinistic Methodist Bookroom, 1956), 162.

In the evening preached at Burnopfield,[125] between Tanfield and Spen, on "Behold the Lamb of God that taketh," etc. [John 1:29]. I met the flourishing Society, and was much refreshed a second time. Returned to Newcastle, and strongly pressed them to constant prayer. I see plainly: " 'tis pray, or perish"!

*Saturday, November 17.* Now, indeed, the rains descend, and the floods come, and the winds blow and beat upon the house.[126] Received a letter from C. G., at D.,[127] half staggered by the boldness of my accusers—God reigneth over the heathen,[128] this is my comfort; and beneath me are the everlasting arms.[129]

At noon set out for Biddick. The snow had made the roads almost impassable for horses. I followed N. Salthouse on foot. Dwelt on my old subject, "These are they that came out of great tribulation" [Rev. 7:14]. For above an hour all were in tears. Another blessed hour was spent in like manner with the Society.

*Sunday, November 18.* Enlarged on that word, "A soldier pierced his side," etc. [John 19:34]. We looked upon him, and could have continued looking and mourning till he appeared in the air.[130]

Walked to Sunderland, and back again. The storm of hail and snow was so violent, that I was often going to lay me down in the road, unable either to walk or stand.

*Monday, November 19.* Brought back a wandering sheep, who had forfeited her pardon by unforgiveness. Received comfort, and wept for joy at the prosperity of our Bristol children, which I heard of in several letters. Walked over the fields to Whickham. The snow was in most places above our knees. After preaching, set out for Horsley in most bitter weather. Rode and walked, till I could do neither, yet got to Horsley by night. But my jaw was quite stiffened and disabled by the snow. Lay down, and got a little strength to preach.

*Tuesday, November 20.* Waded back to Newcastle by one, ofttimes up to my middle in snow.

---

125. Charles spells "Burnup-Field."
126. Cf. Matt. 7:27.
127. This is likely Charles Graves, writing from Donington Park. Graves had accompanied Charles Wesley to Donington Park in 1742, and was now focusing his ministry in the western part of Yorkshire.
128. Cf. Ps. 47:8.
129. Cf. Deut. 33:27.
130. Cf. 1 Thess. 4:17.

Rode, or rather walked, to Plessy, and preached, "It is finished" [John 19:30].

*Thursday, November 22.* Got back to Newcastle, and thence to Whickham, where I spoke of that great and terrible day of the Lord [Joel 2:31]. Many trembled, and some rejoiced in hope of the glory of God. Rode thence to Spen, being so feeble that I could not walk. Yet I was forced to it the last mile, being almost starved to death in the next to impassable ways. I was led, I know not how, by the brethren, up to the knees in snow, the horses ofttimes sinking up to their shoulders.

Surprised at the great number got together in such a season. They did not come in vain, for the Lord comforted their hearts abundantly, and mine also. These were all gathered by John Brown, a simple man whom the Lord has wonderfully raised up for his work.

*Sunday, November 25.* The devil's children made a great disturbance in the time of preaching. I stood on the stairs, and took up the Society one by one, while the mob were ready to tear them in pieces. Satan, one would think, foresaw the blessing we should have together.

*Tuesday, November 27.* At Biddick we had close fellowship with Him in his sufferings, while he cried, "Is it nothing to you, all ye that pass by?" [Lam. 1:12].

Returned, praying, to Newcastle, but almost perished with cold. In the word the Spirit was poured out upon us from on high, and bore down all before it as a mighty flood.

*Wednesday, November 28.* The whole congregation were again broken down by prayer. I put out of the Society all the disorderly walkers; who are, consequently, ready to make affidavit of whatever Mr Broughton pleases.[131] I prayed without ceasing most of this day.

Mr Erskine called on me. I preached, "In the world ye shall have tribulation. But be of good cheer," etc. [John 16:33]. We had peace in Him, in spite of the disturbance of Satan's children.

*Thursday, November 29.* Preached by one of our children dying in the Lord, with tears, and strong desires of going in her place.

---

131. Cf. the November 11, 1744, entry above.

*Friday, November 30.* Mr Erskine left me, but not before he had much strengthened my hands in the Lord. In the evening the waves so lifted up their voice, that we could only sing for half an hour. The most violent of the rioters had been two of our own Society.

# DECEMBER 1744

*Tuesday, December 4.* An hour before preaching-time the mob were so violent, that we thought there could be no preaching that night. They came nigh to break the door. I began speaking abruptly without a text, and God gave me strong words that stilled the madness of the people. Neither was there any breath of opposition during the Society.

*Friday, December 7.* My subject at our watch-night was, "Christ also suffered, leaving us an example" [1 Pet. 2:21]. Toward the end, the power of the Lord dissolved us all into tears.

**Sunday, December 9.** Preached on "Awake, awake, put on strength, O arm of the Lord" [Isa. 51:9], and he did wonderfully answer us in that same hour. Forced to walk to Burnopfield with my sprained leg, through the extreme cold. Expounded Isaiah 35. In the evening our enemies at Newcastle were restrained while I besought them to repent, and believe the gospel [Mark 1:15].

*Tuesday, December 11.* Had asked that at midnight I might rise and praise Him, because of his righteous judgments, and was waked exactly at twelve. Prayed a few minutes, and slept again in peace. Rose again at four, prayed earnestly, and almost rejoiced. Without light or fire, yet felt no cold. At five preached on "Whatsoever things ye ask in prayer, believe that ye receive them, and ye shall have them" [Matt. 21:22]. We were carried out in fervent prayer for ourselves and the whole nation.

Visited Walter Brass, on a bed of sickness. He was once of the Society, but lately turned scoffer and disturber of the word. The Lord hath now set his misdeeds before him, and he cries out vehemently for mercy. Another rioter, J. Wilson, is humbled in like manner, in immediate answer to our prayer last night.

Conferred with a sincere person, who had been turned out of the way by the vain boastings of some whose life contradicted their profession.

In the evening we found a mighty spirit of prayer among the bands, and earnestly cried for the blotting out of all our sins against love.

*Wednesday, December 12.* Rose again at midnight, and prayed with more life than before. John Nelson came.

*Thursday, December 13.* Admitted twenty new members. Took my leave in Acts 20. It was a solemn time of prayer and love.

*Friday, December 14.* Set out, with N. Salthouse, in the severe frost; and on

*Sunday, December 16,* arrived safe at Epworth.

*Monday, December 17.* Wrote thus to a friend:

> My greatest trouble is that I have innocently brought such a burden upon my friends, especially one. Neither can I conceive it possible that this trouble should be wholly removed here. The joint may perhaps be set, but the halting will continue till I come to the land where all things are forgotten.
>
> God, who hath known my soul in adversity, causes me also to know it. That He loves me, I can no more doubt than of his being. He has likewise given me to love others with a pure love; particularly one person, from whom I never expect or desire any farther communication of good, than I do from my mother, or other spirits of just men made perfect. And, however Providence may work, I mean never more to see *that person* (if without sin I may forbear) till we *stand* together at the judgment-seat.

*Tuesday, December 18.* Expounded Revelation 7. All were in tears. All were comforted.

*Wednesday, December 19.* Rode to Sykehouse, and thence to our brother Pindar's.

*Thursday, December 20,* to Birstall.

*Sunday, December 23.* Parted with our brethren in Leeds, commending them to God, and to the word of his grace.[132] There was a

---

132. Cf. Acts 20:32.

general mourning, as if I was taking my last leave. The blessing of the Lord still followed us, both at Morley and at Birstall.

*Friday, December 28.* Preached at Sheffield and Nottingham on my journey, and this evening was refreshed by our brothers [Thomas] Hogg and Butts, who met me at St Albans.

*Saturday, December 29.* Continued in prayer from three to four. Then took horse, with joyful confidence and desire to see London. By seven entered the Foundery. Read prayers at the chapel, and preached from Isaiah 51, with great enlargement. Received much spiritual strength and comfort in the Sacrament.

*Sunday, December 30.* My brother read prayers. I preached on "He shall save his people from their sins" [Matt. 1:21]. At night on "How beautiful upon the mountains are the feet of him that bringeth glad tidings!" [Isa. 52:7]. God gave testimony to his word, and endued my soul with more strength and boldness than ever.

# JANUARY 1745

*Thursday, January [3].*[1] Received a summons from my friend[2] that was with due indifference yet thought it my duty to go, in justice to my own character. I waited upon her, and found Satan at her right hand, good Mrs Ed—[3] I mean. I spoke to her with calm confidence,

above all fear, all anger and all pride.[4]

She expressed her concern. I declared my innocence in general, related my like trial in Georgia, and Ephraem Cyrus's case.[5] Stopped

---

1. MS has "January 4," which is in error.

2. Lady Huntingdon.

3. This is, almost certainly, Catherine Edwin (1702–1773), who was currently a close—but disruptive—friend of Lady Huntingdon (they were later estranged when Edwin affiliated with the Moravians). This is a case of the common practice in the eighteenth century of referring to more mature unmarried women as "Mrs." Unawareness of this practice has led some to confuse references to the unmarried Catherine as being to her sister-in-law, Lady Charlotte Edwin.

4. Cf. Thomas Parnell, "Dedication: To the Right Honorable Robert, Earl of Oxford, and Earl Mortimer," ln. 24, *Poems on Several Occasions* (London: Lintot, 1722), 4: "above all pain, all anger, and all pride."

5. Charles is referring to an incident, recorded in the "Ecclesiastical History" of Sozomen (Book III, ch. 15), where a woman taunted the saintly monastic Ephraem Cyrus (c. 303–373) as being her father. Cf. Samuel Parker, ed., *The Ecclesiastical Histories of Eusebius, Socrates, Sozomen, and Theodorit* (London: Rivington, 1729), 321.

Mrs Ed—'s mouth by saying "If accusations are proofs, you are as much worse than I, as wicked actions are worse than wicked designs." She raged, and sank into sullen silence. My friend said she could not look upon it, or believe me such as I am represented. I found power to suspend my judgment of her, I said, so as neither to condemn nor justify her. She spoke after his Grace,[6] concerning order, etc. I asked what good would have been done at Wednesbury upon that principle; and she fired, so as to lose all charge of herself. I left her without trouble or regret.

This morning the famous Mrs Robinson[7] and others came to beg my pardon. I doubt not but the whole synagogue of Satan[8] will bow down. They showed all the outward signs of repentance.

*Friday, January 4.* All were melted into gracious tears at the Sacrament. Heard of one who had lately received the seal of forgiveness under me, when I was more than usually dead. Expounded John 1 at Short's Gardens, and the power of the Lord was present. Our old Friend [Thomas] Keen was broken to pieces by it.

*Sunday, January 13.* Visited a sister who walks through the valley of the shadow of death and fears no evil.[9] Tasted the sweet consolation and blessedness of tears. I have found these few last days more comfort, both in preaching and prayer, than for some years. Is not our God a very present help in time of trouble?[10]

Today I was with a new creature (of her own making) Mrs Collis who told me "I am glorified already. I shall never die. My body in a little time will feel no pain. I shall be able to walk in the fire, and not be burnt." Many such extravagancies she uttered, which made my flesh tremble. My good brother excuses and palliates, and thinks her a new creature still.

In much distress at the altar, I cast mine eye on that word, "It is good for me to have been in trouble" [Ps. 119:71]. My heart was full of prayer. At last I broke out into tears and strong cries, and all with me. It was indeed a glorious time of visitation.

---

6. I.e., the Archbishop of Canterbury, John Potter.
7. She was likely one of the two women who had sworn a false affidavit against Wesley; cf. the entries for November 11, 1744, and June 29, 1747.
8. Cf. Rev. 2:9; 3:9.
9. Cf. Ps. 23:4.
10. Cf. Ps. 46:1.

*Saturday, January 19.* Prayed with our brother Grey, ready for the Bridegroom, and rejoicing in hope of a speedy dissolution. Preached at the chapel on "Awake, awake, put on strength, O arm of the Lord" [Isa. 51:9], and found, both in the word, and in prayer, and at the altar, the double blessing which now continually attends us.

*Saturday, January 26.* Mr Erskine came to me at Short's Gardens with a message which the Bishop of London had sent to Lady Huntingdon that, if I would come to him, and declare my innocency touching the scandals, and take the Sacrament upon it, he would desire no farther satisfaction, but himself clear me. I immediately consented, and sent my brother advice of it.

*Sunday, January 27.* Paid my last visit to our poor unstable brother Cowper, who is now so *holy in Christ* as to say, "I renounce the doctrine which your brother preaches, and trample it under my feet, as a doctrine of devils." This is what all the German converts come to. Our old friend[11] came as it were to take her leave of the chapel. I discoursed on "These are they that came out of great tribulation" [Rev. 7:14]. Both by the word and at the Sacrament the Lord answered for himself.

Buried a sister, who departed in the Lord. Called the multitude at the Foundery, "Come, for all things are now ready" [Luke 14:17]. Met the bands; and a solemn, mournful assembly it was. I could speak, sing, pray for nothing but death. We mixed our tears and souls together in that love which death cannot violate.

# FEBRUARY 1745

*Friday, February 1.* At our watch-night I described the new Jerusalem (Rev. 21), and great was our rejoicing before the Lord.

*Sunday, February 3.* At the Sacrament and among the bands I was enabled to pour out my soul in prayer, and carried them all with me to the throne of grace.

*Thursday, February 7.* By my brother's advice sent the following declaration to the Bishop of London by the hands of Mr Thomas Butts.

---

11. I.e., Lady Huntingdon. Cf. January 3 entry above.

My Lord

I was informed some time ago that your Lordship had received some allegations against me of one E. J. charging me with committing or offering to commit lewdness with her.

Farther, I have lately heard that your Lordship was pleased to say, "If I solemnly declared my innocence you should be satisfied." I therefore take this liberty, and do hereby solemnly declare that I never did commit lewdness with that person, nor solicit her to it, and that I am innocent in deed, word, and thought touching this thing.

As there are, I hear, other such slanders cast upon me and no less than all manner of evil said against me, I must beg leave farther to declare my innocence as to *all other women likewise*. It is now near 20 years since I began working out my salvation. In all which time God, in whose presence I speak, has kept me *from either* committing *the act of* wickedness (fornication, or adultery) or *even soliciting any person* whatsoever thereunto. *I deny the action*. I deny that I have ever spoken any word prompting any person thereto. *I deny that I have ever harboured any such design in my heart*. If your Lordship requires any further purgation I am ready to declare the same viva voce and to take the blessed Sacrament in proof of this, my declaration.[12]

I am, my Lord, your Lordships' dutiful son and servant. CW

The Foundery
February 7, 1745 [13]

His Lordship, notwithstanding his word, returned me just as much answer as I expected.

*Sunday, February 10.* Received the never-failing blessing at the Sacrament. Our prayer after it, always opens heaven.

*Saturday, February 16.* In a letter to a friend, wrote

I am often weary and faint, but is there not a cause? The loss of all things and life itself is nothing to loss of a friend. If my burden weighs you down I must communicate no more. But whatever becomes of me the foundation stands sure. Farewell my sorrowful friend, for I know I have infected you. Farewell and I long for our meeting in a better world.

---

12. It is not certain that the emphasis in this paragraph is Charles's own.
13. This letter is not included in Jackson.

*Sunday, February 17.* Was strengthened by a zealous Quaker, who informed me he had received the Spirit of adoption in hearing me a year ago, and has walked in the light from that time to this.

*Wednesday, February 20.* In asking, at the chapel, "Is there no balm in Gilead?" [Jer. 8:22] I found, with many others, that there was—and a good physician too, whose power was even then present to heal.

*Sunday, February 24.*[14] We had the spirit of prayer in the Sacrament, as usual. The word at night had great effect. My subject was the returning Prodigal [Luke 15:11-32].

*Tuesday, February 26.* Gave the Sacrament to one on Saffron Hill,[15] and found faith that the Lord was at work. Going down, they asked me to see another dying in the room below. As I entered, I heard her make confession of the faith which she received that moment, as she had told those about her she should, and that she could not die in peace till she saw me. She was full of triumphant joy, and said to me, "I am going to Paradise. It will not be long before you follow me." My soul was filled with *her* consolation.

# MARCH 1745

*Saturday, March 2.* At the chapel expounded, "Thus saith the high and lofty one, that inhabiteth eternity" [Isa. 57:15], and he covered us with a covering of his Spirit.

*Sunday, March 3.* Our hearts were bowed down before the Lord, both in the word and Sacrament.

*Saturday, March 9.* Dined at our brother Arvin's, just after his wife had taken her flight to paradise.

*Sunday, March 10.* Expounded the Woman of Canaan [Matt. 15:22-28], and was carried out after the Sacrament in strong intercession for my departed friends. One of them was there, unknown to me, but went out before my prayer.

---

14. Written "26" and amended to "24" in what appears to be Charles's hand.
15. Saffron Hill Street, just east of Holborn Circus, London.

*Wednesday, March 13.* God gave me strong words at the chapel against the antinomian delusion.

*Saturday, March [16].*[16] Spake with one of the Society, lately a Papist, who is much haunted by her old friends, especially her confessor, who thunders out anathemas against her and threatens to burn me—if he could catch me at Rome. I sent my respects to the gentleman, and offered to talk with him before her, at my own lodgings, or wherever he pleased; but received no answer.

*Thursday, March 21.* Expounded Isaiah 35. Many of our brethren from the Tabernacle were present. Our Lord did not send us empty away,[17] but applied the word of his grace to our hearts.

*Sunday evening, March 24.* Set out for Bristol with Thomas Butts. Lodged on Monday night in Newbury. On *Tuesday, March 26,* came to Mrs Gotley's, at Avon, and the next day to Bristol.

My subject was, "Thy sun shall no more go down by day," etc. [Isa. 60:20]. The Lord sanctified our meeting, and we were comforted by our mutual faith.

*Sunday, March 31.* At five preached in the Room; at eight in Kingswood, on the new Jerusalem [Rev. 21]. Administered the Sacrament to all the Society, and the God, the consolation of Israel, visited us. The whole congregation were moved to cry after him, either through sorrow or through joy.

Rode to Conham. Mr [Charles] Graves read prayers in Mr Wane's chapel. I bade them "Lift up the hands that hung down, and strengthen the feeble knees" [Heb. 12:12]. The word did not return void [Cf. Isa. 55:11]. Walked back to the colliers, and exhorted them to adorn the gospel [Titus 2:10]; then to Baptist Mills, where the children of the devil fled before the sword of the Spirit, which is the word of God.[18]

At our Love-feast in Bristol, spoke of the fruits of faith in strong scriptural words. Sarah Goslin, the mother of our antinomians, was forced to fly for her life. It was a blessed opportunity. The Lord mightily confirmed his word, and thereby ministered his consolations.

---

16. The date is not given in the MS.
17. Cf. Matt. 15:32; Mark 8:3.
18. Cf. Eph. 6:17.

# APRIL 1745

**Wednesday, April 3.** Preached at [South] Wraxall,[19] and found the bread I had cast upon the waters, after many days.[20] Several of my old hearers from Bradford[-on-Avon] were present. One caught hold of me, and cried, "Blessed be the day that ever I saw your face. This was the man, under God, that first opened my eyes." Another, Mrs Taylor, now declared she had received forgiveness in hearing me five years ago. I preached Christ crucified,[21] and we rejoiced as in the days that are past. Returned, with joy and comfort, to Bath, and exhorted them, "Hold fast that ye have already till I come" [Rev. 2:25].

**Thursday, April 4.** Rode to Coleford, a place of colliers lately discovered, and preached in the church-yard on a tombstone. The church would not have contained a quarter of the congregation. I pointed them to "the Lamb of God, who taketh away the sin of the world" [John 1:29]. The poor people followed me to Mr Flowers's, where we wrestled two or three hours in prayer, and would not let him go, except he blessed us.[22]

**Friday, April 5.** Read prayers and preached in the church, crowded within and without. Many followed me to Chilcompton. There I called, on above a thousand gasping souls, "Ho, every one that thirsteth, come ye to the waters" [Isa. 55:1]. Began again and again, after I had, as I thought, concluded.

Returned to Bristol. Was informed that one, lately of our Society, has declared he will make affidavit he himself saw my brother administer extreme unction to a woman, and give her a wafer and say that was her passport to heaven.

**Sunday, April 7.** Found the great blessing after the Sacrament, an ordinance which God always magnifies and honors with his special presence. Prayed by our sister Rogers, just on the wing for paradise. It was a solemn season at the Society, while I spake of death, and the glory which shall follow.

**Tuesday, April 9.** Rode to town and preached at the Foundery, with an enlarged heart, "Sun, stand thou still upon Gibeon!" [Josh. 10:12].

---

19. Charles spells "Wrexal."
20. Cf. Eccles. 11:1.
21. Cf. the note for the September 3–4, 1741, entry above.
22. Cf. Gen. 32:26.

*Friday, April 12.* At the chapel, all the congregation looked upon him they have pierced, and mourned.[23]

*Easter Day, April 14.* With the word, the Spirit of him that raised Jesus from the dead came mightily upon us. For more than half an hour he cried in our hearts. At the Sacrament, also, which the whole Society partook of, we all found, more or less, the power of his resurrection. So again at our Love-feast, we rejoiced together, and felt that the Lord was risen indeed.

*Tuesday, April 16.* Baptised a woman among the leaders, who received the justifying baptismal grace.

We kept the octave, communicating every day; and the Lord never sent us away without a blessing.

*Saturday, April 20.* The power of the Highest overshadowed us, when met in the evening to bewail our sins against light, and pray for a fresh pardon. Most of this week I have spent in confirming the wavering, and God hath blessed me in my deed.

*Sunday, April 21.* While I was declaring, "This is he that came by water and by blood" [1 John 5:6], the Spirit bore strong witness with many hearts. One testified her then receiving the atonement. At the Sacrament we prayed in faith that the sins of the revolting children might be retained—i.e., that while the guilt and power lasted, the misery might last, and they might not be suffered to soothe themselves with a fancied happiness. The Lord was with us in the great power of his love. The cloud stayed upon us when met in band; and they received my solemn warning of the approaching judgments.

*Monday, April 22.* Gave the Sacrament yesterday to two prisoners of hope; and twice today, to two dying believers, who can never die.

*Wednesday, April 24.* Recovered one out of the paw of the antinomian lion. This whole week I have gone on treading him under my feet, through the power of the serpent-bruiser.[24]

*Sunday, April 28.* Expounded Matthew 25, that flail of antinomianism.

---

23. Cf. Zech. 12:10.
24. Cf. Gen. 3:15.

# MAY 1745

*Sunday, May 5.* Preached from 1 Peter 2:12, "Having our conversation honest among the Gentiles, that whereas they speak against you as evil-doers, they may, by your good works which they shall behold, glorify God in the day of visitation." I warned them of that day, already begun, and of that fiery trial approaching.

At the Foundery expounded Ezekiel 9. A great cry followed. Surely there were many present who have the mark in their foreheads [9:4]. The Lord increase their number!

*Wednesday, May 8.* The fast-day. Expounded Zephaniah 1:2 then Joel 2, and lastly those awful words of God to Ezekiel: "Though Noah, Daniel, and Job were in it, as I live," etc. [Ezek. 14:20].

*Tuesday, May 21.* Began examining the classes with my brother, and rejoiced in the success of our past labours. Midst all the rage and havoc of Satan at the Tabernacle, the plague has not come nigh our dwelling.

*Thursday, May 23.* Sent for to Downing Street[25] with my brother. Gave up all hopes of good, when I saw that messenger of Satan[26] standing at our friend's right hand. She urged us, who would believe it, to confess our fault of preaching the gospel, and to submit to the bishops. We promised we would, as soon as we were convinced of our fault. Upon her talking in that miserable way of breaking order, etc., I owned it was contrary to order my having gone to save those poor outcasts of Newcastle, Cornwall and Stafford. This drew out all the old nature, and set her pride in a flame. At first I found myself warm; but immediately recovered, and looked upon her and heard her with the proper affection of grief and pity. We shook off the dust from our feet[27] and departed.

*Friday, May 31.* Visited, at her own desire, a Roman Catholic gentlewoman at Islington who had refused her priest, and would have none but my brother or me. She readily gave up her own merits (which she owned was hell) and the merits of all the saints for

---

25. The London residence of Lady Huntingdon.
26. Most likely Catherine Edwin; cf. the January 3, 1745, entry.
27. Cf. Matt. 10:14; Luke 9:5.

those of Jesus Christ, her only hope, mediator, and Savior. I prayed in faith, and left her not far from the kingdom of heaven.

Kept a watch-night. Dear Howell Harris I carried into the desk, and we sang together and shouted for joy, till morning.

# JUNE 1745

*Tuesday, June 4.* I baptized three adults, who all confessed the ordinance a seal of the covenant of forgiveness.

*Tuesday, June 11.* Much revived by the sight of Mrs Davis's mother departing in peace. For seventy years she lived, if it may be called life, a stranger to the covenant of promise. For these two last years, since faith came by hearing, she has never had a doubt or fear, but walked with Christ, and adorned the gospel. Now she longs to go see him face to face.[28]

*Wednesday, June 12.* Going to bed at Mrs Witham's, I could not rest, but must needs go to the other end of the town. In Holborn I found the reason—a poor man, and countryman, challenged me, who had been converted by occasional hearing us but, through neglect of the means, had fallen from his first love and into poverty. Exhorted him to return to God, gave him somewhat, and parted. The next day he spent in seeking me everywhere, to restore a guinea I had given him by mistake.

*Sunday, June 16.* Expounded Elijah's flight, and pining desire to die [1 Kgs. 19:1-8], and were strengthened by his weakness. My brother Taylor read prayers, and assisted at the truly blessed Sacrament. In the evening also, we had the shout of a king in the midst of us,[29] as at the beginning.

*Monday, [June] 17.[30]* Preached at Brentford in our way to Bristol. The moment our Society met, Jesus appeared in the midst, and we lay an happy hour, weeping and rejoicing, at his feet.

*Wednesday, June 19.* Three miles on this side Salisbury, a still sister came out to meet, and try her skill upon, me. But, alas 'twas labour lost. I knew the *happy sinner*, and all her paces.

---

28. Cf. 1 Cor. 13:12.
29. Cf. Num. 23:21.
30. MS has "May 17," which is in error.

Found my sister [Patty] as a rock in the midst of the waves. Mr Hall's society had all left the Church, and mocked and persecuted her for not leaving it. Many pressed me to preach, but I answered them, "My heart was not *free* to it." At four set out with my sister, and reached Bristol in the afternoon of the next day.

*Friday, June 21.* Sent an account of our affairs here to a friend:

> The work of God goes on successfully. Great is the constancy of them that believe. Neither error nor sin can shake them. Several, since I left this place, have witnessed a good confession in death, particularly a girl of thirteen, and an old sinner of threescore. We had expelled him [from] the Society for drunkenness. And he went on sinning, and repenting, and sinning again, till God laid his chastening hand upon him. After a great agony, he found redemption in the blood of Jesus. He lay some time rejoicing, and testifying the grace of Christ to the chief of sinners. When one said, "Blessed are the dead that die in the Lord," he replied, interrupting him, "Even so saith the Spirit in me." To another, "I am just entering the haven on a broken piece of the ship."
>
> I am just come from giving the Sacrament to a young woman, rejoicing in death with joy unspeakable. The day before my first visit, the Lord revealed himself in her. Her soul seemed all desire and love, "ready to go this moment," as she often testified, yet willing to tarry the Lord's leisure, or even to recover, if it were his will.
>
> I have observed that all our people, without exception, be they ever so dark or weak before, when they come to die, recover their confidence. Would to God every soul, of every Christian denomination, might witness the same confession of eternal life in them when they turn their faces to the wall![31]

*Sunday, June 23,* was a day much to be remembered. I preached to our colliers on Jeremiah 31:1, and received strong faith for the desolate Church of England.

In the Sacrament, the spirit of grace and supplication came down, and we prayed after God that it might reach all our absent brethren. The backsliders we never forget at such gracious opportunities.

Near four hours we were employed in *doing this*, and not one soul, I am persuaded, thought it long.

---

31. Cf. 2 Kgs. 20:2.

I had just time to reach Conham chapel by two. From those words, "I will that they may behold my glory" [John 17:24]. While I was speaking of our Lord's appearing, we were alarmed with the loudest clap of thunder I ever heard. I thought it must have cleft the house. Most of the congregation shrieked out, as if the day of the Lord were come. A thought darted into my heart as quick as the lightning, "What if it should be the day of judgment!" I was filled immediately with faith, stronger than death, and rejoiced in hope of the glory of God. The same spirit rested on all the faithful, while I broke out into singing,

> So shall the Lord the Savior come,
>  And lightnings round his chariot play!
> Ye lightnings, fly to make him room,
>  Ye glorious storms, prepare his way![32]

I went on for half an hour describing that final scene. The heart of every person present, I believe, either rejoiced or trembled. A mixed cry of horror and triumph was heard, till I dismissed them with the blessing.

Afterwards we heard that an house on one side our chapel was almost demolished, both roof and walls, by the thunder-clap. The lead of the windows melted, and six persons struck down to the ground. On the other side of us, a gibbet was split into a thousand pieces.

*Sunday, June 30.* Preached our sister Rogers' funeral sermon, whose blessed life and death were of a piece.

Called on Mr Wane and told him a scandalous tale which his keeper of the chapel had invented of me. I had formerly put her out of the house in Kingswood. He was astonished at her modesty! So was not Mrs Wane, who said to me, " 'Tis in vain to bring me these stories of you, since a gentleman told me to my face that you was caught in bed with another man's wife—and that I was the woman!"[33]

# JULY 1745

*Wednesday, July 3.* Took horse for London. The first night I preached at Cirencester; the two next at Evesham, where I found

---

32. Stanza 6 of "The God of Thunder," by Isaac Watts, which John Wesley had included in *MSP*, 1:206–7. Original is from Watts, *Horae lyricae* (London: Humfreys, 1709), 81.

33. This paragraph is not printed by Jackson.

the Society increased both in grace and number. Was welcomed to London on Saturday evening with the joyful news of Thomas Maxfield's deliverance.

*Sunday, July 7.* Preached on Luke 21:34, and many, I would hope, were stirred up to watch and pray.

*Sunday, July 14.* The Lord set to his seal while I explained, "Who art thou, O great mountain? before Zerubbabel thou shalt become a plain" [Zech. 4:7]. We rejoiced in steadfast hope of the precious sanctifying promises.

*Monday, July 15.* The Lord comforted our hearts by the letters, and confirmed our faith, that the work he is now reviving shall never be destroyed.

*Sunday, July 21.* In our prayer after the Sacrament the heavens dropped down from above, nay, and the skies seemed even to pour down righteousness.

*Monday, July 22.* Gave the Sacrament to our sister H., who is coming to the grave as a ripe shock of corn. A poor trembling tempted soul she has been. But at the approach of death all her fears are vanished, and she lies gasping for the fulness of eternal life.

*Thursday, July 25.* Strongly exhorted the Society to constancy in the faith, and fervency in prayer. Their hearts were melted much, if one may judge by their tears.

*Sunday evening, July 28.* Took leave of the Foundery in those words, which I vehemently wished accomplished, "The redeemed of the Lord shall return, and come with singing into Sion" [Isa. 51:11].

*Wednesday, July 31.* Joined with my brother to examine the Society at Bristol. Mr Gwynne[34] of Garth accompanied us, and rejoiced greatly in the grace given them.

# AUGUST 1745

*Thursday, August 1.* Began our Conference with Mr [John] Hodges, four of our own assistants, Herbert Jenkins, and Mr Gwynne. Continued it five days, and parted in great harmony and love.

---

34. Marmaduke Gwynne (1691–1769), a Welsh magistrate and father of Sarah Gwynne, Charles's future wife.

*Friday, August 2.* At the watch-night our souls were satisfied as with marrow and fatness,[35] while our mouth praised God with joyful lips.

*Wednesday, August 7.* While I was speaking from those words, "The end of all things is at hand" [1 Pet. 4:7], the Lord applied them to our hearts, and we felt the solemn weight of things eternal.

He passed by us again in the bands, and showed us his goodness. For near two hours we tasted the powers of the world to come, in solid, serious joy.

*Saturday, August 10.* Preached at Shepton Mallet, where a great door is opening, and there are many adversaries. One of the devil's drunken champions attempted to disturb us, but my voice prevailed.

They desired me to meet their little Society at an unusual place, to disappoint the mob. I walked forward toward the town, then turned back over the field, to drop the people, and, springing up a rising ground, sprained or broke my leg. I knew not which, but I fell down when I offered to set my foot to the ground. The brethren carried me to an hut, which was quickly filled with the poor people. It was soon noised about the town that I had broke my leg—some said my neck—and that it was a judgment upon me. The principal man of the place, Mr P., sent me a kind message, and his bath-chair to bring me to his house. I thanked him, but declined his offer, on account of my pain, which unfitted me for any company except that of my best friends—the poor. With these I continued praying, singing, and rejoicing for two hours. Their love quite delighted me. Happiest they that could come near to do anything for me. When my strength was exhausted, they laid me on their bed, the best they had. But I could not sleep for pain.

*Sunday, August [11].*[36] Met the Society at six, and took in twenty new members. About eight the surgeon from Oakhill came, and found, in dressing my leg, that it was not broke but violently sprained. Many being come from far to hear the word, I got the brethren to carry me out in a chair, which they set on a table, and I preached kneeling. I thought of Halyburton's "best pulpit,"[37] which

---

35. Cf. Ps. 63:5.
36. MS has "August 12," which is in error.
37. Halyburton used this term for his death bed; cf. Halyburton, *Memoirs*, 201.

alone seemed preferable to this. For near an hour I forgot my maim, and appointed to preach again at Oakhill.

The brethren carried me thither by noon in Mr P.'s chair. My congregation was mostly Dissenters, not wise and rich, but poor and simple, and longing to be taught the first elements of Christ's doctrine. They stood listening in the hard rain, while I showed them "the Lamb of God, who taketh," etc. [John 1:29]. The word was not bound [Cf. 2 Tim. 2:9], but ran very swiftly through their hearts. For an hour I preached kneeling as before, and felt no pain or weariness till it was over. Then my flesh shrunk at the twenty measured miles to Bristol. They set me on the horse, and by night I performed the journey, but in such extreme pain as I have not known with all my broken bones and sicknesses.

*Tuesday, August 13.* Preached from, "They that wait on the Lord shall renew their strength" [Isa. 40:31]. And then, confiding in the promise, went in my chair and lay at Mr Wigginton's, by the water-side.

Between four and five next morning was carried to Captain Philips's vessel, which was filled with our own people chiefly. We spent the day in singing and reading, and by six on

*Thursday morning, August 15th,* landed at Cardiff.

At night, most of the gentry of the town were at the room. I laboured to trouble the careless, as well as comfort the troubled, hearts.

*Sunday, August 18.* Our greatest persecutor lent his chair to carry me to Wenvoe. Indeed, the whole place at present seems turned towards us. But we do not depend on this peace as lasting. Preached at Wenvoe, from Hebrews 12:1, to a weeping audience. My brothers [Philip] Thomas[38] and Hodges administered the Sacrament.

The room at Cardiff was crowded with high and low. I invited them to come thirsty to the waters. The same spirit was with us as in the months that are past. Our Love-feast was a feast indeed!

*Tuesday, August 20.* At the request of the prisoners, I had promised to preach in the gaol. But Mr Michael Richards came first, and threatened and forbade the jailer. If these souls perish for lack of knowledge, Mr Michael Richards, not I, must answer it in that day.

---

38. Philip Thomas was now a curate to John Hodges at Wenvoe.

Carried to Fonmon, with Mr Hodges and Mrs Jones. I once more met the church in her house. We were all melted down by the fire of the word.

*Wednesday, August 21.* This and every evening I got down to the chapel on my crutches, and preached to the family, with fifty harvesters and others that came from far.

*Friday, August 23.* Wrote thus to my brother:

> Once more hear my raven's note—and despise it. I look most assuredly, unless general repentance prevent it, for the day of visitation. Whether my apprehensions have aught divine in them, I never presume to say; neither am I concerned for the credit of my prophecy, or conjecture. But none of you all will more rejoice at my proving what you may call a false prophet than I. For should I prove a true one, I expect Balaam's fate. In great weariness of flesh and spirit I conclude
>
> Your Μάντις κακῶν[39]

*Sunday, August 25.* Mr Gwynne's servant came to show me the way to Garth, but returned without me, my lameness still continuing, or rather increasing, by the use of the British oil, which inflamed and swelled my foot exceedingly. Probably it was the counterfeit sort.

*Monday, August 26.* Admitted several into the Society. Continued preaching twice a day the rest of the month.

# SEPTEMBER 1745

*Sunday, September 1.* Ventured to ride to church, where the minister invited us all to the Sacrament next Sunday, and afterwards made proclamation in the church-yard that no stranger should be admitted. He might as well have excepted me by name. But though I could not be admitted, a notorious drunkard was (as Mrs Jones and other eye-witnesses told me next Sunday). He made much disturbance in the time of service, and was actually drunk when the minister gave him the Sacrament.

---

39. "Prophet of bad things."

*Tuesday, September 3.* Mr Gwynne and Mr [Edward] Phillips[40] of Maesmynis, came to pay us a Christian visit. We had sweet fellowship till the sixth instant, when they departed without me, whom they came to fetch.

*Friday, September 6.* At the hour of intercession we found an extraordinary power of God upon us, and close communion with our absent brethren. Afterwards I found, by letters from London, that it was their solemn fast-day. The night we passed in prayer. I read them my heavy tidings out of the north.

"The lion is come up from his thicket, and the destroyer of the Gentiles is on his way" [Jer. 4:7].

*Sunday, September 8.* The spirit of supplication was given us in the Society for his majesty, King George; and, in strong faith, we asked his deliverance from all his enemies and troubles.

*Monday, September 9.* My three weeks delightful confinement ended, and I returned to Cardiff.

*Wednesday, September 11.* Rose, after a restless night, with a fever upon me, but was forced to take my bed again. How gladly would I have been taken from the evil to come. But alas, my sufferings are scarce begun!

*Saturday, September 14.* My fever left me, and my strength so far returned that I could sit an horse with one behind me. Almost as soon as we set out, my supporter and I were thrown over the horse's head, but neither hurt. My lameness was much mended by three or four days' rest.

*Sunday, September 22.* Met the poor shattered bands, and found the cause of their decay. One of them had drank into the Quakers' spirit, and got all their form, which he laboured to bring into the Society. Preached at Wenvoe, "That ye may be found of him in peace" [2 Pet. 3:14]; then at Fonmon, on that great and terrible day of the Lord [Joel 2:31]. His fear was mightily upon us, but at the Society his love constrained and quite overpowered us. For two hours we wept before the Lord, and wrestled for our Sodom. We shall hear of these prayers another day.

---

40. Charles spells "Philips."

*Monday, September 23.* Having been often importuned to preach at Cowbridge, this morning I set out with sister Jones and others. The gentleman who had invited and promised me the church, took care to be out of town, but left word that the church-doors were open, and, if I pleased to preach there, no man would forbid me. I did not choose to go in a clandestine manner, but sent to the church-wardens, who durst neither deny or grant leave. I therefore preached in a large hall, over against the place where my brother had been stoned.[41] Many attended and, I believe, were pricked at the heart.

*Wednesday, September 25.* After a tedious and dangerous passage, got to shore, and soon after to Bristol. Heard the news confirmed of Edinburgh being taken by the rebels.[42] Saw all around in deep sleep and security. Warned our children with great affection. Our comforts, we expect, will increase with our danger.

*Thursday, September 26.* Tidings came that General Cope[43] was cut off with all his army. The room was crowded in the evening. I warned them, with all authority, to flee to the mountains, escape to the strong tower, even the name of Jesus. Seemed to have strong faith, that the Romish Antichrist shall never finally prevail in these kingdoms.

*Sunday, September 29.* My subject at Kingswood was, "Because thou hast kept the word of my patience, I will also keep thee in the hour of temptation," etc. [Rev. 3:10]; at Bristol, "Fear God, and honor the King" [1 Pet. 2:17].

# OCTOBER 1745

*Tuesday, October 8.* Having left the Society fully warned, I rode to Bath, and exhorted them also to meet God in the way of his judgments. At noon I preached repentance and faith, at the Cross, to the people of Rode.[44] They drank in every word. When I said, "Put away the evil of your doings" [Isa. 1:16], several cried out, "We will,

---

41. Cf. John Wesley, *Journal* (May 7, 1743), *Works* 19:325.
42. The rebels were Jacobite forces led by Prince Charles Edward Stuart (the "Young Pretender").
43. Sir John Cope (1692–1755), commander of the troops loyal to George II.
44. Rode, Somerset. Charles spells "Road."

we will!" When I said, "Be drunk no more, swear no more," etc., they answered, "I will not swear. I will not be drunk again, as long as I live." The ale-house keepers and profligate young men are the most exemplary in their repentance. I dined at the squire's, who seemed amazed, and half converted, at *their* change.

Preached at four to a barn full of simple, hungry, seeking souls. They sunk under the hammer, and melted before the fire of the word.[45]

**Wednesday, October 9.** Met them again in the barn, and wept with them that wept.[46] All were stirred up, and made haste to escape into the ark, because of the stormy wind and tempest.

Preached at Bearfield, after five years' absence, to many of my old hearers. They received the word with all readiness of mind, and will be, I doubt not, a people fearing God and working righteousness.

After preaching in Bath, a woman desired to speak with me. She had been in our Society, and in Christ, but lost her grace through the spirit of offence. Left the fellowship, and fell by little and little into the depth of vice and misery. I called Mrs Naylor[47] to hear her mournful account. She had lived some time at a wicked house in Avon Street. Confessed it was hell to her to see our people pass by to the preaching. Knew not what to do, or how to escape. We bade her fly for her life, and not once look behind her. Mrs Naylor kept her with herself till the morning; and then I carried her with us in the coach to London, and delivered her to the care of our sister Davey. Is not this a brand plucked out of the fire?

**Sunday, October 13.** Warned them earnestly, both at the chapel and the Foundery, of the impending storm.

**Thursday, October 17.** We had twenty of our brethren from Flanders[48] to dine with us at the Foundery, and rejoiced in the distinguishing grace of God toward them.

**Friday, October 18.** Expounded Jer. 3 at the chapel. Some endeavoured to disturb us, by throwing in a cracker, which many took for

---

45. Cf. Jer. 23:29.
46. Cf. Rom. 12:15.
47. Mrs. Mary Naylor (d. 1757), who became a close friend of Charles. See his six-part hymn on her death in *Funeral Hymns* (1759), 49–59 (*Poetical Works*, 6:266–77).
48. Likely soldiers from Belgium supporting the British in the war against France and the Jacobite forces.

a gun discharged. In one minute the people recovered their hurry, and I went for another half hour with double assistance.

*Saturday, October [26].*[49] Dined at Mrs Rich's.[50] The family concealed their fright tolerably well. Mr Rich behaved with great civility. I foresee the storm my visit will bring upon him.

## NOVEMBER 1745

*Sunday, November 3.* Found much life and solemn comfort among the bands.

*Monday, November 4.* At Mrs Sparrow's, waited some days, to renew my strength.

*Friday, November 8.* Preached first in Bexley church, then in the front of the camp near Dartford. Many of the poor soldiers gave diligent heed to the word. One of the most reprobate was pricked at the heart, and entered the Society.

*Saturday, November 9.* A regiment passing by our door, I took the opportunity of giving each soldier a book. All, excepting one, received them thankfully.

*Sunday, November 10.* Expounded Psalm 46, with great enlargement. An officer was present, and by his tears confessed the emotion of his heart. The same power attended the word in the evening; Zephaniah 2. It was a solemn assembly, while we rejoiced in the release of an happy brother.

*Monday, November 11.* Had some of our brethren of the army at the Select Society, and solemnly commended them to the grace of God, before they set out to meet the rebels. They were without fear or disturbance, knowing the hairs of their head are all numbered,[51] and nothing can happen but by the determinate counsel of God.

---

49. MS has "October 27," which is in error.
50. Priscilla Rich (*née* Wilford, c. 1713–1783), the third wife of John Rich (1692–1761), the actor and owner of a theatre in Covent Garden. She converted to Methodism shortly after their marriage in 1744, much to the consternation of her husband. While Priscilla added no children, she helped raise the four surviving daughters from Rich's second marriage.
51. Cf. Matt. 10:30.

*Saturday, November 16.* Prayed with the penitents, all in tears.

*Sunday, November 17.* Brought back (with the extraordinary blessing of God) two wandering sheep from the Germans.

*Saturday, November 23.* Finished examining the classes with my brother, and rejoiced in their steadfastness.

*Saturday, November 30.* Prayed by Bridget Armsted, full of desire to be dissolved. She sent for me some hours after. I found her in a great agony of temptation. We prayed, and God arose, and all his enemies were scattered.

# DECEMBER 1745

*Sunday, December 1.* It was a season of love, a time of great refreshing, at the Sacrament.

*Friday, December 6.* In reading my brother's last *Appeal*,[52] I was drawn out into fervent prayer for him, myself, and all the children whom God hath given us.

*Monday, December 23.* Met my old friend John Gambold at my printer's, and appointed to meet him tomorrow at Dr Newton's. Brought my brother with me. Found the Germans had quite estranged and stole away his heart, which nevertheless relented while we talked over the passages of our former friendship. But he hardened himself against the weakness of gratitude. We could not prevail upon him to meet us again.

*Friday, December 27.* While I discoursed on that word, "The Spirit and the Bride say, 'Come'!" [Rev. 22:17], the whole congregation seemed to hear and answer the divine call.

*Sunday, December 29.* Explained my commission: to open their eyes, to turn them from darkness to light, etc. [Acts 26:18]. An extraordinary power and blessing sealed the word. One of my audience was the famous Mr Chambers, the honest attorney!

---

52. John Wesley, *A Farther Appeal to Men of Reason and Religion; Pts. II & III* (London: Strahan, 1745).

# JANUARY 1746

**Wednesday, January 1, 1746.** The Lord strengthened me at the chapel to stir up many by that word of his, "Let it alone this year also" [Luke 13:8].

**Tuesday, January 7.** Found a blessing in the cluster at Deptford.

**Friday, January 10.** Filled a coach with our friends and, in spite of the toothache, had a pleasant journey to Bristol.

**Sunday, January 12.** Gave the Sacrament at Kingswood, and expressed the vehement desires of our souls in mighty prayer. The word at night was blessed to the quickening of many.

**Tuesday, January 14.** Was much assisted in expounding Job 23; and yet more next morning, in those words, "It is of thy mercy that we are not consumed" [Lam. 3:22]. Found the old blessing and power at Weavers' Hall, while I put them in remembrance of their first love, from Psalm 126.

**Sunday, January 19.** At Baptist Mills there was a great awakening of those that had fallen asleep again. But in the Society the Lord stirred up his power in a wonderful manner, and came to his house. While I was reproving them he gave weight to the words, and for an hour and a half nothing was to be heard but cries and tears, and strong resolutions to return unto the Lord.

**Monday, January 20.** The same blessing we found at Bath, while the Spirit applied the word, "He that endureth to the end, the same shall be saved" [Matt. 24:13].

**Tuesday, January 21.** Preached from Isaiah 35 at Rode, and took the names of near seventy of the Society.

**Wednesday, January 22.** Preached at Bearfield, and [South] Wraxall, in the barn, where we never miss of our Lord's presence. Many women of Canaan cried after him, and seemed resolved to take no denial.[1]

**Thursday, January 23.** While I unfolded those precious promises of grace and glory, John 17, our Lord came down among us and filled us with his consolations.

---

1. Cf. Matt. 15:22-28.

*Wednesday, January 29.* The power of the Highest overshadowed us.[2] All were dissolved into that blessed mourning, so that we wept with the angel, and made supplication, such as the Lord will hear.

# FEBRUARY 1746

*Sunday, February 2.* Had a blessed meeting with our London children at the Lord's Table.

*Monday, February 3.* Opened our new chapel in Wapping, by preaching to a numerous audience, from 1 Cor. 15:1.

*Tuesday, February 4.* Wrote my thoughts to a friend as follows:

> I cannot help expecting the sorest judgments to be poured out upon this land, and that suddenly. You allow us "one hundred years to fill up the measure of our iniquity." You cannot more laugh at my vain fear, than I at your vain confidence. Now is the axe laid to the root of the tree; now is the decree gone forth; now is the day of visitation.[3] It comes so strongly and continually upon me, that I almost think there is God in my prospect of war, famine, pestilence and all the vials of wrath bursting on our heads.

*Wednesday, February 5.* Visited our sister Webb, dying in childbed. Prayed with earnest faith for her. At hearing the child cry, she had broke out into vehement thanksgiving, and soon after fell into convulsions, which set her soul at liberty from all pain and suffering.

*Thursday, February 6.* We sang that hymn over her corpse: "Ah lovely appearance of death,"[4] and shed a few tears of joy and envy.

*Sunday, February 16.* Buried our late sister Adams, who has finished her course with joy; and preached on "Blessed are the dead that die in the Lord" [Rev. 14:13], with great consolation, and desire of following her.

*Friday, February 28.* I invited the weary and heavy-laden to him who hath promised them rest. Many found it then.

---

2. Cf. Luke 1:35.
3. Cf. Luke 3:9; 1 Pet. 2:12.
4. Beginning of Hymn 5, "On the Sight of a Corpse," *Funeral Hymns* (1746), 7–8 (*Poetical Works*, 6:193–95). This collection was published this same month.

# MARCH 1746

*Monday, March 3,* was a day of visitation. God put into my heart good desires, which lasted with power to pray best part of the day.

*Sunday, March 9.* Got abroad again after my painful confinement through the toothache, and officiated at the chapel.

*Thursday, March 13.* God confirmed the word, while I enforced the necessity of a single eye [Matt. 6:22-23].

*Sunday, March 16.* He fulfilled that promise at the Foundery, "Him that cometh unto me, I will in no wise cast out" [John 6:37].

*Tuesday, March 18.* Rejoiced exceedingly to hear of the death of our sister Molly Godwin. Let my latter end be like hers!

*Sunday, March 23.* I explained that best of prayers, if rightly used, "His blood be upon us and upon our children" [Matt. 27:25]. All present, I believe, received then some benefit from his passion.

*Monday, March 24.* In riding to Brentford with our sisters Davey, Alcroft, and Rich, our coach broke down. The only courageous person among us was the only person afraid. Prayed in our return by a dying prisoner of hope, and felt an humble confidence that his eyes shall see the salvation of God.

*Good Friday, March 28.* Every morning of this great and holy week the Lord was at his own feast—but especially this. The word, "Let us also go and die with him" [John 11:16], was written on our hearts. Passed from two to three in solemn prayer at Short's Gardens. Drank tea at my sister Wright's,[5] with Mrs Rich and her two youngest daughters; one [of whom is] the greatest miracle of all accomplishments, both mind and body, that I have ever seen.

*Saturday, March 29.* Administered the Sacrament to a dying sinner, who did run well, but was now groaning out her last breath under the guilt of sin and curse of God. I preached to her the sinner's advocate. She received the faithful saying, and believed the Lord would save her at the last hour.

---

5. That is, his sister Mehetabel, wife of William Wright.

Passed the afternoon at Mrs Rich's, where we caught a physician by the ear, through the help of Mr Lampe[6] and some of our sisters. This is the true use of music.

*Easter Day, March 30.* My text was, "If ye be risen with Christ, seek the things which are above" [Col. 3:1]. The Lord was present, convincing or comforting. We had another blessed opportunity in the evening.

*Monday, March 31.* Preached and administered, notwithstanding a violent purging, which forced me to lie down all day. In the evening I rose and, not being able to stand, preached sitting, with supernatural strength.

# APRIL 1746

*Thursday, April 3.* Prayed by a dying relation (Mrs Richardson[7]) to our mutual comfort.

*Monday, April 7.* My cousin Wilson[8] brought me the joyful news of her mother's release, and last warning words to me.

*Monday, April 14.*[9] Set out with Mr [James] Waller in a chaise for Bristol, [and] on

*Thursday, April 17,* afternoon saluted our friends in the Horsefair. Found the spirit of supplication as soon as I entered the house. Preached on "Hosanna to the Son of David" [Matt. 21:9].

*Sunday, April 20,* was a day of salvation. We had a comfortable Sacrament in Kingswood. I preached with great severity at Conham. The stones cried out on every side, and the Pharisees were offended. At night I expounded Hebrews 9:12, "Neither by the blood of goats and calves, but by his own blood, he entered in once into the holy place, having obtained eternal redemption for

---

6. John Frederick Lampe (1703–1751). Lampe would soon compose settings for some of Charles's hymns on the Christian year: *Hymns on the Great Festivals* (London: M. Cooper, 1746). See Charles's elegy for Lampe in *Funeral Hymns* (1759), 30–31 (*Poetical Works*, 6:246–48).

7. Mary Annesley (b. 1652), the sister of Charles's mother, married Nathaniel Richardson in 1671. This is apparently their daughter-in-law, and the wife of Charles's first cousin.

8. The married daughter of Mrs. Richardson.

9. In the MS the date is incorporated into the text. It has been separated out for clarity.

us." God stood in the midst of the congregation. But in the Society he was still more sensibly present. A loud cry was heard at first. But it sunk lower and lower, into the groans that could not be uttered. This joyful mourning continued two hours. The Spirit of the Lord was upon me as a Spirit of power and love.[10] I thought I could at that time have laid down my life for their[11] salvation. The backsliders were most upon my heart. One such caught hold of my hand in departing, and cried with great earnestness, "I have found my Savior again. He has wrote forgiveness on my heart."

*Monday, April 21.* Expounded Revelation 3:2, 3: "Be watchful, and strengthen the things that remain," etc. Again the power of the Lord was present both to wound and heal. One who had fallen from grace, and lay in the pit of despair three years, was lifted up again, and a new song put in her mouth.

*Wednesday, April 23.* Passed an hour with some of our first children, and found the Spirit of God as in the former days. It continued at Weavers' Hall. But in meeting the women bands I was carried above things temporal. The cloud rested on the tabernacle.[12] The Spirit of supplication was poured ~~out~~ forth. I broke out again and again into effectual prayer, their faith bearing me up. In the midst of strong cryings one was suddenly brought to me, whom I offered up to the throne of grace. It was one who had often strengthened my hands in the Lord. Immediately followed such a burst of divine power as broke all our hearts. All the members suffered with that one member. And God, who knoweth what is the mind of his Spirit, will surely bring back that wanderer to his fold.

*Thursday, April 24.* I declared the promises made to backsliders, and many rejoiced for the consolation. Mary Gee in particular was released, and once more laid hold on eternal life.

*Sunday, April 27.* "This is the day which the Lord hath made. We will rejoice and be glad in it" [Ps. 118:24]. He vouchsafed us at the Sacrament the never-failing spirit of intercession. At Conham likewise he refreshed us in his own house. A vast, quiet congregation

---

10. Cf. 2 Tim. 1:7.

11. The word "their" has been written in after the rest of this sentence, in what does not appear to be Charles's hand.

12. Cf. Num. 9:15.

attended at Baptist Mills to "Wisdom crying without, uttering her voice in the streets" [Prov. 1:20]. The Society was with him again on the mount.

*Tuesday, April 29.* Through many perils came at last to Rode. Showed them at the Cross the end of Christ's coming; namely, "that they might have life," etc. [John 10:10].

*[Wednesday,]*[13] *April 30th.* Preached with double effect. A poor mourner had been crying for mercy all night in the Society house. Conferred with several who have tasted the love of Christ, mostly under the preaching or prayers of our lay-helpers. How can anyone dare deny that they are sent of God? O that all who have the outward call, were as inwardly moved by the Holy Ghost to preach! O that they would make full proof of their ministry, and take the cause out of our weak hands!

Set out in our chaise. Broke it in a slough, and made an hard shift to reach Bradford[-on-Avon] by noon. Preached close and searching on "If any man enter by me, he shall be saved" [John 10:9].

# MAY 1746

*Thursday, May 1.* I endeavoured to strengthen the weak hands. Many rejoiced in sure and steadfast hope that their God will come, and save them. The disconsolate soul (that was at Rode) here found peace and pardon, and rejoiced with joy unspeakable.

*Friday, May 2.* Rode back to Bristol, and was met with the news of our victory in Scotland.[14] Spoke at night on the first words that presented, "He that glorieth, let him glory in the Lord" [1 Cor. 1:31; 2 Cor. 10:17]. We rejoiced unto him with reverence and thankfully observed ~~that~~ the remarkable answer of that petition,

> All their strength o'erturn, o'erthrow,
> > Snap their spears, and break their swords,
> Let the daring rebels know
> > The battle is the Lord's![15]

---

13. MS has "Monday," which is in error.
14. The Jacobite forces were defeated at the battle of Culloden on April 16.
15. "For his Majesty King George," st. 2, lns. 5–8, *Hymns for Times of Trouble and Persecution*, 2 ed. (London: William Strahan, 1745), 55 (*Poetical Works*, 4:64). This was the fifth of fifteen

O that, in this reprieve, before the sword return, we may know the time of our visitation!

*Sunday, May [4].*[16] From preaching to the Conham stocks and stones, I hastened to Baptist Mills, and called, "Come now, and let us return unto the Lord, for he hath torn and he will heal us" [Hos. 6:1]. In the Society exhorted the backsliders to return. We heard a general cry of fear, and grief, and joy, in answer to our prayer, and sweetly felt the most sensible presence of God.

*Sunday, May 11.* He showered down blessings upon us at his table. We were carried out in prayer, especially for the clergy.

*Monday, May 12.* Had a Conference four days with Mr [John] Hodges, Mr [Samuel] Taylor, and our own sons in the gospel.

*Whitsunday, May 18.* We had asked in prayer last night a double blessing for this day, and the answer came. Rejoiced from four to six. The second time I preached in the Wood. In the Sacrament the skies poured down righteousness. Mr Hodges read prayers at Conham. I preached a fourth time to a quiet multitude at the Mills, and then exhorted the Society to walk worthy [of] their holy calling. This might properly be called the Lord's Day.

*Thursday, May 22.* Many heard *h*is[17] voice who stood at the door and knocked [Rev. 3:20]. But in the Society they all seemed ready to open the door.

*Friday, May 23.* Passed two hours with a young clergyman, who is determined to know nothing but Christ crucified.[18] His name is already cast out as evil[19] in his own parish, for endeavouring to do them all the good he can. Our Lord, it seems, is answering our long-continued prayer for labourers.

*Sunday, May 25.* Our Lord was made known to us, as he always is, in the breaking of bread. Let the Quaker and Orthodox *dispute* about the ordinance—our Savior satisfies us a shorter way.

---

"Hymns for Times of Trouble for the Year 1745" that Charles appended to this second edition of an earlier 1744 publication.

16. MS has "May 3," which is in error.

17. The "h" of the word "his" has been underlined several times in the MS, presumably for emphasis.

18. Cf. 1 Cor. 2:2.

19. "As evil" has been inserted above the line in what appears to be Charles's hand.

**Wednesday, May 28.** Reasoned at Bearfield, on "righteousness, temperance, and judgment to come" [Acts 24:25]. The Judge stood at the door, and applied his own awful words, "The trumpet shall sound, and the dead shall be raised" [1 Cor. 15:52].

**Thursday, May 29.** In conference found many of our children in a thriving condition. Not one of those that are justified dreams that he is sanctified at once and wants nothing more.

**Friday, May 30.** In great deadness was revived by praying with one of a fearful heart.

Rode to Wick, and preached forgiveness of sins to the simple-hearted poor. Mr H. and his family were present, and carried me home with them. The large house and garden, the five little children and sweet behaviour of their mother, and above all the open generous temper of Mr H., made me fancy I was got to Fonmon Castle and conversing again with our friend come back from paradise.

# JUNE 1746

**Sunday, June 1.** It rained most part of the day. At Baptist Mills I was told the child of a Papist had much displeased his father by saying, "I believe it will be fair because Mr Wesley is to preach here." But so it was. About five the clouds dispersed, the rain ceased, and we had a blessed opportunity.

**Monday, June 2.** Set out with my charioteer, Mr Waller. Baited[20] an hour at Publow, where the wickedness of one, and the enthusiasm of another, has quite destroyed the work of God. Mr Meriton administered private baptism to a child of our host's, who is escaped once more out of bad hands, and no longer makes the spirit swallow up the letter. By night we got to Coleford.

**Tuesday, June 3.** My morning's congregation drank in every word. Spake with the Society severally. When I saw them last there was scarce a justified person among them. Now fourscore testify their having experienced the pardoning love of God.

Baptised an Anabaptist, and all her fears and troubles fled away in a moment.

---

20. *OED:* (of travelers) "to stop at an inn for food."

Preached at one in the shell of their house. The hearers without were as many as those within, though it rained hard. They are hungry souls, and therefore they shall be filled.

Rode and preached in Shepton Mallet. Spent an hour with the principal man of the town. Met the classes at my host [William] Stone's, and slept in peace.

*Wednesday, June 4.* Driving down a steep hill in our way to Sherborne,[21] the horse stumbled, and threw me out of the seat. I fell on my back upon the wheel; my feet were entangled in the chaise; but the beast stood stock still, so I received no harm, but was only stunned and dirtied. We were four hours going five miles. It rained incessantly, and blew an hurricane this and the day following. By nine at night we were glad to reach W. Nelson's house in Portland.

*Friday, June 6.* Preached to a houseful of staring, loving people, from Jeremiah 50:20. Some wept, but most looked quite unawakened. At noon and night I preached on a hill in the midst of the island.[22] Most of the inhabitants came to hear, but few as yet feel the ~~bitterness of~~ burden of sin, or the want of a Savior.

*Sunday, June 8.* After evening service we had all the islanders that were able to come. I asked, "Is it nothing to you, all ye that pass by?" [Lam. 1:12]. About half a dozen answered "It is nothing to us"—by turning their backs. But the rest hearkened with greater signs of emotion than I had before observed. I found faith at this time that our labour would not be in vain.

*Monday, June 9.* At Southwell, the farthest village, expounded the Song of Simeon [Luke 2:25-32]. Some very old men attended. I distributed a few books among them, rode round the island, and returned by noon to preach on the hill, and by night at my lodgings. Now the power and blessing came. My mouth and their hearts were opened. The rocks were broken in pieces,[23] and melted into tears on every side. I continued exhorting them from seven till ten, to save themselves from this untoward generation [Acts 2:40]. We could hardly part. Left the little Society of twenty members confirmed and comforted.

---

21. Charles spells "Sherburn."
22. Portland is on a peninsula that could be cutoff from the mainland at high tide.
23. Cf. Jer. 23:29.

*Tuesday, June 10.* Came to Axminster, and preached next morning in the bowling-green to above a thousand well-behaved people, on "Come unto me, all that travail," etc. [Matt. 11:28]. Got to Exeter by night.

*Saturday, June 14.* Went forth at Tavistock to call sinners to repentance. A large herd of wild beasts were got together, and very noisy and tumultuous they were. At first I stood on a wall, but their violence forced me thence. I walked to the middle of the field, and began calling, "Wash ye, make you clean," etc. [Isa. 1:16]. The waves of the sea raged so horribly that few could hear. But all might see the restraining hand of God. I continued in prayer mostly for half an hour and walked quietly to my lodgings through the thickest of the King's enemies.

*Sunday, June 15.* Offered Christ once more to a larger audience, who did not seem like the same people. The power of the Lord was present to convince. I endeavoured to strip them of all pretensions to good, insisting that the natural man has absolutely nothing of his own but pure evil, no will or desire to good, till it be supernaturally infused, any more than the devils in hell.

After church I expounded the Prodigal Son [Luke 15:11-32], and many listened to their own history.

Mr [Andrew] Kinsman's Society complained of a brother who had made a division and carried away fifteen of their members. Went to him and his company. They told me they were convinced by reading my brother's books of universal redemption, and therefore met by themselves to avoid dispute and confirm one another in the truth. I persuaded, and carried, them back to their brethren.

*Monday, June 16.* Some of Mr Whitefield's society importuned me to go to Plymouth. I went, resolving to preach only in the streets or fields. A confused multitude were got together, and tolerably quiet, while I showed them the necessity of conversion.

*Tuesday, June 17.* While I preached from Isaiah 1:16, an whole army of soldiers and sailors stood behind me shouting, and blaspheming. A wall of brass was betwixt us.[24] They raged, but could not pass their bounds, or stop the course of the gospel.

---

24. Cf. Jer. 1:18.

The Society were now so exceeding urgent with me that I could not refuse praying with them in their room, and provoking them to love and to good works. I found no difference between them and our children at Kingswood, or the Foundery.

*Wednesday, June 18.* At five expounded in the Tabernacle Zechariah 13:6, "What are these wounds in thy hands?" etc. Then at the dock to above a thousand artless souls, who even devoured the word.

*Thursday, June 19.* Many of the rich heard or seemed to hear me in the evening. In much love I warned the Society against the antinomian errors which they were blindly running into.

*Friday, June 20.* Urged that legal saying of our Lord (as some would call it), "If ye love me, keep my commandments" [John 14:15].

Preached Christ crucified[25] to a multitude at the dock. The word was as a fire, and melted down all it touched. We mourned and rejoiced together in Him that loved us. I have not known such a refreshing time since I left Bristol.

Spake with several in private who had received benefit by the word. One who had found forgiveness, clave to me, and would have gone to any of our Societies which I should advise. But I advised her to stay for a plainer direction.

*Sunday, June 22.* Preached on an hill in Stoke churchyard.[26] It was covered with the surrounding multitude, upward of four thousand by computation. Expounded the Good Samaritan [Luke 10:29-37]. Some reviled at first, on whom I turned and with a few words silenced them. The generality behaved as men fearing God. They followed me with their blessings. One only cursed, and called me Whitefield the second.

Took my leave of Mrs Wheatly and others, whom I greatly love for their love to my brethren Graves, Grinfill, Maxfield—whose bonds they had compassion on.[27] The Lord recompense them in that day!

Our own children could not have expressed greater affection to us at parting. They could have plucked out their eyes and given

---

25. Cf. the note for the September 3–4, 1741, entry above.
26. Stoke is a district of Plymouth, one mile northwest of city center.
27. Cf. the entry for July 23, 1746, below.

them us.[28] Several offered me money, but I told them I never accepted any. Others would have persuaded Mr Waller to take it, but he walked in the same steps, and said their love was sufficient.

*Tuesday, June 24.* Got to Mr Bennet's.[29]

*Wednesday, June 25.* Read prayers and preached in Tresmeer church. They seemed to *feel* the word of reconciliation.

*Thursday, June 26.* Came to Gwennap, and encouraged the poor persecuted sheep by that promise, Zechariah 13:7, 8, 9. The Lord smiled upon our first meeting.

*Sunday, June 29.* Upon examination of each separately, I found the Society in a prosperous way. Their sufferings have been for their furtherance, and the gospel's. The opposers behold and wonder at their steadfastness and godly conversation. Preached the gospel to the poor at Stithians. The poor received it with tears of joy.

My evening congregation was computed upward of five thousand. Preached the pardoning God from the returning Prodigal [Luke 15:11-32], and felt as it were the people sink under the power of Him that sent me. They all stood uncovered, knelt at the prayers, and hung *narrantis ab ore*.[30] For an hour and an half I invited them back to their Father, and felt no hoarseness or weariness afterwards. Spent an hour and an half more with the Society, warning them against pride, and the love of the creature, and stirring them up to universal obedience.

*Monday, June 30.* Both sheep and shepherds had been scattered in the late cloudy day of persecution. But the Lord gathered them again and kept them together by their own brethren, who began to exhort their companions; one or more in every Society. No less then four have sprung up in Gwennap. I talked closely with each, and find no reason to doubt their having been used by God thus far. Advised and charged them not to stretch themselves beyond their line, by speaking out of the Society, or fancying themselves public teachers. If they keep within their bounds, as they promise, they may be useful in the church. And I would to God that all the Lord's people were prophets, like these!

---

28. Cf. Gal. 4:15.
29. Rev. John Bennet (c. 1670–1750).
30. "On the lips of the one who speaks." Cf. Virgil, *Aeneid*, iv.79.

In the evening preached to our dearest children at St Ives, from Isaiah 35 last: "The redeemed of the Lord shall return," etc. He brought us some steps forward on our journey by that meeting.

# JULY 1746

*Thursday, July 3.* At Ludgvan[31] preached Christ crucified.[32] Spake with the classes, who seem much in earnest. Showed above a thousand sinners at Sithney the love and compassion of Jesus towards them. Many who came from Helston, a town of rebels and persecutors, were struck, and confessed their sin, and declared they would never more be found fighting against God.

*Friday, July 4.* At Wendron a huge multitude listened to the invitation, "Ho, every one that thirsteth, come ye to the waters" [Isa. 55:1]. Explained to the infant Society the design of their meeting.

*Sunday, July 6.* At Stithians rebuked the Society sharply, and gave them a fortnight to know their own mind, whether they will serve God or mammon [Luke 16:13].

The woman who keeps the Society house could not be satisfied acquainting me how rich and strong she was in grace, that she could not be proud, could not be deceived, could not fall, etc. I assured her a common harlot was in a far better state. But she was above all reproof, or conviction. "A wild ass used to the wilderness, that snuffeth up the wind at her pleasure. In her occasion who can turn her away?" [Jer. 2:24]. God deliver us from these saints of the devil's making! One such more hinders the work than a hundred drunkards.[33]

At Gwennap near two thousand listened to those gracious words that proceeded out of his mouth, "Come unto me all that travail, and are," etc. [Matt. 11:28]. Half of them were from Redruth, which seems on the point of surrendering to the Prince of peace.

The whole country finds the benefit of the gospel. Hundreds who follow not with us, have broke off their sins, and are outwardly reformed, and though persecutors once, will not now suffer a word to be spoken against this way. Some of those who fell off

---

31. Also called Ludjan. Charles spells "Lidgeon."
32. Cf. the note for the September 3–4, 1741, entry above.
33. This paragraph was not included by Jackson.

in the late persecution desired to be present at the Society. I addressed myself chiefly to the backsliders. God touched their hearts. Several followed me to my lodgings, and desired to be admitted again. Received them back upon trial.

*Saturday, July 12.* Showed them at Morvah (who were growing rich) the farther rest for the people of God [Heb. 4:10], and inculcated the first great lesson of humility.

*Sunday, July 13.* Most of St Just Society were present. I applied those seasonable words, "Will ye also go away?" [John 6:67], with great severity and love. Besought them to cast up the stumbling block of sin, to turn unto the Lord with weeping and fasting and mourning, that the gospel door might be again opened among them. I urged the same thing upon them in the Society-room, and with many tears they promised amendment, and requested me to come to them again.

Went to church at Zennor, and thence to my congregation, whom I showed the twofold rest of pardon and holiness.[34] Talked with their young exhorter Maddern,[35] and advised him to practise, before he preached, the gospel.

At St Ives no one offered to make the least disturbance. Indeed the whole place is outwardly changed in this respect. Walk the streets with astonishment, scarce believing it St Ives. It is the same throughout all the county. All opposition falls before us; or rather, is fallen, and not yet suffered to lift up its head again. This also hath the Lord wrought.

Put a disorderly walker, the first of the kind, out of the Society.

*Friday, July 18.* Preached with much freedom at Wendron. A poor drunkard exclaimed for a few moments, and turned his back. I did not wonder when I heard he was an alehouse-keeper.

*Una cum gente tot annos Bella gero.*[36]

Men of his craft are generally our sworn enemies.

---

34. Probably speaking on Heb. 4:10 again.

35. John Maddern, of Zennor, would become a Methodist itinerant the next year. Charles spells "Madern."

36. "I have waged war on a whole race, for so many years." Virgil, *Aeneid*, i.47.

*Saturday, July 19.* Had a visit from Captain Trounce, the man who last year hindered my brother from preaching; and threw him over the wall.[37]

Rode to Sithney, where the word begins to take root. The rebels of Helston threatened hard. All manner of evil they say of us. Papists we are that's certain; and are for bringing in the Pretender. Nay the vulgar are persuaded I have brought him with me, and James Waller is the man. But a law is to come from London tonight, to put us all down and set £100 upon my head. We had notwithstanding a numerous congregation, and several of the persecutors. I declared my commission to open their eyes, to turn them from [darkness to light], etc. [Acts 26:18]. Many appeared convinced, and caught in the gospel net.

*Sunday, July 20.* Near a hundred of the fiercest rioters were present, who a few months since had cruelly beat the sincere hearers, not sparing the women and children. They were hired by the pious minister for that purpose. Now these very men, expecting a disturbance, came to fight for me, and said, they would lose their lives in my defence. But there was no occasion for their service. All was quiet, as it generally is when Satan threatens most.

Crossed the country to Redruth. Walked through the town, a mile to church, and was surprised by the general civility.

Drew the congregation after me to the field; more than 8000, as was supposed. I expounded the Good Samaritan [Luke 10:29-37]. Surely he has a multitude of patients here.

*Monday, July 21.* I had heard sad accounts of St Just people; that, being scattered by persecution they had wandered into by-paths of error and sin, and been confirmed therein by their covetous, proud exhorter John Bennetts.[38] From St Ives, I came on

*Wednesday noon, July 23,* to his house in Trewellard,[39] a village belonging to St Just. Found about a dozen of the shattered Society, which quickly increased to fifty or sixty.

Perceived, as soon as we kneeled down that there was a blessing in the remnant. We wrestled with God in his own strength from one

---

37. John Wesley's *Journal* account of this incident on July 7, 1745, in Tolcarn does not present Captain Trounce as the main instigator (cf. *Works* 20:78–79).

38. Charles spells "J. Bennet" but not to be confused with Rev. John Bennett. See fn. 29.

39. Charles spells "Trewallard."

till nine (with only the preaching between). I acknowledged God was with them of a truth. My faith for them returned, and I asked, nothing doubting, that the door might again be opened and that "He who hinders might be taken out of the way, as God knew best." This man was once a gentleman of fortune, but is now a poor drunken spendthrift; brother to Dr Borlase, and retained by that dispenser of justice to supply the defect of the laws. This champion they send forth drunk on all occasions. It was he that pressed my brother for a soldier; dragged away Edward Grinfill, though past age, from his business and family, for a soldier and sailor; assaulted Mr Meriton, to serve him the same way; seized on Mr Graves, the third clergyman, in bed, and hurried him on board a man-of-war. In a word, he seems raised up by Satan to support his tottering kingdom, and swears continually there shall never be any more preaching at St Just. For a year and an half Satan has seemed to triumph in his success. So much good may one sinner hinder, if armed with the sins of God's people. In praying for this poor soul, I thought heaven and earth would meet. The spirit of prayer bowed down all before him. We believed the door would be opened for preaching at this time. Between six and seven I cried in the street to about a thousand hearers, "If God be for us, who can be against us?" [Rom. 8:31-32]. The wall of brass surrounded us.[40] None opened his mouth, or appeared on Satan's side. The little flock were comforted and refreshed abundantly.

I spake with each of the Society, and was amazed to find them just the reverse of what they had been represented. Most of them had kept their first love,[41] even while men were riding over their heads, and they passed through fire and water. Their exhorter appeared a solid, humble Christian; raised up to stand in the gap, and keep the trembling sheep together.

I was ready for rest, but none could I find all night, through the multitude of my small bed-fellows. At four I talked with more of the Society, and adored the miracle of grace, which has kept these sheep in the midst of wolves. Well may the despisers behold and wonder. "Here is a bush in the fire, burning, yet not consumed!" [Exod. 3:2]. What have they not done to crush this rising sect? but, lo! they prevail nothing!

---

40. Cf. Jer. 1:18.
41. Cf. Rev. 2:4.

*Non Hydra secto corpore firmior vinci dolentem crevit in Herculem.*[42]

For one preacher they cut off, twenty spring up. Neither persuasions nor threatening, flattery nor violence, dungeons or sufferings of various kinds, can conquer them. Many waters cannot quench this little spark which the Lord hath kindled, neither shall the floods of persecution drown it.

*Thursday, July 24.* Rode with a merry heart to Ludgvan, and called many sin-sick souls to their Physician. Met the Society at Zennor. How unlike those of St Just! Rebuked them sharply. Silenced one of their exhorters. And returned to Trewellard by Friday noon.

*Friday, July 25.* From one to three we poured out our souls in prayer for a nation laden with iniquity. I was led undesignedly to pray for our drunken persecutor, and the Spirit came pouring down like a river. We were filled with the divine presence. I had left my hymn-book in my chamber, and stepped up for it. One came after me with news that Mr Eustick was just coming to take me up. I went down to the congregation, but my friend Eustick was gone, without beating man, woman, or child. He only asked if Mr Wesley was there, for he had a warrant to apprehend him, went out at the other door and told those he met he had been searching all the house for Wesley but could not find him. We supposed he had not got sufficient courage—that is, drink—for his purpose, and expected his return. To make the devil a liar, I began preaching an hour before the appointed time. The flame was kindled in a moment. I had only to speak, and *leave*[43] God to apply. He filled us up to the brim with faith, and love and joy, and power. The Spirit of the Lord lifted up, and caused us to triumph, and tread on all the powers of the enemy.

After a short interval, I received strength to preach again in the court-yard on "Saul, Saul, why persecutest thou me?" [Acts 9:4]. The two-edged sword did great execution.[44] Concluded with that hymn:

---

42. "No, the hydra, as its body was hewn, grew mightier against Hercules." Horace, *Odes*, IV.iv.61–62.

43. The word *leave* is written "LEAVE" in the MS, apparently for emphasis.

44. Cf. Heb. 4:12.

> Glory, and thanks, and praise
>  To Him that hath the key!
> Jesus, thy sovereign grace
>  Gives us the victory;
> Baffles the world, and Satan's power,
> And open throws the Gospel-door.[45]

*Sunday, July 27.* Met the Society at Morvah. Went to church at St Just, and then to my old pulpit, the large stone by brother Chinhall's house. I preached from Matthew 22:1[ff]. All was quiet, till I came to those words, "And the remnant took his servants, and entreated them spitefully, and slew them" [Matt. 22:6]. Then one begun throwing stones. But I went on exhorting them to save themselves from this untoward generation. My discourse was as mixed as the multitude—law, gospel, threatenings, promises, which I trust the Spirit applied to their several cases.

Rode to St Ives, and expounded the Woman bowed down with a Spirit of Infirmity [Luke 13:11-17].

*Monday, July 28.* Began my week's experiment of leaving off tea, but my flesh protested against it. I was but half awake, and half alive all day: and my headache so increased toward noon, that I could neither speak nor think. So it was for the two following days, with the addition of a violent purging, occasioned by my milk-diet. This so weakened me, that I could hardly sit my horse. However, I made a shift to ride to Gwennap and preach and meet the Society. I would have ate afterwards, being very faint and weary, but could get nothing proper.

# AUGUST 1746

*Friday, August 1.* Left two or three of a doubtful character out of the Society at St Ives, not daring to trust them with the honor of God and his people. At the hour of intercession our hearts were moved, and we desired to return to God in weeping, and fasting, and mourning. They promised henceforward to meet the true members of the Church of England at the throne of grace on this day.

---

45. This hymn was in use before formal publication. It appeared as "Another (After Preaching)," st. 1, *HSP* (1749), 1:323–24 (*Poetical Works*, 5:128).

*Saturday, August 2.* At Sithney spoke with one who had been set at liberty from the guilt of sin the first time he heard me, I think, as soon as I had named my text. Preached Christ crucified[46] in the evening, and on *Sunday morning, August 3*, to many who seemed truly desirous to know him.

From evening service at Redruth I rode back to my own church, the valley near our room at Gwennap, and found at least five thousand sinners waiting for the glad tidings of salvation. I bade them to the Great Supper [Luke 14:15-24], in my Master's name and words, and even compelled them to come in.

*Tuesday, August 5.* Preached there again, and rejoiced over those blessed mourners. Some I heard were then filled with all joy in believing.

*Thursday, August 7.* Asked at Trewellard, "What are these wounds in thy hands?" [Zech. 13:6]. The Lord himself answered, and made himself known to us by the marks of his sufferings.

Before preaching I read them the late Act against swearing,[47] of which a hundred had been sent my brother by a justice of peace. I thought his design best answered by reading it in our largest congregations. Last Sunday I read it at Gwennap. I believe it was blessed to many.

Rejoiced over this steady people. Near 150 are gathered again, and knit together in the love of Jesus.

*Friday, August 8.* Met the Society at five, and more of the power of God than ever. I thought he would give us a double portion at parting. We tasted the powers of the world to come,[48] while the Spirit applied his own word, "These are they that came out of great tribulation!" [Rev. 7:14].

Got back to St Ives by one, and humbled ourselves under the mighty hand of God. He did now begin to lift us up. A spirit of mourning ran through our hearts; and again in the evening, while I explained, "The Spirit and the Bride say, Come!" [Rev. 22:17].

*Sunday, August 10.* At Gwennap nine or ten thousand by computation listened with all eagerness, while I commended them to

---

46. Cf. the note for the September 3–4, 1741, entry above.

47. *An Act More Effectually to Prevent Profane Cursing and Swearing* (London: Thomas Baskett, 1746).

48. Cf. Heb. 6:5.

God, and to the word of his grace [Acts 20:32]. For near two hours I was enabled to preach repentance towards God, and faith in Jesus Christ. Broke out again and again into prayer and exhortation. I believed not one word would return empty.[49] Seventy years' sufferings were overpaid by one such opportunity.

Never had we so large an effusion of the Spirit, as in the Society. I could not doubt, at that time, either their perseverance or my own. And still I am humbly confident that we shall stand together among the multitude which no man can number.[50]

*Monday, August 11.* I expressed the gratitude of my heart in the following thanksgiving:

> All thanks be to God,
>   Who scatters abroad,
>   Throughout every place,
> By the least of his servants his savour of grace:
>   Who the victory gave,
>   The praise let him have,
>   For the work He hath done;
> All honor and glory to Jesus alone!, etc.[51]

Preached at St Tudy's,[52] "Repent, and believe the gospel" [Mark 1:15]. Mr Bennet and Thomson were present. As I was concluding, a gentleman rode up to me very fiercely and bade me come down. We exchanged a few words, and talked together more largely in the house. The poor drunken lawyer went away in as good a humour as he was then capable of. Had more difficulty to get clear of a different antagonist, one Adams,[53] an old enthusiast, who travels through all the land, as "Overseer of all the Ministers."

*Tuesday, August 12.* Mr Bennet's church [in Tresmeer] was crowded at night. He read prayers, and I preached on "They that be whole have no need of a Physician" [Mark 2:17].

*Wednesday, August 13.* Offered to preach in Tavistock, but to such sticks and stones as I have not seen, no not at Conham. The words

---

49. Cf. Isa. 55:11.
50. Cf. Rev. 7:9.
51. St. 1 of "Thanksgiving for the Success of the Gospel," *Redemption Hymns*, 5–7 (*Poetical Works*, 4:210–12).
52. Charles spells "St Eudy."
53. This is the John Adams, of Tresmeer, who was eventually confined as a madman. Cf. John Wesley, *Letter to the . . . Bishop of Gloucester*, I.29, *Works* 11:493.

rebounded as from a wall of brass. So great a bar I have seldom felt, and was therefore forced in a quarter of an hour to dismiss them.

*Thursday, August 14.* Many letters I have received from Plymouth, importuning me to visit them in my return. A brother met us on the road thither, and informed me of what I expected, the indefatigable pains Satan has taken to alienate the minds of the people. Yet I complied with the request of Herbert Jenkins, Mr [Andrew] Kinsman's family, and many others, by preaching in their house once more.

*Friday, August 15.* Showed a simple people at the dock the blessedness of mourning, and they tasted it in that hour.

*Saturday, August 16.* Spent the morning in conversing with Mrs Stephens, Mrs Patrick, Mr Hide's family, and other sincere followers after Christ. Baptized a young woman who, *in* the ordinance, lost her burden of sin, and was soon after filled with joy in believing.

*Sunday, August 17.* My subject was, "They that be whole have no," etc. [Mark 2:17]. The number of the sick, I believe, increases. We walked back from the field with the voice of praise and thanksgiving.

*Monday, August 18.* Took boat for the dock with sisters Gregory, Veel, Poppleston, and Herbert Jenkins. In perils by water, in perils among false brethren! The rough, stormy sea tried our faith. Some supernatural courage I had given me for the rest. None stirred, or we must have been overset. In two hours our invisible Pilot brought us safe to land—thankful for our deliverance, humbled for our littleness of faith, and more endeared to each other by our common danger.

Found thousands waiting for the word of life. The Lord made it a channel of grace. Spoke and prayed alternately for two hours. The moonlight added to the solemnity. Our eyes overflowed with tears, and our hearts with love. Scarce a soul but was affected with grief or joy. We drank into one spirit, and were persuaded that neither life nor death, nor things present, nor things to come, shall be able to separate us.[54]

---

54. Cf. Rom. 8:38.

Spent all **Wednesday, August 20th,** at Tavistock, to encourage their poor scattered Society, under the reproach which one had brought upon them all.

**Thursday, August 21.** Published the dying love of Jesus[55] in Tresmeer church; and on

**Friday, August 22,** I enforced the duty (Matthew 7:7) and pleaded the promise, in full assurance of faith. Refreshed by the sight of my brother Thomson. At night I preached in Laneast[56] church, to a people seeking the Lord.

**Sunday, August 24.** Preached morning and evening, not my own words, at St Gennys.

At Mr Bennet's, heard from Captain [James] Hitchens that John Trembath was still alive, but his son Samuel departed in full triumph.[57] His last words were,

> Ready wing'd for their flight
> To the regions of light,
> The horsemen are come,
> The chariots of Israel, to carry me home![58]

**Thursday, August 28.** At Bristol I met my brother returned from Wales.

**Friday, August 29.** The Lord gave me words of comfort for our own dear children in the gospel.

**Sunday, August 31.** In expounding the woman bowed down [Luke 13:11-17] we found the ancient blessing. Concluded the day and month with a joyful Love-feast.

# SEPTEMBER 1746

**Tuesday, September 2.** Preached at Bath and Brentford, where some of our friends met and conducted us to town.

---

55. Cf. the note for the September 3–4, 1741, entry above.

56. Laneast, Cornwall; one of the parishes served by Rev. John Bennet (c. 1670–1750).

57. James Hitchens (Charles spells "Hitchins") was a "tinner" or blacksmith in Gwennap. His son Samuel died on August 16. John Wesley assisted Hitchens in writing an account of the death, published as *A Short Account of the Death of Samuel Hitchens* (London: [Strahan,] 1746). See also Charles's "Hymn on the Death of Samuel Hitchens," *HSP* (1749), 2:74–75 (*Poetical Works*, 5:214–16).

58. "Hosannah to God," st. 7, *Funeral Hymns* (1746), 23 (*Poetical Works*, 6:211).

*Thursday, September 4.* Here I heard that Mr Green,[59] a clergyman, whom my brother had sent for to assist us, was fallen off to the antinomians.

*Thursday, September 11.* Poor Thomas Williams came to beg something of me, on pretence of visiting his father, before the Bishop of London ordained him for a missionary. Got Mr Watkins to assist him, although his promises of repentance had little weight with me.

Talked with a man of the world, in great affliction for the loss of a favourite child. When on the point of committing sin, he had been warned of her death, as if a voice had said, "if you do this thing, I will take away your child." She died in the most triumphant manner, being perfected in the short space of nine years.

*Tuesday, September 16.* Set out in a chaise with Mr Edward Perronet, Mr Watkins, and others, for Shoreham. Preached in our way at Sevenoaks, where we were much threatened, but nothing hurt. At Shoreham Mr Green read prayers. As soon as I began preaching, the wild beasts began roaring, stamping, blaspheming, ringing the bells, and turning the church into a bear-garden. Spoke on for half an hour, though only the nearest could hear. The rioters followed us to Mr Perronet's[60] house, raging, threatening, and throwing stones. Charles Perronet hung over me to intercept my blows. They continued their uproar after we were housed. Our sisters from Sevenoaks feared to go home. But our Lord in some time scattered the beasts of the people, so that they escaped unhurt.

*Friday, September 19.* An opposer desired to see me on his deathbed. Now his voice was changed, and he glad to hear [that] one might know our sins forgiven here, but feared he was too great a sinner to obtain it. I left him waiting for redemption, as a poor trembling publican or harlot.

*Sunday, September 21.* Heard Mr Green preach rank antinomianism. In the evening I cried, in the name of my Lord, "Look unto me, and be ye saved [Isa. 45:22]—from sin, not in it." He owned his own word. To the bands I explained the nature of Christian perfection, another name for Christian salvation. Mr Green sat by and mocked.

---

59. Rev. John Green. Cf. John Wesley, *Journal* (October 4, 1746), *Works* 20:143.

60. Rev. Vincent Perronet (1693–1785), vicar of Shoreham, married to Charity (*née* Goodhew, c. 1690–1763), and father of Edward and Charles.

*Monday, September 22.* Carried him to Newington Green,[61] where he appeared an antinomian barefaced.

*Tuesday, September 23.* He fairly told me, my brother and I preached another gospel, and were therefore accursed.

*Wednesday, September 24.* Prayed by our sister Lincoln, rejoicing, as was thought, in death. The fever had taken away her senses, but not her joy. Still her words were all prayer, or praise.

*Friday, September 26.* Met my brother at Uxbridge. I heard him at our chapel in the evening. He read us an account of another son of James Hitchens, just going to glory;[62] which set us all on fire.

# OCTOBER 1746

*Sunday, October 5.* Had the never-failing presence of our Lord at his table. Encouraged my companions in tribulation at the Foundery by the scriptural prospect of the new Jerusalem [Rev. 21]. Added a few words how they should observe the thanksgiving-day.

*Tuesday, October 7.* Prayed with Edward Perronet, just on the point of receiving faith.

*Thursday, October 9.* The Foundery was filled at four in the morning. I spoke from those words, "How shall I give thee up, Ephraim?" [Hos. 11:8]. Our hearts were melted by the long-suffering love of God, whose power we felt disposing us to the true thanksgiving.[63] It was a day of solemn rejoicing. O that from this moment all our rebellions against God might cease!

*Friday, October 10.* Set out for Newcastle with my young companion and friend, Edward Perronet, whose heart the Lord hath given me. His family were kept from us so long by their mistaken

---

61. Newington Green was an open area halfway between Islington and Stoke Newington, about four miles north of London.

62. Thomas Hitchens died on September 12, less than a month after his brother Samuel. The account which John Wesley helped James Hitchens prepare was also published as *A Short Account of the Death of Thomas Hitchens* ([Bristol: Farley,] 1747).

63. This was the designated public Thanksgiving Day for celebrating the defeat of the Jacobite rebellion. Charles published for the occasion his *Hymns for the Public Thanksgiving Day, Oct. 9, 1746* (London: [Strahan,] 1746).

notion that we were against the Church. We lodged at Tilsworth. I could not rest for my vomiting and purging.

*Sunday, October 12.* At Quinton I preached repentance, from the strongest of all motives, "Turn ye unto the Lord, for he is gracious," etc. [Joel 2:13]. Out of the abundance of my heart my mouth spake, and both preacher and people bowed down to the pardoning God.

In the evening my text at Evesham was, "His blood be upon us, and upon our children!" [Matt. 27:25]. We felt its softening power; and yet more at the Society, where Patty Keech and others were quite overpowered by it.

*Monday, October 13.* Dined at Studley, where some poor drunkards, offended at our singing, endeavoured a while to silence us, but we fairly outsung them. Riding on, I had a narrow escape. A man discharged a gun just over my head, and shot a bird on the opposite hedge, which fell dead at my feet. The shot flew within a few inches of my face. One of our company told us his father had been killed by such an accident.

Much refreshed at Birmingham by my brother James Jones, and the rest of the children whom God hath given us.

*Tuesday, October 14.* Rejoiced once more with our brethren at Wednesbury, who have rest at present, and walk in the comfort of the Holy Ghost. The Lord was with us as in the former days. Late at night came our brother [Robert] Swindells to conduct us to the Cheshire Societies.

*Wednesday, October 15.* Preached at Tipton Green the necessity of taking Christ's yoke upon us [Matt. 11:29]. The few remaining antinomians were present, but they only mocked at God's word and messenger.

Baptized a Dissenter's child. Went forth, and proclaimed my Master in the street. All were deeply attentive. How is the leopard laid down with the kid![64] It was past eight when we came to Penkridge,[65] at the invitation of a brother. He comforted my heart on the way by informing me that his father, aged seventy and a great opposer lately, had come last night to the preaching and returned to his house justified.

---

64. Cf. Isa. 11:6.
65. Charles spells "Pencrage."

We were hardly set down when the sons of Belial beset the house and beat at the door.[66] I ordered it to be set open and immediately they filled the house. I sat still in the midst of them for half an hour. Edward Perronet I was a little concerned for, lest such rough treatment at his first setting out should daunt him. But he abounded in valour, and was for reasoning with the wild beasts, before they had spent any of their violence. He got a deal of abuse thereby, and not a little dirt, both which he took very patiently.

I had no design to preach. But being called upon by so unexpected a congregation, I rose at last and read the first words I met: "When the Son of man shall come in his glory, and all the holy angels with him, then shall he sit upon the throne of his glory" [Matt. 25:31]. While I reasoned with them of judgment to come, they grew calmer by little and little. I then spake to them one by one, till the Lord had disarmed them all. One who stood out the longest I held by the hand, and urged with the love of Christ crucified, till in spite of both his natural and diabolical courage, he trembled like a leaf. I was constrained to break out into earnest prayer for him, and surely the Lord heard and answered. Our leopards were all become lambs, and very kind we were at parting. Near midnight the house was clear and quiet. We gave thanks to the God of our salvation, and slept in peace.

**Thursday, October 16.** Rose much refreshed at four, and preached to a house-full of listening souls. Rode to Congleton, and preached in a yard, and prayed with the little Society, who seem on the brink of the pool.[67] One important sinner, past seventy, was healed, and witnessed it the same hour.

**Friday, October 17.** Directed a quiet multitude at the cross to "the Lamb of God, who taketh away," etc. [John 1:29]. Satan had sent one Smith to this place before me, who begged their charity and railed at the clergy. Yet the poor people heard me gladly. Two ministers were of my audience.

**Saturday, October 18.** At Woodley I invited the weary to Christ [Matt. 11:28]; and on

---

66. Cf. Judg. 19:22.
67. Cf. John 5:1-15.

*Sunday morning, October 19th*, discoursed on "Him that cometh unto me, I will in no wise cast out" [John 6:37].

*Monday, October 20.* Saluted our friends at Birstall.

*Tuesday, October 21.* Preached at Dewsbury, where John Nelson had gathered many stray sheep. The minister did not condemn them unheard, but talked with the persons wrought upon, and narrowly examined into the doctrine taught them, and its effect on their lives. When he found, that as many as had been affected by the preaching were evidently reformed and brought to Church and Sacrament, he testified his approbation of the work, and rejoiced that sinners were converted unto God.

At Leeds called a lamblike multitude to repentance. Many at the Society were unable to suppress their concern. Others, who had more power over themselves, were as no less deeply affected.

*Wednesday, October 22.* Preached in a yard at Keighley on "God so loved the world" [John 3:16]. Here also is the promise of a plentiful harvest. Went on to Haworth. Called on Mr Grimshaw,[68] a faithful minister of Christ, and found him and his wife[69] ill of a fever. She had been a great opposer, but lately convinced. His soul was full of triumphant love. I wished mine in its place. We prayed believing that the Lord would raise him up again, for the service of his church.

I read prayers and expounded Isaiah 35. All listened, many wept, some received comfort. Returned and exhorted the steady Society at Keighley. Lay at a public-house; and I slept, in spite of the serenaders, who entertained my fellow-traveller till the morning.

*Thursday, October 23.* Set out with Edward Perronet and reached Newcastle by Saturday noon.

*Sunday, October 26.* My companion was taken ill of a fever. We prayed for him in strong faith, nothing doubting. Monday and Tuesday he grew worse and worse. On Wednesday the small-pox appeared—a favourable sort. Yet on Thursday evening we were much alarmed by the great pain and danger he was in. We had recourse to our never failing remedy, and received a most remarkable,

---

68. Rev. William Grimshaw (1708–1763), curate of Haworth. Charles's hymn on his death can be found in *Poetical Works*, 6:306–7.

69. Grimshaw's second wife, Elizabeth, who died soon after from this illness.

immediate answer to our prayer. The great means of his recovery was the prayer of faith.

*Friday, October 31.* Rode to Whickham, where the curate sent his love to me, with a message that he was glad of my coming, and obliged to me for endeavouring to do good among his people, for none wanted it more, and he heartily wished me good luck in the name of the Lord. He came with another clergyman, and stayed both preaching and Society. I discoursed on Matthew 11:5.

It was the exemplary behaviour of our Society, with the deaths of two or three, which convinced the ministers that this new sect, everywhere spoken against, is no other than the sect of the Nazarenes,[70] or real Christians.

# NOVEMBER 1746

*Sunday, November 2.* Preached in the street, close to the popish chapel, from Isaiah 1:9, "Except the Lord of hosts had left us a very small remnant, we should have been as Sodom," etc. I put them in mind of their late consternation, and deliverance in answer to the mourning, praying few. God gave weight to my words, which therefore sunk into their hearts. Many in this place, I am persuaded, will thank him with their lives, and not be terrified when the scourge returns.

*Monday, November 3.* Prayer has been made to God without ceasing for my young man, and God hath showed he heard. Today the small-pox turned, and he is better than we could hope in so short a time. It is the Lord's doing, who has given him to his church. Whether he has not also received the sense of pardon in his sickness, let his life, rather than my words, witness.

*Tuesday, November 4.* Preached at Biddick on "How shall I give thee up, Ephraim?" [Hos. 11:8], and the numerous congregation were dissolved in tears. At one I spoke from those words, "Lord, when thy hand is lifted up, they will not see, but they shall see," etc. [Isa. 26:11]. Again my voice was drowned in the general sorrow. We poured out a prayer while His chastening was upon us,

---

70. Cf. Matt. 2:23.

and all lay at his feet weeping. At night many followed the example of the importunate widow.[71]

*Thursday, November 6.* God broke us to pieces with the hammer of his word, Jeremiah 31, and the room was filled with strong cries and prayers that pierced the clouds.

*Friday, November [7].[72]* Preached at Plessy, at Swalwell, and at Whickham, where I got an hour's useful conversation with the two ministers.

*Sunday, November 9.* Was very sensible of the hard frost in riding to Burnopfield, but did not feel it while calling a crowd of sinners to repentance. At my return found Edward Perronet rejoicing in the love of God.

*Wednesday, November 12.* Preached on "Let us come boldly to the throne of grace" [Heb. 4:16]; and the Lord fulfilled the words. I cannot describe what our souls felt while we sat down with Christ in heavenly places.

*Thursday, November 13.* Expounded at Newlands.[73] Here also John Brown has gathered a flock, and suffered greatly for their sake.

*Monday, November 17.* At Biddick preached on "They all shall know me from the least to the greatest" [Jer. 31:34]. The least begin to know Him. When will it spread to the greatest too?

*Wednesday, November 19.* Had much serious talk with the friendly Dr F. Such a physician is truly the gift of God. He seems resolved with his house to serve the Lord.

*Sunday, November 23.* At night I could not preach (through the usual uproar), but only exhort the Society, to which I admitted the backsliders.

*Monday, November 24.* They were greatly moved under the morning word. We observed the day as a day of humiliation. Had a solemn hour of prayer with the mourners. God did not manifest himself so much in joy and comfort, as in power and firmness (which he put into our hearts ) against sin.

---

71. Cf. Luke 18:3.
72. MS has "November 6," which is in error.
73. Charles spells "Newlings."

*Wednesday, November 26.* All seemed overwhelmed with the power of his love. For an hour or two I quite forgot myself, and those that burden me.

*Thursday, November 27.* Rode to Hexham, at the pressing instance of Mr [Thomas] Wardrobe, a Dissenting minister, and others. Walked straight to the market-place, and began calling sinners to repentance. A multitude of them stood staring at me, but all quiet. The Lord opened my mouth, and they drew nearer and nearer, stole off their hats, and listened. None offered to interrupt, but one unfortunate squire, who could get none to second him. His servants and the constables hid themselves. One he did find, and bade him go take me down. The poor constable simply answered, "Sir, I cannot have the face to do it. For what harm does he do?" Several Papists attended, and the Church minister, who had refused me his pulpit with indignation. However, he came to hear with his own ears; and I wish all who hang us first, would, like him, try us afterward.

I walked back to Mr Ord's through the people, who acknowledged, "It is the truth, and none can speak against it." A constable followed, and told me, "Sir Edward Blacket orders you to *disperse* the town" (*depart*, I suppose, he meant) "and not raise a disturbance there." Sent my respects to Sir Edward, and said if he would give me leave, I would wait upon him, and satisfy him. He soon returned with an answer that Sir Edward would have nothing to say to me. But if I preached again, and raised a disturbance, he would put the law in execution against me. I replied, I was not conscious of my breaking any law of God or man; but if I did, was ready to suffer the penalty. That as I had not given notice of preaching again at the Cross, I should not preach again *at that place*, or cause disturbance anywhere. Charged the constable, a trembling, submissive soul, to assure his worship I reverenced him for his office's sake.

The only place I could get to preach in was a cock-pit, and expected Satan would come and fight me on his own ground. Squire Roberts, the justice's son, laboured hard to raise a mob (for whose riot I was to answer). But with a strong hand did our Lord hold down him that is in the world.[74] The very boys ran away from

---

74. Cf. 1 John 4:4.

him, when the poor squire persuaded them to go down to the cock-pit, and cry, "Fire!"

I called (in words then first heard in that place), "Repent, and be converted, that your sins may be blotted out" [Acts 3:19]. God struck the hard rock, and the waters gushed out.[75] Never have I seen a people more desirous at the first hearing.

Passed the evening in conference with Mr Wardrobe. O that all our Dissenting brethren were like-minded! Then would all dissensions cease for ever.

*Friday, November 28.* At six we assembled again in our chapel, the cock-pit. I imagined myself in the Pantheon, or some heathen temple, and almost scrupled preaching there at first; but we found "the earth is the Lord's, and the fullness thereof" [Ps. 24:1]. His presence consecrated the place. Never have I seen greater awe, or sense of God, than while we were repeating his own prayer. Set before their eyes Christ crucified, and crying from the cross, "Is it nothing to you?" [Lam. 1:12]. The rocks were melted into gracious tears. We knew not how to part. I distributed some books among them, which they received with the utmost eagerness. [They] begged me to come again, and to send our preachers to them.

*Sunday, November 30.* Went out into the streets of Newcastle, and called the poor, the lame, the halt, the blind, with that precious promise, "Him that cometh unto me, I will in no wise cast out" [John 6:37]. They had no feeling of the sharp frost, while the love of Christ warmed their hearts.

I took my leave of the weeping flock at Burnopfield in that of Jude, "Now to Him that is able to keep you from falling," etc. [Jude 1:24]. Nothing can be more comfortable than our parting, except our last meeting to part no more.

Preached before the usual time at Newcastle. Yet the mob paid their usual attendance, our Lord still permitting them to try us.

# DECEMBER 1746

*Friday, December 5.* At Ryton[76] preached, "Jesus Christ the same yesterday, to day, and for ever" [Heb. 13:8]. Many hungry souls

---

75. Cf. Ps. 78:20.
76. Charles spells "Righton."

listened with inexpressible eagerness. I was greatly enlarged, and knew not when to end.

*Saturday, December 6.* Visited one of our sick children, Phebe Crosier, and received *her* blessing and prayers.

*Sunday, December 7.* Many from the country increased our joy at the Love-feast. We were carried out in mighty prayer for the Church and nation.

*Sunday, December [14].*[77] Had two or three hours' close conversation with the two ministers at Whickham. At noon I preached in Swalwell to many, now quiet, serious hearers. Here indeed, our Lord hath at last got himself the victory.

*Tuesday, December 16.* Preached the gospel to the poor at Spen, their spirit bearing me up. Next morning we had a double blessing, and diligently poured out our souls before the Lord.

*Thursday, December 18.* Waked between three and four, in a temper I have rarely felt on my birthday. My joy and thankfulness continued the whole day, to my own astonishment. Rode to Hexham. Preached at the Cross, "Repentance towards God, and faith in Jesus Christ" [Acts 20:21]. All opposition was kept down, and the Lord was with us of a truth.

At four attempted to preach in the cock-pit. Satan resented it, and sent, as his champions to maintain his cause, the two butlers of the two justices. They brought their cocks, and set them a fighting. Gave them the ground, and walked straight to the Cross, where was four times as many as the other place could hold. Our enemies followed, and strove all the ways permitted them to annoy us. Neither their fire-works nor their water-works could stop the course of the gospel. I lifted up my voice like a trumpet, and many had ears to hear.

*Friday, December 19.* I took my leave of the dear people at the cock-pit. Called on Mr —[78] at Whickham, whose countenance was changed. He had been with the bishop, who forbade his conversing with me. I marvel the prohibition did not come sooner.

---

77. MS has "December 13," which is in error.
78. This is likely the curate, but Charles omits the surname, giving only a dash.

*Saturday, December 27.* Rode in better weather to Pelton. Talked with each of the Society, and found nothing to reprove among them.

*Sunday, December 28.* Hastened through the snow to Gateshead, and preached out to many, who promise fair for making hardy soldiers of Christ.

*Monday, December 29.* Left these poor languid souls among whom God has been humbling me these many days. He vouchsafed us a blessing at parting. Rode with Edward Perronet and J. Crawford to Biddick. Preached at night and next morning. The Lord gave us a token by which to remember each other.

*Tuesday noon[, December 30].* Preached and distributed books to a few starved souls at Ferryhill.

*Wednesday, December 31.* By three came to Osmotherley. Mr Adams[79] carried us to his house and then to his chapel, where I read prayers and preached repentance and remission of sin in the name of Jesus Christ.[80]

# JANUARY 1747

*Thursday, January 1.* In the evening I preached at Acomb, near York, and exhorted the brethren with great freedom.

*Friday, January 2.* Comforted among our dear brethren and children in Epworth.

*Saturday, January 3.* Waited with Mr Perronet upon the curate,[1] who did not refuse us the Sacrament, as he had my brother.

*Sunday, January 4.* Preached at the Cross, as usual.

*Tuesday, January 6.* Got to Grimsby by three, saluted by the shouting mob. At six began speaking at the room, and the floods lifted up their voice.[2] Several poor wild creatures, almost naked, ran

---

79. His full name may have been Thomas Adams. The details are obscure, but he may have formerly been a Franciscan monk. Cf. John Wesley, *Journal* (28 March 1745), *Works* 20:58, n. 34.

80. Cf. Luke 24:47.

1. Rev. Romley had refused John Wesley the sacrament on January 2, 1743 (cf. *Works* 19:309–11).

2. Cf. Ps. 93:3.

about the room, striking down all they met. I gave myself to prayer, believing God knew how to deliver us. The uproar lasted near an hour. When I told the poor wretches that I shook off the dust of my feet against them, several of them caught at me to drag me down. Others interposed, and kept their companions off. I laid my hand on their captain, and he sat down like a lamb at my feet the whole time. One struck at me, and J. Crawford received my blow, which left on his face the marks of the Lord Jesus.[3] Another of the rebels cried out, "What, you dog, do you strike a clergyman?" and fell upon his comrade. Immediately every man's hand was against his fellow. They fell to fighting and beating one another, till, in a few minutes, they had all driven one another out of the room. I then preached without molestation for half an hour, and walked into the next room. Stayed, reading the Scripture, while the rioters at the door cried they would come in and take their leave of me. I ordered them to be admitted, and the poor drunken beasts were very civil, and very loving. One of the ringleaders, with a great club, swore he would conduct me to my lodgings. I followed him, and he led me through his fellows, to our brother [William] Blow's. They threw but one stone afterwards, which broke the window, and departed.

**Wednesday, January 7.** All was quiet at five. I met the Society, and expelled two disorderly walkers, by reason of whom the truth had been evil spoken of.[4] Immediately the Lord returned to his people, and began reviving his work, which had been stopped among them some time.

At eight I preached again, no man opposing. Heard an excellent sermon at church, it being the national fast-day, on Heb. 11[:7], "By faith Noah, being warned of God," etc. I preached repentance the third time at the room, where many of the rioters stood bound by the restraining hand of God.

God never lets Satan shut the door in one place, but that it may be opened in another. The violence of our enemies at night drove us to preach in the neighboring towns, where the seed fell into good ground.

**Thursday, January 8.** Preached at Grimsby in the morning, and strongly exhorted our Society to adorn the gospel of Christ in all

---

3. Cf. Gal. 6:17.
4. Cf. 2 Pet. 2:2.

things. At parting, our friend the rabble saluted us with a few eggs and curses only.

At Hainton I set forth Jesus Christ before their eyes as crucified.[5] My congregation was mostly Papists, but they all wept at hearing how Jesus loved them.

*Friday, January 9.* Talked severally to the little Society, who are as sheep encompassed with wolves. Their minister has repelled them from the Sacrament, and laboured to stir up all the town against them. And they would have worried them to death, had not the great man of this place, a professed Papist, hindered these good Protestants from destroying their innocent brethren.

By three came safe to Epworth, and was received by Edward Perronet and the brethren as one alive from the dead.

*Sunday, January 11.* Declared, at the Cross, "Except the Lord had left us a very small remnant," etc. [Isa. 1:9]. Preached there again, with greater enlargement, in the afternoon; and at night God comforted us on every side.

*Monday, January 12.* At Sykehouse I preached Christ crucified.[6] Many were comforted, one received the faith that justifies.

*Wednesday, January 14.* I expounded that comfortable promise at Leeds, "On them that fear the Lord, the Sun of righteousness shall rise with healing in his wings" [Mal. 4:2].

*Saturday, January 17.* I met Miss B. in Leeds, whom the Lord convinced this week, the first time she heard the word; and on Thursday night, just as she was dropping into hell, received her into his everlasting arms. She appeared plainly justified. My spirit was much refreshed hereby, and my hands strengthened.

*Sunday, January 18.* In the midst of my discourse, we all broke out into joy and singing. The same comfort at Birstall, and were constrained to own, at our Love-feast, that He had kept the best wine to the last.[7]

*Thursday, January 22.* Preached in a large house at Haworth, but not near large enough. Lodged at my dear brother Grimshaw's.

---

5. Cf. the note for the September 3–4, 1741, entry above.
6. Ibid.
7. Cf. John 2:10.

*Friday, January 23.* Told my host, at parting, that he had feared where no fear was, there being no law either of God or man against his lending me his pulpit. He was much ashamed at having given place to his threatening enemies.

Set out to preach in what were called William Darney's societies. I preached at different places, morning, noon, and night, with much freedom.

*Saturday, January 24.* Rode to Manchester. Baptized a child of Thomas Taylor's, and our brother B. found a divine proof that infant baptism is of God. At Davyhulme had much conversation with our old friend John Boulton.

*Sunday, January 25.* Re-settled the poor shattered Society. One woman delighted me with her scrupulosity, telling me, "she would be of the Society if I would allow her to go to Church. But the Germans used to forbid them." Through the blessing of God, I have brought back these wandering sheep to her pale.

Preached at several places in or near the Peak.

*Friday, January 30.* Preached at Sheffield, where the rioters threatened much, but did nothing.

*Saturday, January 31.* Made up an old quarrel between some of the Society, which had hung on them, like a millstone, for many months.

# FEBRUARY 1747

*Sunday, February 1.* Rode to Rotherham, where I had been stoned through the town the first time of my passing it. Heard a curious sermon, of which I was the unworthy subject. The accuser of the brethren was very fierce indeed. I sat quite composed, till he had concluded. Then walked up to the table, expecting to be repelled, as he had threatened. I prayed the Lord to turn his heart, and he was not suffered to pass me by.

From church I went to our brother Green's, and preached repentance and faith in Jesus Christ, from Isaiah 1:16. Many of the principal people of the town were in a private room. The convincing Spirit went forth, and restrained the madness of the people. I departed in peace.

Warned the hardened sinners at Sheffield from those awful words, "Except the Lord of hosts had left us a very small remnant," etc. [Isa. 1:9]. He filled my mouth with judgments against this people, except they repent, which I trembled to utter. So did most who heard, particularly some of our fiercest persecutors. I found relief and satisfaction in having delivered my own soul, whether they will hear or whether they will forbear.

Repeated my warnings to the Society, and believe they will escape into the ark before the flood comes.

Baptized my host's child, and [we] were sensible of the divine presence.

*Monday, February 2.* Never met with worse way and weather than in riding to Penkridge. About eight at night I was taken down from my horse, and found the congregation just going. The Lord gave me strength from above, though I could neither stand nor go, and held me up to call lost sinners to Him. Rode the next day to Wednesbury.

*Thursday, February 5.* Baptized the child of a Dissenter, which their minister refused to do, because the parents heard us.

Preached in Darlaston at the door of our brother [Jonathan] Jones's house, which had been pulled down in the former riot. The persecutors in this place were some of the fiercest in Staffordshire. I saw the marks of their violence, and thereby knew our people's houses, as I rode through the town. Their windows were all stopped up, etc.

The word was a two-edged sword.[8] The ringleader of the mob was struck down, and convinced of his lost estate. I preached again with double power. The minister's wife[9] I had some talk with afterwards. Her husband has been, in the hand of God, an instrument of quelling the mob. They have been all quiet since their captain drowned himself.

*Friday, February [6].*[10] Put a woman out of the Society for speaking disrespectfully of the minister.

*Sunday, February 8.* At Wednesbury expounded Acts 2:42. The word was sent home to many hearts.

---

8. Cf. Heb. 4:12.
9. Mrs. John Rowley.
10. MS has "February 7," which is in error.

*Tuesday, February 10.* God brought me safe to London.

*Sunday, February 15.* While I was preaching remission of sins, the power of God came down and constrained many to confess it.

*Tuesday, February 17.* Heard of our second house being pulled down at Sheffield, and sympathized with the sufferers. Every day this week our Lord has given testimony to the word of his grace.

*Monday, February 23.* At four set out with Mr Meriton for Bristol.

*Tuesday, February 24.* Between three and four in the afternoon came to Mr Clark's, at the Devizes.

Found his daughter there, our sister Taylor (who has won him to Christ without the word), and a sister from Bath. We soon perceived that our enemies had taken the alarm, and were mustering their forces for the battle. They began with ringing the bells backward, and running to and fro in the streets, as lions roaring for their prey. From the time my brother told me in London, "there was no such thing as raising a mob at the Devizes," I had a full expectation of what would follow. But saw my call, and walked with my brother Meriton and Mrs Naylor to an house where the Society used to meet.

The curate's mob had been in quest of me at several places, particularly Mrs Philips's, where I was expected to preach. They broke open and ransacked her house. But not finding me, marched away to our brother Rogers's, where we were praying and exhorting one another to continue in the faith, and through much tribulation enter the kingdom.[11]

The chief gentleman of the town headed the mob; and the zealous curate, Mr Innys, stood with them in the street the whole time, dancing for joy. This is he who declared in the pulpit, as well as from house to house, that he himself heard me preach blasphemy before the University, and tell them, "If you do not receive the Holy Ghost while I breathe upon you, ye are all damned."

He had gone about several days, stirring up the people and canvassing the gentry for their vote and interest, but could not raise a mob while my brother was here. The hour of darkness was not then fully come.

While his friends were assaulting us, I thought of their ancient brethren, whom we read of [in] Genesis 19:4, "Before they lay down,

---

11. Cf. Acts 14:22.

the men of the city, even the men of Sodom, compassed the house about, both young and old, all the people from every quarter. And they called upon Lot, and said unto him, Where are the men that came unto thee this night? Bring him [sic] out unto us." My own name I heard frequently repeated, with, "Bring him out, bring him out!" Their design was first to throw me into the horse-pond. They continued raging and threatening for the first hour, and pressed hard upon us to break the door. The windows they did break to pieces, and tore down the shutters of the shop. The little flock were less afraid than I expected. Only one of our sisters fainted away, but beneath were the everlasting arms.[12]

Our besiegers had now blocked up the door with a wagon, and set up lights, lest I should escape. Yet a brother got out unobserved and, with much entreaty, prevailed upon the mayor to come down. He came with two constables, one a faithful brother, the other a persecutor, and threatened the rioters. But so softly that none regarded him. It was the Lord who for the present rebuked the madness of the people. They hurried away from us to the inn, where our horses were, broke open the stable door and turned out the beasts, which were found some hours after in a pond, up to their chin in water.

We were at a loss meantime what to do, when God put it into the heart of our next-door neighbor, a Baptist, to take us through a passage into his own house, offer us his bed, and engage for our security. We accepted his kindness, and slept in peace.

*Wednesday, February 25.* A day never to be forgotten! At seven I walked quietly to Mrs Philips's. Began preaching a little before the time appointed, and for three quarters of an hour invited a few listening sinners to Christ. Then the boys with their bells, like the devil's infantry, began; and soon after, his whole army assaulted the house to bring us forth. We sat in a little ground-room, and ordered all the doors to be thrown open. They brought an hand-engine, and began to play into the house. We kept our seats, and they rushed into the passage. Just then Mr Borough, the constable, came, seized upon the spout of the engine, and carried it off in spite of them all. They swore if he did not deliver it, they would pull down the house. At that time they might have taken us prisoners,

---

12. Cf. Deut. 33:27.

for we were in their sight, close to them, and none to interpose. But they hurried out to fetch the larger engine.

Meantime, we were advised to send to Mr Mayor. But Mr Mayor was gone out of town in the sight of the people. This was great encouragement to those who were already wrought up to a proper pitch by the painstaking curate and gentleman of the town, particularly [to] Mr Sutton and Mr Willy, the two leading men, Dissenters.

Mr Sutton lived next door, and frequently came out to the mob to keep up their spirits. Mr Innys was there too, and quite happy on the occasion. Mr Sutton sent word to Mrs Philips that if she did not turn that fellow out to the mob, he would send them to drag him out. Mr Willy passed by again and again, assuring the rioters he would stand by them, and secure them from the law, do what they would.

They now began playing the larger engine, which broke the windows, flooded the rooms, and spoiled the goods. We were withdrawn to a small upper-room, in the back part of the house, *seeing* no way to escape their violence. They seemed under the full power of the old murderer.[13] Our brother who keeps the Society they laid hold on first, dragged him away, and threw him into the horse-pond, and broke his back, as was reported. But another of the Society ran in resolutely among them, and rescued him out of their hands, by little less than a miracle. His wife fell into fits again.

We gave ourselves unto prayer, believing the Lord would deliver us, how or when we saw not, nor any possible way of escaping. Therefore we stood still to see the salvation of God.[14]

As soon as the mob had emptied the engine, they ran to fill it again, keeping strict watch on all sides lest we should escape. One advised us to attempt it through the garden of a persecutor, and I put on my coat on purpose. But could not think it the Lord's way of bringing us forth. Laid aside the design, and saw a troop of our enemies coming up the very way we should have gone.

Every now and then some or other of our friends would venture to us, but rather weakened our hands. So that we were forced to stop our ears, and look up. Among the rest, the mayor's maid came, and told us her mistress was in tears about me, and begged me to disguise myself in women's clothes, and try to make my escape.

---

13. I.e., Satan.
14. Cf. Exod. 14:13.

Her heart had been turned towards us by the conversion of her son. Just on the brink of ruin, God laid his hand on the poor prodigal, and, instead of running away to sea, he entered into the Society, to the great joy and surprise of his parents.

The rioters without continued playing their engine, which diverted them for some time. But their number and fierceness still increased, and the gentlemen plied them with pitchers of ale, as much as they would drink. Mr Meriton hid his money and watch, that it might do good to somebody, he said; for as to the mob, they should have nothing of him but his carcass.

They were now on the point of breaking in, when Mr Borough thought of reading the Proclamation.[15] He did so, at the hazard of his life. In less than the hour, of above a thousand wild beasts, none were left but the guard. They retreated, as we suppose, by the advice of the old serpent[16] who sat observing us at an opposite house, in the shape of a lawyer. We had now stood siege for about three hours, and none but the invisible hand could have kept them one moment from tearing us in pieces.

Our constable had applied to Mr Street, the only justice in town, who would not act. We found there was no help in man, which drove us closer to the Lord, and we prayed by his Spirit, with little intermission, the whole day.

Our enemies, at their return, made their main assault at the back-door, swearing horribly they would have me, if it cost them their lives. Many seeming accidents concurred to delay their breaking in. The man of the house came home, and instead of turning me out, as they expected, took part with us, and stemmed the tide for some time. Then they got a notion that I had made my escape, and ran down to the inn and played the engine there. They forced the inn-keeper to turn out our horses, which he immediately sent to Mr Clark's. This drew the rabble and their engine thither, but the resolute old man charged and presented his gun, till they retreated.

Upon their re-visiting us, Mr Meriton was for surrendering ourselves before the night came on—which, he said, would make them more audacious; and that there might be witness of whatever they did by daylight. But I persuaded him to wait till the Lord should point out the way.

15. That is, the "Riot Act." Cf. the entry for May 26, 1743.
16. Cf. Rev. 12:9.

Now we stood in jeopardy every moment. Such threatenings, curses, and blasphemies I have never heard. They seemed kept out by a continued miracle. I remembered the Roman Senators sitting in the forum when the Gauls broke in upon them,[17] but thought there was a fitter posture for Christians, and told my companion they should take us off our knees.

We were kept from all hurry and discomposure of spirit by a divine power resting upon us. We prayed and conversed as freely as if we had been in the midst of our brethren, and had great confidence that the Lord would either deliver us from the danger or in it. One of my companions (Mrs Naylor) cried out, "It must be so. God will deliver us. If God is true, we are safe."

Told my friend Meriton, "*et haec olim meminisse juvabit*";[18] that our most distant friends were praying for us, and our deliverance would soon occasion many thanksgivings unto God. In the height of the storm, when we were just falling into the hands of the drunken, enraged multitude, he was so little disturbed that he fell asleep.

They were now close to us, on every side, and over our heads, untiling the roof. I was diverted by a little girl, who called to me through the door, "Mr Wesley! Mr Wesley! Creep under the bed. They will kill you. They are pulling down the house." Our sister Taylor's faith was just failing when a ruffian cried out, "Here they are, behind the curtain!" At this time we fully expected their appearance, and retired to the furthermost corner of the room, and I said, "This is the crisis!"

In that moment Jesus rebuked the winds and the sea, and there was a great calm.[19] We heard not a breath without, and wondered what was come to them. The silence lasted for three quarters of an hour before any one came near us, and we continued in mutual exhortation and prayer and looking for deliverance.

If ever we felt faith, it was now. Our souls hung upon that arm which divided the sea.[20] I often told my companions, "Now God is at work for us. He is contriving our escape. He can turn these leopards into lambs;[21] can command the heathen to bring his children

---

17. According to the account of Plutarch (*Life of Camillus*, xxi.2), the senators sat quietly in their ivory chairs, awaiting the Gauls, who massacred them.
18. "Someday it will be pleasant to remember even these things." Virgil, *Aeneid*, i.203.
19. Cf. Matt. 8:26; Mark 4:39.
20. Cf. Isa. 63:12.
21. Cf. Isa. 11:6.

on their shoulders, and make our fiercest enemies the instruments of our deliverance."

In about an hour after the last general assault, the answer of faith came, and God made bare his arm.[22] Soon after three, Mr Clark knocked at the door, and brought with him the persecuting constable. He said, "Sir, if you will promise never to preach here again, the gentlemen and I will engage to bring you safe out of town." My answer was, "I shall promise to do no such thing." "But will you not tell me you have no intention of returning hither?" "Not till you are better disposed to receive me. For, in obedience to my Master, if you persecute me in one city, I will flee to another.[23] But, setting aside my office, I will not give up my birthright, as an Englishman, of visiting what part I please of His Majesty's dominions." "Sir, we expect no such promise, that you will never come here again. Only tell me that it is not your present intention, that I may tell the gentlemen, who will then secure your quiet departure." I answered, "I cannot come now, because I must return to London a week hence. But observe,[24] I make no promise of not preaching here when the door is opened; and don't you say that I do."

He went away with this answer, and we betook ourselves again to prayer and thanksgiving. We perceived it was the Lord's doing, and it was marvellous in our eyes.[25] Our adversaries' hearts were turned. Even Mr Sutton and Willy laboured to take off the mob, and quench the fire themselves had kindled. Whether pity for us, or fear for themselves, wrought strongest, God knoweth. Probably the latter. For the mob were wrought up to such a pitch of fury that their masters dreaded the consequence, and therefore went about appeasing the multitude, and charging them not to touch us in our departure.

I knew full well it was not in their power to lay the devil they had raised, and none but the Almighty could engage for our security. We had hoped to make our escape in the dead of the night, if the house was not pulled down first, and had therefore sent our horses toward Seend,[26] intending to walk after them. But now we

---

22. Cf. Isa. 52:10.
23. Cf. Matt. 10:23.
24. In Jackson's edition the word appears as "OBSERVE." In the MS the word is double-underlined; but this emphasis appears to have been added by Jackson, being in his pencil.
25. Ps. 118:23; Matt. 21:42; Mark 12:11.
26. Seend, Wiltshire, three miles east of Devizes. Charles spells "Seen."

sent for them back, and recovered them before they were got out of the town.

While the constable was gathering his posse, we got our things from Mr Clark's, and prepared to go forth. The whole multitude were without, expecting us. Now our constable's heart began to fail, and he told us he much doubted if the mob *could* be restrained, for that thirty or more of the most desperate were gone down the street and waited at the end of the town for our passing. He should therefore advise us to hide ourselves in some other house, and get off by night. Mr Meriton's counsel was to escape by the back-door, while the mob were waiting for us at the fore-door. I asked counsel of the Lord, and met with that word, "Jesus said unto her, 'Said I not unto thee, if thou wouldest believe thou shouldest see the glory of God?' " [John 11:40]. After reading this, I went forth as easy as Luther to the Council.[27]

We were saluted with a general shout. The man whom Mrs Naylor had hired to ride before her, was, as we now perceived, one of the rioters. This hopeful guide was to conduct us out of the reach of his fellows. Mr Meriton and I took horse in the face of our enemies, who began clamouring against us, and I answering them, when the constable begged me to forbear. The gentlemen were dispersed among the mob to bridle them.

We rode a slow pace up the street, the whole multitude pouring along on both sides, and attending us with loud acclamations. Such fierceness and diabolical malice I have not seen in human faces. They ran up to our horses, as if they would swallow us; but did not know which was Wesley. We felt great peace and acquiescence in the honor done us, while the whole town were spectators of our march.

After riding two or three hundred yards, I looked back and saw Mr Meriton on the ground in the midst of the mob, and two bulldogs upon him. One was first let loose, which leaped at his nose, but the horse with his foot beat him down. The other fastened on his horse's nose, and hung there till Mr Meriton, with the butt-end of his whip, felled him to the ground. Then the first dog, recovering, flew at the horse's breast and fastened there. The beast reared up, and Mr Meriton slid gently off. The dog kept his hold till the flesh tore off. Then some men took off the dogs. Others cried, "Let

27. Charles has Luther's appearance at the Council of Worms (1521) in mind here.

them alone." But neither beast nor man had any farther commission to hurt. I stopped the horse, and delivered him to my friend. He re-mounted with great composure, and we rode on leisurely as before, till out of sight.

Then we mended our pace, and in an hour came to Seend, having rode three miles about, and by seven to [South] Wraxall. The news of our danger was got thither before us, but we brought the welcome tidings of our own deliverance.

Now we saw the hand of Providence in suffering them to turn out our horses; that is, to send them to us against we wanted them. Again, how plainly were we overruled to send our horses down the down, which blinded the rioters without our designing it, and drew off their engines and them, leaving free passage at the other end of the town!

We joined in hearty praises to our Deliverer, singing the hymn, "Worship, and thanks, and blessing," etc.[28]

*Thursday, February 26.* Preached at Bath, and we rejoiced like men that take the spoil. Continued our triumph at Bristol, and reaped the fruit of our labours and sufferings.

# MARCH 1747

*Sunday, March 1.* In riding to Kingswood, Satan had another thrust at me. We were singing the thanksgiving for our deliverance, when our coach overturned. All six were hurt, but none dangerously. The voice of joy and thanksgiving was heard among our beloved colliers, both in the word and Sacrament.

*Friday, March 6.* Took horse at four, and on Saturday afternoon came safe to the Foundery.

*Wednesday, March 11.* Spake with one who once walked in simple faith, but the antinomian tempter has prevailed. Now he expressly renounces us, "who seek to be justified by works."

*Friday, March 13.* Mr M., a young clergyman, was at our watch-night; one who seems inclined to think and judge for himself.

---

28. "Written after a Deliverance in a Tumult," *Redemption Hymns*, 29–31 (*Poetical Works*, 4:237–39).

*Friday, March 20.* Found, by the increase of my audience this morning, that my sharp rebuke of the Society last night has been lost.

*Sunday, March 22.* In the evening we rejoiced as in the day when we came up out of the land of Egypt.

*Tuesday, March 24.* Preached at Shoreham, without molestation. These wild beasts also are tamed; and will, many of them, I doubt not, receive the truth they persecuted.

*Wednesday, March 25.* Stopped one who had crept in among our helpers, without either discretion or veracity.

*Thursday, March 26.* I was walking to J. Ellison's,[29] when a gentleman ran out of his house, and exceedingly pressed me to step in and dine with him. Although pre-engaged, I could hardly deny him, as the person was no other than Mr Daniel Garnault.

*Friday, March 27.* God gave us his blessing, both in the word and Sacrament.

# APRIL 1747

*Sunday, April 12.* Invited many to come in, upon that promise, "In thy seed shall all the nations of the earth be blessed" [Gen. 22:18].

*Monday, April 13.* Met Mr Bateman[30] at our sister Witham's. My heart rejoiced and ached for him. What has he to go through, before he has made full proof of his ministry!

*Thursday, April 16.* He was with me at night in the desk. My text was, "Thy watchmen shall lift up the voice together," etc. [Isa. 52:8]. Great was our rejoicing before the Lord.

*Good Friday, April 17.* We had sweet fellowship with Him in his sufferings; and many cried after Him, being deeply wounded by his dying love.

---

29. It is unclear if this is Charles's nephew, John Ellison (1720–1791), living in London for a time. When Charles's sister Suky left her abusive husband Richard Ellison in 1740, John was sent to Bristol, apparently to apprentice with Felix Farley (cf. his letter of June 9, 1740, to John Wesley; *Works* 26:14). He eventually established a career as an excise officer, married, and settled in Bristol. John Wesley visited him there on July 26, 1783 (cf. *Works* 23:456d).

30. Richard Thomas Bateman was rector of the church of St Bartholomew-the-Great in London, and invited both John and Charles to preach there. Cf. the June 12, 1747, entry.

*Easter Day, April 19.* The Lord gave us, under the word, to know the power of his resurrection; but in the Sacrament he carried us quite above ourselves and all earthly things.

Went forth to an huge, unruly multitude in the fields. The Lord stilled them by the word of his power, and comforted me among the faithful.

*Monday, April 20.* Preached again in the fields, to a solemn assembly.

*Tuesday, April 21.* With Sarah Perrin, in perils by water. Her calmness would not suffer me to fear.

*Wednesday, April 22.* Received an unexpected invitation through Mrs Edwin,[31] but, by Mr Erskine's and Sarah Perrin's advice, deferred accepting it.

*Monday, April 27.* That I might abstain from all appearance of evil,[32] particularly of pride and resentment, I took up my cross, and went in Mrs Rich's coach to Chelsea. Passed an hour or two at Lampe's, before I waited upon one who was once my friend.[33] The first that greeted me was faithful Mrs M—, with her *old professions*; next, Mrs Edwin; and last, *that person*, at whose desire I sang, prayed, dined, exhorted, talked of the times, and took my leave.

# MAY 1747

*Sunday, May 3.* Took my leave of the Foundery and fields for a short season; and on

*Monday, May 4,* set out for Bristol. Overtook Charles Perronet at Brentford, and rode on to Hungerford.

*Tuesday, May 5.* Received fresh strength among our colliers, and brethren in Bristol.

*Wednesday, May 6.* Took Charles Perronet to see the new charge, and picked up some lost sheep—one on the brink of the pit.

---

31. Catherine Edwin; cf. the note for January 3, 1745. Charles spells "Edwyn" this time.
32. Cf. 1 Thess. 5:22.
33. This is apparently Lady Huntingdon, who was staying during this period at her home in Chelsea. Tensions had emerged between Lady Huntingdon and the Wesleys in 1745 over

*Saturday, May 9.* My namesake and charge was taken ill of a fever, which soon appeared to be the small-pox.

*Sunday, May 10.* Stirred up the Society with forcible words, and greatly rejoiced with the faithful at our feast of love.

*Tuesday, May 12.* Gave the Sacrament to my patient, who grows worse and worse.

*Friday, May 15.* Visited a brother, triumphing over death. He had found the door of hope opened the first time I prayed with him, and now is ready to depart in peace.

*Tuesday, May 19.* Expecting the turn of the distemper, I sat up with Charles. The Lord is pleased to try our faith and patience yet further.

*Wednesday, May 20.* At Wick my text was, "In thy seed shall all the nations of the earth be blessed" [Gen. 22:18]. And surely we were all partakers of the blessing in that hour. Near two hours we continued in tears of grief and joy. The justice was as much affected as any of us.

*Friday, May 22.* At our watch-night I asked in faith that the Lord would give his beloved sleep,[34] and he heard and answered the prayer immediately. Our brother Perronet was then in the utmost danger, through the second fever, and delirious for want of rest—ready to enter his rest eternal. But the Lord rebuked the fever, and he fell asleep, and waked late the next morning as one raised from the dead.

*Sunday, May 24.* God gave us, under the word, great strength and resolution against sin.

*Wednesday, May 27.* Preached at the Hall on "The good God pardon every one of you," etc. [2 Chr. 30:18-19], and surely he showed us his great readiness so to do.

*Thursday, May 28, Ascension Day.* We spent from four to seven in triumph with our Lord.

---

their support of "irregular" preaching (see the May 23, 1745, entry). The tensions were exacerbated more recently by Lady Huntingdon's growing alignment with the Calvinist branch of the revival.

34. Cf. Ps. 127:2.

*Friday, May 29.* Having made strict inquiry into the life of each member of the Society, today I left out fifty of them who have not adorned the gospel.

# JUNE 1747

*Monday, June 1.* Rejoiced at Bath with our dear dying brother Yapp. He blessed me, and blessed God that he had ever seen my face. Soon after we left him he returned to his Lord in paradise.

*Wednesday, June 3.* Preached at the chapel in West Street, and rejoiced for the abundant consolation which our Lord administered to us all.

*Thursday, June 4.* Rode over to our friends at Shoreham, a joyful messenger of their son's recovery.

*Friday, June 12.* At St Bartholomew's I expounded Isaiah 40:1, and wrapped them up in the promises.

*Sunday, June 14.* Heard my brother in the fields, and was adding a word of confirmation, when our old friend Mr [John] Green began speaking from a table just behind us. I would not strive, but walked quietly away, and all our children with me.

*Sunday, June 21.* Great multitudes attended in the fields to His cry from the cross, "Is it nothing to you, all ye that pass by?" [Lam. 1:12].

*Friday, June 26.* Expelled one who had taken a bribe for his vote. I hope there is not another like offender in all our Societies.

*[Saturday],*[35] *June 27.* Prayed by our sister [Martha] Somerset, just ready for the Bridegroom. I read prayers at St Bartholomew's, and heard a true gospel sermon from Mr Perronet. I preached there myself on Sunday, "Come, for all things are now ready" [Luke 14:17].

*Monday, June 29.* Joined with Howell Harris, etc., in prayer, and groaned under the burden of this guilty nation.

At Wapping the Lord gave testimony to his own word, "Him that cometh unto me, I will in no wise cast out" [John 6:37]. A woman

---

35. MS has "Friday," which is in error.

cried out, and rushed into the vestry. But her cries continued all the time of preaching. I saw her afterwards in great agony. For *this time* she is no dissembler, although she is Sarah Robinson!

# JULY 1747

*Friday, July 3.* Had our first watch-night at the chapel. Preached on "Looking for, and hastening toward, the coming of the day of God" [2 Pet. 3:12]. His blessing confirmed his word. One who had been slack, but was now returning, heard it, and went home and died!

*Sunday, July 5.* The whole congregation were in tears or in triumph, crying after God or rejoicing in his favour. The cloud rested upon [us] the whole time of communicating. In the evening there was a great shaking among the dry bones,[36] and in the bands the God of all consolation showed himself.

*Wednesday, July 8.* Assisted Mr Bateman at St Bartholomew's. But was quite weighed down with the behaviour of the communicants, so contrary to the apostolical precept, "Let all things be done decently and in order" [1 Cor. 14:40].

*Sunday, July 12.* Our sister Hoffman, setting sail for Jamaica, we commended to the grace of God, and felt we could never be separated from that soul while she and we were united to Christ.

*Friday, July 17.* Gave the Sacrament to a grievous backslider, now crying out of the deep for mercy. Soon after she departed in peace.

*Saturday, July 18.* One received a fresh seal of pardon under the word this morning who was before on the brink of destruction.

*Friday, July 24.* Expounded Rev. 4 at the watch-night. Have not lately known a more solemn season. The place was crowded with strangers, emboldened by the night to hear us. It was near one before we could part.

*Sunday, July 26.* Many hearts were touched by the history of the returning Prodigal [Luke 15:11-32].

---

36. Cf. Ezek. 37:4ff.

# AUGUST 1747

*Sunday, August 2.* My audience in the field seemed to feel the word; and much more those at the chapel, whom I strongly exhorted to continue in the Ship.[37]

*Monday, August 3.* In Mr Richards's school at Reading, preached "the Lamb of God who taketh away the sin of the world" [John 1:29].

*Wednesday, August 5.* Met the bands in Bristol, and the power of God broke in upon us wonderfully.

*Thursday, August 6.* Found it again in the singing with Miss Wells, Miss Burdock, and eight of our preachers.

*Sunday, August 9.* Preached from Luke 14:15 at the Old Orchard[38] (I think for the first time), and we had a great pouring out of the Spirit. It put me in mind of a like season which the first Quakers had at the same place, when many were convinced.

*Sunday, August 16.* Preached again in Moorfields, on "To the Lord our God belong mercies and forgivenesses," etc. [Dan. 9:9].

*Friday, August 21.* Received a second summons from my brother, hastening me to Ireland.

*Monday, August 24.* Parted at the Foundery in fervent prayer, particularly for the conversion of some Romish priest.

*Wednesday, August 26.* Left my old host at Oxford, Mr Evans, and stretched with Charles Perronet to Huntley, seven miles beyond Gloucester.

*Thursday, August 27.* Before five we renewed our strength and our labour. Overtook an hearer of Howell Harris, who conducted us within ten miles of Builth.[39] For the rest of the way the river was our guide. Between eight and nine we found our brother [Edward] Phillips, and were glad soon after to betake ourselves to rest.

---

37. That is, in the Church of England.
38. Originally the orchard of the Dominican Friary, in an area just south of the Horsefair in Bristol that came to be known as "Quakers Friars" because the estate became property of the William Penn family.
39. Builth Wells, Brecknockshire.

*Friday, August 28.* My brother not being come from Ireland, according to appointment, we concluded he was delayed by cross winds, and had an opportunity thereby of resting ourselves and our weary beasts.

At nine I preached in the street, repentance and faith [Isa. 1:16]. The people behaved with great decency. Mr Gwynne came to see me at Mr Phillip's, with two of his family.

My soul seemed pleased to take acquaintance with them. We rode to Maesmynis church. I preached, and Mr Williams[40] after me in Welsh. At four I expounded the Good Samaritan [Luke 10:29-37] in the street, and He was present binding up our wounds. Preached a fourth time at Garth, on "Comfort ye, comfort ye my people" [Isa. 40:1]. The whole family received us as messengers of God; and if such we are, they received Him that sent us.

*Saturday, August 29.* Rode to Llandrindod Wells, and called the burdened souls to Jesus. He gave me to speak both searching and comfortable words. Three ministers were of my audience. Returned to Garth rejoicing. Still no news of my brother. While we were talking of him, he came and brought life and a blessing with him.

*Sunday, August 30.* Preached on a tombstone in Builth churchyard; and again, on the Prodigal Son [Luke 15:11-32]. Then at Garth, on the marks of the Messiah (Matt. 11:5), "The blind receive their sight," etc.

*Monday, August 31.* After preaching at noon in the churchyard, my brother set out for Bristol. I preached there at three, and invited a great multitude to the gospel feast. Then expounded at Garth [on] Simon, the Pharisees, and the woman that was a sinner [Luke 7:36-50].

# SEPTEMBER 1747

*Tuesday, September 1.* Preached at Maesmynis, and again in Builth, on Lam. 1[:12], "Is it nothing to you, all ye that pass by?" Now the great blessing came, even the constraining love of Christ crucified. All were melted down as wax before the fire. I took a sweet

---

40. Rev. Rice Williams (1704–1784), of the nearby parish of Llansantffraed-yn-Elfael, who was now actively supporting the Wesley brothers.

leave of the weeping flock, and plainly found that if we never met again upon earth, yet shall we never be parted.

Returned to Garth, and showed the end of Christ's mission, even to make all mankind happy (Acts 3[:26]). We continued rejoicing in the Lord till past eleven.

*Wednesday, September 2.* At six I met the family, both servants and children, and strongly explained, "I am come that they might have life," etc. [John 10:10]. All seemed to receive my testimony. We left them in body, not in spirit.

Took horse with Mr Gwynne, Mr Phillips, and our guide, a brother from Anglesey.[41] We found the seven miles to Rhayader[42] four good hours' ride. Preached in the church, and laboured to awake the dead, and to lift up the hands that hung down. The minister seemed a man of a simple heart, and surely not eager for preferment, or he would not be contented with his salary of £3 a year. Three or four neighboring clergymen invited me to their churches, whom I had not time to visit. Rode forward to Llanidloes, and pointed a house-full of listening sinners to the all-atoning Lamb [John 1:29].

*Thursday, September 3.* Called near the Town-hall, "Ho, every one that thirsteth, come ye to the waters" [Isa. 55:1]. Rode to Dolgellau, where our dear friends, Mr Gwynne and Phillips, left us.

*Friday, September 4.* Reached Tan-y-Bwlch by nine, and Aber Menai ferry[43] by five. It blew so hard there was no crossing till the tide was out. We waited two hours, part of which I slept on the ground. Then with much difficulty we got into the boat. The hurricane soon drove us out of danger. We rode in the dark over the heavy sands, and in an hour got to a little town in Anglesey. After midnight we came throughly wet to the brother's, where we dried ourselves, and pushed on to Holyhead by seven in the morning, having been in the saddle twenty-five hours.

*Sunday, September 6.* I sent an offer of my assistance to the minister, who was ready to beat my messenger. I went to church, and wondered he did not refuse me the Sacrament.

---

41. Charles spells "Anglesea."
42. Charles spells "Raydor."
43. Running from Caernarfon to Angelsey. Charles spells "Bar-Myni."

After evening service I preached at the request of some gentlemen, who behaved as such, though the vulgar were rude enough.

*Tuesday, September 8.* At ten we embarked. What wind we had was contrary. It increased in the evening, and at midnight was too high for us to sleep. Next morning, *September 9,*[44] we were taken into the smaller packetboat, and by eleven the Lord brought us safe to Dublin.

Here the first news we heard was that the little flock stands fast in the storm of persecution, which arose as soon as my brother left them. The popish mob has broke open their room, and destroyed all before them. Some of them are sent to Newgate, others bailed. What will be the event we cannot tell till we see whether the grand jury will find the bill.

*Wednesday, September 9.* Walked at five in the evening to the shattered room in Marlborough Street, where a few people were met, who did not fear what men or devils could do unto them. God has called me to suffer affliction with his people. The popish mob, encouraged and assisted by the Protestant, are so insolent and outrageous that whatever street we pass through, it is up in arms. The mayor would assist us, but cannot. The grand jury have had the plainest evidence of the riot laid before them: that a mixed rabble of Papists and Protestants broke open our room, and four locks, and a warehouse, stealing or destroying the goods to a considerable value; beat and wounded several with clubs, etc.; tore away the pulpit, benches, window-cases, etc., and burnt them openly before the gate; swearing they would murder us all. Yet it is much doubted whether the grand jury will find the bill! But doth not the Most High regard?

I began my ministry with "Comfort ye, comfort ye my people," etc. [Isa. 40:1]. None made disturbance till I had ended. Then the rabble attended us with the usual compliments to our lodgings.

*Thursday, September 10.* At five all was quiet within doors. But we had men, women, and children upon us as soon as we appeared in the streets. One I observed crying, "Swaddler, swaddler!" (our usual title here), who was a young Ishmael indeed, and had not long learned to speak. I am sure he could not be four years old.

---

44. This part of the entry for September 9 is not separated in the MS from the flow of September 8.

We dined with a gentleman, who explained our name to us. It seems we are beholden to Mr Cennick for it, who abounds in such like expressions as, "I curse and blaspheme all the gods in heaven, but the babe that lay in the manger, the babe that lay in Mary's lap, the babe that lay in swaddling clouts,"[45] etc. Hence they nicknamed him "Swaddler, or Swaddling John." And the word sticks to us all, not excepting the clergy.

Met with Society, and the Lord knit our hearts together in love stronger than death. We both wept and rejoiced for the consolation. God hath sent me, I trust, to confirm their souls, and keep them together in the present distress.

**Friday, September 11.** Met the Society at one, for the first time, and spent an hour in intercession for our nation and Church. We shall hear of these prayers again another day, even the day of the great slaughter, when the towers fall.[46]

I preached morning and evening, this and the following day, no man forbidding me, though every one reviled us, both coming and going.

**Sunday, September 13.** In the strength of the Lord I went forth to Oxmantown Green. Stood under the wall of the barracks, and preached Christ crucified.[47] They all, both Protestant and Papists, gave diligent heed, as to words whereby they may be saved.

Received Sacrament at St Patrick's, and from evening service returned to the Green. Thousands were now assembled to hear the word, and many to hinder them. Our dying Lord applied his own words, "Is it nothing to you, all ye that pass by?" [Lam. 1:12]. In vain did the poor blind Papists rage, and shout, and cast stones. None were suffered to hurt me, or any of the hearers.

The mob waited for me on a bridge. We tried in vain to get a coach, and were therefore forced, when it was dark, to walk home another way, without calling upon our Catholic friends.

**Tuesday, September 15.** Woe is me now, for my soul is wearied because of murderers which this city is full of! The Ormond mob

---

45. "Clout" is here used in the eighteenth-century sense of a piece of cloth or clothing.
46. Cf. Isa. 30:25.
47. This was probably the same sermon as preached later that day; cf. the note on the September 3–4, 1741, entry in vol. 1.

and Liberty mob[48] seldom part till one or more are killed. A poor constable was the last, whom they beat and dragged about till they had killed him, and then hung him up in triumph. None was called in question for it, but the earth covered his blood. Last week a woman was beaten to death by the rabble. But that was all fair, for she was caught picking a pocket, so there is an end of her. No wonder if, in such a place, there should be no justice for Christians. A poor, weakly man of Mr Cennick's society was so abused by his neighbor, who knocked him down and stamped upon his stomach, that he died soon after. The murderer was indeed brought to a trial, but acquitted as usual.

I preached in the evening without interruption, the mob being awed for the present while our bill is depending. The utmost application has been made by them to the jury, and none at all by us. We leave the matter to God. If man does us justice, it is more than we expect.

*Thursday, September [17].*[49] Got a particular account of the late riot. On Sunday, August 30th, a mob of Papists and Protestants assaulted the house where the Society was met after evening service. They met them going out, with sticks and stones, knocked down several, both men and women, and beat them in a barbarous manner. Some escaped the back way. Others retreated to the house and shut the door. The mob broke it open, and another inward door, tore down the desk and forms, carried two large counters, chairs, and part of the wainscot into the street, and openly burnt all but what they stole.

There was a warehouse over the preaching-room, which they broke open and ransacked. Above one hundred pounds' worth of goods they seized as lawful prize, and committed the rest to the flames.

They have often threatened our lives. Mr Paterson they knocked down, and cut in several places while on the ground, then threw him into a cellar and cast stones on him. Mrs Young and many others were treated in the same manner. Half-hour past nine the mayor came with his guard and saw with his own eyes the havoc the mob had made. He readily granted warrants to apprehend them.

---

48. These were Roman Catholic and Protestant factions that had been battling one another in Dublin since 1726.

49. MS has "September 18," which is in error.

Some of the poorest, Papists mostly, were sent to Newgate. But the better sort made a mock of his authority and walked about the town, from alehouse to alehouse, with the constables whom, by drink and money, they had secured of their party.

Our hour of intercession was a solemn season, most present receiving a manifestation of the Spirit, even the spirit of contrition and prayer.

Dined at Mr Powell's,[50] the printer, who informed us that the jury have thrown out the bill. It was no surprise to me. My soul was filled with comfort, and confidence that the Lord would now take the matter into his own hands.

Met Mr Millar the Lutheran minister, a simple, loving man, but not quite so courageous as Martin Luther.

*Saturday, September 19.* Breakfasted at Mr Aggit's and found him full of indignation at the injustice of the jury. He did not seem to know that Christians are looked upon as outlaws in all times and places.

*Sunday, September 20.* After commending our cause to God, walked to the Green. I believed the Lord would make bare his arm in our defence.[51] I called, in his name, "Come unto me, all ye that are weary," etc. [Matt. 11:28]. His power was upon the hearers, keeping down all opposition. I spoke with great freedom to the poor Papists, urging them to repentance and the love of Christ, from the authority of their own Kempis[52] and their own liturgy. None lifted up his voice or hand. All listened with strange attention. Many were in tears. I advised them to go to their respective places of worship. They expressed general satisfaction, especially the Papists. This also hath God wrought.

Returning, we were insulted by a gathering mob, when a Baptist came by and desired us to take shelter in his house. We stayed and breakfasted, and left him quite happy in having protected us from the violence of the people.

The holiday folk were at the Green before me, it being the scene of all manner of diversions on Sunday afternoon. I lifted up my voice, and cried "Ho, every one that thirsteth, come ye to the waters!"

50. Samuel Powell (d. 1772), on Crane Lane. Charles spells "Powel."
51. Cf. Isa. 52:10.
52. Thomas à Kempis (1379?–1471).

[Isa. 55:1]. A great multitude of serious hearers encompassed me, while those who had not ears to hear withdrew on every side to the opposite hill, sat down in rows on the grass, and there remained the whole time. I never saw the hand of God more visible.

*Monday, September 21.* Began examining the classes, and met several who received forgiveness under the word last week. But, justified or unjustified, all are in earnest, and seem made without fear. I have not seen such soldiers before, so young and yet so valiant.

*Wednesday, September 23.* Heard that on Sunday last, after I was gone, the popish mob fell upon the women, but were beaten off by the soldiers. They threaten to come with all their forces next Sunday.

Going to the room, the mob insulted us and forced us to take refuge at Mr Aggit's. He was scandalized at such treatment of a minister of the established Church, and very sure a popish priest, so used, would be succoured by the magistrate. I believe so too. Error of every kind may meet with favour, but the world never did nor ever will tolerate real Christianity.

In our return the people gaped upon us with their mouths, like ramping and roaring lions. What restrains them from tearing us to pieces? They want neither will nor power. The jury have taken off the reins from the many-headed beast. And our Protestant brethren have sold us into their hands who think they would do God service, and merit heaven, by killing us.

*Friday, September 25.* Passed the evening very agreeably at a Baptist's, a woman of sense and piety, and a great admirer of my father's *Life of Christ.*[53]

*Sunday, September 27.* Never have I seen a quieter congregation at the Foundery than we had at the Green, both morning and afternoon. Many of the soldiers were within hearing, though behind the doors and walls, for fear of their officers. The Papists stood like lambs. I quoted Kempis, which makes some of them confident I am a good Catholic.

*Monday, September 28.* Our landlady yesterday nailed up our preaching-room, but we had it opened for the word this morning.

53. Samuel Wesley (1662–1735), *The Life of our Blessed Lord & Saviour, Jesus Christ; an heroic poem* (London: Charles Harper, 1693).

We are now come to close quarters with the enemy, who threatens hard to drive us out of his kingdom.

Had an hour's conference with two serious Quakers, who hold the Head with us, and build on the one foundation.[54]

*Tuesday, September 29.* My subject in the evening was "The kingdom of heaven is at hand. Repent ye, and believe the gospel" [Mark 1:15]. I was led, unawares, to describe the glorious appearing of our Lord; and the word came with power irresistible. The cries of the wounded almost drowned my voice. One, I afterwards heard, received a cure.

At Mr Powell's I met Mr Edwards, landlord of Mr Cennick's preaching-house. He told us he quite disliked his tenants, was resolved to raise the rent, and asked if we should be willing to take the room, if they refused it. We answered, "If they had the first offer, and did not accept of it, we should be glad of the next refusal."

# OCTOBER 1747

*Friday, October 2.* Passed two hours with Mrs Powell, and another Baptist, whom I almost persuaded to give up their faith of adherence, so called, for the faith of the gospel, which works by love, and includes peace, joy, power, and the testimony of the Spirit.

*Sunday, October 4.* At Marylebone Lane I expounded those awful words, "The Lord himself shall descend from heaven with a shout, with the voice of the archangel, and the trump of God" [1 Thess. 4:16]. Many trembled, and some rejoiced in hope of his glory. A Papist behind the wall at first lifted up his voice in curses, but in the end cried out "The Lord bless you!"

*Wednesday, October [7].*[55] Several soldiers ventured to the word, notwithstanding the prohibition. Now and then an officer came by, and stopped to see if any of their men were there. Then they skulked down, kneeling or sitting on the ground, behind the women.

---

54. Cf. 1 Cor. 3:11.
55. MS has "October 8," which is in error.

*Thursday, October [8].*[56] God is daily adding to our number. Today I admitted two more into the Society; one a Papist, whom we caught in the Green.

*Sunday, October 11.* None has made the least disturbance for a week past, whether Protestant or Papist. Only one of the latter flung away in a rage, crying I ought to be stabbed for lumping them all together and telling them they might all be saved, of whatever church or party, if they would return like the prodigal to their heavenly Father.

Began preaching, with great reluctance, at Marylebone Lane, where the Spirit came pouring down like a flood. All present were in tears, either of sorrow or joy. We continued above an hour, singing and crying. A more refreshing time I have not known since I left England.

Spent the evening with Mrs M., a true mourner in Sion, till the Lord, on Wednesday, put the new song in her mouth. She set us all on fire with the warmth of her first love.

*Saturday, October 17.* Passed the day at the house we have purchased near Dolphin's Barn, writing and meditating. I could almost have set up my rest here, but must not look for rest on this side eternity. I heard (as I do every day) of more sinners who have received the atonement.

*Monday, October 19.* Dined at a gentleman's who offered us a large piece of ground to build upon, at a very moderate price. It seems as if the time for building were at hand, now the magistrates are so favourable. The mayor has declared he will send any man to Newgate who only calls after us in the streets. But we are not so vain as to think all the authority of man can long screen those who will live godly in Christ Jesus from suffering persecution.

*Friday, October 23.* Visited a sick man, who has been convinced by reading my brother's sermons, and justified, as far as I can find, by the immediate voice of Christ.

*Sunday, October 25.* Passed three hours at St Patrick's, under my usual burden among the dry bones of the house of Israel.[57] I seldom enter this place but they are ready to drag me out as a profaner of

---

56. MS has "October 9," which is in error.
57. Cf. Ezek. 37:1-14.

the temple. The dean[58] I must except, who has always treated us with great courtesy; looks pleased to see us make the bulk of the communicants; appointed us a set by ourselves; and constantly administers to me first, as the rubric directs.

Opened our new house at Dolphin's Barn by preaching to a great multitude within and without. After preaching five times today, was as fresh as in the morning.

*Monday, October 26,* [Spent time][59] examining the Society, and took in several new ones, and put out others who had been too hastily admitted by our helpers. My hands were strengthened by meeting several who have found the pardoning love of God through my ministry.

*Tuesday, October 27.* Prayed by our sister Baker, whom I had lately checked for her too great contempt of death, as it seemed to me. The trying time is come, yet she keeps her confidence.

*Friday, October 30.* In our return from intercession we were stoned for the length of a street or two. Charles Perronet interposed his back to screen me. Here I received the first blow since I came to Dublin. At our lodgings the mob took their leave of us, without hurting either.

*Saturday, October 31.* Heard the best news of any since our coming hither—that our sister Baker is departed in full triumph. To one who asked her this morning how she did, she answered, "Bravely! Bravely! Never better." The pains of death had then got hold of her, but she smiled on the welcome messenger; took leave of her husband and children with calm joy; expressed great satisfaction at having chosen to suffer affliction with the people of God; confirmed those about her in the same happy choice; and soon after fell asleep, and awoke in paradise.

I called at the house, as well to exhort the survivors as to see the late temple of the Holy Ghost.[60] The happy soul had left a smile upon the clay, to tell where she was gone. We were all comforted in prayer and thanksgiving.

---

58. Francis Corbet (d. 1775) became Dean of St. Patrick's, Dublin, in January 1747, succeeding the long tenure of Jonathan Swift (d. 1745).

59. The words "employed in" are found written above the line at this point in the MS, but the hand is that of Jackson.

60. Cf. 1 Cor. 6.19.

Preached for the last time in Marlborough Street, on "These are they that came out of great tribulation, and washed their robes, and made them white in the blood of the Lamb" [Rev. 7:14]. It was a time of solemn rejoicing in hope of His coming to wipe away all tears from our eyes.

# NOVEMBER 1747

*Sunday, November 1.* At St Patrick's Mr K.[61] entertained us with a discourse so full of low, pitiful lies and nonsense as I never heard from any, except the ingenious Mr Hoblyn.

Preaching five times is not more than twice a day, when the order of Providence calls us to it. My strength do I ascribe unto Thee, and all my success, and all my blessings!

*Monday, November 2.* Admitted five or six into the Society, and among them the soldier who was put under arrest last Sunday for the high crime and misdemeanour of hearing a sermon at the Green. The officer, after much threatening, let him go. But he continues refractory still—that is, resolved to work out his salvation.

*Saturday, November 7.* Prayed by a man near death. When we first visited him, he was quite unawakened; but is now saved from the fear both of death and hell, and waiting for the great salvation of God. We have several such instances of persons departing in the Lord, who never heard the gospel till we preached it to them on their death-beds.

*Tuesday, November 10.* Preached at a new place in Hanbury Lane, next door to a warm antagonist, the Rev Mr N. Therefore we did not expect to be long unmolested. Three nights, however, we have had peace.

*Thursday, November 12.* Hearing the minister had procured a mob to hinder our preaching, I would not suffer any of the preachers or people to expose themselves at Hanbury Lane. At night our adversaries, who till then had expected us in vain, broke into the house and took possession.

---

61. Most likely Rev. James King (d. 1759), Prebendary of Tipper at St Patricks, 1737–1759 (the only prebendary with a last name starting in "K").

*Thursday, November 26.* Spent the day in walking about and taking subscriptions for the building. At night proposed it to the Society, who were glad to give of their little. This and the following day was subscribed upward of £70.

## DECEMBER 1747

*Friday, December 4.* Passed an hour at Mr Millar's, the Lutheran minister, who favoured me with a sight of Count Zinzendorf's famous declaration against my brother and me,[62] and likewise his translation of the New Testament.[63] We looked for St James's epistle, but he was not to be found, the Count having thrust him out of the canon by his own authority.

At midnight I was raised by a dying child, brought into my room to be baptized.

*Sunday, December 13.* We had a large increase of communicants at St Patrick's, mostly of the Society. The good dean expressed his approbation at the sight.

*Monday and Tuesday, December [14 and] 15.* Had great rejoicing over our lately departed sister Witham.[64] Her dying prayers for me I found strengthening my hands, and confirming my hope of shortly following her.

*Wednesday, December 16.* Seldom have I been more alive than in the morning preaching, or more dead than in the evening.

*Saturday, December 19.* Spake from John 1[:12], "As many as receive him, to them gave he power," etc., and warned them against receiving Christ by halves, or so magnifying one of his offices, as to slight or deny the other. The Priest must not swallow up the King, nor the Savior the Lord.

*Wednesday, December 23.* Had a conference with two clergymen concerning this way, which they seemed to believe was no schism,

---

62. This declaration was included in a letter that James Hutton published in *The Daily Advertiser*, August 2, 1745 (letter dated July 24, 1745). A summary of Zinzendorf's comments and John Wesley's letter in reply can be found in *Works* 26:150–51.

63. Nikolaus Zinzendorf, *Eines abermahligen Versuchs zur Übersetzung der historischen Bücher des Neuen Testaments unsers Herrn Jesu Christi* (Büdingen: J. C. Stöhr, 1739).

64. See Charles's published elegy "On the Death of Mrs Elizabeth Witham," *HSP* (1749), 1:282–86 (*Poetical Works*, 5:87–90).

or new religion, but the faith once delivered to the saints. One of them invited me to his lodgings in the college.[65]

*Friday, Christmas Day.* The people met at my lodgings between three and four. It was a day of rejoicing. So were the three following, suitable to the solemn occasion.

*Monday, December 28.* Prayed by a constant hearer of the word, who was joyfully turning his face to the wall.[66] The next morning he departed with that word, "Into thy hands I commend my spirit" [Luke 23:46].

# JANUARY 1748

*Friday, January 15.* Heard more good news from the country, whither we had sent some of our preachers. At Tyrrellspass[1] and the neighboring towns there seems to be a great awakening.

*Wednesday, January 20.* Charles Perronet had, without my knowledge, told the Society last night that he intended to go and ask Mr Cennick if he had any farther pretensions to the house; and if not, he would take it himself for the Society.

Mr Handy brought us glad tidings from the country, which made me eager to go with him.

*Thursday, January 21.* Reproved the Society, who were all melted into tears, especially when I spake of leaving them.

*Friday, January 22.* Troubled to hear one of our children was carried away by the lies of the *still* brethren. Prayed for her in faith, and was relieved immediately. At night the spirit of contrition fell mightily upon us.

*Saturday, January 23.* The answer of prayer returned. Met Mrs M., who humbled herself, asked pardon of God and us, and seemed quite recovered.

*Sunday, January 24.* Preached Christ crucified at the Barn,[2] from

---

65. This is presumably Trinity College, Dublin.
66. Cf. 2 Kgs. 20:2.
1. Charles spells "Tyril's Pass."
2. That is, their new preaching house in Dolphin's Barn.

"They shall look upon me, whom they have pierced, and mourn" [Zech. 12:10]. This Scripture was then fulfilled in many.

*Monday, January 25.* Our brother Gurley and another reported to me the blasphemies of one Connor (of Mr Cennick's Society), who insisted in their hearing that Christ was in an error and called the Trinity a three-headed devil, etc.[3]

*Tuesday, January 26.* Met the Society, with the great power and blessing of God in the midst.

*Friday, January 29.* Administered the Sacrament to an aged woman at Sophy Evans's. It was a solemn season of love.

# FEBRUARY 1748

*Friday, February [5].*[4] Mr Cennick called on me. I asked if he had any hopes of the house. He answered, No. He believed the trustees would never let it [to] them again. Then I said I would, or he should preach in it whenever he pleased. He acknowledged my kindness, and that I had acted fairly throughout this affair.

*Sunday, February [7].* Expounded Wrestling Jacob [Gen. 32:24-31]. Many wept and made supplication to the Angel. I parted from them with regret, though for a few days only, and on

*Monday morning, February [8],* took horse for Tyrrellspass. We overtook a lad whistling one of our tunes. He was a constant hearer, though a Roman, and joined with us in several hymns which he had by heart. Near seven we got, half choked with the fog, to Mr Force's.[5] The town immediately took the alarm and crowded in after us. I discoursed on "A certain man had two sons," etc. [Luke 15:11-32]. These are the publicans that enter before the pharisees. Never have I spoke to more hungry souls. They devoured every word. Some expressed their satisfaction in a way peculiar to them, and *whistled* for joy. Few such feasts have I had since I left England. It refreshed my body more than meat or drink.

---

3. This entry is not included in Jackson.
4. MS has "Friday, February 6." Presuming the day is correct, it was February 5. The next several entries are also off by one day (until February 15 is assigned to both Sunday and Monday), and have been corrected here in square brackets.
5. Charles spells "Fource."

God has begun a great work here. The people of Tyrrellspass were wicked to a proverb; swearers, drunkards, Sabbath-breakers, thieves, etc., from time immemorial. But now the scene is entirely changed. Not an oath is heard, or a drunkard seen, among them. *Aperto vivitur horto.*[6] They are turned from darkness to light.[7] Near *one hundred* are joined in Society, and following hard after the pardoning God.

***Tuesday, February [9].***[8] Rode to Mr Jonathan Handy's at Templemacateer,[9] seven miles from Tyrrellspass, and pointed several of his poor neighbors to the Lamb of God [John 1:29].

***Wednesday, February [10].*** At eight took horse for Athlone. We were seven in company, and rode mostly abreast. Some overtook us, running in great haste, and one horseman, riding full speed. We suspected nothing, and rode on singing, till within half a mile of the town. Mr Samuel Handy and John Heally happened to be foremost, three or four yards out of the line, though I had led the company until then. We were mounting a little hill, when three or four men appeared at the top, and bade us go back. We thought them in jest, till the stones flew. John Heally was knocked off his horse with a stone, fell backward, and lay without sense or motion. Mr Handy, setting spurs to his horse, charged through the enemy and immediately turned upon them again. There were only five or six ruffians on the spot, but we saw many gathering to us from all sides.

I observed the man who had knocked down John Heally striking him on the face with his club, cried to him to stop, which drew him upon me and probably saved our brother's life, whom another blow might have dispatched. They had gathered against our coming great heaps of stones, one of which was sufficient to beat out our brains. How we escaped them, God only knows, and our guardian angels. I had no apprehension of their hurting me, even when one struck me on the back with a large stone, which took away my breath.

One struck Mr Force on the head, at whom Mr Handy made a full blow. He turned and escaped part, yet it knocked him down,

---

6. "Life is lived in an open garden."
7. Cf. Acts 26:18.
8. Charles gives the date halfway through the sentence, in parentheses. It has been moved to the front for clarity.
9. Charles spells "Temple-Macqueteer."

and for the present disabled him. As often as we returned we were driven off by showers of stones. Some were for returning home, but I asked if we should leave our brother in the hands of his murderers.

We rode back to the field of battle, which our enemies had quitted, the Protestants beginning to rise upon them. It seems the Papists had laid their scheme for murdering us at the instigation of their priest, Father Farrell,[10] who had sounded an alarm last Sunday and raised his crusade against us. The man who wounded John Heally was the priest's servant, and rode his master's horse. He was just going to finish the work with his knife, swearing desperately that he would cut him up, when a poor woman from her hut came to his assistance, and swore as stoutly that he should not cut him up. The man half killed her with a blow of John Heally's whip, yet she hindered him till more help came. One Jameson, a Protestant, ran in with a pitchfork and stuck the clerk into the shoulder. The bone stopped it. The man made a second push at him, which was broke by Mr Handy, returned to save his enemy's life. The hedges were all lined with Papists, who kept the field till they saw the dragoons coming out of Athlone. Then they took to their heels, and Mr Handy after them. In the midst of the bog they seized the priest's servant, carried him prisoner to Athlone, and charged the High Constable with him, who quickly let him go. A Protestant met and beat him unmercifully. But he escaped at last, and fled for his life, sorely wounded.

We found John Heally in his blood at the hut, whither the woman and her husband had carried him. He recovered his senses at hearing my voice. We got him to Athlone, had him blooded,[11] had his wounds dressed. The surgeon would take nothing for his pains.

The people of the town expressed great indignation at our treatment. The soldiers flocked about us. They had been ordered by their officers to meet and guard us into town. But we came before our time, which prevented them; and our enemies likewise, or we should have found an army of Romans ready to receive us. The country, it seems, knew beforehand of the design, for the Papists made no secret of it. But by the providence of God none of us, or our enemies, lost their lives.

---

10. Rev. John Farrell (c. 1696–1753) was the priest at St Mary's church, Athlone, from 1723 to 1753. Charles spells "Ferril."
11. The words "had him blooded" have been omitted by Jackson.

I walked down to the market-house, which was filled by a third of the congregation. I removed to a window in a ruined house, which commanded the market-place. The gentlemen, with the minister,[12] and above two thousand hearers, gave diligent heed while I strongly invited them to buy wine and milk without money and without price [Isa. 55:1]. The congregation waited on us to our inn, and many of them out of town with our trusty soldiers. But first the minister and collector came to see us, and inquire after our wounded man; got us to leave information, and promised us justice. The minister acknowledged it was the doctrine of our own Church, accepted some of our books, and bade us God speed.

We marched very slowly for the sake of our patient, till we came to the field of battle. It was stained with blood abundantly. We halted, and sang a song of triumph and praise to God,[13] who giveth us the victory through our Lord Jesus Christ.[14] Here we sent back our guard, and went on our way rejoicing to Moate.[15]

I proclaimed in the street the faithful saying that Jesus Christ came into the world to save sinners [1 Tim. 1:15]. A few stones were cast, and a drum beat to entertain the ladies. In spite of the genteel devil, some impression was made on the vulgar, as their tears testified.

We rode through the noisy ones to Mr Handy's. The voice of joy and thanksgiving was heard in his dwelling; and we magnified the God by whom we escape death.

Among my hearers was the mother of my host, who, after a moral life of near eighty years, is now convinced of unbelief and quietly waiting for the salvation of God.

***Thursday, February [11].*** At Tyrrellspass. Our Barn was filled at night with high and low, rich and poor, whose curiosity brought them from all parts. I showed them their case and their Physician, in the wounded traveller and good Samaritan [Luke 10:29-37]. They listened for two hours, and seemed to feel the weight of the word. Counsellor Low[16] followed us home, and had much serious discourse with us.

---

12. A Rev. T— ; cf. the September 25, 1748, entry.
13. Charles wrote a hymn celebrating this deliverance, which can be found in *Poetical Works*, 8:394–96; it seems unlikely that this was the hymn they sang the same day.
14. Cf. 1 Cor. 15:57.
15. Charles spells "Moat."
16. It appears that Charles wrote "Lo–" and Jackson added the "w" in the MS.

*Friday, February [12].* Spent the morning in conference with the strangers. One, a sensible Roman, seemed satisfied with my answers to his objections, and not far from the kingdom of heaven.[17] Another, who has been a notorious sinner, but a man of reading, went away convinced, and longing to be converted. The counsellor, we heard, had sat up the whole night searching the Scriptures, if these things be so.[18]

At Mr Samuel Handy's I invited many to the Great Supper [Luke 14:15-24]. Two hours passed unperceived, before I could give over.

*Saturday, February [13].* A poor publican was drowned in tears, who constantly attends the word of grace, on which all his hopes depend. Preached at Tullamore, on "O, Israel, thou hast destroyed," etc. [Hos. 13:9]. They received both the legal and gospel saying as the truth of God. Many of the soldiers from Dublin followed us into the house for further instruction, to whom I again declared "The poor have the gospel preached unto them" [Luke 7:22]. It was a time of refreshing, like one of the former days.

*Sunday, February [14].* At Phillipstown expounded the Prodigal Son [Luke 15:11-32]. Above forty dragoons joined me in singing and conference, both before and after. These are all turned from darkness to light, that they may receive forgiveness.[19]

*Monday, February 15.* Visited several at Tyrrellspass, particularly Mrs Wade, aged ninety-five, who counts all things but loss, so she may win Christ, and be found in him, not having her own righteousness.[20] She has continued in the temple for near a hundred years, and in fasting every Friday.[21] How does this shame the young professors, who say they have faith, yet live in a total neglect of Christ's ordinance! She looks every moment for the seal of her pardon, that she may depart in peace.

The next I saw was a venerable couple indeed—the man ninety-six, the woman ninety-eight. He had rejoiced to hear of the great change wrought in the town, and said if he could but see us lifting up our hands in prayer for him, he doubted not but the Lord would

17. Cf. Mark 12:34.
18. Cf. Acts 17:11.
19. Cf. Acts 26:18.
20. Cf. Phil. 3:8-9.
21. Cf. Luke 2:37.

give him the blessing. Till within these two years, he has worked at his loom. He was in all the actions of the last century, at the siege of Londonderry, Limerick, etc.; the greatest Tory-hunter in the country; full of days and scars. His wife retains her senses and understanding. She wept for joy while we prayed over them, and commended them to the pardoning grace of God.

*Tuesday, February 16.* Came to Dublin, half dead with the rain and snow.

*Sunday, February 21.* Had much of our Lord's presence in the word, while the poor blind beggars cried after him on every side. At night the Good Samaritan [Luke 10:29-37] looked upon us. One testified that her wounds were then bound up.

*Monday, February 22.* Visited a poor wretch in Newgate, who is to be burnt next week for coining.[22] The proof against her was not very full, but her life and character cast her. She has lived in all manner of wickedness, and narrowly escaped death before for killing her son-in-law. Justice has now overtaken her, and she cries she is lost forever. I could not well discern whence her sorrow flowed, but found hope for her in prayer.

*Tuesday, February 23.* She was much the same, but vehemently desired our people's prayers, and told me, had she continued hearing the word, she had never come into that misery. But her neighbors had laughed her out of it, and now God had left her to herself.

At the Barn I expounded the Woman with the Bloody Issue,[23] and many seemed not only to press, but to touch him. Their cries pierced the clouds. Three testified that they were healed of their plague. A greater blessing followed us in the Society. Glory be to God who so wonderfully revives his work among us. I trust many shall yet be added to the church, before we part.

*Wednesday, February 24.* At night we were all melted into tears by our dying Lord's expostulation, "Is it nothing to you, all ye that pass by?" [Lam. 1:12], and long continued mourning in sight of his cross.

*Thursday, February 25.* We had wrestled in prayer for the poor criminal, and today I plainly saw the answer returned. Her heart

22. *OED*: counterfeiting, or forgery.
23. See the note on this sermon for the November 5, 1739, entry in volume 1.

was broken in pieces. She had nothing to plead or pay, and all her concern was for her soul. She received the word of reconciliation as the thirsty land doth the dew of heaven, and resolved to spend her last breath in crying after the friend of sinners.

*On Friday, and Saturday, February 26 and 27,* I was again with the woman. Near twenty of the poor wretches pressed in after me. Her tears and lamentations reached both their hearts and mine.

Met with one who has lately received the atonement, and is continually exercised by the contradiction of *poor* sinners, even her own daughters. They abuse and persecute her, not refraining even from blows, for "they have nothing to do with works or the law."

*Sunday, February 28.* Expounded Isaiah 35, and the word was with power, as at the beginning. Many cried under it, and one woman, "I have found forgiveness this moment!" I spake with her afterwards at our sister Baker's, and she told me she was just before quite sunk down in sorrow, when a light was darted into her heart. "It set me a trembling," she added, "and, soon after, a joy came such as I never felt before. I am quite another creature. I am so light, I cannot express it." Her testimony is the more remarkable because she can neither write nor read.

I did not wonder, while passing Newgate, that one struck me on my head with a stone. Preached at two and six at the Barn. The great blessing came at last. My subject was the Woman washing our Savior's Feet [Luke 7:36-50]; and never was he more sensibly present with us. A woman could not forbear declaring openly that her faith had saved her.

*Monday, February 29.* Received fresh comfort by a letter from a Dissenter, testifying that she had found again, under the word, the peace which she had lost for many years. Every day we hear of more children born, which reconciles us to the contrary wind, though it keeps my brother from us.

Sent a brother to the condemned woman, who told him she had been visited by a Romish priest. On his bidding her pray to the Virgin Mary, she answered, "I have an advocate with the Father, Jesus Christ the righteous."[24] The Ordinary was also with her for the first time, and she told him the reason of the hope that was in her.

---

24. Cf. 1 John 2:1.

I heard, from the keeper, that a reprieve was come down, and a pardon expected. Feared it might stop the work of God in her, and was agreeably surprised to find her full of fear and trouble at the news. "O," said she to me, "I am afraid, if my life be spared, that I shall fall from God. I know he would have mercy on me if I die now." In discoursing farther, I perceived very comfortable signs. Some of her words were, "Two days ago I found such a change, as I cannot describe. My heart is so lightened, my trouble and grief quite gone. And in the night, when I pray to my Savior, I feel such a strange comfort and confidence as cannot be expressed. Surely God has forgiven me my sins." I believed it, but took no notice, till the work should prove itself; only exhorted her to watch and pray, lest she should fall from those good beginnings.

# MARCH 1748

*Tuesday, March 1.* Met the woman, released from her chains, both soul and body. She threw herself at my feet, and cried, "O, Sir, under God, you have saved my soul. I have found mercy, when I looked for judgment. I am saved by a miracle of mercy."

In the evening preached on that most important word, "It is finished" [John 19:30], and God set to his seal. One received forgiveness. A man and a woman testified that they had found it at the last preaching. The power of the Lord was wonderfully in the Society. I asked, "Who touched him?"[25] not doubting but some had then received their cure. One, and another, and another witnessed a good confession. Our sister Blammires declared, with great struggling, that she then found power to believe, and blessed the day that ever she saw my face. Others spake in the same manner. And last, Thomas Barnes told me he had recovered his pardon while I was repeating, "There is more joy in heaven over," etc. [Luke 15:7]. The number of the witnesses this night was nine.

*Wednesday, March 2.* At Mrs Gilmore's, a serious Dissenter. Met three others of the same communion who had been lately justified under the word.

---

25. This would be Charles's sermon on the Woman with the Bloody Issue, with particular focus on the account in Mark 5:25-34 or Luke 8:40-56.

*Saturday, March 5.* Showed the poor felons in Newgate what they must do to be saved. One man I have often observed much affected by the word, and extremely officious to wait upon me. This was the executioner, who is half converted by the woman, and shows the most profound reverence for her. I gave him several of our books, which he has read over and over. By profession he is a Papist.

*Sunday, March 6.* I do not remember when we have had a greater blessing than we had this evening in the Society. Near twenty declared the manifestation of the Spirit then vouchsafed them.

*Monday, March 7.* Spake with eleven of them who had received a clear sense of pardon. Another went to his house justified when I discoursed on Wrestling Jacob [Gen. 32:24-31].

*Tuesday, March 8.* My brother landed, and met the Society. God confirming the word of his messenger.

*Wednesday, March 9.* Passed a comfortable hour in conference with some others who have lately stepped into the pool.[26] One was begotten again this evening by the word of his power (Isaiah 53).

*Thursday, March 10.* Three more received their cure.

*Friday, March 11.* My text in the morning was, "The Spirit and the Bride say, Come" [Rev. 22:17]. After great strugglings, one was constrained to cry out, "He is come! He is come! I have him, I have him now, in my heart." A stranger, who stood with his hat on upon the stairs, with all the marks of carelessness, cried out in great astonishment, "Lord bless me! What is this?" and ran away as if the avenger was at his heels. Another testified her having lately found favour, who was, some days since, a grievous sinner—common harlot. But she is washed! God grant she may hold out!

*Sunday, March 13.* In our garden I once more invited them to the Great Supper [Luke 14:15-24]. Many tears were shed at parting. Yet was it a blessed mourning, because we expect to meet again at the great white throne.[27]

*Monday, March 14.* The wind turning full against us gave me an opportunity of preaching again in Ship Street. Heard that our sister

26. Cf. John 5:1-15.
27. Cf. Rev. 20:11.

Preston was yesterday delivered of her burden in singing. This evening Mrs Gilmore received the love of God shed abroad in her heart.[28] A month ago she was a warm opposer. But venturing, out of curiosity, to hear me, the Lord applied his word, and stripped her all at once of her self-righteousness, faith of adherence, and good works. She mourned after him, till now that Jesus has received her among his witnesses.

*Sunday, March 20.* After a week's confinement through the toothache, at two this day entered the packet-boat with John Haughton.

*Monday, March 21.* By three landed at the Head.[29] Passed the night in great pain.

*Tuesday, March 22.* Took horse for our brother [William] Jones's. It was a bright, sunshiny morning; the wind moderate, and in our backs. Came to my guide's by nine, and rode by three to Bol-y-don ferry[30] (sending John Haughton forward to Chester). The wind was now higher, and more ahead of us, blowing full in my swollen face. We overfilled the small old boat, so that

> *Crepuit sub pondere cymba*
> *Futilis, et multam accepit rimosa paludem.*[31]

We flew on the wings of the wind, till we got to the channel. There the motion was so violent that my young horse began prancing, and striving to take the water. I held him with the little strength I had; but an oar lying between us, I had no firm footing, and could not command him at arms' length. His unruliness frightened the other horse, who began kicking, and struck our brother down. I saw the danger that, if my horse got his foot over the boat, it must overset, and had no strength to hinder it. It came into my mind, "Hath God brought me through the sea to be drowned here?"

---

28. Cf. Rom. 5:5.

29. I.e., Holyhead.

30. Departed from present village of Port Dinorwic, Caernarfonshire. Charles spells "Baladon." Also called "Moel-y-don."

31. This is Charles's somewhat faulty memory of Virgil, *Aeneid*, vi.413–14: "*Gemuit sub pondere cymba sutilis, et multam accepit rimosa paludem.*" Charles's version can be translated: "The leaky boat creaked beneath the weight and, full of cracks, took on board much swamp water."

Looked up, and in that moment the horse stood still, and continued so till we reached the shore.

Went early to bed at Caernarfon,[32] and got a little rest.

*Wednesday, March 23.* Overruled, by brother [William] Jones, not to set out till past seven. The continual rain and sharp wind were full in my teeth. I rode all day in great misery, and had a restless, painful night at Tan-y-bwlth.

*Thursday, March 24.* Resolved to push for Garth, finding my strength would never hold out for three more days' riding. At five set out in hard rain, which continued all day. We went through perils of waters. I was quite gone when we came at night to a little village. There was no fire in the poor hut. A brother supplied us with some, nailed up our window, and helped us to bed. Had no more rest than the night before.

*Friday, March 25.* Took horse again at five, the rain attending us still. At eight comforted by the sight of Mr [Edward] Phillips, at Llanidloes. The weather grew more severe. The violent wind drove the hard rain full in our faces. I rode till I could ride no more, walked the last hour, and by five dropped down at Garth. All ran to nurse me. I got a little refreshment, and at seven made a feeble attempt to preach. They quickly put me to bed. Had a terrible night, worse than ever.

*Saturday, March 26,* and the five following days, was exercised with strong pain, notwithstanding all the means used to remove it. My short intervals were filled up with conference, prayer, and singing.

## APRIL 1748

*Sunday, April 3.* Through the divine blessing on the tender care of my friends, I recovered so much strength that I read prayers, and gave the Sacrament to the family. At night my dearest Sally,[33] like my guardian angel attended me. In the loving openness of my heart, without premeditation I asked her "if she could trust herself

---

32. Charles spells "Caernarvon."
33. Miss Sarah ("Sally") Gwynne (1726–1822), whom Charles would marry a year later (see April 8, 1749, entry).

with me for life," and with a noble simplicity she readily answered me "she could."

*Monday, April 4.* Frightened at what I had said last night, I condemned my own rashness and almost wished I had never disclosed my feelings.

Mrs [Sarah] Gwynne carried me out in her chair, and I found my strength sensibly return.

*Tuesday, April 5.* She drove me to Builth. Took horse at three. Mr Gwynne and Miss Sally accompanied me the first hour. Then I rode on alone, weary, but supported. My accommodations at my inn were none the best. I lay restless till midnight, expecting to return, as I had promised in case of a relapse. But toward the morning I dropped asleep, and woke much refreshed at five.

*Saturday, April [9].*[34] In the evening, with God's evident help, I came safe to the Foundery.

*Easter Day, April 10.* Joined my brethren on this and the seven following days, to show forth the Lord's death, and he never once sent us empty away.[35]

Dined at Counsellor [William] Glanville's,[36] a brand lately plucked out of the fire.

*Thursday, April 14.* Met another poor publican, Colonel Gumley,[37] who has just now entered the kingdom and is brimful of his first love.

*Saturday, April 16.* Gave the Sacrament to our sister King, inexpressibly happy at the approach of death.

*Tuesday, April 19.* I had communicated my embryo intentions to my brother while in Ireland, which he neither opposed, nor much encouraged. It was then a distant first thought, not likely ever to come to a proposal; as I had not given the least hint, either to Miss Gwynne or the family. Today I rode over to Shoreham, and told Mr [Vincent] Perronet all my heart. I have always had a fear, but no *thought*, of marrying, for many years past, even from my first

---

34. MS has "April 8," which is in error.
35. Cf. Matt. 15:32; Mark 8:3.
36. Charles spells "Glanvil."
37. Colonel Samuel Gumley (d. 1763), of Chertsey. Gumley was converted on this very day, under the preaching of George Whitefield, at the London house of Lady Huntingdon.

preaching the gospel. But within this twelvemonth that thought has forced itself in, "How know I whether it be best for me to marry or no?" Certainly better now than later. And if not now, what security that I shall not then? It should be now, or not at all.

Mr Perronet encouraged me to pray, and wait for a providential opening. I expressed the various searchings of my heart in many hymns on the important occasion.

*Friday, April 22.* Mrs Colvil was at the chapel. I discoursed on the Pharisee and Publican [Luke 18:9-14]. The divine power and blessing made the word effectual, and broke down all before it.

*Wednesday, April 27.* My text was "There be many that say, Who will show us good?" etc. [Ps. 4:6]. The Lord was mightily present in his awakening power.

*Friday, April 29.* Mrs Rich carried me to Dr Pepusch,[38] whose music entertained us much, and his conversation more.

## MAY 1748

*Sunday, May 1.* The cup of blessing was the communication of his blood, the bread broken of his body, to his disciples at the chapel.

*Thursday, May 5.* Baptized Elizabeth Cart in the river at Cowley,[39] and she washed away all her sin and sorrow.

*Tuesday, May 10.* Came to Bristol, bruised a little with a fall.

*Friday, May 20.* At the watch-night I discoursed on Jacob wrestling with the Angel [Gen. 32:24-31], and many were stirred up to lay hold on the Lord, like him.

*Sunday, May 22.* The whole multitude wept to hear how Jesus loved them, while I urged his passionate question, "Is it nothing to you, all ye that pass by?" [Lam. 1:12].

*Thursday, afternoon, May 26.* Set out for London, and on Saturday reached it. The first good news I heard from Mrs Boult, that our old friend Mrs Sparrow is at last departed in the Lord.

*Tuesday, May 31.* Attended her mortal part to the grave.

38. John Christopher Pepusch (1667–1752), organist at Charterhouse school in London.
39. Cowley, Middlesex.

# JUNE 1748

*Sunday, June 5.* Fulfilled my friend's last request, by preaching her funeral sermon, on Micah 7:8, "Rejoice not against me, O mine enemy. When I fall, I shall arise. When I sit in darkness, the Lord shall be a light unto me." I spoke as freely of her faults as virtues— her love of the world, and final victory over it. The hearers appeared deeply affected.

*Friday, June 10.* Returned to Bristol.

*Sunday, June 12.* Preached to several thousands in the Orchard, with great strength, both of body and spirit.

*Thursday, June 16.* Visited the brethren in Cardiff, Llanmaes,[40] Cowbridge, etc., and exhorted them to strengthen the things that remain.

*Monday, June 20.* Returned with Kitty Jones[41] to Bristol. Mr Gwynne and Miss Sally were got there a little before me. Till

*Saturday, June 25.* Carried them to see my Christian friends, my principal ones especially at Kingswood. Today I asked and obtained permission to speak to her mother.

*Sunday, June 26.* In the word, and Sacrament, and Love-feast, the Lord made our souls as a watered garden.

*Tuesday, June 28.* Quite spent with examining the classes, I was much revived in singing with Miss Burdock and Sally.

*Thursday, June 30.* Comforted in all our trials by that blessed promise, "The third part I will bring through the fire" [Zech. 13:9].
Set out with Mr Gwynne and his daughter to visit the church in London. Preached at Bath with great liberty, and carried away our faithful sister Naylor.

# JULY 1748

*Saturday, July 2.* Lodged my fellow-travelers in the Foundery.

---

40. Charles spells "Lanmase."
41. Catherine ("Kitty") Jones (b. 1736), daughter of Robert and Mary, of Fonmon Castle.

*Sunday, July 3.* Took the field, and was not sent a warfare on my own cost. At the chapel preached, "I reckon the suffering of the present time not worthy to be compared," etc. [Rom. 8:18]. Both now and at night we had a great spirit of contrition among us.

*Tuesday, July 5.* Carried my guests to Mrs Blackwell[42] and Dewal[43] at Lewisham, and thence to my most worthy friend in Shoreham.[44]

*Friday, July 15.* My text at the watch-night was, "I say unto all, Watch!" [Mark 13:37]. Great reverence we felt in the presence of our Lord.

*Monday, July 18.* Baptized good old Mrs Pearce by immersion, at four in the morning.

*Tuesday, July 19.* Rose at three, and called our friends. The Lord sent us a great deliverance, as a token for good. Mary Naylor had shut the door of their bed-chamber, and left the key in the inside. Sally wanted something out which Mary Naylor would have put her by; but, on Sally's still desiring it, she called the man to break open the door. He said he would go see his horses, and come. She insisted upon his doing it just then, which he did, and they found the sheet on fire, through Molly's dropping the snuff of a candle. Had the man stayed, the whole Foundery might have been in a flame.

Set out at four with Mr Gwynne and Sally. At eleven, in Windsor, my horse threw me with violence over his head. My companion fell upon me. The guardian angels bore us in their hands, so that neither was hurt. Saw the castle and palace with insensibility. No sight, we trust, will satisfy us, but that of Moses from Mount Pisgah.[45] By seven came to Reading, and preached in great bodily weakness.

*Wednesday, July 20.* My old desire of escaping out of life possessed me all day. By three we got to Oxford. Walked about the colleges. Met a poor servitor of St John's, James Rouquet, who is not ashamed to confess Christ before men. Preached in the evening on

---

42. Elizabeth Blackwell (*née* Mowland, d. 1772), lived in The Limes manor at Lewisham. The hymn that Charles wrote upon her death can be found in *Poetical Works*, 6:323–31.
43. Mrs Hannah Dewal (d. 1762). Charles's hymn on her death can be found in *Poetical Works*, 6:318–23.
44. Vincent Perronet.
45. Cf. Deut. 34:1-4.

"Ye are my witnesses" [Isa. 43:10], and lodged with our old friend Mr Evans.

*Thursday, July 21.* Gave the Sacrament to Mrs Neal (one who received the atonement in reading my sermon before the University[46]), and had sweet fellowship with our Lord and his members.

*Friday, July 22.* At five took horse with Mr Gwynne, Sally, and Mrs Boult. Reached Cirencester before two. Preached in a yard from "The redeemed of the Lord shall return, and come with songs," etc. [Isa. 51:11]. I was pierced through with desires of complete redemption, which broke out in tears and words that affected them in like manner. I could gladly have dropped the body in that hour.

*Saturday, July 23.* Set out at half-hour past four. Rode four miles, when Mrs Boult's horse, walking on the plainest ground, fell and broke her arm. We carried her to an inn just by, and sent J. Griffith back for a surgeon. By seven we left her, her arm set and her mind stayed on Christ, and came to Bristol in the cool of the evening.

*Sunday, July 24.* Rose from my boards at four. Carried Sally to Kingswood. Began the Sacrament with fervent prayer and many tears, which almost hindered my reading the service. Broke out into prayer again and again. Our hearts were all as melting wax. Administered to our sisters Robertson and Rutter, sorely bruised by an overturn into a pit; yet they would not lose the Sacrament.

Received letters from Cork loudly calling me thither. My heart was at once made willing, and I had my commission. Joined in earnest prayer for success. Preached a third and a fourth time in the shell of our house,[47] with supernatural strength.

*Tuesday, July 26.* Dined at the Fishponds with faithful Felix Farley. At night I preached in the Orchard to many serious souls. There was a coach with Mrs Knight,[48] Miss Cheyne,[49] Mr Edwin,[50]

---

46. I.e., "Awake Thou that Sleepest" (*Sermons*, 211–24).

47. The preaching-room at the Horsefair was in the midst of remodeling to enlarge it.

48. Anne Knight (*née* Robinson) was the daughter of William Robinson (1677–1720) of Rokeby, and widow of Robert Knight (d. 1744), cashier of the South Sea Company.

49. Almost certainly Margaret Cheyne, of Bath; daughter of Dr George Cheyne (d. 1743), a good friend of Lady Huntingdon and an acquaintance of John Wesley.

50. Charles Edwin (1699–1756), member of parliament for Glamorgan, 1747–1756 (and husband of Lady Charlotte Edwin).

and Sir William Bunbury.[51] The latter challenged me for his old school-fellow, in the face of the sun, and was not ashamed to join heartily in our hymns.

*Wednesday, July 27.* They attended again, while I expounded the Good Samaritan [Luke 10:29-37].

*Thursday, July 28.* Waited upon Miss Cheyne first, and then on Mrs Knight, at the Wells.[52] Both assented to the truth. The latter sent for her brother, my old friend Robinson,[53] of Christ Church. He called me to defend the lay-preachers, and would fain have brought me to confess we *sent* them. I declared the matter of fact, that when God had sent any one forth, and owned him by repeated conversions, then we durst not reject him. He talked with great candour, and remains of his old kindness for me.

*Friday, July 29.* Preached over against the assembly room to the most polite audience I have ever been honored with. The ladies in their coaches were surprisingly patient, while I told them "one thing is needful" [Luke 10:42]. A servant who behaved rudely, Sir William Bunbury seized and delivered over to a constable. Some young officers made a disturbance, whom I rebuked and silenced.

Ran with fresh strength to the shell of our room, and continued preaching, singing, rejoicing till midnight.

*Sunday, July 31.* Baptized a woman in Kingswood, and trembled at the descent of the Holy Ghost. All present were more or less sensible of it, especially the person baptized. Joined in the Lord's Supper, and had his never-failing presence. So again at our first Love-feast in the New Room.[54] For two hours we were sensible of Christ in the midst.

# AUGUST 1748

*Monday, August 1.* Set out at five for Garth. Lodged at Abergavenny.

---

51. Sir William Bunbury (c. 1710–1764), 5th baronet of Bunbury, vicar of Mildenhall, Suffolk, was a classmate of Wesley at Westminster School.

52. Hotwells, Somerset, about one mile west of Bristol, which had become a favored gathering place for the gentry for the summer social season.

53. Richard Robinson (1709–1794) of Rokeby, who entered Christ Church with Charles in 1726, was currently rector of Elton, Yorkshire. He became Archbishop of Armagh (1765–1794).

54. With the remodeling complete, Charles now refers to it as the "New Room."

*Tuesday, August 2.* In the afternoon Mrs Gwynne received us with a cordial welcome.

*Thursday, August 4.* Rode with Sally to the Wells,[55] and preached in their assembly room to the gentry, clergy, and others, inviting them to the superlative happiness of religion.

*Sunday, August 7.* Maesmynis church being too narrow, I preached in the churchyard the promised Spirit of grace and supplication [Zech. 12:10]. His comforts refreshed our souls, and more abundantly still in the Sacrament that followed.

*Monday, August 8.* Mr Gwynne, with Miss Sally and Betsy,[56] accompanied me as far as Llanidloes. I preached with great enlargement. The poor people received the word with tears of joy. Parted with tears from my dearest friends, and rode on with Mr [Edward] Phillips to Machynlleth.

*Tuesday, August 9.* From three in the morning till eight at night on the road. Had sweet fellowship with my friends in prayer.

*Wednesday, August 10.* Left Caernarfon at five. Found the boat just going off, full of unruly oxen. Waited an hour for its return, which I passed in earnest prayer for my friends. Near seven landed in a strange, intricate country, where I could procure no guide, or direction, as often as I lost my way. At last Providence sent me one that understood English, and rode several miles out of his way, to put me in mine. I gave him some advice and books, both [of] which he thankfully received.

I continued in the right road while it was impossible to get out of it, and no longer. Blundered on through the sands, especially some near the town, where, if the sea had been out, I should have ended all my journeys. Passed by several ships, and cross the channels, till my horse, without my care or counsel, brought me to Holyhead soon after two.

Here I heard the boat went off at ten this morning. It was a trial of my patience, and I almost wished I had stayed with my friends, rather than wait here till Saturday, the soonest that any packet can go. The boats are all on the other side.

---

55. Llandrindod Wells, a popular spa town.
56. Elizabeth ("Betsy") Gwynne (b. 1730), younger sister of Sally.

I quickly saw God's design. He has found me time for retirement, in which I can both write and pray for those who are to me as my own soul.

The hour of prayer I passed among the rocks, presenting my friends at the throne. Towards six I sunk to sleep, the body pressing down the soul; but still my fellowship with them was not interrupted. A few neighbors joined us at my private lodgings, in family prayer.

*Thursday, August 11.* Passed the day in my prophet's chamber, or closet, among the rocks. Only in the evening I walked up the mountain, and wandered in a wilderness of rocks with my inseparable friends.

*Friday, August 12,* was another solid day which I spent in retirement; only allowing half an hour, after public worship, for Mr [Thomas] Ellis the minister, in provoking each other to love and good works.

*Saturday, August 13.* Took boat in a very rough sea, which washed us thoroughly, while toiling to come up with the vessel. At eleven we set sail. God sent us a wind out of his treasury, the fairest we could have, which by nine brought us smoothly and safely into Dublin Bay.

*Sunday, August 14.* At five walked to the preaching room, and gave them a welcome word of exhortation. Great was our rejoicing, and mutual faith, and fellowship in the Spirit.

Met them again, and my brother, at St Patrick's. The number of communicants was much increased since my departure. Preached in our garden at two. The power of the Lord was present as at the beginning. Met all the lively Society, to our mutual consolation— consolation which words cannot express.

Mr [William] Lunell could not be satisfied without my lodging under his roof. I mourned with him that mourned under Ezekiel's trial: "Son of man, behold, I take away the desire of thine eyes with a stroke" [Ezek. 24:16]. She died triumphant.[57] He lost his Benjamin too; the child accompanying the mother to paradise.

*Tuesday, August 16.* Reproved the slack, and encouraged the orderly walkers. Their prayers, I trust, will follow me to Cork.

---

57. William Lunell's second wife, Anne (*née* Gratton), had just died. Charles's epitaph for her, "On Mrs Lunell," can be found in *Poetical Works*, 8:436.

*Wednesday, August 17.* Set out in the hard rain. My horse, the roughest I ever rode, shook all the strength out of me before I got to Tyrrellspass. There our sister Force[58] and the rest received me right gladly. Preached on the blood of sprinkling [Heb. 12:24], and met the poor neglected Society. Our preachers had all left them for Cork, where is now the widest door.

*Thursday, August 18.* Rode to Ballyboy,[59] where an hospitable Quaker received us with open arms. Broke through my great reluctance and preached, in his house, the atoning Lamb of God [John 1:29]. He opened my mouth, and the hearer's hearts.

*Friday, August 19.* It rained the whole day. The road was one continued quagmire. Made an hard shift to reach Roscrea by ten. Some of the town caught me leaving it, and demanded their debt of the gospel. A mixed crowd of Papists and Protestants filled the market house. I called them (never with more authority) to Jesus Christ. Then rode on in the rain, rejoicing with my dropping companion. By nine we hardly reached Cashel.

Here we met with poor entertainment, having no way to dry our clothes. I put off my great coat, and got a little sleep.

*Saturday, August 20.* Rose cheerfully between two and three. Put on my clothes, wet and weighty enough. Had some intervals of fair weather, and got, by seven in the evening, to Cork. Was wishing for rest at some private house, when Mr Harrison, the printer, came and invited me to his. I took a sweat, and rose at my usual time.

*Sunday, August 21.* At five found a congregation of some thousands on the marsh,[60] and spoke from Luke [24:46], "Thus it is written, and thus it behoved Christ to suffer," etc. They devoured every word with an eagerness beyond description. I advised them all to go to their several places of worship, and went myself to Christ Church. It is the largest church in Cork, yet quite full. The communion kept us till near ten.

Much good has been done already in this place. Outward wickedness has disappeared, outward religion succeeded. Swearing

---

58. This time Charles spells "Fource."
59. Charles spells "Balliboy."
60. Hammond's Marsh, an open area, which four years later became the site of a Methodist chapel.

is seldom heard in the streets. The churches and altars are crowded to the astonishment of our adversaries. Yet some of our clergy and all the Catholic priests take wretched pains to hinder their people from hearing us.

At five took the field again, but such a sight I have rarely seen! Thousands and thousands had been waiting some hours, Protestants and Papists, high and low. The Lord endued my soul, and body also, with much strength to enforce the faithful saying "that Jesus Christ came into the world to save sinners" [1 Tim. 1:15]. I cried after them for an hour, to the utmost extent of my voice, yet without hoarseness or weariness. The Lord, I believe, hath much people in this city.[61] Two hundred are already joined in a Society.

*Monday, August 22.* The congregation was on the marsh before me, near three thousand loving, listening, unawakened souls, whom I urged to repent, that their sins might be blotted out [Acts 3:19].

At present we pass through honor and good report. The chief persons of the town favour us. No wonder then that the common people are quiet. We pass and repass the streets, pursued by their blessings only. The same favourable inclination is all round the country. Wherever we go, they receive us as angels of God.[62] Were this to last, I would escape for my life to America.

Many are turned from their outward sins, and if they went no farther the saints of the world would like them well enough. When the power of godliness, the forgiveness of sins, the gift of the Holy Ghost, is preached, many will fall off. But as yet the work is very superficial. Not one justified person have I yet found.

Passing by the marsh at five, I saw hundreds waiting there for the word; and was told it was their custom from the beginning; and that last Sunday many were there from one in the morning.

I declared, with divine assistance, "One Thing is Needful" [Luke 10:42]. The sin-convincing Spirit was present. He struck the hard rock, and the waters gushed out.[63] The assizes brought many strangers. I did not spare them, and they bore my plainness of speech. Several of the better sort, particularly two justices, thanked and wished me success.

---

61. Cf. Acts 18:10.
62. Cf. Gal. 4:14.
63. Cf. Ps. 78:20.

*Tuesday, August 23.* Laboured to convince my hearers of unbelief. More and more are awakening out of sleep. In the evening near a dozen clergymen attended. I would all our brethren would do us the same justice of hearing before they judge us.

*Wednesday, August 24.* By a clergyman's advice, I went to wait on the bishop. He was not at his palace. The housekeeper begged a few words with me. She trembled exceedingly, and struggled to speak, and at last told me her whole life. From twelve years old she had had violent conflicts with the old murderer.[64] She seemed a chosen vessel, one who, like Obadiah, had served God from her youth. I told her what she wanted, even faith and forgiveness. She received my saying with all readiness of mind; begged me to let her have the prayer I used for her; wept and rejoiced; and sent me away with many thanks and blessings.

In the evening expounded Blind Bartimeus [Mark 10:46-52] to as genteel an audience as I have ever seen. Several ministers of all denominations, the governor's lady, and many strangers attended out of various motives. The word did not return void. Some of the clergy acknowledged it was the truth.

I designed to have met about two hundred who have given in their names for the Society, but such multitudes thronged into the play-house that it occasioned great confusion. I perceived it was impractical, as yet, to have a regular Society.

*Thursday, August 25.* Here is indeed an open door, such as was never set before me till now. Even at Newcastle the awakening was not so general. The congregation last Sunday was computed above ten thousand. As yet there is no *open* opposition, though the people have had the word two months. Nay, it is not impossible but their love may last two months longer, before any number of them rise to tear us in pieces.

Met a neighboring justice, and had much serious conversation with him. He seems to have a great kindness for religion, and determined to use all his interest to promote it. For an hour and half continued calling the poor blind beggars to Jesus. They begin to cry after him on every side, and we must expect to be rebuked for it.

*Friday, August 26.* Spake severally with the candidates for a Society. All seem awakened, none justified. But who hath despised

---

64. I.e., Satan.

the day of small things?[65] This is, I doubt not, the seed of a glorious church.

Waited on the bishop[66] at Riverstown, and was received with great affability by himself and family. After dinner rode back to Cork. Drank tea with some well-disposed Quakers, and borrowed a volume of their dying sayings[67]—a standing testimony that the life and power of God was with them at the beginning; as it might [be] again, were they humble enough to confess their want.

*Saturday, August 27.* Had much discourse with Mr C[otrell?],[68] a sensible, pious clergyman, one after my own heart in his love to our desolate Mother. Clear in the doctrine of faith. He gave me a delightful account of the bishop. Yet I do not find it good for me to be countenanced by my superiors. It is a snare and burden to my soul. All day long I was bowed down by my late conversation, and stripped of every good desire, especially of preaching. Sometimes our waiting on great men *may* do good, or prevent evil. But how dangerous the experiment! How apt to weaken our hands, and betray us into an undue deference and respect of persons! The Lord send to them by whom He will send. But hide me still in disgrace or obscurity.

Set upon in the street by a Romish priest for words which, *he was told,* one of our preachers spoke against him. I tried to undeceive him, but he was too loud, and too fond of showing his learning (as far as Latin went), to hear reason. However, we parted without coming to blows.

*Sunday, August 28.* From early Sacrament I went to Mr H., an *honest attorney,* and with him to Passage, five miles from Cork. There Justice P. received us, and used all his authority with others to do the same. He sent word to the Romish priest that, if he forbade his people hearing me, he would shut up his mass-house, and send him to gaol for one year at least. Several of the poor Romans ventured to come, after the justice had assured them he would himself take off the curse their priest had laid upon them. I exhorted

---

65. Cf. Zech. 4:10.

66. Jemmett Browne (1702–1782) was Bishop of Cork at this time.

67. This would be one of the series titled *Piety Promoted: in a Collection of Dying Sayings of many of the People called Quakers.* The first three slim volumes were published by John Tomkins between 1701 and 1706. Four more volumes were added by other editors by 1736.

68. Probably Rev. Edward Cotrell, rector of Marmullane.

all alike to repentance toward God and faith in Jesus Christ [Acts 20:21], and staked my own salvation upon it that he who believes, whether Papist or Protestant, shall be saved. Hastened back to the marsh. On seeing the multitudes, I thought on that of Prior,

> Then (baseness of mankind!) then of all these
> Whom my dilated eye with labour sees.[69]

How few will own God's messengers when the stream turns! Now they all received me with inexpressible eagerness. I discoursed on the Good Samaritan [Luke 10:29-37], and took occasion to vindicate the Methodists from that foulest slander—that they rail against the clergy. I enlarged on the respect due to them, prayed particularly for the bishop, and laid it on their consciences to make mention of them in all their prayers.

I had appointed part of the Society to meet me in a private house. But the people so crowded in, there was no room for me. Their love at present as effectually prevents our assembling as their hatred will by and by.

*Tuesday, August 30.* Mr [John] Stockdale drove me to Rathcormack.[70] Mr [Richard] Lloyd, the minister, offered me his church; but agreed with me that I had better preach out, or I should lose all the Papists. They flocked with the Protestants to the market-house, where I strongly urged them to repentance and the obedience of faith [Acts 20:21]. The great man of the place and his lady employ all their authority to promote true vital Christianity. The Romish priest is so intimidated that he dares not forbid his people hearing us. Were every magistrate in Ireland like this, what a multitude of poor Catholics might be turned from darkness to light![71]

*Wednesday, August 31.* In conference, I found one who had received forgiveness in the Sacrament. Two or three more have been justified under the word. Another last Monday.

Passed an useful hour with Mr C[otrell?]. He rejoiced at my having preached in his parish last Sunday. If our brethren were like-

---

69. Matthew Prior, "Solomon on the Vanity of the World," lns. 335–36, *Poems on Several Occasions. A New Edition, with some additions* (London: T. Johnson, 1720), 430. In line one, however, Prior's original text reads "vileness" instead of "baseness."
70. Charles spells "Rathcormuck."
71. Cf. Acts 26:18.

minded, how might their hands be strengthened by us! But we must have patience, as he observed, till the thing speaks itself and, the mist of prejudice being removed, they see clearly that all our desires is the salvation of souls and the establishment of the Church of England.

Talked with a poor innocent girl, who constantly hears the word, but in great fear of the priest. I hope in a little time she will be bold to judge for herself, and save her own soul, without asking any man's leave.

Invited many sinners at the marsh to Him who has promised them the rest of pardon, holiness, heaven.[72] They seem to taste the *good* word. One told me after it that from the time I spake to her at the palace she had expected the blessing every moment, and was sure beyond the possibility of a doubt that she should have it. "I seem," said she, "to be laying hold on Christ continually. I am so light, so happy, as I never was before. I waked, two nights ago, in such rapture of joy, that I thought, 'Surely this is the peace they preach.' It has continued ever since. My eyes are opened. I see all things in a new light. I rejoice always." Is not this the language of faith, the cry of a new-born soul? But prayed over her that the Lord might confirm it, and was greatly comforted with her consolations.

# SEPTEMBER 1748

*Thursday, September 1.* I met the infant Society for the first time in an old play-house. Several were there from two in the morning. One received forgiveness in Jonathan Reeves's first prayer. Our Lord's presence consecrated the place. I explained the nature of Christian fellowship. God knit our hearts together in the desire of knowing Him.

The people are now ripe for the gospel, which I therefore preached from Isaiah 35, to the poor hungry mourners. Heard that one received the atonement on Monday. Behold, a troop cometh! The angel is come down, the water is troubled, and many are just stepping into the pool.[73]

Spoke with some who told me they had wronged their neighbors in time past, and now their conscience will not let them rest till they

---

72. Likely speaking on Matt. 11:28-30.
73. Cf. John 5:4.

have made restitution. I bade them tell the persons injured, it was this preaching compelled them to do justice.

One poor wretch told me, before his wife, that he had lived in drunkenness, adultery, and all the works of the devil for twenty-one years; had beat her every day of that time, and never had any remorse till he heard us; but now he goes constantly to church, behaves lovingly to his wife, abhors the thing that is evil, especially his old sins. This is one instance out of many.

An alderman heard me tonight in a covered chair. Met part of the Society, who are fully convinced that without present forgiveness they cannot be saved.

Called on Mr C[otrell?], who told me he had had a great battle with his brethren, who confidently averred, "affidavit was made of that wicked brother of mine running away with another man's wife at Athlone." I rejoiced at the report, as a sign that the god of this world is alarmed for his kingdom in danger. How will he and his servants rage by and by! Hitherto they seem asleep, but the witnesses of Jesus are rising to rouse them.

Walking to the marsh, I overtook Mrs N., who broke out into strong confession of the faith she received yesterday morning under the word. I marvel not that her daughter says "she is gone distracted." You might as well stop the tide as her testimony. She rides on the high places of the earth. She speaks in the plerophory of faith; she lives in the spirit of triumph. One of her expressions was, "I do not walk, but fly; and seem as if I could leap over the moon."

The marsh was covered with high and low, rich and poor. The gospel had free course, not a word returned empty.[74]

One followed and told me he had found the Lord in the word this morning.

I had much discourse with the young woman above-mentioned, and found she was in Christ before me. But her not using my expressions hindered my perceiving it. Some of her words were:

> From the time you spake to me of forgiveness, I have been praying for it day and night, in continual joy. I am inexpressibly happy. All my temptations are gone. I tread on all the power of the enemy.

---

74. Cf. Isa. 55:11.

From twelve years old I have walked with God, and found him in all my ways, in every place, and business, and company. In all my words I find him prompting me. From my infancy he has been my guide and instructor. When I would have spoken to the bishop or others, he checked me with that thought, "I will bear all my burdens till the Lord himself delivers me." Many things he has taught me to pray for, which I did not myself understand at the time of my asking, nor fully till the answers came.

I have been urged with that question, "Could you die for the gospel of Jesus Christ?" And when I would have put it by, it still followed me, and the Lord insisted upon my answer. While I have sat at work, it came into my mind, *"These fingers will never corrupt in the grave: I must die for the truth!"* I replied, "But how can it be, Lord? We are all Christians. Who is there to persecute us now?" This thought pursues me still, that I am to suffer for my Savior, and I should *grudge* the dying in my bed.

I never felt more powerful, piercing words. They brought their own evidence, and left me no room to doubt God's special love to this soul. They also confirmed my continual expectations of sufferings.

*Saturday, September 3.* My text was, "I, even I, am he that blotteth out thy transgressions, for my own sake" [Isa. 43:25]. I felt, as it were, their spirits sink under the word of grace.

From six to eight I attend those that would speak with me. The first who accosted me was a poor soldier, with, "O, Sir, I have found the blessing!" I asked, "What blessing?" "Why, the blessing you preach—the forgiveness of my sins." "How do you know that?" "I am sure of it. I cannot doubt of it. I feel it in my heart." "When and how did you receive it?" "Yesterday morning under the word. I strove, and strove hard, before I could lay hold on it. But at last I did venture upon Christ. *I put on boldness*, and did believe; and that moment all my sins were taken away, as you would take the coat from my back. I went home rejoicing, and told my wife, and persuaded her to believe like me. She fell a-crying and praying for an hour together, and then she got it too. My mother is not far from it; only for fear of one sin she dares not venture."

His artless confession was confirmed by his wife, who has found the pearl at the same time with him.[75] His brother found it last Sunday.

---

75. Cf. Matt. 13:46.

Joyce Baily informs me she received the blessing yesterday morning through the Spirit applying that word, "Ask, and it shall be given you" [Matt. 7:7].

Exhorted some of the Society, and found them all on full stretch after Christ.

*Sunday, September 4.* Expounded the Prodigal Son [Luke 15:11-32] to thousands of listening sinners, many of whom, I am assured, are on their return, and will never rest till they rest in the arms of their Father.

*Monday, September 5.* More, I hear, are added to the church. Two at the Sacrament yesterday. Two in the Society. One overtook me going to the cathedral[76] and said, "I have found something in the preaching, and cannot but think it is forgiveness. All my sins sunk away from off me in a moment. I can do nothing but pray, and cry, 'Glory be to God!' I have such a confidence of his love as I never knew. I trample all sin and sorrow under my feet." I bade him watch and pray, and expect greater things than these.

Our old master the world begins to take it ill that so many desert and clean escape its pollutions. Innumerable stories are invented to stop the work, or rather repeated, for they are the same we have heard a thousand times, as well as the primitive Christians: "All manner of wickedness is acted in our Society, except the eating of little children." My advice to our people is, "Answer them not a word."

The Romish priests go more secretly to work, deterring their flock by the penalty of a curse. Yet some venture to hear us by stealth.

Took horse for Bandon, with my loving lawyer and his wife, who has lately received Christ, as her language and life declare.

On the road I made the following hymn, for the Roman Catholics in Ireland

Shepherd of souls, the great, the good, etc.[77]

By ten we came to Bandon, a town of Protestants only. Several Papists from the old neighborhood attended me to the market-house.

---

76. St Fin Barre's cathedral, Cork.
77. Charles did not publish this hymn during his life, but it can be found in *Poetical Works*, 8:397–400.

I stood on a scaffold and called, to about a thousand wild, gaping people, "Behold the Lamb of God," etc. [John 1:29]. Four ministers confessed it was the truth. All seemed hugely pleased, and rejoiced that I should preach again in the evening at the other end of the town.

The whole town was then gathered together, with many out of the country. My text was, "I send thee to open their eyes, to turn them from darkness to light" [Acts 26:18]. Three of the ministers were present again, and the provost, or governor of the town, with many of the better sort, in the opposite houses. I was enabled to speak closely, both to pharisees and publicans. Many of the latter wept.

*Tuesday morning (September 6),* between four and five, was surprised to find as numerous an audience as last night's. Breakfasted with the only family of Quakers in the town. They behaved with that love and zeal which we meet with in all *the Friends,* till their worldly-wise and envious brethren pervert them, and make their minds evil affected towards us.

Two men from Kinsale came to press me thither. I expounded the Prodigal Son [Luke 15:11-32], but could not get through half of it. They drank in every word. In the evening I began again with a sore throat, an heavy heart, and a feeble body. To them that have no might, God increaseth strength.[78] For an hour and an half I strongly called the weeping prodigals to their heavenly Father. Many Romans were present, and others who had not been near a church for years.

Spent an hour in the town hall with some hundreds of them, in prayer and singing. They were impatient to have a Society, and to take the kingdom of heaven by violence.[79] I commended them to the grace of God, and departed, laden with their blessings.

Rode to Kinsale with my trusty lawyer, and at noon walked to the market-place. The windows were filled with spectators rather than hearers. Many wild-looking people stood with their hats on in the street. The boys were rude and noisy. Some well-dressed women stood behind me, and listened. My text was, "Go out quickly into the lanes and streets of the city, and bring in the poor, the lame," etc. [Luke 14:21]. I did most earnestly invite them all to

---

78. Cf. 2 Cor. 12:9.
79. Cf. Matt. 11:12.

the Great Supper. It was fallow ground, yet the word was not all lost. Several settled into serious attention. Others expressed their approbation. A few wept.

I was followed to my lodgings by a *devout* soldier, one of our Society in Dublin, who keeps his integrity. Some others called, and convinced me God hath not left himself without witness in this place.

In the evening the multitude so trod on one another that it was some time before they could settle to hear. I received a blow with a stone on the side of my head, and called on the person to stand forth and, if I had done him any wrong, to strike me again. This little circumstance increased their attention. I lifted up my voice like a trumpet, and showed the people their transgressions, and the way to be saved from them. They received my saying, and spake well of the truth. A sudden change was visible in their behaviour afterwards, for God had touched their hearts. Even the Romans owned "none could find fault with what the man said." Only one did most bitterly curse me, and all that should ever pray for me.

*Thursday, September 8.* The rain drove us to the market-house, a far more convenient place for preaching. I was surprised to find such a multitude in such weather. They sank down on every side into a just sense of their wants.

The next time several of the better rank of Romans came to hear for themselves, and a whole army of soldiers. All were profoundly silent as soon as I opened my mouth in the words of our dying Lord, "Is it nothing to you, all ye that pass by?" [Lam. 1:12]. The love of Christ crucified bore down all before it.

A lady of the Romish church would have me to her house. She assured me the governor of the town (called the Sovereign), as soon as he heard of my coming, had issued out orders that none should dare disturb me; that a gentleman, who offered to insult me, would have been torn to pieces by the Romans, had he not fled for it; and that the Catholics, in general, are my firm friends.

It is worth observing that in Kinsale I am of every religion. The Presbyterians say I am a Presbyterian; the Church-goers, that I am a minister of theirs; and the Catholics are sure I am a good Catholic in my heart.

Returned to Cork. Here the witnesses increase, so that we lose count of them.

*Friday, September 9.* Got the whole morning to myself, and my beloved friends in Wales. Had sweet fellowship with them in reading their letters, and saw them, as it were, all about me at the throne of grace.

*Saturday, September 10.* A man and his wife laid hold on me and said, "We have followed you from Bandon, to Kinsale, and hither. And if we had not found you here, our hearts are so warm toward you, we would have followed you to Dublin, and all the world over." They so urged me to come once more to Bandon that I could not refuse. Some from Middleton and Youghal pressed me to them also.

In conference, met a gentlewoman who has lately received forgiveness, when she was scarcely seeking it.

Preached, at the south prison, "What must I do to be saved?" [Acts 16:30] and made a collection for the prisoners.

Prayed a second time with Sally Gwynne,[80] a sincere mourner, just ready for *the consolation.*

Met the extraordinary young woman, strong in the Lord, impatient to sell all. I charged her to continue in her calling, and wait upon Him for direction.

*Sunday, September 11.* Heard a plain, useful sermon at St Peter's against judging. Such crowds at church and Sacrament were never seen before. So immediately is the gospel, the power of God, saving from sin. Multitudes, from their first hearing it, left off to do evil and learnt to do well.[81]

Much refreshed by part of the Bishop of Exeter's late charge to his clergy, worthy to be written in letters of gold:

> My brethren, I beg you will rise up with me against only[82] moral preaching. We have been long attempting the reformation of the nation by discourses of this kind. With what success? Why, with none at all. On the contrary, we have very dexterously preached the people into downright infidelity. We must change our voice; we must preach Christ and him crucified. Nothing but the gospel is,

---

80. This is not his future wife, but an Irish woman with the same name. It is clear that Charles notes the irony, because he wrote the name in larger script than normal.

81. Cf. Isa. 1:16-17.

82. The word "only" has been written in above the line. It is not clear if the hand is that of Charles himself. "Only" was not found in the original document that Charles is quoting.

nothing will be found to be, the power of God unto salvation, besides. Let me, therefore, again and again request, may I not add, *let me charge you*, to preach Jesus, and salvation through his name; preach the Lord who bought us; preach redemption through his blood; preach the saying of the great High Priest, "He that believeth shall be saved." Preach repentance towards God, and faith in our Lord Jesus Christ.[83]

*Monday, September 12.* Got to Bandon by eleven. My poor woman and her husband soon found me out, and carried me to their house in triumph. The neighbors flocked in, and we had indeed a feast of love. A prodigal came, who had been a monster of wickedness for many years, but is now returned to the Father. So are more of the town, who were wicked to a proverb.

I spake with a woman whom the word has wounded, and convinced that God is among the Protestants. She was bred a Protestant, but turned young to the Romans, and has continued with them these twenty years. She told me she never could rightly believe that any man could forgive her her sins. But Jesus Christ has the power, she is persuaded, and therefore returns to those who preach forgiveness in His blood.

Invited above four thousand sinners to the Great Supper [Luke 14:15-24]. God hath given them the hearing ear. I went to Mrs Jones's,[84] a widow-gentlewoman, as teachable as a little child; determined to promote the work of God to the utmost of her power. All in the place *seem* like minded, except the clergy. O why should they be the last to bring home their King?

It grieved me to hear the poor encouragement given last Sunday to the crowds that flocked to church, which some of them had never troubled for years. We send them to church to hear ourselves railed at and, what is far worse, the truth of God.

*Tuesday, September 13.* We parted with many tears and mutual blessings. I rode on to Kinsale. Here also the minister, Mr Parkinson,

---

83. Wesley is quoting a single-sheet flyer that was distributed in August 1748 purporting to be an extract from the charge George Lavington, Bishop of Exeter (1746–1762), had just given to the clergy in his diocese. This extract, which seemed to show some approval of Methodism, was fictitious. Indeed, Lavington accused the Methodists of promoting the fraud—a charge Lady Huntingdon helped disprove. Lavington's response was to publish his three-part *The Enthusiasm of Methodists and Papists Compared* (London: Knapton, 1749–1751).

84. The wife of John Jones, who had twice been provost of Bandon.

instead of rejoicing to see so many publicans in the temple, *enter-tained* them with a railing accusation of me as an impostor, incendiary, and messenger of Satan. Strange justice, that Mr Parkinson should be voted a friend of the Church, and I an enemy, who send hundreds into the Church, for him to drive them out again.

At noon I discoursed on the Prodigal Son [Luke 15:11-32]. Many approved by silent tears. I could not dismiss them without a word of advice, how to behave toward their enemies, persecutors, and slanderers.

*Thursday, September 15.* After proclaiming liberty to the captives[85] at Cork, took horse for Middleton. Preached there at noon to an attentive congregation, who pressed me much to come again.

Rode on to Youghal, a seaport town twenty Irish miles from Cork. Went forth to the strand. A wild multitude following almost crowded me and one another to death. While I described our Lord's passion, the waves subsided, the noise ceased, and they earnestly listened to His last dying cries.[86] The minister (as well as people) testified his satisfaction, saying, as I am told, "These gentlemen have done a great deal of good. There is need enough of them in Youghal."

Lodged at Mr Price's, a friendly Dissenter who, with his family, received me cordially for my work's sake.

*Friday, September 16.* The rain quickened our pace to Middleton. Here my audience was thrice as numerous as yesterday. The town-hall could not contain them. All listened to their own history in the Prodigal [Luke 15:11-32], and begged hard for a continuance of the gospel.

The power of the Lord was present in the Society at Cork. I marvel not that Satan so hates it. We never meet but some or other is plucked out of his teeth.

Riding with the wind and rain in my face has brought back my old companion the toothache. I feared it would hinder my taking leave of the people. But let my Lord look to that.

*Saturday, September 17.* After a restless night of pain, rose to confer with those that desired it. A woman testified that the Lord

85. Cf. Isa. 61:1.
86. Cf. the note on the September 3–4, 1741, entry above.

spoke peace to her trembling soul at the Sacrament; Thomas Warburton, that faith came by hearing, and now he hates all sin with a perfect hatred and could spend his whole life in prayer.

Stephen Williams witnessed that, "Last night I found my heart burdened and bursting in your prayer. But I repeated after you, till my speech was swallowed up. Then I felt myself as it were fainting, falling back, and sinking into destruction. When on a sudden I was lifted up, my heart was lightened, my burden gone, and I saw all my sins at once, so black, so many, but all taken away. I am now afraid of neither death, devil, or hell. I am happier than I can tell you. I know God has for Christ's sake forgiven me."

Two others, in whom I found a real work of grace begun, were Papists till they heard the gospel; but are now reconciled to the Church, even the true, invisible church, or communion of saints, with whom is forgiveness of sins. A few of these lost sheep we pick up, but seldom speak of it, lest our own good Protestants should stir up the Papists to tear us in pieces.

At Mr Rolt's, a pious Dissenter, I heard of the extreme bitterness of his two ministers, who make it their business from house to house to set their people against the truth, and threaten all that hear us with excommunication. So far beyond the Papists are these *moderate men* advanced in persecution.

*Sunday, September 18.* Rose, as I laid down, in pain, which confined me the whole day. I prayed God to suspend it, if it was his will I should speak an useful word at parting with his people. I went to meet them at five, for a few minutes. The marsh was quite covered. Above ten thousand, as was supposed, stood fixed in deep attention. Not a breath was heard among them all. I faintly read my text (Acts 2:42), "And they continued," etc. They observed my weakness, and prayed me strong. I urged them to walk as the first followers of Christ. My words sunk into their hearts, and melted them into tears. For two hours we wept and rejoiced together; commended each other again and again to God.

I mentioned with honor the behaviour of our own clergy, not one of whom has publicly spoken the least word against us. I had told them before, and now I told them again, that persecution will arise because of the word. Great confidence and love the Lord gave me for them, and we parted most triumphantly, with the voice of joy and thanksgiving.

*Monday, September 19.* Rose at two, refreshed as with wine, and set out with Robert Swindells. My pain was kept off by the prayer of those I left behind. Reached Cashel by night. Our host, a serious Roman, and his neighbor, an hearty loving Quaker, made us forget our journey.

*Tuesday, September 20.* Reached Templemore by nine. Met several clergy, who were attending the Archbishop, come to confirm. Preached at my inn door. The people behaved better at the end than the beginning.

Found the twelve miles to Roscrea good six hours' riding; the rain attended us all the way. At five came to Mr White's, sated with travelling. But I had not time to rest, the people demanding me. My knees and eyes failed me, so that I could neither stand nor see. Leaned on a door, and called, "Is it nothing to you, all ye that pass by?" [Lam. 1:12]. The word was not weak, like me.

*Wednesday, September 21.* By four we got to Mountmellick. Preached in the market-house to a crowd of poor, convinced sinners. Could mention nothing but pure promises. They received the word as souls gasping for God.

*Thursday, September 22.* Took in thirty new members. Rode to B—, at the pressing instance of a clergyman, who met, carried me home, and, after fairly proposing his objections, and attending to my answers, allowed me to speak with great closeness and particular application.

By four we came to Mr Jackson's in Birr. I preached "the Lamb of God that," etc. [John 1:29]. The power of the Highest overshadowed us.[87] One gentlewoman sunk down at Jesus' feet. Most seemed affected.

*Friday, September 23.* Talked with my host's brother, a publican indeed! A monster of wickedness lately, but now so changed that all the town is alarmed by it. At five preached in a barn of Mr Wade's near Aughrim; seldom with greater power. Left a young woman in the pangs of regeneration.

*Saturday, September 24.* By one the Lord brought us safe to our beloved brethren in Athlone. No Father Farrell, or his volunteers,

---

87. Cf. Luke 1:35.

withstood our entrance. The door is wide opened, at the expense of one life indeed, if not more. For the first news I heard was that the poor big-bellied woman who covered John Healy from his enemy is lately dead of the blows she then received.

Preached in the market-house, and met the Society in a barn, which a well-disposed Roman lends us, to the great dissatisfaction of his fellows. Our poor lambs were all in tears, mourning after Jesus.

*Sunday, September 25.* Examined each of the Society, who make upward of two hundred. A soldier followed, and told me, "that while I was talking to them, an horrible dread overwhelmed him. He *knew* I was a servant of God; saw himself as called to the bar; felt the burden of all his sins; shook, every bone of him, and trembled exceedingly, for fear of God's judgments." I could not hinder his falling down again and again at my feet, under such piercing apprehensions of God, the righteous Judge, as made me envy his condition.

Accepted of an invitation from the Rev Mr T.; comforted the mourners at the market-house by all the precious promises of the gospel, summed up in Isaiah 35.

Dined with Mr R., a gentleman of the Romish persuasion till he heard my brother; since which, both he and his house, with several others, are come over to the Church of England and, what is far better, to the power of godliness.

In the evening preaching the great blessing came. The cries of the wounded spirits cannot be described. The place rung with loud calls for "mercy, mercy!" I concluded, and began again, and again; then sung, and prayed, and sung, not knowing how to give over.

*Monday, September 26.* Took leave in those solemn words, which reached their hearts: "And now, brethren, I commend you to God," etc. [Acts 20:32]. At three came safe to our dear friends at Tyrrellspass. It should not be forgot that the condemned soldier told me at parting that the Lord had absolved him.

*Tuesday, September 27.* Found much life in applying those words, "Behold, I stand at the door, and knock" [Rev. 3:20]. Took horse for Dublin. Young Mr Wade accompanied me three or four miles. His mother died last week in peace. He is swiftly following her, through the last stage of a consumption. Has not yet attained, but *knows* he shall not depart till his eyes have seen *His* salvation. I commended him to the Lord Jesus, and appointed to meet him next in paradise.

I rode on alone, yet not alone. My noon hour of prayer refreshed my spirit. My absent friends were never *less* absent. Came before night to Dublin.

*Wednesday, September 28.* Breakfasted with Mrs Folliard, whom I left mourning, and found rejoicing in Christ her Savior. The Society is in a flourishing condition. Spent from twelve to one as usual, in our garden, with my Christian friends. They never fail to meet me at the throne, in my retirement.

*Friday, September 30.* At night our Lord pierced many hearts with his dying cries.[88] Two received faith, many a deeper sense of his love.

# OCTOBER 1748

*Saturday, October 1.* It was the first time of my meeting the bands. The Lord was with us, and we rejoiced unto him with reverence.

*Sunday, October 2.* One received the blessing under the word. As soon as the Society was met, the fire was kindled. Three or four testified the grace of our Lord, which they then first experienced. A poor revolter who, like Demas,[89] had forsaken us, stealing in this evening, found mercy unexpected. His servant at the same time *felt* her sins forgiven, and gave God the glory. So did two or three more. Eight or nine confessed their faith openly. I believe all present rejoiced either in hope or in possession of their Savior.

*Friday, October 7.* Met at Mr Lunell's an old Dutch Quaker who seemed to have deep experience of the things of God. At two Mr Lampe and his wife called, and were overjoyed to see me. I cannot yet give up my hope that they are designed for better things than feeding swine—that is, entertaining the gay world.

*Saturday, October 8.* The wind brought in a packet boat, then sunk away into a dead calm. However, we attempted at night to get out to sea. The particulars I sent to a friend:[90]

---

88. Cf. the note for the September 3–4, 1741, entry above.
89. Cf. 2 Tim. 4:10.
90. The journal letter for this period identifies the recipient as Mr Lunell.

Holyhead, October 10th

My very dear Brother

I did not tell you at parting, that I never had a stronger apprehension of evil near. On Saturday evening, half-hour past eight, I entered the small boat. We were two hours getting to the vessel. There was not then water to cross the bar. So we took our rest till eleven on Sunday morn. Then God sent us a fair wind, and we sailed smoothly before it five knots an hour. All things promised a speedy, prosperous passage. Yet still I found *the* burden upon my heart, usual in times of extreme danger.

Towards evening the wind freshened upon us, and we had full enough of it. I was called to account for a bit of cake I had ate in the morning, and thrown into violent exercise. Up or down, cabin or deck, made no difference. Yet in the midst of it I perceived a distinct and heavier concern for I knew not what.

It was now pitch-dark, and no small tempest lay upon us. The captain had ordered in all the sails. I kept mostly upon deck till half-hour past eight, when, upon my inquiry, he told me he expected to be in the harbour by nine. I answered we would compound for ten. While we were talking, the mainsail (as I take it) got loose, and flew overboard as [if] it would drag us all after it. The small boat at the same time, for want of fastening, fell out of its place. The master called, "All hands upon deck," and thrust me down into the cabin. Within a minute we heard a cry above, "We have lost the mast!" A passenger ran up, and brought us worse news, that it was not the mast, but the poor master himself, whom I had scarcely left when the boat, as they supposed, struck him overboard. From that moment he was seen and heard no more. My soul was bowed before the Lord. I knelt down, and commended the departing spirit to His mercy in Christ Jesus. I adored His distinguishing goodness. "The one shall be taken, and the other left" [Matt. 24:40]. Thought of those lines of Young:

> No warning given! unceremonious death!
> A sudden rush from life's meridian joys,
> A plunge opaque beyond conjecture![91]

The sailors were so confounded they knew not what to do they did. The decks were strewed with sails, boat, etc; the wind shifting

---

91. This quote is from "Night II" of Edward Young's *The Complaint, or Night Thoughts on Life, Death and Immortality* (London: Dodsley, 1742–1745); but Charles is quoting from the slightly abridged form that John reprinted (without Young's permission!) in *MSP* (see 2:260).

about; the compass they could not get at; nor the helm for some time. We were just on the shore, and the vessel drove where or how they knew not. One of our cabin-passengers ran to the helm, gave orders as captain till they had righted the ship. But I ascribe it to our invisible Pilot, that we got safe to the harbour soon after ten. The storm was so high, we doubted whether any boat would venture to fetch us. At last one answered, and came. I thought it safer to lie in the vessel. But one calling, "Mr Wesley, you must come," I followed, and by eleven found out my old lodgings at Robert Griffith's.

*Monday, October 10.* Blessed God that I did not stay in the vessel last night. A more tempestuous one I do not remember. Wrote a thanksgiving hymn:

> All praise to the Lord,
> Who rules with a word, etc.[92]

At half-hour past nine took horse with my host, in a perfect hurricane. Were wet through in less than ten minutes. But I rode on, thankful that I was not at sea. By one reached the Bull's Head.[93] Paid off my extorting guide, and trusted Providence to conduct me over the Welsh mountains. Rode near three miles before my genius for wandering prevailed. Then I got out of the way to Bol-y-don ferry, but was met by a Welsh child, and set right again. Near five I entered the boat with a clergyman, and others, who crowded our small, crazy vessel. The water was exceeding rough, our horses frightened, we looking to overset every moment. The minister acknowledged he was never in the like danger. We were half drowned in the boat. I sat at the bottom with him and a woman, who stuck very close to me, so that my swimming would not have helped me. But the Lord was my support, and I cried out to my brother clergyman, "Fear not. *Christum et fortunas vehis!*[94] The hairs of our head are all numbered.[95] Our Father sits at the helm."

Our trial lasted near half an hour. Then we landed, wet and weary, in the dark night. The minister was my guide to Caernarfon;

---

92. Cf. "Thanksgiving for a Deliverance from Shipwreck," *HSP* (1749), 2:235–36 (*Poetical Works*, 5:378–79).
93. An inn in Llangefni, Anglesey, seven miles west of Menai.
94. "You carry Christ and fate." Julius Caesar was said to have encouraged the captain of a war ship during a storm with the words "*Caesarem Vehis*"—"you carry Caesar."
95. Cf. Matt. 10:30; Luke 12:7.

and by the way entertained me with the praises of a lay-preacher he had lately heard, and talked with. He could say nothing against his preaching, but heartily wished him ordained. His name, he told me, was Howell Harris. He carried me to his own inn, and at last found me out, which increased our intimacy.

*Tuesday, October 11.* Set out at break of day. Missed my way as soon as I could, but quickly recovered it. Rode on with a cheerful heart in the bright, sunshiny day to a small village three miles beyond Tan-y-Bwlch. From three to nine I enjoyed myself in solitude.

*Wednesday, October 12.* Set out at six; got to Dolgellau by nine. Took a guide for the first hour, and then came by myself triumphantly to Machynlleth. Here I got another guide, who soon led me out of all way. We wandered over the mountains at random, and I was quite reconciled to the thought of taking up my lodging there. But Providence sent us directors again and again, when we most wanted them. We rode down such precipices that one false step would have put an end to all our journeys. Yet the Lord brought us through all, and by seven we rejoiced to find ourselves in Llanidloes.

*Thursday, October 13.* Soon after five set out in the dark with a brother, who by eight delivered me over to Mr [Hugh] Edwards, curate of Rhayader. He could get no horse for love or money, and therefore waited on me on foot to Garth. Met our dearest friends there by twelve, in the name of the Lord, and rejoiced and gave thanks for his innumerable mercies. At seven I preached with life and faith, and at ten rested from my labours.

*Friday, October 14.* Rested the whole day, only riding out for an hour, to pray by a sick, helpless publican. Preached morning and evening to the family; I hope not in vain, but miss my Cork congregation.

*Saturday, October 15.* Mr [Rice] Williams read prayers at Llansantffraed.[96] I preached from Matt. 11[:28], "Come unto me, all that are weary," etc. We were all in tears after Him who promises us rest. An happier time have I not known; no, not at Cork or Bandon. Returned with the night to Garth.

---

96. Llansantffraed-yn-Elfael, Radnorshire. Charles spells "Llansaintfraid."

*Sunday, October 16.* Preached there at eight, and in Maesmynis church at eleven. It was a solemn season of love, and yet more so at the Sacrament. At Builth I published the end of Christ's coming; namely, "that they might have life" [John 10:10]. Preached a fourth time, at Garth, and set the terrors of the Lord in array against the unawakened.

*Monday, October 17.* Rode with Mr Gwynne to Builth and, preaching there at noon, returned to our little church at Garth.

*Tuesday, October 18.* Rode to Maesmynis with most of the family, and enforced those triumphant words of the departing Apostle, "I have fought a good fight," etc. [2 Tim. 4:7]. Great consolation was thereby administered to us. Forty sincere souls, whom the storm could not discourage, joined in receiving the Lord's Supper. It was a Passover much to be remembered. All were melted down in prayer. We were not unmindful of our absent brethren, or of those that travel by water. The church about us was rocked by the tempest. But we had a calm within. O that it might last till we all arrive at the haven! Preached the third time at Builth, and once more at Garth.

*Wednesday, October 19.* Preached again in Llansantffraed church, and took leave of our family in the evening.

*Thursday, October 20.* Set out with brother [Edward] Phillips in the dark and rain. Had not rode a quarter of a mile before I was struck through with pain as with a dart. Whether it was the rheumatism in my shoulder, or what else, I know not. But it took away my breath in an instant, and stopped my progress. I lay some time on my horse, unable to bear the least motion, but determined not to turn back till I fell off. In a few minutes I could bear a foot-pace, and then a small trot. As the rain increased my pain decreased. I was quickly wet to the skin, but some fair blasts dried me again, and in five hours I got well to Bwlch.

After an hour's rest took horse again, and came swiftly to Usk, before five. We went early to bed. Rose at three the next morning.

*Friday, October 21.* Set out soon after five, and by eight were brought safe to the New Passage. Were from ten to twelve crossing, and came to Bristol between one and two.

Called on Mrs Vigor,[97] uncertain if she was escaped out of the body. Found her (or rather her shadow) still in the vale, and was much comforted by her calm desire of dissolution. She has no doubt of God's finishing his work in her soul before he calls her hence. But he has, I am persuaded, more work for her to do.

Passed the afternoon among my friends, who are much alive unto God. Called on a listening audience, "Rejoice with me, for I have found the sheep that was lost" [Luke 15:6], and we did rejoice with all the angels in heaven over our younger brethren in Ireland.

*Saturday, October 22.* Rode over to our children in Kingswood, and was much comforted by their simplicity and love.

At night the leaders brought me a good report of the church in general. They walk as becometh the gospel.[98]

*Sunday, October 23.* Our Lord met us at his own table, and our souls lay low and happy at his feet.

In [the] Society the Lord comforted us on every side. It was like one of the former days. We were brought a large step on our journey to Sion.

*Monday, October 24.* Met the select band[99] for the first time. The cloud overshadowed us, and we all said, "It is good to be here!"[100]

Rode to Coleford under a great burden. What would I not have given to escape preaching? But as soon as I opened my mouth the skies poured down righteousness. In the Society we seemed all rapt up. A cloud of witnesses arose. Five or six received forgiveness, and testified it. We rejoiced with joy unutterable. My body was quite spent. Mr Phillips did not much commend our accommodations. Our chamber looked very ghastly, scarce affording a prophet's furniture. Our bed had but one thin quilt to cover us.

*Tuesday, October [25].*[101] Rode to Paulton, where my horse cast me to the ground with such violence as if I had been shot out of an engine. I lay breathless for some time. They set me up on the horse,

---

97. Mrs Elizabeth Vigor (d. 1775), widowed mother of Francis Vigor, became a close friend of Charles and Sarah Wesley; cf. Charles's mournful poem on her death, *Poetical Works*, 6:341–42.
98. Cf. Phil. 1:27.
99. The select band was for leaders and those who had experienced sanctifying grace.
100. Cf. Matt. 17:4.
101. MS has "October 26," which is in error, and remains one day off for the next two entries.

and led me to Bristol. Got a surgeon to dress my arm and hand, which were much bruised, and my foot crushed.

*Wednesday, October [26].* Woke with a stiff neck and aching bones, which did not interrupt my business, public or private. Preached at night with enlargement of heart.

*Thursday, October [27].* Preached at five with some pain in my breast, which wears off more and more.

# NOVEMBER 1748

*Wednesday, November 2.* At sister Perrin's the Spirit helped our infirmities in mighty prayer, and filled us with divine confidence. I had then no doubt, even of my own perseverance.

*Friday, November 4.* Imparted my design to Mrs Vigor, who advised me with all the kindness and freedom of a Christian friend.

*Monday, November 7.* Had tender sympathy with a sick, absent friend, Mrs B. L., and much of the divine presence in praying for her.

*Thursday, November 10.* Expounded Isaiah 35 at the Foundery, and lost all my burdens among my brethren.

*Friday, November 11.* My brother and I having promised each other (as soon as he came from Georgia) that we would neither of us marry, or take any step towards it, without the other's knowledge and consent, today I fairly and fully communicated every thought of my heart. He had proposed three persons to me: Sarah Perrin, M. W., and Sarah Gwynne; and entirely approved my choice of the last. We consulted together about every particular, and were of one heart and mind in all things.

*Saturday, November 12.* Waited on Dr Cockburn, who paid me £50, part of the legacy which my old friend Mrs Sparrow left me.

*Monday, November 14.* Rejoiced over our sister [Sarah] Peters, whose spirit was on the wing for paradise.

*Wednesday, November 16.* At the hour of intercession the Lord looked upon us, and we lay a long time at his feet weeping. Talked with my brother about a provision, in case I married, and he said "the church could not afford it." Then, I thought, the church did not deserve a gospel minister.

*Friday, November 18.* Consulted old Mr [Vincent] Perronet, who thought a few of my particular friends might subscribe what would be sufficient for my maintenance, and offered himself to set the example.

*Monday, November [21].*[102] Set out with Mr Waller for Bristol; and on Wednesday met our Lord there, in the midst of his disciples.

*Friday, November 25.* Visited our sister Amos, supposed to be near death. Her joy was so great the earthen vessel could scarce contain it. Her love and thanks and blessings on me lifted up my hands and heart. I offered up myself, with my absent friends, in fervent, faithful prayer.

*Monday, November 28.* Rode to Cardiff.

*Tuesday, November 29.* Mr James[103] overtook us at Fonmon. Both at Cardiff and here was much assisted in preaching.

# DECEMBER 1748

*Thursday, December 1.* Rose at two, and, after prayer, set out with Mr James. The moors were almost impassable. Yet we got to Brecon soon after three.

*Friday, December 2.* By nine found them at Garth, singing, and was most affectionately received by all, especially Mrs Gwynne.

Advised with Sally how to proceed. Her judgment was that I should write to her mother.

While the family was at dinner, I got some of *my* flock together, Miss Betsy [Gwynne], Molly Leyshon,[104] Betty Williams, and faithful Grace Bowen,[105] with whom I spent a comfortable hour in prayer. In the evening I pressed upon them, with much freedom,

---

102. MS has "November 22," which is in error.
103. This is likely Thomas James, a Brecon attorney and early supporter of the Methodist movement.
104. Molly Leyshon (d. 1750) was Sally Gwynne's cousin. Her mother was Mary Leyshon (*née* Gwynne, d. 1774), the sister of Marmaduke Gwynne. Charles spells "Leyson."
105. Grace Bowen (d. 1755), nurse for the Gwynne family. See Charles's two-part hymn on her death in *Funeral Hymns* (1759), 24–28 (*Poetical Works*, 6:239–44).

that blessed advice, "Acquaint thyself now with God, and be at peace" [Job 22:21].

**Sunday, December 4.** Rode with Sally and Betsy to Maesmynis. Our Lord administered strong consolation to our souls by the word and Sacrament. At Builth, also, we were all melted into tears. Preached at Garth with the same blessing. Took farther counsel with Sally, quite above all guile or reserve. Afraid of making the proposal. The door of prayer was always open.

**Monday, December 5.** Spake with Miss Becky [Gwynne], who heartily engaged in the cause, and at night communicated it to her mother, whose answer was, "she would rather give her child to Mr Wesley than to any man in England." She afterwards spoke to me with great friendliness above all suspicion of underhand dealing (the appearance of which I was most afraid of), said she had no manner of objection but "want of fortune." I proposed £100 a year. She answered, her daughter could expect no more.

**Wednesday, December 7.** Preached twice a day, and never with more liberty.

**Thursday, December 8.** A little tried by the brutishness of my friend Phillips,[106] who got my advocate, M—n,[107] over to his side. But their buffetings did me no great harm.

Mr Gwynne leaving the whole to his wife, I talked the matter fully over, and left it wholly with her to determine. She behaved in the most obliging manner, and *promised her* consent, if I could answer for £100 a year.

**Friday, December 9.** Prayed and wept over my dear Miss Becky, in great pain. She begged me not to leave them tomorrow.

**Saturday, December 10.** Mr Phillips called me, whom I mildly put by. Preached the next day, with great utterance and emotion. Talked once more with Mrs Gwynne, entirely open and friendly. She promised to tell me if any new objection arose, and confessed, "I had acted like a gentleman in all things."

---

106. Edward Phillips was interested in Sarah Gwynne himself. His close relationship with Wesley did not survive the marriage of Charles and Sarah.

107. Likely John Meriton.

*Monday, December 12.* Took a cheerful leave, and set out with Harry and Mr Phillips, somewhat milder. His only concern now was for the people. Them also, I told him, my brother and I had taken into the account, and I had taken not one step without my brother's express advice and direction. We lodged at Usk.

*Tuesday, December 13.* Rejoiced with my Christian friends in Bristol.

*Thursday, December 15.* Preached at Bath, in my way to London.

*Friday, December 16.* Soon after four set out with Mr Jones, in thick darkness and hard rain. We had only one shower, but it lasted from morning till night. By half hour past eight we got, in sad plight, to Calne. Left it within an hour, as wet as we came to it, sore against my companion's will, who did not understand me when I told him, "I never slack my pace for way or weather." In a quarter of an hour we were wet from head to foot, the rain driving in our faces. On the Downs the storm took my horse off his legs, and blew me from his back. Never have I had such a combat with the wind. It was labour indeed to bear up against it.

No foot of earth unfought the tempest gave.[108]

Many times it stopped me as if caught in a man's arms. Once it blew me over a bank, and drove me several yards out of the road before I could turn. For a mile and an half I struggled on, till my strength was quite spent. There was little life in either me or my companion when we came to Hungerford. We dried ourselves, and I scarcely persuaded him to go on to Newbury. There I was forced to leave him, and push forward to Woolhampton by seven.

*Saturday, December 17.* Took horse by four, by starlight. Such cheerfulness of heart, such a sense of joy and thankfulness, I have seldom known. For five hours I quite forgot my body. Thomas Hardwick met me at Maidenhead, with a post-chaise, and carried me to Brentford, when my last reserve of strength was gone. By four found my brother at the Foundery, and rejoiced his heart with the account of my prosperous journey.

---

108. A slight revision of Samuel Wesley, Jr., "To the Memory of the Right Rev Francis Gastrell," ln. 233, *Poems* (1736), 136. Original: "No Spot of Earth unfought the Hero gave."

He had advised me to make the experiment directly, by going to Garth, and talking with Mrs Gwynne. Her negative (or his, or Sally's) I should have received as an absolute prohibition from God. But hitherto it seems as if the way was opened by particular Providence.

*Monday, December 19.* So my wise and worthy friend at Shoreham thought when I communicated to him the late transactions. As to my own judgment I set it entirely out of the question, being afraid of nothing so much as trusting my own heart.

*Wednesday, December 21.* Talked with Mr Blackwell,[109] who very freely and kindly promised to assist in the subscription of £100 a year. I thought it better to be obliged for a maintenance to ten or a dozen friends, than to five hundred or five thousand of the people.

In the morning discoursed on Thomas's confession, "My Lord, and my God" [John 20:28]; and in the evening on the divine testimony, "This is my beloved Son," etc. [Matt. 3:17].[110] Great life and power accompanied and applied the word.

*Friday, December 23.* Visited our brother [Alexander] White, who has again found mercy on his death-bed, which is to him a triumphal chariot.

*Saturday, December 24.* Disclosed my affair to good Perronet, who most violently opposed, offered me his sister; appeased by little and little; at last offered his utmost assistance.

*Christmas Day.* Told Mr [William] Holland, who was much for it; as are all to whom I have yet communicated it, except Mrs Cart. We rejoiced in the glad tidings, "To us is born a Savior" [Luke 2:11], and yet more in the Sacrament were filled with all peace and joy in believing.

*Tuesday, December 27.* One received the pardoning love of God under the word this morning.

*Friday, December 30.* Met Mr Blackwell with my brother, who proposes £100 a year to be paid me out of the books.

---

109. Ebenezer Blackwell (d. 1782), a partner in Martin's Bank, London. The hymn that Charles wrote upon Blackwell's death can be found in *Poetical Works*, 6:353–56.

110. While there are parallel accounts in Luke and Mark, Wesley quotes the Matthew account below (May 13, 1750). The emphasis on God bearing witness suggests Wesley is dealing with the baptismal account in Matthew, rather than the Transfiguration (17:5).

*Saturday, December 31.* The more I pray, the more assured I am. God will not suffer the blind to go out of his way. He was with us at his own table, in solemn power. My ministrations were never more lively, never more blessed to my own and the people's souls.

I married Thomas Hardwick and Sally Witham. We were all in tears *before* the Lord.

Rejoice to hear of our brother White's translation. Described it in the following hymn:

> O what a soul-transporting sight
> Mine eyes today have seen,
> A spectacle of strange delight
> To angels and to men!, etc.[111]

# JANUARY 1749

*Tuesday, January 3.* My brother wrote as follows to Mrs Gwynne.[1] I enclosed it in my own, and sent both letters, after offering them up to the divine disposal.

Buried Alexander White, and preached on "I have fought the good fight, I have finished my course," etc. [2 Tim. 4:7]. We were all partakers of His joy.

*Monday, January 9.* Visited sister Smith, sick and in pain, but her pain was swallowed up in love. "Were I to choose," said she, "I should choose death. But let my Lord choose for me. I want nothing but his love."

*Friday, January 13.* Read undisturbed a letter from Mrs Gwynne, dissatisfied with my brother's proposal. Visited Mr Perronet the next day. He has indeed acted the part of a father, another proof whereof is this letter of his to Mrs Gwynne.

Shoreham, January 14, 1748 [2]

Madam

As the trouble of this proceeds from the most sincere friendship, I have reason to believe you will easily excuse it.

---

111. Cf. "On the Death of Alexander White," *HSP* (1749), 2:83–86 (*Poetical Works*, 5:224–28).

1. Despite this apparent introduction, the text of what John wrote is not given in the MS Journal. Moreover, John's letter does not appear to be extant.

2. This dating is in "old style." It is really January 1749.

Give me leave then, Madam, to say, that if you and worthy Mr Gwynne are of opinion that the match proposed by the Revd. Mr Charles Wesley be of God, neither of you will suffer any objections drawn from this world to break it off. Alas, Madam, what is all this world, and the glories of it? How little does the world appear to that mind, whose affections are set on things above! This state is what I trust you are seriously seeking after. I am sure it is a state worth every Christian's seeking after, and what every Christian must seek after, if ever he hopes to get to heaven.

I have a daughter now designed for a pious gentlemen whose fortune is not half that of our friend's, and yet I would not exchange him for a Star and Garter.[3] I only mention this that I might not appear to offer an opinion which I would not follow myself.

However, I have been hitherto speaking as if Mr Wesley's circumstances really wanted an apology. But this is not the case. The very writings of these two gentlemen are, *even at this time, a very valuable estate*; and when it shall please God to open the minds of people more, and prejudice is worn off, it will be still much more valuable. I have seen what an able bookseller has valued a great part of their works at, which is £2,500, but I will venture to say, *that this is not half their value.* They are works which will last and sell while any sense of true religion and learning shall remain among us. However, as they are not of the same nature with an estate in land, they cannot be either sold or pledged without the most manifest loss and inconvenience.

I shall trouble you, Madam, no farther than only to add that from the time I had the pleasure of seeing Miss Gwynne at my house, I have often had her upon my mind. I then perceived so much grace and good sense in that young lady, that, when this affair was first mentioned to me, I could not help rejoicing at what promised so much happiness to the church of God.

May that God, in whose hands are the hearts of the children of men, direct all of you in such a manner as may tend to the promoting His honor, and the kingdom of his dear Son. I am, with great respect to worthy Mr Gwynne, yourself, and good family, Madam,

Your very sincere and affectionate friend and servant,

Vincent Perronet

---

3. I.e., for a duke.

*Monday, January 23.* Received letters from Garth, consenting to our proposals.

*Saturday, January 28.* I married William Briggs and Elizabeth Perronet, who seem quite made for each other.

*Tuesday, January 31.* Found life and comfort in the small remnant at Deptford.

# FEBRUARY 1749

*Tuesday, February 14.* Assisted to preach twice a day the last fortnight, and pitied an unhappy friend for her confident assertion that the Lord is departed from me. Let the rest of her words and actions be buried in eternal oblivion.

At four this morning set out for Garth, with my brother and Charles Perronet. At Kensington my horse threw me. My foot hung by the spur. My company were gone before, when a servant flew to my help, and I rose unhurt.

*Wednesday, February 15.* Dined at the Rector of Lincoln's.[4] Waited on our Dean[5] and others. All extremely civil.

*Friday, February 17.* Our wanderings through the bogs etc. ended at eight in the evening. Sally met me before I entered the house with news that her brother[6] was come, and very vehement against the match. Yet he received us with great courtesy.

*Saturday, February 18.* Mrs Gwynne was extremely open and affectionate; has fought my battles against her own relations, particularly her son, who has behaved very violently towards her. Miss Becky told him he might think it a great honor done him by my proposal. Mrs Gwynne, my brother, and I had a conference. He repeated his proposals and agreed to make them good, being entirely reconciled to the settlement, for which Mr Gwynne and Mr Perronet were to be the trustees.

*Sunday, February 19.* Returned to Garth from the Sacrament at Maesmynis. Mr Howell Gwynne was very obliging. Drove his

---

4. Euseby Isham.
5. John Conybeare.
6. Howell Gwynne (1718–1789).

father to church, where we heard a good sermon. Had a conference with my brother and Sally. She promised to let me continue my vegetable diet and travelling.

*Monday, February 20.* Mr Howell Gwynne was now as affable as the rest; said he had nothing to object, and behaved as if his heart was entirely turned towards us.

*Tuesday, February 21.* My brother and Charles Perronet left us. I stayed a week longer, preaching twice a day.

*Sunday, February 26.* Mrs Gwynne assured me she should not change; talked freely of our marriage, and would have got me to promise not to go again to Ireland. But Sally would not let me, saying she should be glad herself to visit the many gracious souls in that country.

*Monday, February 27.* Commended them once more to God, and took horse with Harry. It rained all day, yet we reached Usk by night, and the next morning breakfasted at Bristol.

# MARCH 1749

*Friday, March 3.* Met George Whitefield, and made him quite happy by acquainting him with my design.

*Monday, March 6.* Mentioned it to the select band, desiring their prayers, not their advice.

*Friday, March 10.* Prayed by happy Sally Huntington. The approach of death has put all her troubles to flight.
Miss Burdock (to whom I told my affair) expressed the strongest approbation. Had a very solemn watch-night.

*Thursday, March 16.* Rode with Charles Perronet in a day and an half to London. Expounded, in bodily weakness, Hab. 3[:17], "Though the fig-tree shall not blossom," etc. The power of the Lord was present, and great love we felt towards each other.

*Saturday, March 18.* Returning from Shoreham, I narrowly escaped being crushed to death by a dray on London Bridge.

*Sunday, [March] 19.*[7] An extraordinary blessing attended the word preached both at the chapel and every other place. In the Sacrament I was constrained to pray again and again, with strong cryings and tears. So it was every day of this *great and holy week.*

*Easter Day, March 26.* The convincing and comforting Spirit reached our hearts, both in the word and Sacrament.

In the evening I took my leave of the Society, who express a general satisfaction in my intentions. Surely, both Jesus and his disciples are bidden.

*Wednesday, March 29.* Having by the help of Mr [Samuel] Lloyd and his lawyers settled everything to Mrs Gwynne's wish, I set out at three with Charles Perronet for Bristol, in my way to Wales. Lodged the first night at Oxford.

*Thursday, March 30.* Took horse again at seven, and God prospered our journey to Cirencester. Expounded Rom. 8:32, and met the Society, to our mutual comfort.

*Friday, March 31.* My text in the morning was, "If ye then be risen with Christ, seek the things which are above, where Christ sitteth at the right hand of God" [Col. 3:1]. He strongly drew our hearts after Him, as the tears of many testified.

I stopped to pray by an aged woman, who lay a-dying, and knew not God. She then received faith to be healed. By two we came to Felix Farley's, and soon after to Kingswood, where we found our beloved sisters Murray and Davey, who joined us in prayer and joyful thanksgiving.

# APRIL 1749

*Saturday, April 1.* Just as we were setting out for Wales, my brother appeared full of scruples, and refused to go to Garth at all. I kept my temper, and promised "if he could not be satisfied there, to desist." I saw all was still in God's hands, and committed myself to Him.

*Sunday, April 2.* The Lord opened my mouth to apply those weighty words, "If ye then be risen with Christ, seek the things which are above" [Col. 3:1].

7. MS has "May 19," which is in error.

I had wrote our friends notice that I should be at Cardiff tomorrow, and on Tuesday or Wednesday at Garth. But found my brother had appointed to preach in several places till Friday, which I did not take kindly.

*Monday, April 3.* He seemed quite averse to signing his own agreement. Yet at five we set out with an heavy heart. Our brother Thomas met us on the Welsh side. Before five I came, weary, faint, oppressed, to Cardiff, and lay down, being unable to stand.

*Tuesday, April 4.* Met Mr [John] Hodges at Fonmon. He asked me, "My brother, what are you seeing in this thing? Happiness? Then you will be sadly disappointed. If an help and comfort only, look up to God and he will surely give it you." Heard my brother at the castle, and again in the morning.

*Wednesday, April 5.* Lodged with him at Llantrisant.

*Thursday, April 6.* Was his hearer at five, and nine, and twelve, in Aberther church. By seven we got to Brecknock.[8] An hour after, Mr [Thomas] James came. Waited with him on Mr [Edward] Williams the surrogate for a licence.[9] He was extremely civil, refusing his fees from a brother clergyman.

*Friday, April 7.* Rose at four, and got ~~some~~ an hour for prayer and the Scripture. That word in particular came with power to my heart, "Thus saith the Lord, 'if my covenant be not with day and night, and if I have not appointed the ordinances of earth and heaven, then I will cast away the seed of Jacob, and David my servant . . . for I will cause their captivity to return, and will have mercy upon them' " [Jer. 33:25-26].

Came to Garth by nine, found them at breakfast. Almost equally welcome to all. We talked over matters with Mrs Gwynne, and all my brother's fears were scattered. Read over the settlement. Mrs Gwynne proposed a bond, till it could be signed. My brother signed the bond and Miss Becky and Miss [Molly] Musgrave witnessed it.

We crowded as much prayer as we could into the day.

---

8. Another (older) name for Brecon.
9. This marriage license survives, held at MARC (ref. DDCW 6/49).

# SATURDAY, APRIL VIII, 1749[10]

Sweet day! so cool, so calm, so bright,
The bridal of the earth and sky![11]

Not a cloud was to be seen from morning till night. I rose at four;
spent three hours and an half in prayer, or singing, with my
brother, with Sally, with Becky. At eight I led MY SALLY[12] to
church.[13] Her father, sisters, Lady Rudd,[14] Grace Bowen, Betty
Williams, and, I think, Billy Tucker[15] and Mr James, were all the
persons present. At the church-door I thought of the prophecy of a
jealous friend, "that if we were even at the church-door to be married, she was sure, by revelation, that we could get no farther." We
both smiled at the remembrance. We got farther. Mr Gwynne gave
her to me (under God). My brother joined our hands. It was a most
solemn season of love! Never had I more of the divine presence at
the Sacrament.

My brother gave out the following hymn

     1. Come thou everlasting Lord,
       By our trembling hearts adored;
       Come, thou heaven-descended Guest,
       Bidden to the marriage-feast!

     2. Sweetly in the midst appear,
       With thy chosen followers here.
       Grant us the peculiar grace,
       Show to all thy glorious face.

     3. Now the veil of sin withdraw,
       Fill our souls with sacred awe,
       Awe that dares not speak or move,
       Reverence of humble love.

---

10. Written in all capitals in the MS, with a clear intention for emphasis.
11. "Virtue Altered from Herbert," st. 1, HSP (1739), 9 (Poetical Works, 1:10).
12. So written in the MS, with a clear intention for emphasis.
13. The Llanlleonfel parish church in Garth.
14. Lady Elizabeth Rudd (c. 1706–1802); widow of Sir John Rudd (d. 1739), 4th baronet, of
Aberglassney; and (since 1740) wife of Howell Gwynne, so Sally's sister-in-law. She apparently retained her titled name because there were no other heirs to the Rudd title.
15. William Tucker, of Sithney, who was traveling with John Wesley.

4. Love that doth its Lord descry,
   Ever intimately nigh,
   Hears whom it exults to see,
   Feels the present Deity.

5. Let us on thy spirit rest,
   Dwell in each devoted breast;
   Thou with thy disciples sit,
   Thou thy works of grace repeat.

6. Now the ancient wonder show,
   Manifest thy power below;
   All our thoughts exalt, refine,
   Turn the water into wine.

7. Stop the hurrying spirit's haste,
   Change the soul's ignoble taste;
   Nature into grace improve,
   Earthly into heavenly love.

8. Raise our hearts to things on high,
   To our Bridegroom in the sky;
   Heaven our hope and highest aim,
   Mystic marriage of the Lamb.

9. O might each obtain a share
   Of the pure enjoyments there;
   Now, in rapturous surprise,
   Drink the wine of Paradise;

10. Own, amidst the rich repast,
    Thou hast given the best at last;
    Wine that cheers the host above,
    The best wine of perfect love![16]

He then prayed over us in strong faith. We walked back to the house, and joined again in prayer. Prayer and thanksgiving was our whole employment. We were cheerful without mirth, serious without sadness. A stranger, that intermedleth not with our joy,

---

16. "A Wedding Song," *Hymns for the Use of Families* (Bristol: Pine, 1767), 172–73 (*Poetical Works*, 7:196–97).

said, "It looked more like a funeral than a wedding." My brother seemed the happiest person among us.

*Sunday, April 9.* We all partook of the Lord's Supper, and our souls were satisfied with his comforts. Spent good part of the day in writing letters. Heard my brother at night.

*Monday, April 10.* At four my brother took his leave of us. Passed the day in prayer, chiefly with my dearest friend. In the afternoon Mr [Roderick] Gwynne of Glan Bran[17] came to visit them. He took no notice of me, or I of him. Explained at night the happiness of religion from Prov. 3. and invited them to partake of it.

*Tuesday, April 11.* Rode with Mr Phillips to Builth. The Lord applied his most precious promise, "I will pour out the Spirit of grace and supplications" [Zech. 12:10].

Discoursed at Garth, with delightful enlargement, on "The One Thing Needful" [Luke 10:42].

*Sunday, April 16.* Preached constantly the last week at Garth; only once at Llansantffraed. Carried my beloved Sally to Maesmynis. We had sweet fellowship in the Sacrament and in prayer. Rode on to Llansantfraed, and preached a third time at Garth, with a close application on watching unto prayer [1 Pet. 4:7].

*Monday, April 17.* The Lord was never more with me than he was at Builth, while I spake from those words, "These are they that came out of great tribulation" [Rev. 7:14]. All the hearers were in tears, but it was a blessed mourning.

*Thursday, April 20.* Took my leave of Garth in those words of our Lord, "Be thou faithful unto death, and I will give thee a crown of life" [Rev. 2:10].

*Friday, April 21.* Took horse with Sally, Betsy, and my father. Slept at Abergavenny.

---

17. "Glanbran" has been added, apparently in the hand of Charles Wesley, to an empty space in the MS Journal. Glan Bran (i.e., Llanfair-ar-y-bryn) is an estate on the west bank of the Bran River, about one mile southwest of Cynghordy, Carmarthenshire. This estate was inherited by Roderick Gwynne (1695–1772), the brother of Marmaduke, in 1734.

*Saturday, April 22.* Cheerfully left my partner for the Master's work, and rode on with Harry to Bristol. We made so much haste that I left all my strength behind me. Was glad to go to bed as soon as I came in.

*Sunday, April 23.* Dr Middleton sweated, blooded, vomited me. Yet on Monday I attempted to preach; but my body failed.

*Wednesday, April 26.* Received strength to urge my hearers to come boldly to the throne of grace. The word was quick and powerful. Had a second blessing among the bands.

*Thursday, April 27.* I had prayer for a blessing upon the word this day, and God heard and answered, while I expounded John 17. There was scarce a soul present that was not broken down.

*Friday, April 28.* Some letters from Garth brought life with them. I prayed and wept over the beloved writers.

In the evening proceeded in my exposition of John 17. And still our Lord owned the words for His.

*Saturday, April 29.* "They that seek me early shall find me" [Prov. 8:17]. This word was made good to the morning audience.

*Sunday, April 30.* Had a solemn, joyous Sacrament in Kingswood. At Conham I thundered, "O ye dry bones, hear ye the word of the Lord" [Ezek. 37:4].

# MAY 1749

*Monday, May 1.* Never since I preached the gospel have I been more owned and assisted of God than now. He is always with me in the work of the ministry. Therefore I live by the gospel.

*Thursday, May 4.* Preached at Cirencester and Oxford, in my way to London, which I reached on Saturday afternoon.

*Sunday, May 7.* At the chapel my subject was, "The end of all things is at hand" [1 Pet. 4:7]; at the Foundery, "Thou shalt show me the path of life" [Ps. 16:12, BCP]. The word was really a means of grace to our souls. Met the Society in very great love, which was only increased by my change of condition. I am married to more than one or one thousand of them.

*Monday, May 8.* Found a blessing in examining the classes. Left out a careless girl, and her mother came abusing me with horrid oaths and curses. Satan, I perceived, did not like our work.

Heard, in the evening, that old Mr Adams had brought two constables for me. The poor men were hugely civil and hugely frightened; said they would not see me, but I might send bail. John Heally had threatened him in the morning, if he forced his way into the house again, to put him in the bathing-tub. I had shut the door upon him. Justice Fielding had very wisely granted him a warrant against me.

I chose to have a hearing of it directly, and went with Mr Perronet, Hoy, [Robert] Windsor, Briggs, and John [Heally], to the next justice, Mr Withers. He received us with great civility; said, "I am sorry, gentlemen, this has happened; but assure you, you shall have no farther trouble, only your bail." On mentioning Adams, "What!" cried he, "that old man who makes disturbance in the streets? I saw him yesterday raising a riot, and he commanded me to attend him in the name of the Lord. I wonder my brother Fielding would grant a warrant to such a madman. He did not consider the consequence." After ten Mr Adams came. The justice examined the warrant particularly, and showed it was no assault. Asked, "Did they threaten your life?" "No, but Heally threatened to duck me," said the old man; abused the justice, told him I had bribed him, and would have been sent to Newgate for so saying, had we not interposed.

The justice assured [us] he would take care of him, if ever he molested us more; made the clerk give back his fees; marked the warrant, "Litigious, malicious, vexatious, false"; discharged the bail, and promised us all the assistance in his power on all occasions.

*Friday, May 12.* Waited on him again, hearing Adams had got me presented at Hick's Hall. The justice said I need give myself no trouble about it; he should be there himself. The next day the bill was thrown out.

*Whitsunday, May 14.* Preached the promise of Christ and the Father [Acts 1:4-5], with the demonstration of that Spirit; and received it *partly* with the Sacrament. Our brother Thomson partook with us, and declared "he was in heaven!"

*Tuesday, May 16.* A woman, in baptism, received both the outward visible sign and the inward spiritual grace.

*Friday, May 19.* Joined in the Lord's Supper with our happy dying sister Kempthorn.

*Monday, May 22.* Left London at two in the afternoon, and came to Bath on Tuesday evening.

*Thursday, May 25.* My exhortation was blessed to the Society at Bristol. On mention of the persecution in Cork, a spirit of sympathy ran through all our hearts.

*Saturday, May [27].*[18] Hired a small horse near my worthy Friend Vigor's, such an one as suited a stranger and pilgrim upon earth.

*Sunday, May 28.* Had a glorious time at Kingswood, never better.

*Monday afternoon, May 29.* At Mrs Dicken's in Bath I met Miss Stonehouse, the sister of my old friend. Shall I ever meet my poor dear George again? Preached to a very fine audience, whom I did not spare.

# JUNE 1749

*Friday, June 2.* Took horse at two, and got to Hereford by one. At half-hour past three my beloved Sally, with Mrs Gwynne and her[19] sister Peggy,[20] found me at the Falcon. We sang, rejoiced, and gave thanks till Mr and Mrs Hervey came. After dinner drank tea at their house, and went to see the cathedral. I wanted work, but there was no door opened.

*Saturday, June 3.* Carried my companion to Ludlow, to which the family lately removed. My mother and sisters Becky, Betsy, [Mary] Baldwyn,[21] received me as I expected. Brother Duke[22] and the Captain[23] could not be civiller.

---

18. MS has "May 29," which is in error.
19. Written "Sally with [her mother and] sister Peggy." The words in brackets have been struck through and amended above the line as given, in what appears to be Charles's hand.
20. Margaret ("Peggy") Gwynne (1733–1752).
21. Mary [Gwynne] Baldwyn, Sarah's oldest sister.
22. Marmaduke Gwynne, Jr. (b. 1722).
23. Captain Edward Baldwyn, Mary's husband.

*Sunday, June 4.* The pulpit was refused me. But not the Sacrament. In the afternoon the boys began gathering, and throwing eggs and stones. Mr Gwynne sent for the bailiff, who himself fetched the refractory constable, and seized the ringleader of the mob. This quelled the increasing riot.

I preached, with tolerable quiet, on "Repent, and believe the gospel" [Mark 1:15].

*Monday, June 5.* With more enlargement, and to a better behaved congregation, from, "Behold the Lamb of God, who taketh," etc. [John 1:29]. I stood at the door; got one stone at last.

*Tuesday, June 6.* Drove my wife to visit Captain Baldwyn, and very gently overturned without hurting her in the least. My hearers at night were very tumultuous, yet could do no mischief.

*Thursday, June 8.* Preached at the market-place in Leominster, "Is it nothing to you, all ye that pass by?" [Lam. 1:12]. All appeared quite eager to hear. Exhorted about forty serious people in an house at Ludlow to work out their salvation [Phil. 2:12-13]; and the blessing of the Lord was with us.

*Friday, June 9.* Rode with Sally to Leominster, and expounded Isaiah 55 in the market-place. The minister was there again. All serious, some visibly affected. Dr Young entertained us till we got to Coleford, late at night. It was fair time. With difficulty we got a private lodgings.

*Saturday, June 10.* Came by noon to our dear Mrs Vigor's. The Lord welcomed us there, and at night among the leaders, with the blessing of peace.

*Sunday, June 11.* Preached first in the streets, and then at Kingswood. My partner and all present rejoiced in the Consolation of Israel [Luke 2:25-32].

*Tuesday, June 13.* Felt every word I spoke this morning. What comes from the heart usually goes to the heart.

*Wednesday, June 14.* Threw away some advice on an obstinate preacher (James Wheatley). For I could make no impression on him, or in any degree bow his stiff neck.

*Thursday, June 15.* Spake in conference with a woman admitted lately among the witnesses of pardoning love. At night preached "Jesus Christ, the same yesterday, to day, and for ever" [Heb. 13:8]. Most of the congregation were in tears. Many cried after Him. Some even fainted under the sense of his love.

*Monday, June 19.* Found much life in the select band. James Jones was carried out in fervent prayer for my partner and me.

Carried her to Captain [John] James's, where Miss Burdock helped to increase our joy in the Lord.

*Friday, June 23.* Expounded Moses' wish[24] at the watch-night; and the Lord came down into many faithful hearts.

*Saturday, June 24.* We waited on Dr Middleton, who received us very cordially. All look upon my Sally with my eyes.

*Wednesday, June 28.* Read the Society an account of the persecution at Cork. All were inflamed with love, grief, pity. We parted in the spirit of prayer.

*Thursday, June 29.* Carried my companion by Bath, to Seend. Many listened to the word of grace.

*Friday, June 30.* Lodged six miles short of Marlborough.

# JULY 1749

*Saturday, July 1.* She was quite spent with heat and fatigue, when John Heally and Thomas Hardwick met us at Salt Hill with two chaises. Between eight and nine we got to our lodgings in Moorfields. Who should wait at Mrs Boult's to receive us, but Mrs —, as if she came to atone for her past misbehaviour, like cursing Shimei meeting David.[25]

*Sunday, July 2.* The chapel was excessively crowded, while our Lord applied his own saying, "Behold, I stand at the door and knock," etc. [Rev. 3:20]. Many heard, and testified that they heard, His voice. Satan came with the sons of God, in the shape of an old

---

24. This was likely on Moses' request to see God's glory and for God's presence to go with the people as they prepared to leave Mount Sinai (see Exod. 33:12–34:9).
25. Cf. 2 Sam. 16:5-6.

perjured enthusiast. I ordered him (Mr Adams) to be taken quietly out of the church whenever he appeared to disturb the work of God. Colonel Gumley was weak enough to be offended, and went out too. But the Lord did not depart.

He was with us again in his word, "O Israel, thou hast destroyed thyself" [Hos. 13:9]; and at our feast of love.

*Wednesday, July 5.* God, by his word this morning, ministered strong consolation to those in the wilderness.

*Thursday, July 6.* Disowned John Healy before the Society, for beating the poor old madman.

*Saturday, July 8.* Mr [Vincent] Perronet having come to see my partner, today we returned with him to Shoreham. There I left her with such as knew her value, and hastened back to meet the penitents.

*Sunday, July 9.* Closed the busy, blessed day with Dr Young and faithful John Downes.

*Monday, July 10.* Dined with the preachers, and was troubled of at James Wheatley's obstinacy. He is gone to the north, expressly contrary to my advice. Whither will his wilfulness lead him at last?

*Thursday, July 13.* Fetched my feeble companion from Shoreham.

*Friday, July 14.* Returning from the watch-night, I found her extremely ill.

*Wednesday, July 19.* Gave the Sacrament to our old sister Batchelor, rejoicing in pain and sickness. I found brother Pike still happier, because nearer the haven where he would be.

*Thursday, July 20.* At Ned[26] Perronet's met Mrs Vazeille, a woman of a sorrowful spirit.

*Sunday, July 23.* Preached a funeral sermon over sister Bouquet and brother Pike, departed in the Lord, and added a seasonable word at their graves.

---

26. "Ned" is Charles's nickname for Edward Perronet; others, including Edward's father, apparently referred to him as "Ted." Cf. letter in November 4, 1749, entry below.

*Monday, July 24.* I was riding over Hounslow Heath with my wife behind me, when an highwayman crossed the road, passed us, and robbed all the coaches and passengers behind us. By Wednesday evening God blessed our coming in to Bristol.

*Saturday afternoon, July [29].*[27] Mr B—n, with a troop of his friends, came to visit us at our lodgings in Stokes Croft. Poor N. S., at the sight of so many predestinarians, fell into a transport of passion and grief. I tried to pacify her with counsel and prayer. At night we were honored with a crowd of the great vulgar, between forty and fifty of them in their coaches.

*Sunday, July 30.* Our worthy brother Grimshaw assisted at Kingswood, and partook of our feast.

I preached, in a field near Lawrence Hill, the word of power and truth and reconciliation.

At the Society we seemed filled with the spirit of love and of prayer.

# AUGUST 1749

*Thursday, August 3.* Our conference this week with Mr Whitefield and Mr Harris came to nought; I think through their flying off.

*Friday, August 4.* Kept a watch-night, but dismissed the people at ten, as an alarm was gone forth of the colliers rising.

*Saturday, August 5.* Gave the Sacrament to a dying sister— unjustified till very lately, now ready for the Bridegroom. Then to Sarah Perrin, desiring neither life nor death, but that God might be magnified.

*Sunday, August 6.* With my partner, and all our Kingswood children, exceedingly comforted at the Lord's table, my mouth being opened in strong exhortation and fervent prayer.

*Monday, August 7.* At six took horse with Sally for Ludlow, and Thomas Butts, and Captain James, my brother, and Grace Murray overtook us before we reached the Passage. Near nine we took up with a sorry lodging two miles short of Hereford.

---

27. MS has "July 28," which is in error.

*Tuesday, August 8.* Dined with our hospitable friends in Ludlow.

*Wednesday, August 9.* Several of the gentry listened to my brother at night.

*Thursday, August 10.* My brother, having signed the settlement, set out at four with Grace Murray and James Jones. Thomas Butts and I took horse at six. It rained all day. Preached at Evesham with much life. The next evening met my brother and Grace Murray, who came through Birmingham to Oxford, and on.

*Saturday, August 12.* Attended him to London.

*Tuesday, August 15.* We had the satisfaction of two hours' conference at Mr Watkins's, with that loving, mild, judicious Christian, Dr [Philip] Doddridge.

*Tuesday, August 22.* Preached at Evesham with great effect.

*Wednesday afternoon, August 23.* Rejoiced to find Sally and the rest well at Ludlow. Continued with them a week, preaching the gospel with little fruit.

*Wednesday, August 30.* At nine set out with Sally, Becky, Betsy, and Peggy. Preached in Leominster, from Isaiah 61, with a blessing, even the blessing of the gospel. Lay at Hereford, whence Becky returned home.

*Thursday, August 31.* Lodged at Thornbury.[28]

# SEPTEMBER 1749

*Friday, September 1.* By eleven saluted our Friend Vigor. Saw my house, and consecrated it by prayer and thanksgiving.[29] Spent an hour at the preaching-room in intercession. Began the hour of retirement with joint prayer. Alone, in some measure sensible of the divine presence. Opened the book on those words, "While they spake, Jesus stood in the midst of them, and said, Peace be unto you" [Luke 24:36]. At six ~~my~~ our first guests, Mrs Vigor and her sisters,

---

28. Thornbury, Gloucestershire, twelve miles north of Bristol.
29. This is the house still present on Charles Street, Bristol, in which Charles and Sarah would live for the next twenty years.

passed an useful hour with us. I preached on the first words I met, Rom. 12:1, "I beseech you therefore, brethren, by the mercies of God, that ye present your bodies a living sacrifice," etc. The power and blessing of God was with us. Half-hour past nine I slept comfortable in my own house, yet not my own.

*Saturday, September 2.* Family prayer at eight. Began the New Testament. Passed the hour of retirement in my garden, and was melted into tears by the divine goodness.

*Sunday, September 3.* Sally accompanied me to our feast in Kingswood. Poor Betsy was kept away by illness.

*Monday, September 4.* Rose with my partner at four. Both under the word and among the select band we were constrained to cry after Jesus with mighty prayers and tears.

Sang this hymn in my family:

1. God of faithful Abraham, hear
        His feeble son and thine,
    In thy glorious power appear,
        And bless my just design:
    Lo! I come to serve thy will,
        All thy blessed will to prove;
    Fired with patriarchal zeal,
        And pure primeval love.

2. Me and mine I fain would give
        A sacrifice to Thee,
    By the ancient model live;
        The true simplicity;
    Walk as in my Maker's sight,
        Free from worldly guile and care,
    Praise my innocent delight,
        And all my business prayer.

3. Whom to me thy goodness lends
        Till life's last gasp is o'er,
    Servants, relative, and friends,
        I promise to restore;
    All shall on thy side appear,
        All shall in thy service join,
    Principled with godly fear,
        And ~~witnesses~~ worshippers divine.

> 4. Them, as much as lies in me,
> I will through grace persuade,
> Seize, and turn their souls to Thee
> For whom their souls were made;
> Bring them to the atoning blood,
> (Blood that speaks a world forgiven,)
> Makes them serious, wise, and good,
> And train them up for heaven.[30]

In the evening was that word fulfilled, "Him that cometh unto me, I will in no wise cast out" [John 6:37], by the reception of a poor sinner to the favour of God in Christ Jesus.

*Thursday, September 7.* As often as I minister the word, our Lord ministers his grace through it. He blessed me also in private, as well as family, prayer, and conference with my Christian friends. In a word, whatsoever I do prospers.

*Sunday, September 10.* There was a multitude of guests at our Lord's Supper; and none of them, I would hope, sent empty away.[31]

*Friday, September 15.* My throat grew worse and worse, so that I could not preach in the evening.

# OCTOBER 1749

*Sunday, October 22.* Rode with Mr Waller and my family to Kingswood. After the Sacrament, we found the usual spirit of prayer.

*Wednesday, October [25].*[32] Among my hearers today at Bath were a son of Lord Chief Justice Lee;[33] my old school fellow, Sir Danvers Osborn;[34] and Lord Halifax.[35] They behaved decently, and were particularly taken with the singing. In the evening God sent forth his awakening power, and his fear fell on all that heard the word.

---

30. Charles did not publish this personal hymn written to celebrate their new home, but it can be found in *Poetical Works*, 8:401–2.

31. Cf. Matt. 15:32; Mark 8:3.

32. MS has "October 24," which is in error.

33. William Lee (b. 1726) was the son of Sir William Lee (1688–1754), who served as Lord Chief Justice, 1737–1754.

34. Danvers Osborn (1715–1753), 3rd baronet; married to Lady Mary Montagu, the sister of Lord Halifax; and currently MP of Bedfordshire.

35. George Montagu-Dunk (1716–1771), 2nd Earl of Halifax (1739–1771).

*Thursday, October 26.* Visited my house in peace.

*Saturday, October 28.* Heard that my brother was come. Troubled and burdened, yet went to him. No love or joy or comfort in the meeting. No confidence on either side. He did not want to talk with me. Came home and then was much comforted in prayer with Perronet and Jones.

*Sunday, October 29.* Dead, dead, dead at the Sacrament. Rode back quite miserable, through [David] Trathen's information that he had seen and been locked up with Grace Bennet,[36] and [he] was still desirous to marry. Mournful discourse with Sally. Lost all strength and heart; weighed down to the earth. Went to talk with him; the effect παροξυσμός.[37]

*Monday, October 30.* Sent a sad account to Mr Perronet:

Dear Sir:

I write out of the fulness of my heart. Last Saturday our friend came hither. I went heavily to see him. He spoke very slightly of the fatal letter, insensible both of his own folly and danger, and of the divine goodness in so miraculously saving him. Yesterday I assisted him at the Sacrament, but my mouth was stopped all day, my hands hung down, and my heart fainted. At night we had a second weary παροξυσμός. Forced by his impatience, I had showed him my account of what has lately happened, though I judged it far better to defer it till his passion should be laid and his eyes opened. It had the effect I expected. He denied the whole. "William Shent's account was all lies. Jane Keith's was all lies. His only was all true. He had been in no fault at all, in no passion or inordinate affection, but had done all things well, and with the utmost calmness and deliberation. He had been no temptation; the church and work in no danger. That was nothing but my needless panic." As soon as I could recover my astonishment, I told him plainly he was given up to Jewish blindness of heart; that the light which was in him was darkness; that God would overcome; but wherefore should he be smitten any more? I declared I would cover his nakedness as long as I could, and honor him

---

36. The former Grace Murray, now married to John Bennet (1715–1759).

37. παροξυσμός is probably used here by Charles with the negative sense of "a sharp disagreement" or "irritation"; though the rather more positive "a stirring up" or a "provoking" or "encouraging," perhaps in love (cf. Heb. 10:24), is also possible.

before the people; and if I must at last break with him, would retreat gradually, and hide it from the world. He seemed pleased with the thought of parting. Though God knows, as I told him, that I had saved him from a thousand false steps. And still I am persuaded we shall stand or fall together. If he would not foresee the consequence of marrying, I said, he must marry and feel them afterward, while lying at the mercy of the good bishop of Exeter. What the end of this thing will be only God knoweth, but the cloud at present hanging over us looks very black.

*Tuesday, October 31.* I had designed to preach, but towards the time lost all strength and heart.

# NOVEMBER 1749

*Thursday, November 2.* Heard him preaching, but how unlike himself!

*Saturday, November 4.* Letter to Mr Perronet:

Dear Sir

Since I wrote last, my soul has been exceeding sorrowful, and dragged down my body with it. I had fully designed to stand in our friend's place, and labour more abundantly till his spirit should revive, and his strength and reason return. But his added to my own was a burden too heavy for me to bear. My own you may suppose implies my partner's, to whom this affliction will perhaps prove fatal, so Dr Middleton says he has reason to fear. She was struck down upon my departure September 18, and my return in such weight of evil has well nigh completed the ruin. One cause of rejoicing I shall have, if she is taken from the evil to come. But alas for him who seethes the kid in its mother's milk.[38] Yesterday he took my wife into his room, told her he almost scrupled to say what he was going to say, yet broke through the scruple, and read her his own account, trying all he could to make a difference between her and me. She could say nothing to his confident assertions, though the grossest misrepresentations and falsifications of facts. This last act of unkindness wounded me more than all the rest. Your son Ted is come and confirms all my account, told us

---

38. Cf. Exod. 24:36.

that our friend has acted with most miserable weakness and imprudence, proposed marriage to one at Leeds, said where ever he came he was going to be married. Talked to him of coming straight to Kingswood and marrying his servant there immediately, and asked him whether he thought I should stay with him afterward. Ted honestly told him that neither he nor I should continue with him, if he acted so basely.

*Wednesday, November 8.* Set out for London, with my brother and Ned Perronet. In perils of robbers, who were abroad, and had robbed many the night before. We commended ourselves to God, and rode over the [Hounslow] Heath, singing.

*Friday, November 10.* Kept a joyful watch-night at the Foundery.

*Sunday, November 12.* Heard that our sister [Martha] Somerset was gone to glory.

God, who giveth power to them that faint, was with my mouth, and strengthened me to preach the word with success.

*Friday, November 17.* Had a conference of three days at Ned Perronet's. Old Mr Perronet was present, and well he was, for my brother flew out when contradicted, crying "If he must not have so much authority, he would have none at all." Mr Perronet hardly believed him. I modestly proposed that question "How far is your or my will a law to our preachers." But it was touching a sore place, meddling with the *arcana imperii*.[39] He showed the utmost uneasiness and impatience, telling me in Greek (on my urging the question) that I should ruin all, and threatening again to run away and live beyond [the] sea. Once more our good old friend humoured and stroked him into tolerable temper. I saw there was no good to be done, and half resolved I would never be at another conference.

Examined the classes, and returned in great bodily pain to Bristol.

# DECEMBER 1749

*Friday, December 1.* Hardly reached my own house, quite exhausted as I was with pain of body and vexation of spirit.

---

39. "State secrets."

Had little power for several days, and less inclination to preach. My greatest comfort was the conversation of a few faithful friends, such as Mrs Vigor, Sarah Perrin, Mrs [Anne] Davis, and Suky Burdock.

*Wednesday, December 13.* Answered a soothing letter of Mr Perronet's:

Dear Sir,

I thank you for speaking to my brother, but in vain do you refer me to him for the result of your conference. I am no longer of his council, since he and I were together. All the security I desired, which you then thought reasonable, was his bare word that he would not take a step of so general importance without advice. He has brought down my strength, and I am next to useless. For when I preach, which is very seldom, my word is without power or life. My spirit is that of the whole people. All are faint and weary. All seem on the brink of desperation.

*Monday, December 18.* My birthday. FORTY[40] years long have I now grieved and tempted God, proved him, and seen his works. I was more and more sensible of it all day, till I quite sunk under the burden.

*Saturday, December 23.* Letter to Mr Perronet:

Reverend and Dear Sir,

Charles was exactly right in telling me. Your last was the voice of despairing friendship. You said nothing to the purpose of satisfying me, because you had nothing to say. Neither am I now surprised by your last. *Nulla mali nova mi facies inopinave venit.*[41] I expected no other than our friend's rejecting me out of his council, refusing to advise with me at all about marriage, which is the same as if he had wrote *res tuas tibi habito.*[42] I must strive indeed to "believe the best," or even to hope it. The cry of nature is . . . *occidit, occidit spes omnis!*[43] For I know with whom I have to do. Advise him against his inclination, he answers "wouldst thou

---

40. Charles would actually have been 42 that day; cf. the December 18, 1736, entry.

41. "You cause no new evil to come unanticipated before me." Cf. Virgil, *Aeneid*, vi.103–5, "*non ulla laborum, o virgo, nova mi facies inopinave surgit.*"

42. "I consider that to be your matter [, not mine]." Note that this was a standard Latin formula for divorce.

43. "Every hope is lost, is lost." Horace, *Odes*, IV.iv.70–71.

heave up Olympus?" He is resolved, I very well know, to make all sure the next time. His late deliverance by my ministry, and present silence of the world, gives ground to hope God will save him yet, in spite of himself. It is *dignus vindice nodus*.[44] High time for God to lay his hand, and send deliverance out of Sion. Lord, we are opprest, undertake for us. We know not what to do, but our eyes are unto you. Arise, O God, and maintain thine own cause.

*Sunday, December 24.* Preached with a little strength. Exhorted the Society with more.

*Christmas Day.* The room was full as it could contain! We rejoiced from four to six, that "to us a Son is born, to us a Child is given" [Isa. 9:6].

Received the Sacrament at the college.[45] In the evening, all were melted down at our solemn Love-feast.

## JANUARY 1750

*Monday, January 1.* At four in the morning our room was excessively crowded, while I proclaimed the gospel year of Jubilee. We did not part without a blessing.

*Friday, January 12.* Preached (with the old power) on "Said I not unto thee, if thou wouldst believe, thou shouldst see the glory of God?" [John 11:40]. Generally, my hands hang down, and I am so feeble in mind that I cannot speak.

*Sunday, January 14.* The Spirit helped our infirmity at Kingswood. Sacrament. A daughter of our brother Grimshaw's[1] was just departed in the Lord, being perfected in a short space.

*Wednesday, January 31.* We were waked at two by a clap of thunder, unusually loud and terrible. My partner was much frightened.

## FEBRUARY 1750

*Thursday, February 1.* Walked with her to Dr Middleton's. The rain a little quickened our pace.

---

44. "A knot worthy [of God] to untie." Horace, *Art of Poetry*, 191.
45. That is, Bristol Cathedral, on College-Green. This seat for the Bishop of Bristol was commonly referred to as "Bristol College."
1. Jane Grimshaw (1737–1750), of Haworth.

*Saturday, February 3.* She miscarried.

*Sunday, February 4.* Brought my friend Grimshaw home with me, comforted for his happy daughter. Had unlooked-for life in preaching.

*Thursday, February 8.* There was an earthquake in London.

*Friday, February 9.* Letter to Mr Perronet:

> Sally is slowly recovering her strength after her miscarriage last week. How far it was occasioned by our late affliction I cannot say, but my brother has cast poison into my cup of temporal blessings, and destroyed as far as in him lay all my future usefulness to the Church. Yet still I strive against the stream, and beat the air, dragging myself to the work without love or zeal or faith for it. So the poor people here find it, and so it will be if I come to London.
>
> My great comfort is, God does not want me. Let him send whom he will send. He hath sworn that the earth shall be full of his glory; and all things, persons, events, whether good or evil shall work together for this end, till the mystery of God is fulfilled.[2] Once I had great zeal and strong desires to be used as an instrument in his work, but now I only desire to rest and stand upon my lot at the end of the days.[3]

*Tuesday, February 13.* Preached with a little strength at Bearfield, and the next day with more at Freshford. The spirit of the people helped me. An old lady of fourscore received me into her house. We spent the time in prayer and singing. Stephen Naylor, a poor backslider, had another call to repentance, and seemed resolved to close with it. I invited, at night, many burdened souls to Christ, and his healing power was greatly present, and refreshed every weary spirit.

*Sunday, February 18.* Carried my sister Betsy to Kingswood, where the Lord visited us again and feasted us at his table.

*Monday, February 19.* My wife had recovered strength for her journey. We set out with our sisters Betsy and Peggy. Could not reach Newnham Passage[4] till past seven. It was then quite dark. The boat on the other side refused to come over. We were got to the

---

2. Cf. Rev. 10:7.
3. Cf. Dan. 12:13.
4. Ferry over the River Severn at Newnham, Gloucestershire.

edge of the bank, the usual place of embarking, when Providence sent a man to stop us. He informed us that the rains had choked up the river with two banks of sand, and where we were going was all quicksands. We followed him, with great difficulty, to another part of the river. My horse sunk up to the shoulders, but, with a violent plunge, struggled out. The boatmen at last took pity on us; came over, and with much pains carried us into the boat, and landed us safe on the opposite shore.

By *Wednesday, noon, February 21,* God conducted us safe to Ludlow. For the five following days I received fresh strength for the work, and rejoiced in some measure that the gospel had free course.

*Tuesday, February 27.* Preached in their new room at Evesham, and not without a sensible blessing. Met my brother the next day at Oxford.

# MARCH 1750

*Thursday, March 1.* Rode to London. Ned Perronet supplied me with a lodging. <u>Soon after my arrival Mr Blackwell called on me and with all his weakness recommended implicit obedience to my brother</u>.

*Sunday, March 4.* Visited old Lydia White on her death-bed. She accosted me, "Thou blessed of the Lord, art thou come? I did not expect to see my dear minister till we met in paradise. You and your brother are the instruments of my salvation. I have known the grace of the Lord Jesus long ago. Now I am entering into his glory. He has told me so. I am full of his joy now." Her words strengthened my hands, as I found at the chapel, speaking on those words, "Blessed is the man that endureth temptation" [James 1:12]. They sunk into many hearts. <u>Stood siege again from Mr Blackwell, a weak well-meaning man, giving him the hearing and answering only with my leg.</u>

*Monday, March [5].*[5] Prayed by my sister Wright,[6] a gracious, tender, trembling soul; a bruised reed, which the Lord will not break.

---

5. Charles has not given the date in the MS.
6. This is his sister Mehetabel (Hetty), married to William Wright. She would die March 21.

*Thursday, March 8.*[7]

*Friday, March 9.* Many flocked to the morning word, and were yet more stirred up thereby. Have scarce ever seen so many at intercession. At the chapel I preached on the occasion, from Psalm 46, with very great awakening power.

*Saturday, March 10.* Expounded Isaiah 24, a chapter I had not taken much notice of till this awful providence explained it: "Behold, the Lord maketh the earth empty, and maketh it waste, and turneth it upside down, and scattereth abroad the inhabitants thereof. [ . . . ] The foundations of the earth do shake. The earth is utterly broken down, the earth is clean dissolved, the earth is moved exceedingly. The earth shall reel to and fro like a drunkard, and shall be removed like a cottage; and the transgression thereof shall be heavy upon it; and it shall fall, and not rise again" [Isa. 24:1, 18-20].

Prayed by our sister Lewis, quietly expecting her release. Preached at Snowsfields, and urged them to enter into the Rock, now the Lord is risen to shake terribly the earth.

*Sunday, March 11.* My spirit and many others' seem revived by the late judgment. The word is with the accustomed power, both at London and Deptford, and wherever I minister it.

*Wednesday, March 14.* Found my sister Wright very near the haven; and again on Sunday, the 18th. Yet still in darkness, doubts, and fears, against hope believing in hope.[8]

Preached to a vast attentive multitude over our brother Hoy's grave. As he lived the life, he died the death of the righteous.[9] O might my last end be like his!

*Wednesday, March 21.* At four called on my brother Wright. A few minutes after her spirit was set at liberty. Had sweet fellowship with her in explaining at the chapel those solemn words, "Thy sun shall no more go down, neither shall thy moon withdraw itself. For

---

7. Charles gave the date, marked with an asterisk, and then left a full page and a half blank. He obviously intended to insert more detail at some point, undoubtedly about the earthquake that hit London that day. Cf. his *Hymns Occasioned by the Earthquake, March 8, 1750* (London: [Strahan], 1750).

8. Cf. Rom. 4:18.

9. Cf. Num. 23:10.

the Lord shall be thine everlasting light, and the days of thy mourning shall be ended" [Isa. 60:20]. All present seemed partakers both of my sorrow and my joy.

*Monday, March 26.* Followed her to her quiet grave, and wept with them that wept.[10]

# APRIL 1750

*Wednesday, April 4.* Saw several happy souls, in spite of their feeble, sick, or pained bodies. One I visited yesterday died in the faith soon after.

Mrs E.[11] came to the chapel-house, as usual, an hour before the service. I perceived she had been with *the Brethren* in her self-sufficiency and utter impatience of contradiction.

Fear filled our chapel, occasioned by a prophecy of the earthquake's return this night. I preached my written sermon on the subject,[12] with great effect, and gave out several suitable hymns. It was a glorious night for the disciples of Jesus.

*Thursday, April 5.* At four I rose after a night of sound sleep, while my neighbors watched. I sent an account to Mrs Gwynne, as follows:

> The late earthquake has found me work. Yesterday I saw the Westminster end of the town full of coaches, and crowds flying out of the reach of divine justice, with astonishing precipitation. Their panic was caused by a poor madman's prophecy: last night they were all to be swallowed up. The vulgar were in almost as great consternation as their betters. Most of them watched all night; multitudes in the fields and open places, several in their coaches. Many removed their goods. London looked like a sacked city. A lady, just stepping into her coach to escape, dropped down dead. Many came all night knocking at the Foundery door, and begging admittance for God's sake. Our poor people were calm and quiet, as at another time.

*Saturday, April 7.* Visited a dying sister, speechless yet full of earnest love, as her looks and signs confessed. Among the penitents, our Lord visited us in a spirit of prayer and contrition.

---

10. Cf. Rom. 12:15.
11. Possibly Mrs. Ewsters.
12. *The Cause and Cure of Earthquakes* (London: [Strahan,] 1750); see *Sermons*, 225–37.

*Sunday, April 8.* Buried our brother Somerset, who came to the grave as a ripe shock of corn in its season. He has now overtook his companion, and death can no more separate them.

*Monday, April 9.* Visited Mrs Colvil at St Anne's Hill. Much delighted with the wood, much more with the company. I did not think there was any such creature upon earth as a girl of twelve years old without guile and without vanity.[13]

Another was gathered into the garner. I buried her earthly part— for a short season.

*Sunday, April 15.* Met Mr Salmon's *Foreigner's Companion through the Universities of Cambridge and Oxford*, printed 1748,[14] and made the following extract, p 25:

> The times of the day the University go to this church, are ten in the morning, and two in the afternoon, on Sundays and holidays, the sermon usually lasting about half an hour. But when I happened to be ~~there~~ at Oxford, in 1742, Mr Wesley, the Methodist, of Christ Church, entertained his audience two hours, and, having insulted and abused all degrees, from the highest to the lowest, was in a manner hissed out of the pulpit by the lads.

And high time for them to do so, if the historian said true. But, unfortunately for him, I measured the time by my watch, and it was within the hour. I abused neither high nor low, as my sermon in print will prove.[15] Neither was I hissed out of the pulpit, or treated with the least incivility, either by young or old.

What then shall I say to my old high-Church friend, whom I once so much admired? I must rank him among the apocryphal writers, such as the judicious Dr Mather, the wary Bishop Burnet, and the most modest Mr Oldmixon.[16]

---

13. This would be Miss Mary Digges (1737–1829), who lived with Mrs Colvil. In 1756 Charles would perform her marriage to Lord Robert Manners (1721–1782).

14. Thomas Salmon (1679–1767), *Foreigner's Companion through the Universities of Cambridge and Oxford* (London: W. Owen, 1748).

15. Charles Wesley, *A Sermon Preached on April 4, 1742 before the University of Oxford* (London: Strahan, 1742). This is "Awake Thou that Sleepest" in *Sermons*, 211–24.

16. Charles is comparing Salmon to Cotton Mather (1663–1728), who was infamous for his support of the witch trials in Salem, Mass.; Gilbert Burnet (1643–1715; Bishop of Salisbury, 1689–1715), whose portrayal of his supporters and friends in *History of His Own Times* spawned charges of misrepresentation and naiveté; and John Oldmixon (1673–1742), a strongly biased whig historian who notoriously accused his opponents of falsifying an edition of Clarendon's standard *History of the Rebellion*.

*Friday, April 20.* Found my Sally well among her friends at Ludlow. She rejoiced my heart with her account of Molly Leyshon,[17] whom she saw triumphant in her last hour. Here is another blessed soul gone to paradise with a good report of us.

Continued ten or eleven days, mostly preaching every night and morning, here or at Leominster. The latter part of the time a prisoner of pain.

## MAY 1750

*Wednesday, May 2.* Took horse at three, and came weary to Bristol by night.

*Friday, May 4.* Hearing the Moravians had been soliciting some of our children, I exhorted them this evening to "put on the whole armour of God" [Eph. 6:11-17], and his power was present to confirm the souls of the disciples.

*Sunday, May 6.* The Lord was with us as in the former times, both at the Sacrament and while I applied to thousands that word, "Thou fool, this night shall thy soul be required of thee" [Luke 12:20].

Doubted whether I should again warn the Society against the Moravians. Led unawares to mention them. Read some of their miserable hymns; spoke of our children, both the living and the dead; commended my brother; pleaded with them in words not my own. Our hearts were knit together in love which neither men nor devils shall dissolve.

*Sunday, May 13.* Baptized Hannah, Mrs Gibbs's maid, and the whole congregation with her were conscious of the descent of the Spirit, who bears witness with the water.[18]

Spake with two of the Society whom the Moravians had inspired with their own spirit of self-conceit. They were wiser than their old teachers. Not because they keep God's commandments, for those they have nothing to do with. I was grieved for the pride and blindness of their hearts, but the Lord lifted me up, and many others, by his word "This is my beloved Son, in whom I am well

17. Cf. Charles's epitaph "On Miss Molly Leyson," *Poetical Works*, 8:436.
18. Cf. 1 John 5:6-8.

pleased" [Matt. 3:17]. We joyfully received the record which God hath given of his Son, and believed—without the Brethren's leave.

*Tuesday, May 15.* Set out with Mrs Vazeille, etc., for Ludlow, and the next day saluted our friends there. During our nine days' stay, they showed her all the civility and love that they could show, and she seemed equally pleased with them.

*Thursday, May 24.* My Sally was so very ill in the evening, that I gave up the hope of her company to town. But the next morning,

*Friday, May 25,* she would go, notwithstanding we all dissuaded her. At eight we mounted. Had fair weather after last night's excessive rain. She mended every stage. I preached in the evening at Worcester.

*Saturday, May 26.* Our brother Watson met us with a chaise, and carried Mrs Vazeille and Sally to Mrs Keech's in Evesham by noon. Mr [James] Waller and I rode by them. Preached with life and liberty.

*Sunday, May 27.* Accepted the mayor's offer of the town-hall. The door was quite open. Many gentry and others listened to the word of life. So again in the evening. Rejoiced with the Society, whose enemies God has made to be at peace with them.

*Monday, May 28.* Saw Blenheim[19] in our way to Oxford. Our old friend Mr Evans received us with his wonted hospitality.

*Tuesday, May 29.* Showed Mr Waller and Mrs Vazeille the buildings and gardens. Gave the Sacrament to Mrs Neal, a true daughter of affliction. Preached again at night.

*Wednesday, May 30.* Had a long day's journey to St Anne's [Hill]. It was past nine before we got under shelter. Mrs Rich was there, who, with our old friends, received us gladly.

*Thursday, May 31.* Mr Waller and Mrs Vazeille went to town.

# JUNE 1750

*Saturday, June 2.* We took up our quarters for eight or nine days at Mrs Vazeille's.[20]

---

19. I.e., Blenheim Palace, Woodstock, Oxford. It was built between 1705 and 1722.
20. Mary Vazeille lived on Threadneedle Street in London.

*Whitsunday, June 3.* <u>Weighed down all day by my brother's</u> <u>threatenings to marry. O why did he ever preclude himself from it?</u> <u>Why did he publish his rash book against it?</u>[21]

*Monday, June 4.* Preached at the chapel with the usual blessing <u>but continued feeble and faint in my mind the whole week.</u>

*Thursday, June 7.* Carried Sally to see our old friends at Newington Green. It is remarkable that the first time Mrs Stotesbury[22] ever saw her, she said within herself, "That person is to be my minister's wife."

*Monday, June 11.* Paid our friends at St Anne's [Hill] a short visit, and returned the next day.

*Wednesday, June 13.* Fetched back my hostage from Chertsey.

*Monday, June 18.* Called on Mrs Dewal at Croydon, and drove on to Westerham,[23] where we met an hearty welcome from Mr Waller's mother and sister Dudley. Walked in Mr Turner's, and then in General Campbell's,[24] gardens. He appeared, carried us into his house, and entertained us with great courtesy.

*Tuesday, June 19.* Rode back to the Foundery, and read the letters.

*Thursday, June 21.* Took horse at three, and *waked* them at Westerham. Passed the day with them in the gardens, reading, singing, and conversing.

*Friday, June 22.* Met a daughter of my worthy old friend Mr Erskine's[25] at the Foundery. She was deeply wounded by the sword of the Spirit.[26] Confessed she had turned many to Deism, and feared there could be no mercy for her.

*Saturday, June 23.* A woman whom I baptized perceived her sins

21. John Wesley, *Thoughts on Marriage and a Single Life* (Bristol: Farley, 1743).

22. Mrs Mary Stotesbury (d. 1759). See Charles's poem celebrating her life in *Funeral Hymns* (1759), 18–20 (*Poetical Works*, 6:232–33).

23. Charles uses the common shorter name "Westram."

24. John Campbell (c. 1693–1770), who was currently a Lieutenant General of the British Dragoons, and later the 4th Duke of Argyll. His estate was at Combe Bank, just outside of Westerham.

25. James Erskine had one daughter, Mary (1714–1772), who married John Keith, 3rd Earl of Kintore.

26. Cf. Eph. 6:17.

to be then washed away. Found much of the spirit of contrition among the penitents.

*Sunday, June 24.* My text was, "Comfort ye, comfort ye my people, saith the Lord" [Isa. 40:1], and his consolations were not small with us. At the Sacrament they abounded. Poor Mrs C— told me she was in an agony, the pangs of labour nothing to what she felt.

I believe God owned me more this day on account of one who, in an abusive letter, had affirmed, that the Lord was departed from me.

*Thursday, June 28.* Prayed by our faithful brother Hogg, just departing in the Lord, and to him. <u>Read letters from my brother, not yet married in Ireland. Yet enabled to preach with great success</u>.

*Friday, June 29.* The Scriptures for the day were much blessed to my comfort. My mouth and heart were both opened to preach the word. The presence of the Lord made it a solemn Sacrament.

I visited the widow (Hogg) in her affliction, and tried to turn it into the right channel.

Continued in watching and prayer till one.

# JULY 1750

*Monday, July 2.* Buried our late brother Hogg, and preached at his grave to a countless multitude on "These are they that came through great tribulation," etc. [Rev. 7:14]. The Lord gave me utterance, and them the hearing ear.

*Monday, July 9.* Administered the Sacrament to a dying believer; lately called, but now made equal to them that have borne the heat and burden of the day.

*Wednesday, July 11.* Preached a written sermon at Spitalfields,[27] on my beloved friend and brother Hogg.[28] The chapel was crowded, and the house of mourning was turned to an house of great rejoicing.

---

27. Spitalfields is an area about one mile north of Tower Bridge that was settled by French Huguenot refugees in the late seventeenth century. In 1750 the Methodists took over one of the Huguenot chapels on Grey Eagle Street, and referred to it as Spitalfields chapel.

28. This sermon does not appear to have survived. However, Charles also published at this time a letter that Thomas Hogg had written to him in 1741 detailing his religious conversion: *A Short Account of God's Dealings with Mr Thomas Hogg* (London: Strahan, 1750). Appended to this letter is a hymn by Charles "On the Death of Thomas Hogg, June 29, 1750," and a short epitaph (pp. 11–12).

*Monday, July 16.* Rode to St Anne's [Hill], and returned in such a storm of thunder, lightning, and rain, as I hardly remember to have seen out of America.

*Wednesday, July 18.* Had the satisfaction of bringing back to Mr Erskine his formerly disobedient daughter. She fell at his feet. It was a moving interview. All wept. Our heavenly Father heard our prayers.

I preached immediately after on "And I, if I be lifted up from the earth, will draw all men unto me" [John 12:32]. We had a double blessing and power. Poor Jane Cox said she was even compelled to receive Christ.

*Friday, July 20.* Kept a solemn watch-night at Spitalfields.

*Sunday, July 22.* After evening service set out with Robert Windsor. Got two or three hours' rest at Mr Manning's,[29] and,

*Monday, July 23,* breakfasted with Mr Evans in Oxford. Lodged at Worcester; and, by eight on

*Tuesday morning, July 24,* found Sally well at Ludlow. Every evening we retired to pray together, and our Lord's presence made it a little church.

*Saturday, July 28.* Wrote to Mrs Gwynne, earnestly beseeching her to do all in her power to reconcile her son and daughter.

*Tuesday, July 31.* The word I preached this day at Leominster was accompanied with the power and blessing of God.

## AUGUST 1750

*Tuesday, August 7.* At seven set out with Sally for Bristol, without the consent of the rest. It rained small rain till we came to Leominster, and so most of the way to Ross.[30]

*Wednesday, August 8.* It rained hard soon after we set out, but quickly gave over. We had a rough, dangerous passage at Framilode.[31] Dined at Cambridge Inn.[32] Had trying journey,

---

29. Rev. Charles Manning (1714–1799), vicar of Hayes, Middlesex.
30. Ross-on-Wye, Herefordshire.
31. Charles spells "Frommelow."
32. In Cambridge, Gloucestershire.

driven by the wind, and battered by the rain.[33]

Sally was frightened with the thunder, which often forced us to trees and huts for shelter. Yet at seven, by the assistance of God, we entered our own house in peace.

*Friday, August 10.* Sally accompanied me in my visits to the sick.

*Sunday, August 12.* The Lord met us, who remembered him in his ways.

*Monday, August 13.* Met my sister Hall[34] in the churchyard, and carried her to the room. I had begun preaching when Mr Hall walked up the room, and through the desk, and carried her off with him. I was somewhat disturbed, yet went on.

*Wednesday, August 15.* He came up again, calling me by my name. I fled, and he pursued, but could not find me in my lurking place.

*Tuesday, August 28.* Many rejoiced in hope, our Lord applying that precious promise, "I will allure her, and will bring her into the wilderness, and will speak comfortable unto her" [Hos. 2:14].

# SEPTEMBER 1750

*Saturday, September 1.* Finished Rapin's *History*,[35] which has cured me, in some degree, of the prejudices of education.

*Sunday, September 2.* Baptized Hannah Skinner. He remembered His promise, "Lo, I am with you" [Matt. 28:20].

*Tuesday, September 4.* Carried Sally to Mr Haynes. Preached with an enlarged heart, as I always do at Wick.

*Wednesday, September 5.* My worthy friend Mr Evans looked upon us in his return to Oxford.

---

33. Thomas Parnell, "The Hermit," ln. 96, *Poems*, 170.
34. That is, his sister Patty, who was apparently trying to leave her unfaithful husband.
35. Paul Rapin de Thoyras (1661–1725), *The History of England, as well ecclesiastical as civil*, 15 vols. (London: Knapton, 1727–1731). This was the text assigned at Kingswood school. Charles later bought his own set of the twenty-volume fourth edition, which can be found (with his inscription) in MARC (ref. CW79–98).

*Sunday, September 9.* Proclaimed to a great multitude in the Orchard, "Christ the way, the truth, and the life" [John 14:6]; and left, I humbly hope, a blessing behind me.

*Monday, September 10.* Set out with Sally, and parted; she for Ludlow, I for London; where I arrived on Wednesday morning.

*Thursday, September 13.* Met my brother and the stewards.

*Friday, September 14.* Met James Hervey[36] at the Tabernacle, and in the fellowship of the Spirit of love.

*Sunday, September 16.* A great number of communicants perceived the Lord present. He gave us his blessing at our Love-feast also. Restless all night, through a boil rising on my neck.

*Monday, September 17.* Rose at two and set out for the north. Beyond Islington my mare threw and fell upon me. Held on as far as St Albans, and was then forced to lie down. Yet could not sleep, day or night.

*Tuesday afternoon, September 18.* With much difficulty got back to London.

*Friday, September 28.* Continued in great pain for several days, till the boil broke.

Passed three days at Newington Green, and found benefit by my physic and fresh air. Mr Waller and his sisters frequently called, and rejoiced with the church in our house.

# OCTOBER 1750

*Sunday, October 7.* Got out to the chapel on this and every Lord's Day. The rest of the month confined to the house mostly. Dr [Samuel] Wathen attended me constantly, till both my neck and swollen hand were quite well.

*Monday, October 29.* Set out with Mr Waller and [George] Bridgins.[37] Slept the first night at Oxford, the second at Moreton.[38]

---

36. James Hervey (1714–1758). See Charles's hymn on Hervey's death in *Funeral Hymns* (1759), 61–63 (*Poetical Works*, 6:279–81).
37. Charles spells "Bridgin."
38. Moreton in Marsh, Gloucestershire.

*Wednesday, October 31.* By ten came to Evesham, and had great comfort in praying over our sick brother Watson. Lodged at Worcester, and was refreshed with the little handful at sister Blackmore's.

# NOVEMBER 1750

*Thursday, November 1.* Preached in Ludlow, where I stayed the whole month, exercised by severe and unexpected trials. One night (November 28) Mr Waller fell into convulsions, through the distractions of his mind. I was on the point of following him. Betsy and Juggy[39] fainted away. Confusion reigned throughout the family.

# DECEMBER 1750

*Saturday, December 1.* Rode out with Miss Becky to meet Mrs Allen and Mrs Dudley, and brought them to Ludlow.

*Sunday, December 2.* Encouraged a poor girl to seek for her cure from Him who had wounded her. She has the outward mark too, being daily threatened to be turned out of doors by her master—a great swearer, and strict Churchman; a constant communicant, and habitual drunkard.

*Tuesday, December 4.* Mr Waller's wedding-day.[40] How unlike my own! Rose, after a sleepless night, in the spirit of heaviness. Prayed for them and with them. Soon after eight they were married; "And 'twas my ministry to deal the blow!"

*Friday, December 7.* Left the house of woe, and the next day rejoiced to find myself among my friends at Bristol.

*Sunday, December 9.* Visited my sick friends, four of them in the triumph of faith. Sister Page was almost overpowered, had desired to live only to see me. She began recovering from our praying together.

The Society seemed filled with consolation. It was a glorious time, and made me forget my late sorrows and sufferings.

---

39. "Juggy" was the nickname for Joan Gwynne (b. 1728), one of Sally's sisters.
40. James Waller was marrying Betsy Gwynne, the younger sister of Charles Wesley's wife Sally.

*Monday, December 10.* Visited our sister Arnett, aged eighty-six, just ripe for glory; and a child[41] of brother [John] Walcam's, departing in the spirit of praise and love.

*Sunday, December 16.* Two went home from the word justified.

*Sunday, December 23.* Gave a close exhortation to the Society, which seemed to sink into every heart.

*Tuesday, Christmas Day.* Rejoiced from four to six, with as many as our room could contain. Then rode to Newbury with T. Hamilton. Eating, immediately he fainted away. I found myself going, and prevented it by a vomit.

*Thursday, December 27.* Did not reach the Foundery till eleven. Found Sally at Mrs Allen's.

*Friday, December 28.* Officiated at Spitalfields chapel. One received forgiveness with the Sacrament.

# [JANUARY] 1751

*Tuesday, January 1.* Began the new year as usual, with the voice of joy and thanksgiving.

*Wednesday, January 2.* Visited a sick believer, who talked of death as of going to sleep. "When I think of the grave," said she, "I think it is a sweet, soft place. But my spirit shall mount above."

Mr Waller having always insisted on our sojourning with him a while, when he should have an house of his own, I carried Sally thither, to her two inseparable sisters, Betsy and Peggy.

*Friday, January 4.* Spent the evening at Mrs Colvil's, and left my partner there.

*Sunday afternoon, January 6.* Mrs Colvil and Miss Digges[1] brought her me back. We had the pleasure of frequent visits from them.

*Sunday, January 13.* Preached at Hayes church,[2] morning and

---

41. Elizabeth Walcam (b. 1733); cf. the account of her death in John Wesley's *Journal* (June 1, 1751), *Works* 20:389–90.
1. Charles spells "Degge."
2. Hayes, Middlesex, where Charles Manning was vicar.

evening, on "Come unto me, all that labour" [Matt. 11:28], and "Behold the Lamb of God, that taketh away," etc. [John 1:29]. They were patient, at least, of the truth. Rode back to town and heard my brother exhort the Society. I thought he misspent his strength in trifles.

*Monday, January 14.* Mr Waller's three sisters were at our family prayers; in which I was even overwhelmed with their burden, and constrained to warn them with tears and vehement expressions of my fear and sorrow. The arrows of conviction pierced one of their hearts. The others were rather confounded than alarmed.

*Thursday, January 24.* Heard my brother again in the Society. A poor society indeed! His words were quite trifling.

*Sunday, January 27.* Preached at the Foundery with great severity. Betsy was amongst my hearers, but alas her hunger for righteousness and the word is all gone.

*Wednesday, January 30.* Got an hour's very useful conversation with Lady Piers.[3]

# FEBRUARY 1751

*Saturday, February 2.* My brother, returned from Oxford, sent for and told me *he was resolved to marry!* I was thunderstruck, and could only answer he had given me the first blow, and his marriage would come like the *coup de grace*. Trusty Ned Perronet followed, and told me the person was Mrs Vazeille! One of whom I had never had the least suspicion. I refused his company to the chapel, and retired to mourn with my faithful Sally. Groaned all the day, and several following ones, under my own and the people's burden. I could eat no pleasant food, nor preach, nor rest, either by night or by day.

*Sunday, February 3.* Gave the Sacrament, but without power or life. No comfort in it, no singing between, no prayer after it.

*Thursday, February 7.* My excessive cough helped to pull me down, and then a sore throat. My companion sympathized with me too sensibly.

---

3. Lady Comelia Gertrude Piers (*née* Pigott), wife of Sir John Piers (d. 1747), 4th baronet of Tristernagh Abbey.

*Thursday, February 14.* She was often in great pain, especially today. I watched by her in great distress, but could not remove her pain by sharing it. Sent for Mr [Samuel] Wathen, who prescribed what gave her immediate relief. I gave God, who heareth prayer, the glory.

*Sunday, February 17.* Dragged myself to the chapel, and spoke on those words, "Thy sun shall no more go down," etc. [Isa. 60:20]. The whole congregation seemed infected by my sorrow. Both under the word, and at the Sacrament, we wept and made supplication. It was a blessed mourning to us all.

At the Foundery heard my brother's lamentable apology, which made us all hide our faces. Several days afterwards I was one of the last that heard of his unhappy marriage.

*Monday, February 18.* Carried Sally out of the confusion to Mrs Colvil's.

*Sunday, February 24.* After Sacrament, Mr Blackwell fell upon me in a manner peculiar to himself, beating, driving, dragging me to my dear sister.

*Wednesday, February 27.* My brother came to the chapel-house with his wife. I was glad to see him. Saluted her. Stayed to hear him preach, but ran away when he began his apology.

# MARCH 1751

*Friday, March 1.* Miss Hardy related my brother's apology that "in Oxford he had an independent fellowship, was universally honored, etc., but left all for the people's sake, returned to London,[4] took up his cross, and married; that at Oxford he had no more thought of a woman than any other animal upon earth, but married to break down the prejudice between the world and him!" His easily won lady sat by.

He said "I am not more sure that God sent his Son into the world, than that it was his will I should marry."

*Saturday, March 9.* Felt great emotion in the word, both morning and evening.

---

4. The shorthand is just "n."

*Thursday, March 14.* Saw the necessity of reconciliation with my brother, and resolved to save the trouble of umpires.

*Saturday, March [16].*[5] Called on my sister; kissed and assured her I was perfectly reconciled to her, and to my brother.

*Monday, March 18.* Finished Marcus Antoninus,[6] having learnt from him, I hope, some useful lessons, particularly not to resent, not to revenge myself, not to let my peace lie at the mercy of every injurious person.

*Tuesday, March 19.* Brought my wife and sister together, and took all opportunities of showing the latter my sincere respect and love.

*Thursday, March 21.* At four in the morning met the watchman, who told me the first news of the Prince's death.[7]

*Friday, March 22.* With my brother. Said I desired entire reconciliation, that all the advantage Satan had gained was owing to our want of mutual confidence, that I did not believe him in so dangerous situation as he was before his marriage. He owned his promise to Molly Francis and Miss Lundy. Was in good humour and high spirits, talked freely and fully, would fain have had me engage for the year to come but I declined it.

*Monday, March 25.* Visited one on his death-bed who had been converted from Deism, and washed in the blood of *his* Redeemer.

# APRIL 1751

*Tuesday, April 9.* Spent a week with Mrs Colvil and Miss Digges, chiefly in reading, singing, and prayer.

*Saturday, April 13.* Passed the evening with Sally at Mr I'Anson's,[8] and saw the Prince's funeral pass. The house was full of strangers. We joined in many suitable hymns till near midnight.

---

5. MS has "March 15," which is in error.
6. Marcus Aurelius, *The Commentaries of the Emperor Marcus Antoninus, containing his maxims of science, and rules of life,* translated by James Thomson (London: T. Parker, 1747). Charles's signed copy of this work can be found in MARC (ref. CW65).
7. Prince Frederick, son of King George II, died on March 20, 1751.
8. Sir Thomas I'Anson (c. 1701–1764), a legal adviser and friend of the Wesleys, who had a home in Westminster, and another about two miles north of Tunbridge Wells, Kent.

*Monday, April 15.* Heard Lovybond preach, most miserably! By how many degrees are such preachers worse than none!

*Sunday, April 21.* God was present in the word and Sacrament, as in the months that are past, when the candle of the Lord was upon our heads.

*Monday, April 22.* <u>Met sister Hall[9] and her son[10] at the Foundery, and received them as kindly as I could. She had been invited by my brother, who left no orders for her reception, nor took any notice afterwards.</u>

*Thursday, April 25.* Our Lord again confirmed his word, "In the world ye shall have tribulation, but be of good cheer," etc. [John 16:33].

*Friday, April 26.* After intercession, met John Hutchinson,[11] and engaged him for the next day. Then laboured to stir him up to do the first works.

*Sunday, April 28.* Buried our sister Pocock, a silent, secret, unpretending Christian, who died the death, as she lived the life, of the righteous. Strongly warned the bands against sin and apostasy.

*[Tuesday],[12] April 30.* Took horse in the afternoon, Mr [Samuel] Lloyd and Sally in the chaise, and lodged at Thomas Hardwick's.

## MAY 1751

*Wednesday, May 1.* I rode to Lewisham, and thence to the Foundery; went to bed ill.

*Thursday, May 2.* Returned to Sally at Brentford, my purging violent as before.

---

9. Patty was again seeking to leave Westley Hall.

10. This is Westley (or Wesley) Hall Jr, the only child of Patty to survive early childhood. John and Charles supported him for a boarding school, where he unfortunately contracted smallpox and died at the age of fourteen; cf. Charles's poems on this death in *Funeral Hymns* (1759), 20–23 (*Poetical Works*, 6:234–37).

11. This is the son of John and Sally Hutchinson, leading Methodists in Leeds. Charles develops a deep concern for the younger John's spiritual health and is deeply shaken by his death in 1754. Cf. the three hymns written in the latter context, in *Funeral Hymns* (1759), 8–14 (*Poetical Works*, 6:221–28).

12. MS has "Friday," which is in error.

*Friday, May 3.* Set out with her for St Anne's [Hill], was driven back by the rain.

*Saturday, May 4.* Carried my companion thither, and rode back to town having first corrected Mrs Colvil's will. She had left my brother two hundred pounds a year, before his marriage.

*Sunday, May 5.* Met my sister[13] at Mrs Emery's, and walked with her to chapel. She had been told I said I did not love my brother, nor ever should.

My subject was, "In me ye shall have peace" [John 16:33], and He did even in that hour extend to us peace like a river. In the afternoon rode to St Anne's [Hill].

*Monday, May 6.* Mr Lloyd paid us a visit. Passed our time no less usefully than agreeably, in reading and singing. He and I witnessed to Mrs Colvil's will.

*Wednesday, May 8.* Set out in a post-chaise for Bristol. Heard, in passing Reading, that our friend Mr Richards was departed in peace. Lay at Newbury the first night, the second at Calne, and on

*Friday, May 10,* came safe with Sally to Charles Street. Our friends Vigor, Davis, etc., were there to welcome us. We were much drawn out in prayer.

*Sunday, May 12.* With Sally at Kingswood, greatly quickened by that promise, "The third part I will bring through the fire" [Zech. 13:9]. In the Sacrament we were swallowed up in the spirit of prayer. Met my sister at the Horsefair, and behaved to her *as such*— gave an earnest exhortation to repentance.

*Tuesday, May 14.* Showed her, both at my own house, and the houses of my friends, all the civility in my power.

*Friday, May 17.* The congregation was melted into blessed mourning through the word.

*Sunday, May 19.* Preached out to a vast multitude on "Thanks be to God, who giveth us the victory" [1 Cor. 15:57]; was carried out to the unawakened wholly. The Society seemed much alive to God.

---

13. Here and in the next several instances Charles is referring to his sister-in-law, Mrs Mary Wesley.

*Wednesday, May 22.* Rode with Sally to Wick, and received the never-failing blessing.

*Thursday, May 23.* Returning by the widow Jones's, I asked her daughter at the door how she was. "Just alive," she answered me, "and no more." I lighted, and prayed over her earnestly with tears, as sent to minister the last blessing to an old friend, torn from us by false brethren. She was full of hope and love and prayer for me, and desire to be dissolved. I went on my way rejoicing.

*Tuesday, May 28.* My very good old friend Mrs Cradock came to see me, with Mrs Motte. We sang, and conversed, and prayed (particularly for their Lady[14]) as in the former days. In the evening, Mrs Jones of Fonmon called, and told me her Ladyship would be very glad to see me.

*Thursday, May 30.* Sally resolved to bear me company to Newcastle. *Deus vertat bene!*[15] Wrote to John Bennet to meet us.

# JUNE 1751

*Saturday, June 1.* In the fear of God, and by the advice of my friends, I went once more to visit Lady Huntingdon.[16] She expressed great kindness toward me, as did all the family; spoke much and well of sufferings, etc. My heart was turned back again, and forgot all that is past. The Spirit of love is a spirit of prayer, and sealed the reconciliation.

*Sunday, June 2.* Baptized Sarah and Elizabeth, a Quaker and a Baptist, before a full congregation. All were moved by the descent of that Spirit. Many wept, and trembled, and rejoiced; the persons baptized, most of all.

*Monday, June 3.* My wife accepted her Ladyship's invitation, and went with me to see her. We employed an hour or two in very useful conversation, and singing, and prayer. Our old friend appeared

---

14. Lady Huntingdon, who was staying at her house in Clifton, Gloucestershire, two miles west of Bristol, near Hotwells.

15. "God, turn it to good."

16. Having resisted earlier overtures (cf. the April 27, 1747, entry), Charles is here trying to renew more positive connection with Lady Huntingdon (which served to strain further his relationship with his brother).

as such. Seemed taken with Sally, and said "Mrs Wesley, I will come to see you." Appointed the next day.

*Tuesday, June 4.* Instead of proceeding in Ezekiel, I expounded Heb. 10:38, "Now the just shall live by faith. But if he draw back, my soul shall have no pleasure in him." Saw the reason with Mr Hall. He came up toward the desk. Mr Hamilton stopped him. I gave out an hymn. He sang louder than us all. I spoke sharply of his apostasy, and prayed earnestly for him. Desired their prayers for me, lest, after preaching to others, I myself also should be a castaway. He walked away, turned back, threatened. The people were all in tears, and agony of prayer.

Spent an hour in prayer with our sisters Perrin, Design, Robertson, T. Hamilton, and Charles Perronet, making particular mention of my brother and Lady Huntingdon. From five to seven she and her daughters[17] spent with us.

*Sunday, June 9.* At eight in the evening I preached with life and freedom to a great multitude at Poynt's Pool.[18]

*Monday afternoon, June 10.* At sister Crockar's, on "God, having raised up his Son Jesus, sent him to bless you," etc. [Acts 3:26].

*Tuesday, June 11.* Our sister Selby brought me a letter from our brother [Richard] Pearce at Bradford[-on-Avon], pressing me to bring James Wheatley thither, to answer some horrible practices of his.

*Wednesday, June 12.* Rode to Bradford[-on-Avon]. Talked with our brother Pearce, then with Miss [Mary] Bradford and another of the *abused* persons. Preached on "Having our conversations honest among the Gentiles" [1 Pet. 2:12]. Spoke kindly to Jo. Hewish and got from him his *Book and Licence to preach.* I wish he were the only worthless, senseless, graceless man to whom my brother had given the same encouragement under his hand.[19]

*Thursday, June 13.* Preached close and severe warnings. Advised Hewish to leave off preaching, which he promised to do. Talked

---

17. The daughters were Elizabeth Hastings (1731–1808) and Selina Hastings (1737–1763).

18. Northeastern suburb of Bristol, just outside of Lawford's Gate. Charles spells "Points Pool."

19. The last two sentences of this entry are not printed by Jackson.

with more women whom James Wheatley had treated in the same vile manner. Met the rest at Wick, in all seven. What they told me, they repeated more at large to Sarah Perrin and Mary Naylor. Prayed with strong faith and tears by our mournful, dying brother Cottle.

Rode to Freshford, and urged them to come boldly to the throne of grace [Heb. 4:16]. The Lord was with my mouth.

*Friday, June 14.* Kept the hour of intercession at Bristol. Bowed down under the mighty hand of God. Carried James Wheatley to my house and set before him, in tender love and pity, the things which he had done. At first he was stubborn and hard, but relented afterwards. Seemed willing to confess, satisfied of my good will.

*Sunday, June 16.* Baptized a young Quaker at Kingswood, and then we all joined in the Lord's Supper. He was mightily present in both sacraments, and afterwards gave me words to shake the souls of those that heard.

*Monday, June 17.* Sally set out for Ludlow.

*Wednesday, June 19.* Carried my brother home. Offered to join with him heartily and entirely. Consulted what to do with Wheatley.

*Thursday, June 20.* Got Wheatley again to my house, and talked with him as he was able to bear.

*Friday, June 21.* Administered the Sacrament to Lady Huntingdon, Sarah Perrin, etc, ~~with~~ under a deep and solemn awe of the divine presence.

Found my sister in tears. Professed my love, pity, and desire to help her. Heard her complaints of my brother. Carried her to my house, where, after supper, she resumed the subject, and went away comforted.

*Saturday, June 22.* Passed another hour with her in free affectionate conference, then with my brother, and then with both together. Our explanation ended with prayer and perfect peace.

*Sunday, June 23.* Lady Huntingdon, with Mrs Edwin[20] and Mrs Knight, desired admittance to our Love-feast. My mouth was opened in exhortation and prayer. Afterwards I introduced my sister to her Ladyship and the rest, who received her with great friendliness.

---

20. Catherine Edwin; cf. the note for January 3, 1745.

*Tuesday, June 25.* My brother and I carried James Wheatley, at his own request, to Bearfield. Mrs [Mary] Deverel and sister Bradford proved their charge to his face. He pleaded guilty, yet justified himself. I walked with him apart. He threatened to expose *all* our preachers; who, *he said*, were like himself. Conferred with my brother, and drew up our resolution in writing that he should not preach. Put him on reading it before Wheatley and the women. Wheatley absolutely refused to submit. Then, said I, bear witness I am pure from the blood of this man.[21] We reasoned with him in vain, and at last told him he might preach where Christ was not named (such a place as Norwich, my brother added.) He insisted on preaching occasionally in our Societies.

Transcribed the declarations taken from their mouths.

*Wednesday, June 26.* With Lady Huntingdon; Sarah Perrin declared the matter. She much approved of what had been done, strengthened our hands, proposed writing to Wheatley herself; quite cordial to advise, and to bear our burden. We were enabled to pray earnestly for the divine direction and blessing.

*Thursday, June 27.* We talked again with stiff-necked James, but prevailed nothing. He was resolved to preach. Neither would he discover which of the preachers it was whom, he *said*, he knew to be a gross sinner.

Communicated with my brother and sister at Lady Huntingdon's.

*Friday, June 28.* James Wheatley having, to screen himself, traduced all the preachers, we had him face to face with about ten of them together. And Thomas Maxfield first, then each of the others, asked him, "What sin can you charge me with?" The accuser of the brethren[22] was silent in him, which convinced us of his wilful lying. However, it put my brother and me upon a resolution of strictly examining into the life and moral behaviour of every preacher in connexion with us; and the office fell upon me.

I set out for this purpose on *Saturday, June 29, 1751.* Francis Walker and Sarah Perrin accompanying me. Lodged at Ross that night. Overtook Sally the next day at Ludlow, by two, unhurt by the incessant rains.

---

21. This sentence is not printed by Jackson.
22. Cf. Rev. 12:10.

Preached to as many as the hall and parlour could contain. They seemed increased in earnestness as well as number. I found unexpected life and comfort among them, and the following evening had still more reason to hope that my past labour ~~among~~ has not been in vain.

# JULY 1751

*Friday, July 5.* Between six and seven set out with Sarah Perrin, my wife, and sister Becky, and honest Francis Walker. Coming to Worcester in the afternoon, we heard the rioters had been at the room on Monday evening, in expectation of me, and made great disturbance. I doubted all along whether I had any business here at this time. Yet, at the desire of the poor people, went to their room at seven. Almost as soon as I began the mob interrupted. But in spite of their lewd, hellish language, I preached the gospel, though with much contention. They had no power to strike the people as usual, neither did any molest us in our way home.

*Saturday, July 6.* We were hardly met, when the sons of Belial[23] poured in upon us, some with their faces blacked, some without shirts, all in rags. They began to "stand up for the Church," by cursing and swearing, by singing and talking lewdly, and throwing dust and dirt all over us; with which they had filled their pockets, such as had any to fill. I was soon covered from head to foot, and almost blinded. Finding it impossible to be heard, I only told them I should apply to the magistrates for redress, and walked up stairs. They pressed after me, but Mr Walker and the brethren blocked up the stairs, and kept them down. I waited a quarter of an hour, then walked through the midst of them to my lodgings, and thence to the mayor's.

I spent an hour with him, pleading the poor people's cause. He said he had never before heard of their being so treated—that is, pelted, beat, and wounded, their house battered, and windows, partitions, locks broke; that none had applied to him for justice, or he should have granted it; that he was well assured of the great mischief the Methodists had done throughout the nation, and the great riches Mr Whitefield and their other teachers had acquired;

---

23. Cf. 1 Sam. 2:12.

that their societies were quite unnecessary, since the Church was sufficient; that he was for having neither Methodist nor Dissenters.

I easily answered all his objections. He treated me with civility and freedom, and promised, at parting, to do our people justice. Whether he does or not, I have satisfied my own conscience.

At ten we took horse for Tipton Green. Our brother Jones gave me a melancholy account of the Society at Wednesbury, which, from three hundred, is reduced to seventy weak, lifeless members. Those who had borne the burden and heat of the day, and stood like a rock in all the storms of persecution, were removed from their steadfastness and fallen back into the world, through vain janglings. Well had it been for them if the Predestinarians had never come hither.

*Sunday, July 7.* Preached out to a numerous congregation, whom I could not look upon without tears. My text was Rev 3:3, "Remember therefore how thou hast received and heard, and hold fast, and repent." Out of the abundance of my heart my mouth spake,[24] and called them back to their first love and first works. It was a solemn season of sorrow. The Lord, I trust, knocked at many hearts, which will hear his voice, and open to him again.[25] He stirred up the faithful remnant to pray for their backsliding brethren, and their prayers shall not return empty.

Another hour I employed in earnestly exhorting the Society to repentance.

*Monday, July 8.* Preached at five with much freedom, and hope of their recovery. In the afternoon the curate met me—a well-disposed youth, just come from college, where his tutor, Mr [Edward] Bentham, gave him an early prejudice for true religion. He invited me to his lodgings, joined with us in serious conversation and singing, and seeming ready for all good impressions.

At six I preached on Bromwich Heath[26] to a multitude of the poor, who heard me gladly, and knew not when to leave off.

*Tuesday, July 9.* The many hearers at Dudley seemed to drink in every word.

---

24. Cf. Matt. 12:34.
25. Cf. Rev. 3:20.
26. Charles spells "Bromidge Heath."

*Wednesday, July 10.* Exhorted them at Wednesbury to "lay aside every weight," etc. [Heb. 12:1]. Joined with the brethren in fervent prayer for a general revival.

*Thursday, July 11.* Examined the classes and rejoiced to find them all orderly walkers. Received some backsliders upon trial; and prayed by a sick sister, quietly waiting for full redemption.

Dined in Darlaston, at our brother [Jonathan] Jones's uncle's. The master was gone to his house not made with hands, and left a good report behind him. He was a good and hardy soldier of Jesus Christ, bold to confess Him before men; for whose sake he suffered the loss of all things, and continued faithful unto death.[27] The people are a pattern to the flock:

> Meek, simple followers of the Lamb;
> They live and speak and think the same.[28]

By their patience and steadfastness of faith they have conquered their fiercest adversaries. God gives them rest, and they walk in his fear and comforts, increasing daily both in grace and number.

I preached to most of the town, and pressed them to "come boldly to the throne of grace" [Heb. 4:16]. My spirit was greatly assisted by theirs. Those without seemed all given into my hands. The Society was all in a flame of love. They made me full amends for my sorrow at Wednesbury.

*Friday, July 12.* Took my leave of them at Wednesbury, exhorting them to continue in the apostles' doctrine, and in fellowship, etc. [Acts 2:42]. Sarah Perrin met, and found much grace among, the women. Half a dozen more wandering sheep I gathered in, and restored to their brethren. Preached at Birmingham to several of the better rank, who received the word with a ready mind.

*Saturday, July 13.* At morning and at noon my mouth was opened to make known the mystery of the gospel.

*Sunday, July 14.* Examined the Society, who adorn the gospel of Christ. Heard a good sermon at church, about using the world as not abusing it. But alas! it supposed the congregation to be Christians.

---

27. Cf. Phil. 3:8; Rev. 2:10.
28. "Primitive Christianity," st. 2, *HSP* (1749), 2:333 (*Poetical Works*, 5:480). In the original the second line is in the past tense and ends with an exclamation mark.

I preached at five before brother Bridgins's door. We expected a disturbance, but the power of the Lord was over all.

The cloud stayed on the assembled Society. The word of exhortation went from my heart to theirs. The Spirit helped us to pray, especially for some at Bristol, and our souls were like a watered garden.

*Monday, July 15.* At five took horse with our brother Bridgins, an old disciple past eighty. Lay at Duffield.

*Tuesday, July 16.* At two rejoiced to meet some of our dear children in Sheffield. I encouraged them by that *most* glorious promise, "Behold, he cometh with clouds, and every eye shall see him" [Rev. 1:7]. The door has continued open ever since Mr Whitefield preached here, and quite removed the prejudices of our first opposers. Some of them were convinced by him, some converted, and added to the church. "He that escapes the sword of Jehu shall Elisha slay" [1 Kgs. 19:17].

*Wednesday, July 17.* Preached at Rotherham, and met, to my comfort, several solid believers. Talked severally with the growing Society. Returned, and preached in the streets at Sheffield, without life or power, to a wild, tumultuous rabble. Equally dead at the Society.

*Thursday, July 18.* Rode toward Barley Hall. Baited three hours at our sister Booth's,[29] and laboured all the time to strip an old, self-righteous pharisee. At last our Lord got himself the victory. We left her in tears and deep convictions, a greater miracle of grace than the conversion of a thousand harlots!

Dined at Barley Hall with our dear sister Johnson (a widow indeed) and her six sons and daughter, all believers. I had heard at Sheffield that the Society here was come to nothing. Yet the word was attended with the blessing which never failed me in this place, and I felt the Lord was not departed. I was still more agreeably surprised in examining the Society to find near seventy earnest souls, most of them believers and grown in grace. But who can stand before envy? The preacher that brought up an evil report of them, had it from some of Sheffield, who, through prejudice and jealousy, would always hinder our preaching at this place. How cautious

---

29. This would be Elizabeth Booth of Woodseats, Yorkshire.

should we be in believing any man! I marvel not now that my ~~word was~~ mouth was stopped at Sheffield.

*Friday, July 19.* Preached once more to this lively, loving people, and left them sorrowful, yet rejoicing. We had a pleasant ride to Wakefield, where our brother Johnson received us joyfully. He himself was sick of a fever. But the Lord makes his bed, and he waits upon Him, without trouble, care, or choice.

By five we were welcomed to Leeds by our sister [Sally] Hutchinson and others. I preached at eight, to many more than the house could hold. The Lord gave us a token for good.

*Saturday, July 20.* The leaders informed me that, of the two hundred and fifty members of the Society, every one could challenge the world, "Which of you convinceth me of sin?" [John 8:46].

Visited a faithful brother, whose wife and sister were drawing back. We laboured to restore them, in the spirit of meekness, and the Lord added weight to our words. They departed for a while, we trust, that we might receive them again for ever.

At eight I preached the gospel to a multitude of poor sinners, unfeignedly poor, and hungering after righteousness.

*Sunday, July 21.* Preached, in the shell of our house, on Zech. 4[:9], "The hands of Zerubbabel have laid the foundations," etc. Rode to Birstall, where John Nelson comforted our hearts with his account of the success of the gospel in every place where he has been preaching, except Scotland. There he has been beating the air for three weeks, and spending his strength in vain. Twice a day he preached at Musselburgh, to some thousands of *mere* hearers, without converting one soul.

I preached at one, to a different kind of people. Such a sight have I not seen for many months. They filled the valley and side of the hill, "as grasshoppers for multitude" [Judg. 6:5]. Yet my voice reached the most distant, as I perceived by their bowing at the holy Name. Not one appeared unconcerned. I directed them to "the Lamb of God that," etc. [John 1:29]. God gave me the voice of a trumpet, and sent the word home to many hearts.

After evening service I met them again, but much increased, and lifted up my voice to comfort them by the precious promises; which were then fulfilled in many. The eyes of the blind were opened, the ears of the deaf unstopped, the lame men leaped like harts, and the tongue of the dumb sang.[30]

The Society, collected from all parts, filled their new room; whom I earnestly exhorted to walk as becometh the gospel [Phil. 1:27].

*Tuesday, July 23.* Showed the believers at Leeds how they ought to walk, from, "Ye are the salt of the earth," etc. [Matt. 5:13]. In the evening preached repentance and forgiveness, in the name of Jesus, to a mixed multitude of rich and poor.

Visited a sick sister, destitute of all things, yet triumphing over want, sickness, death.

*Wednesday, July 24.* Preached at Woodhouse, faint and ill, as before a fever. So I told Sally, yet strove to hold up, till I had wrote, with many tears, to my dear John Hutchinson. At eight the fever came.

*Thursday, July 25.* Was carried to Miss Norton's, who quitted her house for us and Sarah Perrin.

*Friday, July 26.* John Nelson assured me that above seventy had died in triumph, out of Birstall Society only.

*Sunday, July 28.* My fever increasing, I judged it incumbent on me to leave my thoughts concerning the work and instruments, and began dictating to Sarah Perrin the following letter.[31]

*Monday, July 29.* Dr Milner constantly attended me. Had some discourse with Paul Greenwood, an Israelite indeed; glad to work with his hands, as well as to preach.

# AUGUST 1751

*Thursday, August 1.* Mr Polier, a minister from Switzerland, was brought to me by my doctor. He inquired thoroughly into our affairs. I told him all I knew of the Methodists, with which he appeared fully satisfied. He seemed a man of learning and piety. In the evening we were strongly drawn out in prayer for him.

---

30. Cf. Isa. 35:5-6.
31. Charles's letter is not actually given in the MS. Rather, there is a gap of about a page and a third. Charles was evidently planning to transcribe the letters at a later stage.

*Friday, August 2.* I had missed my fit through taking the bark.[32] Today my purging returned and threatened to bring my fever, yet God kept it off.

*Saturday, August 3.* Was enabled to ride out, and to confer with the preachers and others.

*Sunday, August 4.* Found my strength sensibly increase in the fresh air. Spent an hour with the women leaders, and appointed them to meet as a band.

*Monday, August 5.* Went to the room, that I might hear with my own ears one of whom many strange things had been told me. But such a preacher have I never heard, and hope I never shall again. It was beyond description. I cannot say he preached false doctrine, or true, or any doctrine at all, but pure, unmixed nonsense. Not one sentence did he utter that could do the least good to any one soul. Now and then a text of Scripture, or a verse quotation, was dragged in by head and shoulders. I could scarce refrain from stopping him. He set my blood a-galloping, and threw me into such a sweat, that I expected the fever to follow. Some begged me to step into the desk, and speak a few words to the poor dissatisfied hearers. I did so, taking no notice of Michael Fenwick, late superintendent of all Ireland!

I talked closely with him, utterly averse to working, and told him plainly he should either labour with his hands, or preach no more. He hardly complied, though he confessed it was his ruin, his having been taken off his business. He complained of my brother. I answered I would repair the supposed injury by setting him up again in his barber's shop. At last he yielded to work, so it might be *in private.*

Thomas Colbeck brought Eleazer Webster to me. I spoke in vain to a self-hardened slave of sin, and silenced him.

*Tuesday, August 6.* Prayed with the Society, in solemn fear of God present. It seemed as if He spoke with an articulate voice, "Return to me, and I will return unto you" [Mal. 3:7]. My faith was greatly strengthened for the work. The manner and instruments of carrying it on I leave entirely to God.

---

32. Cinchona, known popularly as "Jesuits bark" or "Peruvian bark," is a source of quinine.

*Wednesday, August [7].*[33] Took horse for Newcastle with Sally, Sarah Perrin, Miss Norton, and William Shent. Could get no farther than Topcliffe. Found an aged woman reading [Thomas à] Kempis. Asked her the foundation of her hope. She simply answered, "A good life." I endeavoured to teach her better, and preached Christ the Atonement, as the only foundation. She received my saying with tears of joy. We joined in fervent prayer for her. All the family seemed much affected. I found myself refreshed in body as well as soul, and easily rode on to Sandhutton.

We were no sooner in the house than it began to pour down, and continued raining till we set out next morning.

*Thursday, August 8.* Rested at Durham.

*Friday, August 9.* By noon our travels ended at Newcastle. My companions are better both in mind and body for their long journey.

I preached, but very feeble, on "The third part I will bring through the fire" [Zech. 13:9]. Preaching, I perceive, is not now my principal business. God knoweth my heart, and all its burdens. O that he would take the matter into his own hand, though he lay me aside as a broken vessel!

*Sunday, August 11.* Felt the fever hanging about me all day, notwithstanding the bark which I continue taking. The Society appeared lively and solid. I vehemently exhorted them to watch and pray, as well for the labourers as themselves, that none of us might bring a reproach upon the gospel.

*Monday, August 12.* Had much discourse with a brother from Scotland, who has preached there many weeks and not converted one soul. "You may just as well preach to the stones," he added, "as to the Scots." Yet, to keep my brother's word, I sent William Shent to Musselburgh. Before he went he gave me this memorable account of their late trial at Leeds:

> At Whitecote Hill,[34] three miles from Leeds, a few weeks since, as our brother [Jonathan] Maskew was preaching, a mob arose, broke the windows and doors, and struck the constable, Jacob Hawley, a brother. On this we indicted them for an assault; and the ringleader of the mob, John Hillingworth, indicted our

---

33. MS has "August 6," which is in error.
34. Whitecote Hill is in northwest Leeds. Charles spells "Whitecoat Hill."

brother the constable, and got persons to swear the constable struck him. The grand jury threw out our indictment, and found that against us. So we stood trial with them on Monday, July 15th, 1751, and the recorder, Richard Wilson, Esq., gave it in our favour, with the rest of the court. But the foreman of the jury, Matthew Priestly, with two others, Richard Cloudsley and Jabez Bunnil, would not agree with the rest, being our avowed enemies; the foreman Mr [John] Murgatroyd's great friend and champion against the Methodists.

However, the recorder gave strict order to a guard of constables to watch the jury, that they should have neither meat, drink, candles, nor tobacco, till they were agreed in their verdict. They were kept prisoners all that night and the next day, till five in the afternoon, when one of the jury said he would die before he would give it against us. Then he spoke closely to the foreman concerning his prejudice against the Methodists, till at last he condescended to refer it to one man. Him the other charged to speak as he would answer it to God in the day of judgment. The man turned pale, and trembled, and desired another might decide it. Another (Jo. Hardwick) being called on, immediately decided it in favour of the Methodists. After the trial, Sir Henry Ibison, one of the justices, called a brother, and said, "You see God never forsakes a righteous man. Take care you never forsake Him."

While the trial lasted, hundreds of our enemies were waiting for the event, who showed by their fierceness what they designed, had we lost our cause. They intended to begin with pulling down our house. But thanks be to God, who hath not delivered us over as a prey into their teeth.

The judge of the court was Richard Wilson, Esq., Recorder of Leeds; the justices: J. Frith, Mayor, Alderman Micklethwait, Alderman Denison, Alderman Sawyer, Alderman Smith, Alderman Brooks; Jury: Matthew Priestly, Richard Cloudsley, Jabez Bunnil, H. Briscoe, W. Wormill, Richard Cockell, Joseph Naylor, Joseph Inkersley, George Dixon, Richard Sharp, W. Upton, and Joseph Hardwick. Four witnesses against, six for, us.

*Tuesday, August 13.* Rode with my little family to Sunderland. Examined the Society of about a hundred, most of whom received the atonement in meeting their classes—an argument for such meetings as I cannot get over. At seven I preached in a large convenient room, filled with attentive souls, on whom I called, "Behold the Lamb of God," etc. [John 1:29]. For an hour and a half my strength held out.

*Wednesday, August 14.* At nine set out, and, in half an hour's riding, overtook a woman and girl leading an horse. She begged us to help them up, and forward them on their way. We did so. But the horse turned with them again, and rode back toward Sunderland. We had the riders to pick up again, and remount. Their horse we put between us. But he broke through a gap, and galloped back. When he had shook them off, he stood still. I bade my companion take up the girl behind him, hoping the horse would carry the woman alone; but in vain, though we all beat the poor beast to drive him on. He kicked and flounced, till he had dismissed his rider. I then said, "Surely, good woman, God withstands you. You are going somewhere contrary to his will. I can compare your horse to nothing but Balaam's ass.[35] What can be the meaning of it?" She answered, "Sir, I will tell you all, for there must be something extraordinary in the great pains you have taken for me. That child I had by a gentleman, who promised me marriage, but since married another, because [she is] richer than me. I am going to try if he will do anything for the child and me. But I fear it is not pleasing to God." I asked what she had to live upon. She told me she was married to a blacksmith, had a child by him, and it was but low with them. I advised her to take God's warning, and utterly renounce the first wicked man; to spend the rest of her days in repentance, and working out her salvation; gave her something, and recommended her to a sister in Sunderland. She seemed overwhelmed with joy and gratitude, mounted with her child, and the horse carried them quietly home.

*Friday, August 16.* Heard J. J., the drummer, again, and liked him worse than at first. He might perhaps have done good among the soldiers. But to leave his calling and set up for an itinerant was, in my judgment, a step contrary to the design of God, as well as to his own and the Church's interest.

At seven I walked toward Ouse Burn[36] to meet the classes. But my strength totally failed me by the time I got to Sandgate,[37] where I rested at a brother's till I had recovered strength to return.

---

35. Cf. Num. 22.

36. Industrial area just outside the walls of Newcastle Upon Tyne, in valley of the Ouse Burn River where it enters the River Tyne. Charles spells "Ewe's Bourn."

37. Sandgate was on the southwestern edge of Newcastle at that time, on the bank of the River Tyne, and the home for the keel men.

At three I was sent for by the gaoler's wife to a poor wretch under sentence of death for murdering his own daughter of fourteen. Never have I spoke to a more hardened, ignorant, stupid sinner. He utterly denied the fact. I prayed for him, but with little hope.

After preaching at the Orphan House,[38] I commended him to the prayers of the congregation, and we found free access to the throne.

At my next visit I perceived little change in him, only he suffered me to speak and said nothing of his innocency.

*Sunday, August 18.* Heard Jonathan Reeves at Sheep Hill, and added a few words in confirmation of his. Returned to Newcastle comforted.

Preached in great weakness. At our Love-feast the spirit of supplication was given, and the poor murderer brought to our remembrance. I have not been more refreshed for this many a day.

*Tuesday, August 20.* Preached in the prison, on "Christ hath redeemed us from the curse of the law," etc. [Gal. 3:13]. Still I could not discern any signs of true repentance in the poor man, though he is to die tomorrow. He persists in his innocence, but confesses he deserves far worse punishment at the hands of God. I prayed over him with tears, and told him our next meeting would be at the judgment-seat.

I was ready to wonder why Providence had directed me to him, and engaged his people to pray for him, when one informed me that, while I was earnestly praying for him in the congregation, a woman had received forgiveness. Many other good ends may be answered, which we do not know. At least our prayer shall turn again into our own bosom. At night I was drawn out again in prayer for him, and continued instant therein for half an hour. The people were deeply affected. It is impossible for so many prayers to be lost.

*Wednesday, August 21.* The first news I heard this morning from Jonathan Reeves was that he had been, with John Downes and others, visiting the poor malefactor, and they verily believed he had found mercy. He told them his heart was so light, he could not express it, and he was not in the least afraid to die. Two days before,

---

38. The Orphan House was the first Methodist building in the north of England, built in 1743 to serve as the principal base in that region. It stood just outside of the town walls in Newcastle, on the west side of what is now Northumberland Street.

Jonathan Reeves had talked an hour and an half with him, and put him in great fear. But now he appeared quite calm and resigned, and so continued to the last moment.

Took horse at nine for Horsley, leaving Jonathan to attend the execution, and bring us word. He overtook us in the afternoon with the same account of his convert, who showed all the marks of repentance and faith in death.

Passed the afternoon with Mr Carr, a young minister from Scotland, and our brother and sister Ord from Hexham. Preached at 7, quite overcome with the heat. By noon returned to Newcastle.

*Friday, August 23.* Spake with our brother Allen, an exhorter, whom one would fain have persuaded to forsake his business. I persuaded him to continue in it.

*Saturday, August 24.* At one I set out with Sally, Sarah Perrin, Miss Norton, etc. Preached at Durham, repentance and faith in our Lord Jesus [Acts 20:21].

*Sunday, August 25.* Communicated at the Abbey. Preached in a yard, to many quiet hearers, "Behold the Lamb of God, that taketh away," etc. [John 1:29]. Enlarged much at the Society.

*Monday, August 26.* Lodged at Thirsk.

# SEPTEMBER 1756[1]

*Friday, September 17th, 1756.* At seven I left Bristol with John Downes, and came to Wallbridge[2] by two. In the evening several attended the word, and seemed stirred up to watch and pray [Luke 21:36]. I spake to each of the little steady Society. Forty-three have kept together for years, under the care of our brother Watts. There are no disputes or disorders among them. I added a few

---

1. In the MS Journal Charles has a page with the date August 27, 1751, at the top that is left blank. It then skips to September 1756. (Recall from our Introduction that the material from November 29, 1753, to August 13, 1754, which Jackson included in his edition was not part of the MS Journal.) This large lacuna reflects that after 1751 Charles dramatically reduced the amount of his traveling. This was due in part to the desire to be closer to his family. However, it also reflected the strained relationship between Charles and his brother John. This final section in the MS Journal, for the last quarter of 1756, details Charles's one further tour of the Methodist work in northern England.

2. Charles spells "Walbridge."

words, exhorting them to continue steadfast in the communion of the Church of England. We were much refreshed, and parted in great love.

*Saturday, September 18.* Set out at six, and in three hours reached Cheltenham. The twelve miles thence to Evesham cost us near six hours. But we rode the short (that is, the vale) way, and have taken our leave of it for ever. By four we got, weary enough, to Mr Canning's. The preaching-room was full. I exhorted them to watch and pray always, that they might be counted worthy to escape all these things which shall come to pass, and to stand before the Son of Man [Luke 21:36]. Again at seven next morning, and at five in the evening, they received my saying, the Lord applying his own word, both to awaken and to confirm.

I went to church morning and afternoon, and between the services visited three or four of the Society who had been disabled, by age and infirmity, from assembling with their brethren, and were therefore neglected as not belonging to them. Wrote their names again in the Society-book, with Mr Canning's family, and J. Watson's, who seemed all resolved to do the first works.[3]

I did not forget to confirm the brethren in their calling—that is, to live and die in the Church of England.

*Monday, September 20.* After commending them to God and to the word of his grace [Acts 20:32], rode with our loving guide, J. Watson, toward Birmingham. At Studley he left us, full of his former zeal, and resolved to carry fire among his neighbors of the village to which he is removed.

About two we got to Birmingham, and soon after heard at the door Mr I'Anson's voice. He brought life with him. As a watchman of Israel, I warned a numerous audience of the sword coming [Ezek. 33:1-6]. The word seemed to sink into their hearts.

I had not time to meet the Society, but in conversing with several I conceived fresh hopes that they will at last become a settled people. Some who had forsaken us I received in again.

*Tuesday, September 21.* The Lord gave us a parting blessing. Mr I'Anson's chaise kept pace with us to Ashby,[4] where our brother

---

3. Cf. Rev. 2:5.
4. Ashby de la Zouch, Leicestershire.

Adams received us joyfully. The wild beasts here are tamed at least, if not converted. None molested while I pointed them to the Lamb of God, who taketh away the sin of the world [John 1:29]. We prayed earnestly for the conversion of these hardened sinners. I was comforted with the little company of twenty-one, who meet to build up each other. Great life and love was in the midst of them.

*Wednesday, September 22.* Warned them of the impending judgments, and left them standing on the watchtower [Ezek. 33:1-6]. We passed a profitable hour at Donington Park, with Mr H. Mr I'Anson attended us five or six miles on our way to Nottingham, which we reached by two. I spent the afternoon in taking down the names of the Society, and conversing with them. We rejoiced to meet once more after so long a separation. My subject, both at night and in the morning, was, "I will bring the third part through the fire" [Zech. 13:9]. It was a time of solemn rejoicing. There had been, twelve months ago, a great revival and increase of the Society. But Satan was beginning again to sow his tares.[5] My coming at this season will, I trust, be the means of preventing a division.

*Thursday, September 23.* It rained hard all night. John Downes's lame horse detained him at Nottingham, by which the poor people got another sermon day. At seven I set out in the rain with a blind guide, who at last blundered out his way to Sheffield. Here also I delivered my own soul, and the people seemed awakened and alarmed. I spake plainly and lovingly to the Society of continuing in the Church and, though many of them were Dissenters and Predestinarians, none were offended.

*Friday, September 24.* I had left William Shent sick in Charles Street. But to my great surprise, entering brother [William] Green's at Rotherham this morning, the first person I set eyes on was William himself. The Sunday after I left him he had had another fit of his ague. Yet on Monday morning he *would* needs mount his horse, and ride homeward. He had only one visit from his ague on the road, and grew stronger and stronger by virtue of prayer, more than of physic.

---

5. Cf. Matt. 13:25.

When I was last here the Society were on the brink of a separation, through a party for Mr Whitefield and Mr [John] Edwards. They proposed it to honest Mr Cousins, whose opposing quashed it at that time. I then advised them to go to Church. The weak and wavering were confirmed; three or four of the others offended, and said I made the Church Christ. After preaching as awakening as I could, I plainly told the Society that "there was no salvation *out of the church*; that is, out of the mystical body of Christ, or the company of faithful people." When I had fully explained myself on this head, we were all of one mind and heart. They then *suffered* the word of exhortation, and were even glad when I said unto them, "Let us go into the house of the Lord" [Ps. 122:1].

*Saturday, September 25.* I encouraged them by that precious promise, "I will bring the third part through the fire" [Zech. 13:9], and parted in great love. At eight I preached on the same subject at Barley Hall, and found there the never-failing blessing. Rode on with William Shent, who was threatened last night with the return of his fever. I was at a loss for a companion to York when, in passing through Hunslet, one called after me. I turned, and saw Mr Crook,[6] who told me Dr Cockburn[7] was at his house and had waited for me this week, to carry me to York. We lighted, and spent a delightful hour with the Doctor (my old schoolfellow) and him, both in their first love—both full of life, and zeal, and simplicity. Mr Crook pressed me to assist him at the morning Sacrament.

*Sunday, September 26.* At seven I preached to the people at Leeds on "Thy kingdom come" [Matt. 6:10; Luke 11:2]. The disciples lifted up their heads. Walked with Dr Cockburn to Hunslet. Mr Crook insisted on my preaching, which I did again, from the same words. His congregation seemed to make no opposition to the truth. There were hundreds of communicants, mostly of Mr Crook's awakening.

We passed an hour and an half at his house, with the voice of joy and thanksgiving.[8] Then he pressed me into the service again. His church, which holds nearly as many as our preaching-house, was filled from end to end. At his desire, I preached on those words,

---

6. Henry Crook (1708–1770), curate of Hunslet.
7. Dr. Thomas Cockburn (d. 1768), apparently a classmate of Charles at Westminster School, who later moved to Jamaica.
8. Cf. Ps. 42:4.

"His blood be on us, and on our children" [Matt. 27:25]. Our Lord turned the curse into a blessing.

I doubted my strength, yet set out for Leeds. The room was excessively crowded, both within and without. I was very faint, as I mentioned my text, "When these things begin to come to pass, then look up," etc. [Luke 21:28]. My little strength I increased by using it, and the word refreshed both soul and body. The hearers were variously affected. O that all may be found watching![9]

I could speak of nothing but love in the Society, for I felt nothing else. Great was our rejoicing over each other. Satan, I believe, has done his worst, and will get no farther advantage by exasperating their spirits against their departed brethren. They were unanimous to stay in the Church, because the Lord stays in it, and multiplies his witnesses therein more than in any other church in Christendom.

*Monday, September 27.* I was surprised at the numbers that flocked to the early preaching, and eagerly received that saying of our Lord, "Behold, I come as a thief. Blessed is he that watcheth and keepeth his garments" [Rev. 16:15].

Breakfasted with Miss Norton, and found nothing in my heart towards her but love. She was not so evil-affected towards her forsaken brethren as I expected. Nothing can ever bring such as her back, but the charity which hopeth all things, beareth all things, endureth all things.[10]

Several came to confer with me, particularly Benjamin S. I had great satisfaction with him. While we were drinking tea at a brother's, Mr Edwards found me out. We talked freely and lovingly, till the time of preaching. I walked with him to the house. Mr Crook was another of my hearers. My text was, "His blood be on us, and on our children" [Matt. 27:25]. The power of the Lord was present more than yesterday. I went to the Church-prayers, with several who have been long dealt with to forsake them utterly. They will stand the firmer, I hope, for their shaking.

*Tuesday, September 28.* Set out with the Doctor and William Shent for York. The rain brought back poor William's ague. I preached from Hab. 3:2, "O Lord, revive thy work." The crowd made our room excessively hot, but that did not hinder their attention.

---

9. Cf. Luke 12:37.
10. Cf. 1 Cor. 13:6-7.

*Wednesday, September 29.* Our preacher stationed here had quite left off preaching in the morning. Many told me I could not get a congregation at five, but I found it otherwise. The room was almost full while I explained, "Being made free from sin, and become the servants of God, ye have your fruit unto holiness, and the end everlasting life" [Rom. 6:22]. I insisted largely on freedom from sin, as the lowest mark of faith, and the necessity of labouring after holiness. The hearers appeared much stirred up.

Spent the day in conferring with all comers. The Doctor's house was open to all, and his heart also—his whole desire being to spread the gospel.

*[Thursday],[11] September 30.* My subject was John 5:14, "Afterward Jesus findeth him in the temple, and said unto him, Behold, thou art made whole. Sin no more, lest a worse thing come unto thee." I warned them against that sweet doctrine, "Once in grace, always in grace," but not in a controversial way. Pointed out some of the infinite ways whereby they might forfeit their pardon. Exhorted them to go to Church, that they might be found of Jesus in the temple, and above all to pray always, that that word might be written on their hearts, "Go and sin no more."

The day was well spent in making up a difference which the sower of tares[12] had occasioned among the principal members of the Society.

Between six and seven I got the Society together, with many out of the country, and for two hours showed them how they ought to walk.[13] They gladly received instruction.

# OCTOBER 1756

*Friday, October 1.* Preached again to the awakened, and perceived the word take place. Breakfasted with T. Brooke,[14] who has once more left the Brethren. Went with him to the Minster[15] which he constantly frequents. I met, at his house, Miss T—, earnestly

---

11. MS lists this too as "Wednesday," which is in error.
12. Cf. Matt. 13:25.
13. Cf. 1 Thess. 4:1.
14. T. Brooke and his wife were the pioneers of the Society in Thirsk.
15. The popular name for the Cathedral Church of St Peter's, York.

seeking salvation. The means of awakening her was *Theron and Aspasio.*[16]

Heard that the young woman who cried out last night under convictions was the same hour delivered into the glorious liberty of God's children.

Passed an hour at Mr D.'s, and answered his candid objections. Had an opportunity of vindicating my old friend Benjamin Ingham. 'Tis hard a man should be hanged for his looks—for the *appearance* of Moravianism. Their spirit and practices he has as utterly renounced as we have; their manner and phrase cannot so soon be shaken off.

Found out *Mercy Bell,* and had sweet fellowship with her. I marvel not that the Friends (so fallen from their first simplicity) cannot receive her testimony.

We had a most triumphant watch-night. Began between seven and eight. The enemy did not like our employment, and stirred up his servants without to interrupt us. But our voices prevailed. We sung the "Hymns in a Tumult "[17] with great calmness and consolation. Mr Williamson's[18] maid was deeply wounded. The shout of a king was in the midst of us,[19] and the people thought it full early to part at eleven.

*Saturday, October 2.* The whole day was spent in singing, conference, and prayer. I attended the choir service. The people there were marvelously civil, and obliged me with the anthem I desired, Hab. 3, "a feast for a King," as Queen Anne called it. Mr Williamson walked with me to his house in the face of the sun. I would have spared him, but he was quite above fear. A pious, sensible Dissenter clave to us all day, and accompanied us to the preaching. I discoursed on my favourite subject, "I will bring the third part through the fire" [Zech. 13:9]. We glorified God in the fire, and rejoiced in hope of coming forth as gold.

*Sunday, October 3.* From five till near eight I talked closely with each of the Society. Then, on Mr Williamson's request, preached on

---

16. James Hervey, *Theron and Aspasio,* 2 vols. (Dublin: Robert Main, 1755). This was a pointedly Calvinist Methodist work by one of John Wesley's former students.

17. A set of four hymns at the end of *Hymns for Times of Trouble and Persecution* (London: Strahan, 1744), 43–47 (*Poetical Works,* 4:51–56).

18. Rev. William Williamson (d. 1758), vicar of St Mary Bishophill Junior, York.

19. Cf. Num. 23:21.

the ordinances from Isaiah 64:5, "In those is continuance, and we shall be saved." I dwelt longest on what had been most neglected: family prayer, public prayer, and the Sacrament. The Lord set to his seal, and confirmed the word with a double blessing. I dismissed them at nine. Our preachers had often kept them till near ten, and thereby hindered their going to Church.

Received the Sacrament at the Minster. It was a solemn passover. They were forced to consecrate twice, the congregation being doubled and trebled through my exhortations and example. Glory be to God alone! I found great faith to pray for him that consecrated, and heard afterwards that it was Mr B., one who had known the Methodists from their rise at Oxford and was no enemy to them. I expect (if I hold out myself) to meet that soul in paradise.

Went to Mr Williamson's church. He read prayers as one that felt them, and beckoned me. According to our private agreement, I stepped up into the pulpit, when no one expected it, and cried to a full audience, "The kingdom of God is at hand. Repent ye, and believe the gospel" [Mark 1:15]. They were all attention. The word did not return void, but accomplished that for which it was sent. Neither is he that planted anything, neither is he that watereth.[20]

Dr Cockburn carried me in his chair to Acomb. I lost my voice in the rain, and could not, without much straining, cry, "Behold the Lamb of God, that taketh away the sin of the world" [John 1:29]. A clergyman[21] and the gentry of the place were present. The rain dispersed us in half an hour. I attempted to meet the Society at York, but could not speak to be heard. We got thereby a longer evening at the hospitable Doctor's. Mr Williamson and his family, etc., were helpers of joy.

*Monday, October 4.* I took my leave in the words of the Apostle, "The grace of God which bringeth salvation hath appeared unto all men, teaching us," etc. [Titus 2:11]. From hence I strongly pressed the obedience of faith. We parted in body only.

Through God's blessing on my week's stay among them, I hope 1) peace and love are restored, 2) they will recover their rising again at five; 3) they are brought back again to Church, and Sacrament, and family prayer.

---

20. Cf. Isa. 55:11, 1 Cor. 3:7.
21. Likely John Coates (c. 1716–1782), vicar of Acomb, 1740–1765.

Dr Cockburn and his lady attended me to Tadcaster, where I found both voice and strength to point many earnest souls to the all-atoning Lamb [John 1:29]. The gentry listened as well as the poor. Both dismissed me with blessings.

It rained as soon as we took horse. We were quickly wet to the skin, the high wind driving the storm full in our faces. I was most concerned for poor William Shent, and forced him to stop at the first house. There I reproved a countryman for swearing, and gave a word of advice, which was kindly taken. We took refuge again at Seacroft, and enjoyed the last fair hour which brought us to Leeds by two. I renewed my strength against preaching-time. After which I met the leaders, and earnestly exhorted them to set a pattern to the flock.

*Tuesday, October 5.* At five preached in William Shent's shop. Breakfasted at Miss Norton's. There Mr [John] Edwards assured me he had "never *desired* any one of our children to leave us." Doubtless they did it of their own mere motion. No one ever dealt ~~with~~ or took any pains with them about it. No one ever spoke against the Church to unhinge them. They dropped into his mouth (as our first children into the Count's) without his ever suspecting it.

If he has robbed us of our children, I bless God to find he has not robbed us of our peace and love. He several times expressed his readiness to preach in our Societies. I only answered the people could not trust him, that he would not do in every place as he has done in Leeds.

I endeavored to treat him with due respect and love, according to our rule. "If it be possible, as much as in you lies, live peaceably with all men" [Rom. 12:18].

Passed the day at Mr Crook's, who told me his experience. I cannot doubt of his having known the pangs of the new birth. Our brethren question it, because he does not use all their phrases, and cannot follow all their violent counsels. I begged him to do nothing rashly; least of all, to go from his post, preaching everywhere like us.

Drank tea at a sister's who has been as the troubled sea ever since the separation, and as rough towards all, especially her husband, as Mr Edwards is smooth. I laboured to quiet her, and she was sensible of the great advantage Satan had gained over her. Alas for the man by whom the offence cometh![22]

---

22. Cf. Matt. 18:7.

Walked to Hunslet with William Shent, and heard Mr Crook expound in the church. Dined with him, and was provoked by his zeal. Returning, I found Joseph Tucker at my lodgings, and threw away some words on one wiser in his own eyes than seven men that can render a reason.[23] He entirely justified Mr Edwards. Therefore I can have no confidence in him that he will not do, were it in his power, as Mr Edwards has done.

Henry Thornton came to spend an hour or two with us, and we sharpened each other's countenance. At six I met the leaders, and inquired into the behaviour of each member of the Society. Upwards of forty Mr Edwards has carried off, but not by *desiring* any to leave us. I carried them with me to prayers, and wished them to follow my example, by carrying the whole Society to Church with them. Returned to the room, and explained the believer's privilege, 1 Peter 1[:5], "Kept by the power of God through faith unto salvation."

*Thursday, October 7.* After a most tempestuous night, I preached to a few whom the hurricane could not keep from the word.

Had more talk with Joseph Tucker who frankly confessed if any of our Societies should desire him to take charge of them, as a distinct body, he should not refuse them. I told him plainly that the ground of all such designs was pride. But my words were spoken into the air.

After church set out in a storm for Seacroft, and rode on to Aberford. My old friend Mr Ingham was labouring in the vineyard. But I had the happiness to find Lady Margaret[24] at home, and their son Ignatius. She informed me that his round takes in above four hundred miles; that he has six fellow-labourers, and one thousand souls in his Societies, most of them converted. I sincerely rejoiced in his success. Ignatius would hardly be pacified at my not preaching. We passed an hour and an half very profitably, and set out again. The rain met and drove us to a tree for shelter. We narrowly missed several heavy showers, and got safe back to Seacroft before night.

Soon after, our dearest brother [William] Grimshaw found us, and brought a blessing with him. I preached from Luke 21[:34-36],

---

23. Cf. Prov. 26:16.
24. Lady Margaret Hastings (1700–1768), sister-in-law of Lady Huntingdon, was the first of the Hastings family to befriend the Methodists, and married Benjamin Ingham in 1741.

"Take heed to yourselves," etc., and farther enforced our Lord's warning on the Society. I strongly exhorted them to continue steadfast in fellowship with each other, and the whole Church of England. Our hearts were comforted and knit together.

*Friday, October 8.* We had another blessed hour with them, before we left this lively people. Continued till one in conference with my worthy friend and fellow-labourer, a man after my own heart! Whose love of the Church flows from his love of Christ. With such may my lot be cast in both worlds!

Spent an hour in intercession for the Church and nation. I exhorted the many persons present to continue instant in this prayer, and mark the answer and the end!

Rode with my faithful brother Grimshaw to Bramley. Preached in a large barn (now a convenient chapel) to a multitude of serious souls, who eagerly received our Lord's saying, "Look up, and lift up your heads," etc. [Luke 21:28].

*Saturday, October 9.*[25] They all seemed broad awake when I called again in the morning, "Watch ye, therefore, and pray always," etc. [Luke 21:26]. Their spirit quickened mine. We had sweet fellowship together. I have no doubt but they will be counted worthy to escape, and to stand before the Son of Man.[26]

Returning to Leeds, I met my brother Whitefield, and was much refreshed by the account of his abundant labours. Waited on him to our room, and gladly sat under his word. Preached myself at Rothwell. Their large house was full, though it was an harvest-day. I warned them of the impending storm,[27] with much freedom and faith for the sincere, concluding with a warm exhortation to continue in the Ship.

*Sunday, October 10.* From Isaiah 64:5, "In those is continuance, and we shall be saved," I earnestly pressed the duties of constant communicating, of hearing, reading, practising the word, of fasting, of private, family, and public prayer. The Society I advised to continue in fellowship and never more give place to the sower of tares,[28] the divider of the brethren. I spoke healingly of the breach;

---

25. In the MS the date is incorporated into the text. It has been separated for clarity.
26. Cf. Luke 21:36.
27. This was likely a sermon on Ezek. 33:1-6.
28. Cf. Matt. 13:25.

told them how to behave toward Mr [Charles] Skelton, and the rest who have rose up to draw away disciples after them; and insisted on that apostolical precept, let all your things be done in charity.[29] I did not mention the author of the late division, being convinced he left us for bread. The Spirit of love and union was in the midst of us.

I came to Birstall before noon. My congregation was less by a thousand or two, through George Whitefield's preaching today at Haworth. Between four and five thousand were left to receive my warning from Luke 21. After church we met again. Every soul seemed to hang on the word. Two such precious opportunities I have not enjoyed this many a day. It was the old time revived. A weighty spirit ran through the congregation, and they stood like men prepared to meet the Lord.

*Monday, October 11.* After preaching at five to this solid people, I returned to Leeds, and spent an hour with the leaders. They informed me that my late exhortations have stopped some who were on the point of going over to Mr Edwards's society, and brought others back to the Church-ordinances. A woman in particular, after hearing me on Sunday morning, went to Church, which she had long forsaken, and received a manifestation of Jesus Christ in the prayers. I earnestly pressed them to recommend to their brethren, both by advice and example, the neglected duties of family and public prayer, and to watch over the flock with all diligence.

Hearing Mr Whitefield and Mr Grimshaw were returning to our watch-night, I waited for them at their lodgings, with zealous, humble, loving Mr Crook. It rained so hard, that Mr Whitefield was agreeably surprised at eight to find our house as full as it could cram. They forced me to preach first, which I did from Zech. 13[:9], "The third part I will bring through the fire." My brother George seconded me in the words of our Lord: "I say unto all, Watch" [Mark 13:37]. The prayers and hymns were all attended with a solemn power. Few, if any, I hope, went unawakened away.

*Tuesday, October 12.* I took my leave of Leeds in prayer at William Shent's. Some having ascribed the division to him, I examined that matter to the bottom, having talked largely with all parties,

---

29. Cf. 1 Cor. 16:14.

especially Miss Norton and Mr Edwards himself. Upon the whole, I am convinced that the ground of all was Miss Norton's hatred to William Shent. This induced her to draw away Mr Edwards from us. He could not resist the temptation of a certain provision for his family. Interest blinded his eyes, so that the means to his end seemed right and honest to him, though base and treacherous to us. As for William Shent, I do not find he did more than every upright man would have done on this occasion. He watched to counteract them who were daily seducing our children. He gave early notice to my brother of their design, and thereby drew all their resentment upon himself—as every honest preacher will *qui cum ingeniis conflictatur ejusmodi.*[30] Since the separation (Mr Edwards's friend informed me) he had behaved with such mildness and discretion as has kept the rest of the flock together, when violence or harsh treatment might have scattered them all.

Preached in Wakefield at ten, to a quieter audience than I have ever met with there.

Took a friendly leave of Miss Norton, who assured me some of our ablest preachers were entirely in Mr Edwards's interest. *Nec nihil, nec omnia.*[31]

Rode to Joseph Bennet's, near Dewsbury, and preached very awakening to a mixed, attentive congregation. My vehement exhortation to the Society was on the usual subject, "continuance in the word,"[32] and in prayers, family and public. Passed the evening with Jonas Eastwood.[33] I would gladly part with five hundred Methodists, to be ordained, and useful like him.

**Wednesday, October 13.** The word at Birstall was clothed with power, both to awaken and to confirm. My principal concern is for the disciples, that their houses may be built on the rock, before the rains descend.[34] I hear in most places the effect of the word. But I hearken after it less than formerly, and take little notice of those who say they receive comfort, or faith, or forgiveness. Let their fruits show.

Preached at night, and rejoiced in steadfast hope of being brought through the fire [Zech. 13:9].

---

30. "Who is involved with characters like that" (cf. Terence, *The Lady of Andros*, 93).
31. "Neither nothing, nor everything."
32. Cf. John 8:31.
33. Former headmaster of Kingswood, and then assistant curate at Dewsbury.
34. Cf. Matt. 7:24-27.

*Thursday, October 14.* Baptized a Dissenter's child, and set out with faithful Titus Knight for Halifax. A mixed multitude listened to the word: "When thy judgments are in the earth, the inhabitants of the world will learn righteousness" [Isa. 26:9]. I have not found so great freedom in any place as this, where I expected least. Set out in hard rain for Bradford.[35] My subject there was Hab. 3:2, "O Lord, revive thy work," etc. Many Dissenters were present. Some of them, I believe, were reached, for I spake in irresistible love, and warned them to flee from the wrath to come.[36]

*Friday, October 15.* After preaching, I gathered into the fold a wandering sheep, whom John Whitford's pride and folly had scattered. Having lost her first love, she married an unconverted man; whereupon the Society gave her up for lost. I rejoiced to find her miserable in prosperity, and restless to recover her only happiness.

Found comfort in the first lesson at Church (Wisdom 5). Could be glad to attend the public prayer constantly, for my own as well as for example's sake.

The preaching-house was filled with those that came from far. Our Lord did not send them empty away.[37] A girl of fourteen (who had walked from Birstall) told me she seemed carried under the word, as out of the body. What to call the manifestation of the Spirit then given her, time and temptation will show.

Near two hours more we rejoiced at a primitive Love-feast.

*Saturday, October 16.* Breakfasted again with my lost sheep that is found,[38] for whose sake chiefly I believe myself sent to Bradford. Last night at the Love-feast she recovered her shield.[39] Took my leave of the brethren in that promise, "He that endureth to the end, the same shall be saved" [Matt. 10:22]. Rode with faithful Thomas Colbeck to Keighley.

Found at four a large, handsome room well filled. Did my office as a watchman [Ezek. 33:1-6], and delivered my own soul. Mr Grimshaw assisted at the Society. I recommended family-religion with all my might. For near an hour and an half the cloud stayed on the assembly.[40]

---

35. Bradford, Yorkshire.
36. Cf. Matt. 3:7; Luke 3:7.
37. Cf. Matt. 15:32; Mark 8:3.
38. Cf. Luke 15:6.
39. Cf. Eph. 6:16.
40. Cf. Num. 9:11.

*Sunday, October 17.* We had no room to spare at six in the morning, while I commended them to God, and to the word of his grace [Acts 20:32]. Preached a second time at Haworth (Mr Grimshaw reading prayers), from Psalm 46:8-9,[41] "O come hither and behold the works of the Lord, what destruction he hath brought on the earth. He maketh wars to cease in all the world," etc. My mouth was opened to declare the approaching judgments, and the glory which shall follow, when the Lord is exalted in all the earth. The church, which had been lately enlarged, could scarce contain the congregation, who seemed all to tremble at the threatenings, or rejoice in the promises, of God.

We had a blessed number of communicants, and the Master of the feast in the midst. I prayed and exhorted afterwards. Our hearts were lifted up to meet Him in his glorious kingdom.

After an hour's interval we met again, as many as the church walls could contain. But twice the number stood without, till the prayers were over. Then I mounted a scaffold and, lifting up my eyes, saw the fields white unto harvest.[42] We had prayed for a fair day, and had the petitions we asked. The churchyard, which will hold thousands, was quite covered. God gave me a voice to reach them all. I warned them of those things which shall come to pass, and warmly pressed them to private, family, and public prayer; enlarged on the glorious consequences thereof, even deliverance from the last plagues, and standing before the Son of Man. I concluded, and began again, for it was an accepted time. I do not remember when my mouth has been more opened, or my heart more enlarged.

A young preacher of Mr Ingham's came to spend the evening with me at Mr Grimshaw's. I found great love for him, and wished all *our* sons in the gospel were equally modest and discreet.

*Monday, October 18.* He accompanied us to Heptonstall, where I preached at ten on Isaiah 64:5, "In those is continuance, and we shall be saved." I was very faint when I began. The more plainly did it appear that the power was not of man, but of God.[43] I warned them of the wiles of the devil, whereby he would draw them away from the Church and the other means of grace. I spake as the oracles

---

41. Charles wrote "46:5," which is in error for both the AV and BCP.
42. Cf. John 4:35.
43. Cf. 2 Cor. 12:9.

of God, and God gave testimony, bowing the hearts of all present, except a few bigoted Baptists. Went on our way rejoicing to Ewood.[44]

There the hard rain cut short my discourse from Ezek. 9. Mr Allen could not leave us yet; but rode with us next morning,

*Tuesday, October 19,*[45] as far as Gaulksholme.[46] I stood on a scaffold at the foot of a *Welsh* mountain, having all the people in front, and called, "Behold the Lamb of God, who taketh away the sin of the world" [John 1:29]. The word was as a two-edged sword.[47] I knew not then that several Baptists were present, a carnal, cavilling, contentious sect, always watching to steal away our children, and make them as dead as themselves. Mr Allen informed me that they have carried off no less than fifty out of one Society, and that several Baptist meetings are wholly made out of old Methodists. I talked largely with Mr Grimshaw how to remedy the evil. We agreed, 1. That nothing can save the Methodists from falling a prey to every seducer but CLOSE[48] walking with God in all the commandments and ordinances, especially the word and prayer— private, family, and public; 2. That the preachers should be allowed more time in every place to visit from house to house, after Mr Baxter's manner;[49] 3. That a small treatise be written, to ground and preserve them against seducers, and lodged in every family.

We came to Bolton with the night. Above forty of this poor shattered people still keep together. Many of those without flocked to the word. In great bodily weakness I warned them to fly to the city of refuge. Tried to calm the spirits of our children, and we were comforted together through hope of our Lord's appearing.

*Wednesday, October 20.* Talked kindly to poor John Whitford, who seemed quite sick of his separate congregation, so headstrong and untractable—so like their humble slave and teacher! His principles as well as spirit have cut off his retreat.

*Vestigia nulla retrorsum*[50]

---

44. Likely Ewood, Lancashire, about one mile south of Blackburn.
45. In the MS the date is incorporated into the text. It has been separated for clarity.
46. John Wesley describes this as a lone house set on the side of an enormous mountain (*Journal* [July 20, 1759], *Works* 21:210). It was one mile southwest of Todmorden, Lancashire.
47. Cf. Heb. 4:12.
48. So written in block capitals in the MS.
49. Richard Baxter, *Gildas Salvianus, The Reformed Pastor; showing the nature of the pastoral work, especially in private instruction and catechizing* (London: Robert White, 1656).
50. This is a proverb taken from Horace's fable "The Fox and Lion" (*Epistles*, I.i.74–75). It

when once a Methodist preacher has abused both ours and our children's confidence, by setting up for himself. This he could never think of, till the salt had lost its savour.[51]

The rain quickened our pace to Manchester. Took up my lodgings at Mr Philips's. My subject at night was, "When these things begin to come to pass, then look up" [Luke 21:28]. Many Arian and Socinian Dissenters were present, and gnashed upon me with their teeth, while I preached the coming of Jesus Christ, the one eternal self-existing God, to take vengeance on them, and on all his enemies, who would not have him to reign over them.

*Thursday, October 21.* I finished my discourse to our Lord's disciples. Parted with my right hand, my brother and bosom-friend, Grimshaw. Breakfasted at Mrs Fanshaw's, and rejoiced to find that, though she had left us, she had not utterly forsaken God. Her soul has suffered loss, yet her good desires remain. Here my old friend [John] Boulton found me out, and confirmed his love to me.

From church I went to dine with our sister Rider, still waiting for the consolation of Israel.[52] I drank tea with Dr [John] Byrom, and was hard put to it to defend my brother's book against Mr Law.[53] We got at last to a better subject, and parted, not without a blessing.

At night I discoursed on Titus 2:11. Spoke close and home on practical faith and relative duties; but more closely still to the Society.

It seems the famous Mr Roger Ball[54] is now among them, picking up their pence and their persons. They were smit with admiration of so fine a man (Thomas Williams himself was nothing to him[55]), and invited him to settle with them. Another new preacher they have also got, a young Baptist, who is gathering himself a meeting out of them, like the Baptist teachers who have borrowed so many of Mr Grimshaw's children. Our Society in Manchester was upward of two hundred, but their itching ears[56] have reduced them to half the number.

---

translates literally "no signs of returning." But it came to mean proverbially "There is no turning back."

51. Cf. Matt. 5:13.

52. Cf. Luke 2:25.

53. John Wesley, *A Letter to the Rev Mr Law; Occasioned by Some of His Late Writings* (London: [Strahan,] 1756).

54. Originally a member of the Dublin Methodist society, whom the Wesley brothers came to regard as antinomian and unscrupulous.

55. Cf. the May 2, 1744, entry above.

56. Cf. 2 Tim. 4:3.

To these I showed the melancholy state of the members of the Established Church, who are the most unprincipled and ignorant of all that are called Protestants, and therefore exposed to every seducer who thinks it worth his while to turn them Dissenters, Moravians, or Papists. I told them, "Of all the members of the Church of England the poor Methodists are most exposed, because serious, and therefore worth stealing; and of all the Methodists those of Manchester are in the greatest danger, because the most unsettled and unadvisable." I challenged them to show me one Methodist who had ever prospered by turning Dissenter. I asked what would become of them when my brother should die. Whether they would not then be scattered, and broken into twenty sects, old and new? To prevent this, I advised them 1) to get grace, or the love and power of God, which alone could keep and establish their hearts; 2) to continue in all the means of obtaining this, especially the word, and prayer of all kinds—to read the Scriptures daily, to go constantly to Church and Sacrament.

I make more allowance for this poor shattered Society because they have been sadly neglected, if not abused, by our preachers. The leaders desired me not to let Joseph Tucker come among them again, for he did them more harm than good by talking in his *witty way* against the Church and clergy. As for poor John Hampson, he *could* not advise them to go to Church, for he never went himself. But some informed me that he advised them *not* to go. When we set the wolf to keep the sheep, no wonder that the sheep are scattered.

Our brother Johnson tells me, since he sent the people back to Church two have received forgiveness in the prayers there, and two more in the sermon of a Church minister. There are now three sound preachers in these parts. If they continue steadfast, they may undo the great evil which the unsound preachers have done, and confirm our children in their calling.

I cannot leave them in so unsettled a condition; and therefore intend, with God's leave, to spend another week among them. Talked with the leaders, and earnestly pressed them to set an example to the flock by walking in all the commandments and ordinances.

Wrote my thoughts to my brother as follows:

Mr Walker's[57] letter deserves to be seriously considered. One only thing occurs to me now which might prevent in great measure

---

57. Samuel Walker (1714–1761), rector of Truro; cf. his letter to John Wesley (September 5, 1755) in *Works* 26:582–86.

the mischiefs which will probably ensue after our death, and that is *greater, much greater, deliberation and care in admitting preachers.* Consider seriously if we have not been too easy and too hasty in this matter. Let us pray God to show us if this has not been the principal cause why so many of our preachers have lamentably miscarried. Ought any new preacher to be received before we know that he is grounded, not only in the doctrines we teach, but in the discipline also, and particularly in the communion of the Church of England? Ought we not to try what he can answer a Baptist, a Quaker, a Papist, as well as a predestinarian or Moravian? If we do not insist on that στοργή[58] for our desolate mother as a prerequisite, yet should we not be well assured that the candidate is no enemy to the Church?

Is it not our duty to stop Joseph Cownley, and such like, from railing and laughing at the Church? Should we not now, at least, shut the stable-door? The short remains of my life are devoted to this very thing, to follow our sons (as Charles Perronet told me we should you) with buckets of water, to quench the flame of strife and division, which they have or may kindle.

*Friday, October 22.* After preaching I talked with several of the Society, particularly a young woman, who seemed quite over-whelmed with the love of Christ, which she received yesterday in private prayer. I went to St Ann's[59] prayers, and thence to the Room. Began our first hour of intercession. Many more than I expected were present. I gave an exhortation, showing the end of our meeting every Friday, as Englishmen and members of the Church of England, to deprecate the national judgments, and to pray for the peace of Jerusalem.[60] I have rarely known so solemn an assembly. They were pleased to hear that we design to continue meeting every week.

I went thence to seek that which was lost, poor H. O.[61] He made me very happy by his misery, and restlessness to return. Once more, I trust, there will be joy in heaven over him.[62]

Began in the evening to expound the whole armour of God (Eph. 6[:11-17]). After I had done, the famous Mr Ball lifted up his voice—

---

58. "Affection," or "love."
59. St Ann's church, an early eighteenth-century addition to Manchester.
60. On May 17, 1756, Britain had declared war on France, leading into the Seven Years War.
61. The "H" is clear in the MS, but Charles almost certainly is referring to Adam Oldham, who was indeed restored (see the October 31 entry below).
62. Cf. Luke 15:7.

and a magnificent voice it was. I bade our people depart in peace, which they did. The enemy roared some time in the midst of the room (not congregation) threatening me for scandalizing him and depriving his family of their bread. I believe he is defrauded of his prey through my coming in *ipso temporis articulo*[63] when he promised himself a good provision out of our Society. No wonder Satan rages at his disappointment.

I met the Society in calm love. There was no farther need of my mentioning Satan's apostle, for he has sufficiently showed himself. The snare is thereby broken, and the simple souls delivered. I lovingly exhorted them to stand fast in one mind and one spirit, in the old paths or ways of God's appointing [Phil. 1:27]. Hence forth they will not believe every spirit.[64] The Lord establish their hearts with grace.

Experience convinces me more and more that the Methodists can never prosper, or even stand their ground, unless they continue steadfast in the ordinances. The Society here used to be scattered on the Lord's day in the fields, or sleeping in their houses. This invited all the beasts of the forest to devour them. Suffice the time that is past. We are not ignorant now of Satan's devices.[65]

*Saturday, October 23.* Proceeded to expound the whole armour of God [Eph. 6:11-17]. We were a little too early for Mr Ball and his friends, two of whom last night had laid violent hands on me. One *was* a sister of ours, till her curiosity betrayed her into the hands of Mr Ball.

Breakfasted at brother [Richard] Barlow's, and rejoiced in the remembrance of his blessed sister, now in glory. For seven years she adorned the gospel in all things.

Took horse with brother Philips for Hayfield, which we reached by one. The sun shone all day without a cloud, to the great comfort of the poor husbandmen. I found at Hayfield just such a family as *was* once at Fonmon Castle.[66] The master indeed was absent, but had left word that his church and house expected me.

I preached at seven to an house full of the parishioners, on "Repent ye, therefore, and be converted, that your sins may be blotted

---

63. "The very same moment of time."
64. Cf. 1 John 4:1.
65. Cf. 2 Cor. 2:11.
66. Charles is visiting John Baddeley (1706–1764), rector in Hayfield and a Methodist sympathizer.

out," etc. [Acts 3:19]. I did not spare them. They bore my plain speaking. The awakened were much comforted.

The voice of joy and thanksgiving is in the habitations of the righteous. I thought I was got back to Mr [Robert] Jones's castle. We continued our triumph two hours longer, and could hardly part at last, and not without grudging our bodies their necessary rest.

*Sunday, October 24.* Spent from seven to eight in advising and praying with the sincere, whom Mr Baddeley has divided into classes like ours. Read prayers at ten, and preached "The One Thing Needful" [Luke 10:42]. The Lord filled my mouth with awakening words. I never spake more convincingly. All seemed to feel the sharp two-edged sword.[67]

The church was fuller than was ever known in a morning. But in the afternoon it was crowded every corner of it. I tasted the good word while reading it. Indeed the Scripture comes with double weight to me in a church. If any pity me for my bigotry, I pity them for their blind prejudice, which robs them of so many blessings.

My text was Lam. 1:12, "Is it nothing to you, all ye that pass by? Behold," etc. The love of Christ crucified melted many hearts. I addressed myself by turns to the unawakened, the sincere, and the backsliders. For an hour God enabled me to speak with convincing and comforting power. After the psalm, began again, and recapitulated the whole. Why does God always accompany the word with a double blessing when preached in the church? Is it a sign that he is leaving or that he is returning to it? I have never been more assisted since I left Bristol, than in this church, and Mr Crook's, and Mr Williamson's. Those of the Methodist preachers who have faith and patience may, by and by, have all the churches in England opened to them. Got another blessed, lively hour with the Society. Then my whole stock of strength was exhausted.

*Monday, October 25.* From six to seven I warned and exhorted them with many tears, tasting the bitterness of life, and the various evils we are still to be brought through. By eleven returned to Manchester.

Here I rejoiced to hear of the great good Mr Whitefield had done in our Societies. He preached as universally as my brother. He warned them everywhere against apostasy, and strongly insisted

---

67. Cf. Heb. 4:12.

on the necessity of holiness *after* justification, illustrating it with this comparison: "What good would the King's pardon do a poor malefactor dying of a fever? So, notwithstanding you have received forgiveness, unless the disease of your nature be healed by holiness, ye can never be saved." He beat down the separating spirit, highly commended the prayers and services of our Church, charged our people to meet their bands and classes constantly, and never to leave the Methodists or God would leave them. In a word: he did his utmost to strengthen our hands, and deserves the thanks of all the churches for his abundant labour of love.

I consulted the leaders what could be done for this unstable people. Richard Barlow and the rest ascribed their fickleness to their neglect of the means, particularly going to Church, and "when we advised them to it, they would answer us, 'The preachers do not advise us to go, neither do they go themselves.' " Nay, some spoke against it, even Mr [Christopher] Hopper and those we most confided in. As for Joseph Tucker, they assured me his whole conversation wherever he came was to ridicule both the Church and the clergy. And John Haughton is just now informed by a faithful sister from Cork that James Deaves continues the same vile treacherous practice, and lately made a mock of the Sacrament before all the Society.[68] My brother and I must wink very hard not to see the hearts of such men.

*Tuesday, October 26.* My *former* friend Mr [John] Clayton read prayers at the old church,[69] with great solemnity.[70] Richard Lucas returned from Bolton. Informed me that John Hampson had been scattering his firebrands there also, mocking the people for going to "*Old Peg*," as his fellows and he call our Church. What should hinder him from providing for himself and growing family when opportunity serves by following Mr Edwards's example? Or what security can we have that all the preachers of his mind will not do the same? I am incapable of trusting them till they are convinced of their pride and treachery.

But what should we do in the meantime? Trust the flock to them, as superintendents? Enlarge their power of doing mischief? Or retrench

---

68. The preceding two sentences are omitted by Jackson.
69. The Collegiate Church of St Mary, St Denys, and St George, in central Manchester (now the cathedral).
70. Jackson omitted the remainder of this paragraph, and all of the next.

it? Is it not high time for us *to be* what we profess, ministers and guardians of the Church of England? Should we leave York to the mercy of Mr Johnson? Newcastle to Jacob Rowell and Joseph Cownley? Ireland to James Deaves? And why not then Bristol to Charles Perronet, and London to Ned [Perronet]? By doing nothing we give up all into the enemy's hands.

Spent the day in writing letters at sister Fanshaw's, whom I have received again into the fold. She had never left us in heart, but the cares of the world interrupted her outward fellowship. She seems now resolved to live and die with the poor afflicted people of God.

Made up a quarrel of many months' standing between two sisters. The occasion of it was absolutely nothing. Such is the subtlety of our adversary!

After preaching I examined three of the most wavering classes, and persuaded all, except the Dissenters, to go back to Church and Sacrament. The treacherous dealers have dealt very treacherously. Even *before* our departure the grievous wolves are entered in, not sparing the flock. How much more, *after* our departure, will men arise of ourselves, speaking perverse things, to draw away disciples after them!

*Wednesday, October 27.* I preached from Rom. 6[:22], "But now being made free from sin, and become the servants of God, ye have your fruit unto holiness, and the end everlasting life." The Lord confirmed his word with a double blessing.

Went with John Haughton to the old church, as usual. Preached at six. Then met, and lovingly reproved, the Society. Talked with more of the classes, and could find only two who would not take advice. Amalek had smote the hindmost,[71] so I let Amalek take them, at least while they prefer Mr Ball to all the Methodists. The rest, a few Dissenters excepted, determined to live and die with us in the communion of the Church of England.

*Thursday, October 28.* Mr Fanshaw dragged his feeble body to the early preaching. After all his wanderings and backslidings, we have received him again, as we trust, for ever.

Preached at noon near Davyhulme, with great enlargement, to a simple-hearted people, who made me some amends for my long exercise at Manchester.

---

71. Cf. Exod. 17:8-13.

Passed the remainder of the day with some Manchester friends who are not of the Society. The unsteadiness of our children has kept many from venturing among us.

Began our watch-night exactly at seven, and concluded a quarter before eleven. Hereby we had more time with less inconvenience, and the whole congregation stayed from first to last. I expounded the Ten Virgins [Matt. 25:1-13]. The solemn power of God rested upon us. It was one of the happiest nights I have known.

Was constrained to write the following letters:

To Mr Grimshaw

Manchester, October 29th.

I could not leave this poor shattered Society so soon as I proposed. They have not had fair play from our treacherous sons in the gospel, but have been scattered by them as sheep upon the mountains. I have once more persuaded them to go to Church and Sacrament, and stay to carry them thither the next Lord's day.

Nothing but grace can keep our children, after our departure, from running into a thousand sects, a thousand errors. Grace, exercised, kept up, and increased in the use of all the means, especially family and public prayer, and Sacrament, will keep them steady. Let us labour, while we continue here, to ground and build them up in the Scriptures, and all the ordinances. Teach them to handle well the sword of the Spirit, and the shield of faith.[72] Should I live to see you again, I trust you will assure me, there is not a member of all your Societies but reads the Scripture daily, uses private prayer, joins in family and public worship, and communicates constantly. "In those is continuance, and we shall be saved" [Isa. 64:5].

To my beloved brethren at Leeds, etc.

Grace and peace be multiplied! I thank my God, on your behalf, for the grace which is given unto you, by which ye stand fast in one mind and in one spirit. My Master, I am persuaded, sent me unto you at this time to confirm your souls in the present truth, in your calling, in the old paths of gospel ordinances. O that ye may be a pattern to the flock for your unanimity and love! O that ye may continue steadfast in the word, and in fellowship, and in breaking of bread, and in prayers (private, family, and public) till we all meet around the great white throne!

---

72. Cf. Eph. 6:16-17.

I knew beforehand that the Sanballats and Tobiahs[73] would be grieved when they heard there was a man come to seek the welfare of the Church of England. I expected they would pervert my words, as if I should say, *"The Church could save you."* So, indeed, you and they thought, till I and my brethren taught you better, and sent you *in* and *through* all the means to Jesus Christ. But let not their slanders move you. Continue in the old ship. Jesus hath a favour for our Church, and is wonderfully visiting and reviving his work in her. It shall be shortly said, "Rejoice ye with Jerusalem, and be glad with her, all ye that love her. Rejoice for joy with her, all ye that mourn for her" (Isaiah 66:10, etc.).

Blessed be God, ye see your calling. Let nothing hinder your going constantly to Church and Sacrament. Read the Scriptures daily in your families, and let there be a church in every house. The word is able to build you up. And if ye watch and pray all ways, ye shall be counted worthy to stand before the Son of Man.[74]

"Watch ye, therefore; stand fast in the faith; quit yourselves like men; be strong. Let all your things be done in love" [1 Cor. 16:13-14].

I rejoice in hope of presenting you all in that day. Look up, for your eternal redemption draweth near.[75]

As the people here leave work at twelve, we pitched upon that hour for our intercession. Many flocked to the house of mourning; and again the Lord was in the midst of us, making soft our hearts, and helping our infirmity to pray.[76] We never want faith in praying for King George, and the Church of England.

I recovered another straggler, as I do every day. The enemy has had a particular grudge to this Society. His first messenger to them was a *still sister*, who abounded in visions and revelations. She came to them as in the name of the Lord, and forbade them to pray, sing, or *go to Church*. Her extravagance at last opened their eyes, and delivered them from the snare of mysticism. Then the Quakers, the predestinarians, the dippers, desired to have them to sift them like wheat.[77] They were afterwards thrust sore at by Mr [John] Bennet, [Thomas] Williams, [James] Wheatley, [William] Cudworth, [John] Whitford, [Roger] Ball. It is a miracle that two of them are

---

73. Cf. Neh. 4:1-3.
74. Cf. Luke 21:36.
75. Cf. Luke 21:28.
76. Cf. Rom. 8:26.
77. Cf. Luke 22:31.

left together. Yet, I am persuaded, the third part will be brought through the fire [Zech. 13:9].

Examined more of the Society. Most of them have known the grace of our Lord Jesus Christ. Several received it at Church; one in the Litany, another in the Lord's Prayer—with that word, "Thy kingdom come," Christ came into his heart. To many he has been made known in the breaking of bread.[78]

**Saturday, October 30.** Dined with my candid friend and censor Dr Byrom. I stood close to Mr Clayton in church (as all the week past), but not a look would he cast towards me;

So stiff was his parochial pride,[79]

and so faithfully did he keep his covenant with his eyes, not to look upon an old friend when called a Methodist.

**Sunday, October 31.** Spake from five to seven with the rest of the classes. Left out Richard Glover, with his second wife, whom he has married, contrary to my advice, when his first was scarce cold in her grave. This scandalous practice, seldom named among the heathen, should never be tolerated among Christians. I refused tickets to James and Elizabeth Ridgworth, till they should have enough of Mr Ball. All the others were willing to follow my advice, and go constantly to Church and Sacrament. The Dissenters I sent to their respective meetings.

At seven I found freedom to explain and enforce Isaiah 64:5, "In those is continuance, and we shall be saved." It struck eight before I had got half through my subject. Breakfasted with a wanderer, and brought him back to his brethren. We were all at the Old Church. Heard a good sermon from Mr Clayton on constant prayer, and joined to commemorate our dying Lord. Mr M.,[80] the senior chaplain, sent for me up to the table, to administer first to me, with the other clergy. I know not when I have received a greater blessing. The addition of fourscore communicants made them consecrate twice or thrice. A few of our Dissenting brethren

---

78. Cf. Luke 24:35.

79. Cf. Matthew Prior, "Paulo Purganti and His Wife," ln. 52, *Poems*, 103: "And stiff was her parochial pride."

80. It was actually the Fellows of the Collegiate Church who presided at Eucharist. Charles is most likely referring to Thomas Moss, one of these Fellows.

communicated with us, and confessed to me afterwards that the Lord met them at his table. It was a passover much to be remembered. We renewed our solemn covenant with God, and received fresh strength to run the race set before us.

Dined at Adam Oldham's. The first *was* become last, but is now, I hope, becoming first again.[81] I re-admitted both him and his wife into the Society, with several others who were fallen off.

From the new church [St Ann's] walked to our crowded room, and once more *preached up* the ordinances. Now the long-delayed blessing came. The skies as it were poured down righteousness. The words I spoke were not my own, therefore they made their way into many hearts.

I received double power to exhort the Society (now upwards of one hundred and fifty members), and *believed for them* that they will henceforth walk in all the commandments and ordinances of the Lord blameless.

# NOVEMBER 1756

*Monday, November 1.* Met about a score of the Dissenters at four, and administered the Lord's Supper, to the great consolation of us all.

Took my leave in the promise we wait for, "I will bring the third part through the fire" [Zech. 13:9], and left a blessing behind me. Mr Philips attended me as far as Stone. The heavens smiled upon us all day.

*Tuesday, November 2.* Took horse at seven, and came safe by two to my old friend Francis Ward in Wednesbury. At night I enforced the divine counsel, Isaiah 6:20: "Come, my people, enter thou into thy chambers, and shut thy doors about thee. Hide thyself as it were for a little moment, until the indignation be overpast. For, behold, the Lord cometh out of his place to punish the inhabitants of the earth for their iniquity." I found much freedom of love among my oldest children, and they readily received my warnings;

*(Wednesday, November 3)*[82] which I repeated the next morning from Psalm 46. Employed the morning in visiting the sick and shut

---

81. Cf. Matt. 20:16; Mark 10:31; Luke 13:30.
82. In the MS the date is incorporated into the text. It has been separated for clarity.

up. Three or four stragglers I gathered in. Comforted our sister Spittle, left with five small children by her husband, who was lately killed in a coal-pit, by the earth falling in. No death could be sudden to him. John Eaton was killed by falling into a pit. His daughter [Mrs] Edge told me she was warned by a repeated dream of his death, and begged him in vain not to go out that morning.

While I was talking with her, a woman came in and accosted me in such a bold, violent manner that I told her I did not like her spirit. This raised and called it forth. She quickly *showed* herself a Nicolaitan[83] by her boisterous, shocking antinomian *assurance*. I told her she was a false witness for God, to which she horribly answered, "If I am a liar, God himself is a liar." I shut up the discourse with, "Get thee behind me, Satan!"[84]

I was much assisted, both at one and at seven, to warn many listening souls of the flood coming. There was great life in the Society. *All* the first, I am confident, shall not become last.[85]

*Thursday, November 4.* I left that promise upon their hearts, "I will bring the third part through the fire" [Zech. 13:9], and took horse with James Jones. Encouraged the remnant at Birmingham with the same words, and rode on to Worcester.

About a score I had left here some years ago, twelve of whom are fallen off to the Quakers, seeking the living among the dead.[86] I described the last times to between forty and fifty at our sister Blackmore's, and it was a solemn time of refreshing.

*Friday, November 5.* Set out before day with faithful John Dornford. Lodged at Cambridge Inn; and, by eleven on Saturday morning, November 6th, God brought me safe to my friends in Bristol.

---

83. Cf. Rev. 2:6.
84. Cf. Matt. 16:23; Mark 8:33; Luke 4:8.
85. Cf. Matt. 20:16; Mark 10:31; Luke 13:30.
86. Cf. Luke 24:5.

# INDEX OF PERSONS

Abdey, Judge, of Nottingham, 2:401

Acourt, Mrs, of London, 1:171

Adams, John, of Tresmeer, 2:472

Adams, Mr, of Ashby-de-la-Zouch, Leicestershire, 2:624

Adams, Mr, of London, 2:574, 578

Adams, "Sister" (d. 1746), of London, 2:454

Adams, Thomas, of Osmotherley, 2:485

Aggit, Mr, of Dublin, 2:509, 510

Ainsworth, Robert (1660–1743), of London, 1:102

Alcroft, "Sister," of London, 2:455

Allen, Mr, of Newcastle Upon Tyne, 2:637

Allen, Mrs, of London, 2:600, 601

Amos, "Sister," of Bristol, 2:560

Anderson, Chryssy, of London, 1:169

Angel, George, of London, 1:295

Anne, Queen (1665–1714), 2:628

Annesley, Anne, of Islington (sister of Susannah Wesley), 1:160

Appee (also Apie or Appy), Peter, of Holland, 1:33, 88; 2:403

Archbishop of Canterbury. *See* John Potter, William Wake

Arnet, Rev George (d. 1750), vicar of Wakefield (Charles spells "Arnett"), 2:388

Arnett, "Sister" (b. 1664/5), of Bristol, 2:601

Arnold, Benjamin, sailor, 1:50

Arthur, Mr, of Kingswood, 1:277

Arvin, Mr, of London, 2:436

Ash, Mrs, of London, 1:260

Ashton, Mr, of Bristol (?), 2:378

Aspernell, Mrs Bilhah (c. 1774), of London (Charles spells "Billal Aspernel"), 1:264

Augustine of Hippo, 1:191

Austin, Margaret, of London, 1:234

Ayers, Mrs, of Bristol, 1:194, 195

Ayling, Anne, of Bristol, 1:292

B., Miss, of Leeds, 2:487

B., Mr, of Manchester, 2:629

B., Rev, of the "Minster," York, 2:629

B., "Sister" (d. 1744), of Bristol, 2:420

B—n, Mr, of Bristol, 2:579

Baddeley, Rev John (1706–1764), rector of Hayfield, 2:641, 642

Baddiley, George, of London, 2:337

Baily, Joyce, of Cork, 2:544

Baker, "Sister," 2:513, 523

Baldwyn, Captain Edward, of Diddlebury Hall, 2:575, 576

Baldwyn, Mr, of London, 1:101

Baldwyn, Mrs Mary (*née* Gwynne, b. 1720), of Diddlebury Hall, 2:575

Ball, Roger, of Dublin and beyond, 2:638, 646

Barber, "Sister," of London, 1:238

Barlow, Richard, of Manchester, 2:641, 643

Barnes, Thomas, of Dublin, 2:524

Barr, Miss, of Bristol, 2:407

Barraby, Mary, of London, 1:256

Barrow, Hannah, of Bristol and Kingswood School, 1:271, 300

Barton, Mr and Mrs, of Islington, 1:115

Batchelor, "Sister" (d. 1749), of London, 2:578

Bateman, Rev Richard Thomas (c. 1713–1760), rector of St Bartholomew-the-Great, London, 2:498, 502

Bates, Arthur, of Wakefield, 2:388

Battely, Rev Oliver (b. 1697?), of Oxford and curate at Cowley (Charles spells "Bateley"), 1:85

Baxter, Richard (1615–1691), 1:359; 2:637

Beacher, Rev Henry, rector of Temple Church, Bristol, 1:275

Belcher, Jonathan (1681/2–1757), colonial governor of Massachusetts (1730–1741), 1:56

Bell, Mercy, of York, 2:628

Bell, Richard, of London, 1:164

Bell, Mrs Richard, of London, 1:154

Benham, Mary, of London, 1:260

Bennet, Edward, of Sheffield, 2:344

Bennet, Grace (née Murray) (1716–1803), 2:583

Bennet, John (1715–1759), itinerant, 1:251; 2:394, 400, 583

Bennet, Rev John (c. 1670–1750), of Tresmere, 2:408, 464, 474

Bennet, Joseph, near Dewsbury, 2:634

Bennetts, John (d. 1765), of St Just (Charles spells "J. Bennet"), 2:467

Benson, Martin (1689–1752), Bishop of Gloucester (1734–1752), 1:83

Benson, Mrs, of Cheshunt, Hertfordshire, 1:83

Bentham, Edward ("Ted," 1707–1776), of Oxford, 1:98; 2:612

Bernard, Mrs, of Epworth, 2:354

Beutiman, Margaret, of London, 1:134

Beveridge, William (1637–1708), Bishop of St Asaph (1704–1708), 1:132, 163, 233

Bèze, Théodore de (1519–1605), 1:308

Biddle, Mrs, of London, 1:177

Bidgood, Hannah, of Sticklepath, 2:408

Bird, Elizabeth, of London, 1:261

Bishop of London, 1:72, 78, 150, 162, 165, 168, 178, 179, 185; 2:399, 434, 475. See also Gibson, Edmund

Black, Joseph, of Bristol, 1:209

Blacket, Sir Edward, of Hexham, 2:482

Blackmore, "Sister," of Worcester, 2:600, 649

Blackwell, Ebenezer (d. 1782), of Lewisham, 2:563, 589, 603

Blackwell, Mrs Elizabeth (née Mowland, d. 1772), of Lewisham, 2:531

Bladen, Colonel Martin (1680–1746), of London, 1:69

Bladworth, Ann, of Bristol, 1:201

Blammires, "Sister," of Dublin, 2:524

Blow, William, of Grimsby, 2:486

Böhler, Peter (1712–1775), Moravian, 1:97, 99–101; 2:243

Bonnel, Mr, of Stanton Harcourt, 1:89

Booth, Elizabeth, of Woodseats, 2:614

Boreman, Thomas, of London, 1:260

Borlase, Rev Dr Walter (1694–1776), rector of Ludgvan and vicar of St Just, 2:411, 413, 468

Borough, Mr, constable of Devizes, 2:491, 493

Boult, Mrs, of London, 2:529, 532, 577

Boulton, John, of Davyhulme, 2:488, 638

Bouquet, "Sister," of London, 2:578

Bourn, Jane, of London, 1:258

Bourn, Richard, of Bristol, 1:202

Bovey, Miss Rebecca, of Savannah, Georgia, 1:33

Bowen, Elisabeth, of London, 1:242

Bowen, Grace (d. 1755), of Garth and Ludlow, 2:560, 570

Bowers, Thomas, of London, 1:172

Boyce, Mr, of Berkswell (father of Susan), 1:91

Boyce, Susan, of Berkswell, 1:91

Bradford, Miss Mary, of Bradford-on-Avon, 2:608

Branford, Miss, of London, 1:136, 256
Branker, Mary, of Bristol, 1:215
Brass, Walter, of Newcastle, 2:430
Bray, John, of London, 1:101, 153, 160, 163–64, 169, 171, 174, 176–77, 184, 227, 233, 235, 246, 248; 2:356, 373
Bray, Mrs John, of London, 1:101, 112–13
Bridge, Christopher (b. 1712), of Boston and Cambridge, 1:56, 59
Bridgins, George (b. 1661), of Birmingham (Charles spells "Bridgin"), 2:599
Briggs, William (1722–c. 1788), of London, 1:566
Brimble, "Sister," of Bristol, 1:314
Briscoe, Mr H., of Leeds, 2:619
Bristow, E., of London, 1:244
Broad, Anne, of London, 1:256
Brockmer, John Paul, of London (Charles spells "Brockmar"), 1:143
Brockmer, Mrs John Paul, of London (Charles spells "Brockmar"), 1:143
Bromley, Mr [William], 1:79
Brook, Mrs Esther, of Bristol, 1:203
Brooke, T., of Thirsk, 2:627
Brooks, Alderman, of Leeds, 2:619
Broughton, Thomas (1712–1777), fellow of Exeter College, Oxford, 1:xxii, 100; 2:427
Brown, Elizabeth ("Betty"), of Bristol, 1:204
Brown, John (1712–1794), of London, 1:114–15, 260; 2:429, 481
Brown, John (c. 1717–1808), of Tanfield Lea, 2:429, 481
Brown, Mary, of Bristol, 1:209
Browne, Jemmett (1702–1782), Bishop of Cork (1745–1772), 2:539
Buck, Mr, Justice of Peace, Rotherham, 2:346
Bunbury, Sir William (c. 1710–1764), vicar of Mildenhall, 2:533
Bunnil, Jabez, of Leeds, 2:619
Burdock, Sally ("Suky"), of Bristol, 1:219, 586

Burnet, Gilbert (1643–1715), Bishop of Salisbury (1689–1715), 2:592
Burnet, "Sister," of London, 2:424
Burnham, Mr, of London, 1:133, 182
Burton, E., Justice of the Peace, Wakefield, 2:397
Burton, Rev John (1696–1771), rector of Maple-Durham, trustee of Georgia Colony, 1:89
Burton, Mr, of London, 1:114–15
Burton, Mrs, of London, 1:133, 154
Butcher, Mrs ["Sister"], of London, 1:158
Butler, Joseph (1692–1752), Bishop of Bristol (1738–1750), 1:218
Butts, Thomas, of London, 2:402, 432, 434, 437, 579, 580
Byrom, Dr John (1692–1763), of Manchester, 1:xxii, 116; 2:424, 638

C—, Mrs, of London, 2:596
Calvin, John (1509–1564), 1:203, 292, 308–309, 328–29; 2:404
Cameron, Mrs, of Marshalsea, 1:173
Campbell, General John (c. 1693–1770), of Westerham, 2:295
Canning, Mr, of Evesham, 1:221, 225, 229; 2:623
Canning, Mrs, of Evesham, 1:225
Cannon, Mrs, of London, 1:295
Capell, Mr, of London, 1:151
Carne, Rev Charles (b. c. 1708), rector of St Athan and Llanmaes, 1:321–22
Carpenter, Lord George (c. 1695–1749), trustee of the Georgia Colony, 1:70
Carr, Mr and Mrs, of Bath, 2:341
Carr, Rev, from Scotland, 2:622
Cart, Mrs Elizabeth, of London, 2:529
Carter, Richard (c. 1713–1737?), of Oxford, 1:80
Cary, Rev, vicar in Bristol, 1:277, 280
Castle, Mary, of Birstall, 396–98
Causton, Thomas, of Frederica, Georgia, 1:39, 43
Cellier, Elizabeth (fl. 1680), 1:41
Cennick, Hannah, of Bristol, 1:270, 305

Cennick, John (1718–1755), itinerant, 1:174–81, 292

Chad, Mrs, of Bristol, 1:216

Chadwick, Mr, of London, 1:86, 93

Chambers, Mr, of London (famous "honest attorney"), 2:452, 648

Chapman, George (b. 1710), of London, 1:115

Chapman, Mrs, of London, 1:129

Chapone, Sarah ("Sally," née Kirkham, 1699–1764), 1:82

Checkley, John, of Boston (Charles spells "Chicheley"), 1:56–59, 72, 155

Checkley, Mrs John, of Boston, 1:58

Cheyne, Margaret, of Bath, 2:532–33

Chinhall, Mr, of St Just, 2:470

Chow, Martin, of London, 1:265

Chrysostom, Saint John (d. 407), 1:223

Church, Sarah, of London, 1:258

Cicero, Marcus Tullius, 1:16, 235, 271

Claggett, Miss Elizabeth ("Betsy," b. 1715), of London and Broadoaks, 1:128, 152

Claggett, Mrs Martha (1691–1773), of London and Broadoaks, 1:128

Claggett, Miss Susanna ("Sukey," b. 1723), of London and Broadoaks, 1:128

Claggett, Wyseman (d. 1741), of London and Broadoaks, 1:137

Clancy, Janet, of Bristol, 1:208

Clansy, Jane, of Bristol, 1:196

Clark, Mr, of Devizes, 2:490, 493, 495–96

Clark, Mr, of London, 1:243

Clayton, Anne, of Bristol, 1:201

Clayton, John (1709–1773), of Manchester, 2:643

Cleminger, Mrs, of Oxford, 1:145

Cloudsley, Richard, of Leeds, 2:619

Coates, Rev John (c. 1716–1782), vicar of Acomb, 2:629

Cob, Don Ignacio, Commander of Spanish infantry, St Augustine, Florida, 1:35, 37

Cockburn, Dr Thomas (d. 1768), of York, 2:625

Cockburn, Mrs Thomas, of York, 2:630

Cockburn, Dr William (1669–1739), of London, 1:69, 98, 100, 104; 2:625, 629–30

Cockell, Richard, of Leeds, 2:619

Colbeck, Thomas (1723–1779), of Keighley, 2:617, 635

Cole, Anne, of Bristol, 1:202

Colerick, Rev Thomas (d. 1761), vicar of St John's church, Cardiff (Charles spells "Coldrach"), 1:323

Collis, Mrs, of London, 2:433

Colvil, Mrs, of St Anne's Hill, 2:529, 592, 601, 603–604, 606

Colwell, Mrs, of Frederica, Georgia, 1:4

Comenius, Johann Amos (1592–1670), 1:264

Connor, Jane, of Bristol, 1:218

Connor, Mary, of Bristol, 1:218

Connor, Mr, of Dublin, 2:517

Conybeare, John (1692–1755), Dean of Christ Church, Oxford (1733–1755), 1:79; 2:566

Coombs, Thomas, of Oxford (Charles spells "Combes"), 1:148

Cope, Sir John (1690–1760), 2:449

Corbet, Rev Francis (d. 1775), Dean of St Patrick's, Dublin, 2:513

Corney, Captain of the Hannah, 1:69, 72, 74–75

Cossart, Heinrich Friedrich [Henry] (1714–1763), Moravian, 1:181, 185

Cotrell, Rev Edward, rector of Marmullane, 2:539

Cotteril, Mr, of Islington, 1:172

Cottle, Mr, of Bradford on Avon, 1:213; 2:609

Coulston, Mr, of Bristol, 1:192

Cousins, Mr, of Rotherham, 2:625

Cownley, Joseph (1723–1792), itinerant, 2:640, 644

Cowper, Anne (d. 1743), of London, 2:372

Cowper, Mr, of London, 2:434

Cox, Jane, 2:597

Cox (or Cocks), Lady Mary (*née* Bethel), 1:85

Cox, Sir Robert, 1:85

Cr—, Justice, of Bristol, 1:330

Cradock, Mrs, of Bristol, 2:607

Craven, Mr, of London, 1:294

Crawford, J., of Newcastle upon Tyne, 2:485–86,

Crease, Mary, of Bristol, 1:218

Crease, W., of Bristol, 1:218

Crispe, Lady Elizabeth (*née* Sayer, d. 1741), of Islington (Charles spells "Crisp"), 1:159

Crispe, Mary (1722–1751) (Charles spells "Crisp"), 1:159. *See also* Stonehouse, Mrs Mary

Crispe, Sir John, 1:159

Critchet, Cordelia, of London, 1:252–53

Crockar, "Sister," of Poynt's Pool, 2:608

Cromwell, Oliver (1599–1658), 1:268

Crook, Rev Henry (1708–1770), curate of Hunslet, 2:625–26, 630, 631, 633, 642

Crook, John, 1:293

Crosier, Phebe, of Ryton, 2:484

Crouch, Mr (Thomas?), of London, 1:166, 169, 238, 245, 248, 252

Crowe, Dr William (c. 1691–1743), rector of St Botolph's church, 1:154

Cudworth, William (1718–1763), of London, 2:646

Cutler, John (1713–1771), of Boston and Cambridge (son of Dr Cutler), 1:56, 59–61, 69

Cutler, Dr Timothy (1684–1765), rector of Christ Church, Boston, 1:55–56

D., Mr, of York, 2:628

Dale, James, of Penzance, 2:411

Dalrymple, John (1673–1747), 2nd Earl of Stair, 2:405

Dandy, Mr, of London, 1:136

Daniel, Mrs, of London, 1:170

Darney, William (d. 1774), itinerant, 2:488

Davenport, Rev Addington (1701–1746), of Scituate, Massachusetts, 1:57

Davey, "Sister," of London, 2:450, 455, 568

Davis, Anne (d. 1775), of Bristol, 1:198, 292; 2:586

Davis, Elizabeth (d. 1741), of Bristol, 1:198

Davis, Matthew, of Bristol, 1:200

Davison, Samuel, of Frederica, Georgia, 1:5, 7–8, 16, 19

Dawson, Mr and Mrs Robert, of London, 1:238, 241

Day, Alderman, of Bristol, 1:280

Dean of Christ Church. *See* Conybeare, John

Deaves, James (fl. 1750–1790), itinerant, 2:643–44

Deer, John, of St Nicholas, Wales, 1:286, 327

Delagall, Ensign, British naval officer serving Oglethorpe in Georgia, 1:35

Delamotte, Charles (1714–1786), 1:20, 86–88, 94, 111, 156, 233

Delamotte, Mrs Elizabeth (1685–1771), of Blendon Hall, 1:86

Delamotte, Miss Elizabeth ("Betty/ Betsy") (1710–1780), 1:88, 128

Delamotte, Miss Esther ("Hetty") (1712–1779), 1:88, 193

Delamotte, Miss Mary ("Molly") (b. 1729), 1:94

Delamotte, Mr Peter (d. 1749), of Blendon Hall, 1:88

Delamotte, William ("Jack/Jacky") (1718–1743), 1:103, 122, 124, 126, 129, 132, 134, 141, 149

Dempsey, Charles, of Frederica, Georgia, 1:37, 39

Denison, Alderman, of Leeds, 2:619

Deschamps, Jenny, of Bristol, 1:276

Deschamps, John, of Bristol, 1:194, 197

Designe, Susanna (b. 1712), of Bristol (Charles spells "Design"), 2:338

Deverel, Mary, of Bradford on Avon, 2:610

Dewal, Mrs Hannah (d. 1762), of Lewisham, 2:511, 531, 595

D'Ewes, John, of Wellesbourne (Charles spells "Dews"), 1:81

Dicken, Mrs, of Bath, 2:575

Dickenson, Goody, of Bexley, 1:126

Dickenson, Rebecca, of Bristol, 1:218

Dickinson, John, of London, 1:261

Digges, Miss Mary (1737–1829), of St Anne's Hill (Charles spells "Degge"), 2:592, 601, 604

Dixon, George, of Leeds, 2:619

Dodd, Anne, in Marshalsea prison, 1:162

Doddridge, Rev Dr Philip (1702–1751), 1:182; 2:580

Doleman, John, of Bristol, 1:317

Dornford, John, 2:649

Downes, John (1722–1774), itinerant, 2:392, 406, 425, 578, 621–22, 624

Drummond, "Friend," of Gloucester (a female Quaker), 1:189

Dudley, Captain, of Dudley, 2:383

Dudley, Mrs, of Westerham, 2:600

Dupee, Mrs, of London, 1:254

Dupee, Stephen, of London, 1:234

Dyson, Rev Edward, chaplain of Scottish Highlanders in Georgia, 1:30

E—, Mr, 1:xxi

Eastwood, Jonas, of Dewsbury, 2:634

Eaton, John (1692?–1753), of Wednesbury, 2:649

Edgcomb, "Sister," of Bristol, 2:338

Edge, Mrs, of Wednesbury (daughter of John Eaton), 2:649

Edmonds, John (1710–1803), of London (Charles spells "Edmunds"), 1:101

Edwards, Rev Hugh, curate of Rhayader, 2:556

Edwards, John (1714–1785), itinerant, 2:625–26, 630–31, 633–34, 643

Edwards, Mr, of Dublin, 2:511

Edwin, Catherine (1702–1773), 2:432, 440, 499, 609

Edwin, Sir Charles (1699–1756), MP for Glamorgan (1747–1756), 2:532

Edwin, Lady Charlotte (née Douglas, d. 1774), 2:432, 532

Edzard, Astrea, of London, 1:261

Egginton, Mrs Edward, of Wednesbury, 2:355, 383

Egginton, Rev Edward (c. 1693–1743), vicar of Wednesbury, 2:355, 383

Egmont, Sir John Perceval (1683–1748), 2:383

Elliot, Justice, of Islington, 1:172

Ellis, Mr, of Ebley, 1:190

Ellis, Mr, of Markfield, 2:373

Ellis, Rev Thomas (1712–1792), of Holyhead, 2:535

Ellison, J., of London, 2:498

Ellison, John (1720–1791), nephew of Charles Wesley, 2:498

Ellison, Richard, 2:498

Emery, Mrs, of London, 2:606

England, Mrs, of Bristol, 1:195, 202, 205

Erskine, James (1679–1754), Lord Grange, 2:403, 405, 429–30, 434, 499, 595, 597

Essen, Mrs, of London, 1:77

Eustick, Mr, of Trewellard, 2:469

Evans, Margaret, of Bristol, 2:204

Evans, Sophy, of Dublin, 2:517

Evans, William, of Oxford, 2:503, 532, 594, 597–98

Eveleigh, Samuel, of Charlestown, South Carolina (Charles spells "Eveley"), 1:46

Every, Mr, churchwarden in Bristol, 1:215

Ewsters, Mary (b. 1723), of London (Charles spells "Eusters"), 1:178, 258, 263

Ewsters, Mrs, of London (Charles spells "Eusters"), 1:178, 182, 226, 246; 2:591

Exall, William, of London, 1:141, 172

F., Dr, of Newcastle, 2:481

Fanshaw, Mr, of Manchester, 2:644

Fanshaw, Mrs, of Manchester, 2:638, 644

Farley, Felix (d. 1753), of Bristol, 1:269, 290, 319, 327; 2:369, 378, 404, 423, 498, 532, 568

Farrell, Rev John (c. 1696–1753), priest at St Mary's church, Athlone (Charles spells "Ferril"), 2:519, 551

Fenwick, Michael (d. 1797), itinerant, 2:617

Ferguson, William, Captain of Highlander scout boat, Georgia, 1:29–30

Field, Elisabeth, of Bristol, 1:215

Fielding, Justice, of London, 2:574

Fish, William, of London, 1:137

Fitzwalter, Lord; Benjamin Mildmay (1672–1756), 1:71

Flatman, Captain, Marshalsea prison, London, 1:161

Flowers, Mr, of Coleford, 2:439

Folliard, Mrs, of Dublin, 2:553

Ford, Mrs, of Oxford, 1:269

Force, Mrs, of Tyrrellspass (Charles spells "Fource"), 2:536

Force, Stephen, of Tyrrellspass (Charles spells "Fource"), 2:517–18

Fox, Mr, of Oxford, 1:145

Francis, Molly, of Bristol, 2:604

Frank, gardener for Rev Piers, 1:123

Franklyn, Mr, of Thaxted, 1:174

Frazier, William, Scottish Highlander, in Georgia, 1:31

Frederick, Prince (d. 1751), son of King George II, 1:87; 2:604

Frewin, Richard, M.D. (c. 1681–1761) of Christ Church, Oxford (Charles spells "Fruin"), 1:98–99

Frith, J., mayor of Leeds, 2:619

Fry, Mary, of Bristol, 1:196

Furth, Arthur, of Birstall, 2:397

G—, Mr, of Bristol, 1:312

G., Mr A., of Pool, 2:360

Gambel, Eleanor, of London, 1:265

Gambold, Mrs Elizabeth (d. 1744), of Stanton Harcourt (mother of John), 1:89

Gambold, Rev John (1711–1771), vicar of Stanton Harcourt, 1:80, 85, 97, 148; 2:452

Gambold, Miss Martha (1713–1741), of Stanton Harcourt (sister of John), 1:82

Ganson, Sir John, of London (Charles spells "Gunson"), 1:167, 172, 263

Garden, Ensign, in Sheffield, 2:344

Garden, Rev James (d. 1772?), rector of Slingsby, Yorkshire and curate of Hovingham, 2:370

Gardener, Dr, of Boston, 1:59

Garnault, Daniel, of London, 2:498

Gaseath, "Sister," of Bristol, 1:325

Gates, Anne, of Islington, 1:250

Gee, Mary, of Bristol, 2:457

Gell, Robert (1595–1665), 1:318

George II (1683–1760), King of Great Britain, 1:87; 2:392, 449, 604

Germain, Michael, of Frederica, Georgia, 1:5

Germain, Mrs Michael, of Frederica, Georgia, 1:2

Gershom, Mr, of London, 1:77

Gibbons, Dr, of Boston, 1:59

Gibbs, Mrs, of Bristol, 2:593

Gibson, Edmund (1669–1748), Bishop of London (1723–1748), 1:68, 163

Gilmore, Mrs, of Dublin, 2:524, 526

Glanville, William (1651?–1747), of Plough Court, Fetter Lane, London (Charles spells "Glanvil"), 2:528

Glascott, Thomas, of Cardiff, 1:284

Glover, Richard, of Manchester, 2:647

Godly, Rachel, of Bristol, 1:203

Godwin, Molly (d. 1746), of London, 2:455

Gonzalez, Don Manuel, Secretary to the Spanish Governor, Florida, 1:37

Goslin, Sarah, of Bristol, 2:437

Goter, Richard, of London, 1:182, 215

Gotley, Mrs, of Avon, 2:437

Gough, Sarah, of Bristol, 1:209

Graham, Anne, of London, 1:177

Graham, Mr, first mate of Captain Indivine, 1:52

Granil, Mrs, of Bristol, 1:211

Granville, Anne (1707–1761), 1:77

Granville, Bernard (1700–1776), Duke of Albemarle, 1:81

Graves, Charles Caspar (1717–1787), of Oxford, 1:82, 85, 152, 185, 232; 2:356, 428, 437

Graves, Richard (1715–1804), of Oxford, 1:91

Greaves, Dr Thomas (1683–1747), of Charlestown, Massachusetts (Charles spells "Graves"), 1:57

Green, Rev John, of London, 2:475

Green, William (d. 1777), of Rotherham, 2:624

Greenaway, Mr, Newgate prison, 1:139

Greenwood, Paul (d. 1767), itinerant, 2:616

Gregory, Mary, of Bristol, 1:218, 329; 2:473

Grevil, Elizabeth (née Whitefield, b. 1713), of Bristol, 1:192, 198, 200, 279, 312

Grey, Mr, of London, 2:434, 596

Griffith, J., 2:532

Griffith, Robert, of Holyhead, 2:555

Grimshaw, Mrs Elizabeth (d. 1746), of Haworth, 2:479

Grimshaw, Jane (1737–1750), daughter of William and Elizabeth, 2:587

Grimshaw, Rev William (1708–1763), curate of Haworth and itinerant, 2:479, 487, 579, 587–88, 631–33, 633, 635–38, 645

Grinfill, Edward, of St Just, 2:463, 468

Gumley, Colonel Samuel (d. 1763), of Chertsey, 2:528, 578

Gurley, Mr, of Dublin, 2:517

Gurney, Mr, 2:341, 393

Gwynne, Miss Elizabeth ("Betsy," b. 1730), sister of Sally, 2:534, 560, 600

Gwynne, Howell (1718–1789), brother of Sally, 2:566–67, 570

Gwynne, Miss Joan ("Juggy," 1728–1786), sister of Sally, 2:600

Gwynne, Margaret ("Peggy," 1733–1752), sister of Sally, 2:575

Gwynne, Marmaduke (1691–1769), of Garth and Ludlow, 2:444, 447–48, 504–505, 528, 530–32, 534, 557, 560–61, 565–66, 570, 576

Gwynne, Marmaduke, Jr (b. 1722), brother of Sally, 2:575

Gwynne, Mary (b. 1720), sister of Sally, See Baldwyn, Mrs Mary

Gwynne, Rebecca ("Becky," 1724–1798), sister of Sally, 2:561

Gwynne, Roderick (1695–1772), of Glan Bran, uncle of Sally, 2:572

Gwynne, Mrs Sarah (1695–1770), of Garth and Ludlow, 2:534, 560–61, 563–64, 566–69, 575, 591, 597

Gwynne, Sarah ("Sally," 1726–1822), 2:528, 530–32, 534, 547, 559–61, 565. See also Wesley, Mrs Sarah

H., Miss, of Bath, 2:404

H., Mr, of Cork, 2:539

H., Mr, of Donington Park, 2:624

H., Mr and Mrs and family, of Wick, 2:460

H., Mrs, of Oxford, 1:181

H., B., of Bristol, 1:297

H., B., of London, 1:295

H., "Sister" (d. 1745), of London, 2:444

Haddock, Thomas, of London, 2:261

Hagson, J., of London, 1:165

Hales, John, 2:382

Hales, Dr Stephen (1677–1761), trustee of Georgia Colony, 1:69, 78

Hall, Joseph (1574–1656), Bishop of Exeter (1627–1641), Bishop of Norwich (1641–1656), 1:1, 93

Hall, Mrs (d. 1738), of London, 1:144

Hall, Mrs Martha ("Patty," née Wesley, 1706–1791), 1:249; 2:370, 442, 598, 605

Hall, Rev Westley (1711–1776), brother-in-law of Charles, 1:68, 80, 85, 94–95, 103, 178, 232, 256–57; 2:356, 370, 442, 598, 605, 608

Hall, Westley (or Wesley), Jr (1742–1757), nephew of Charles Wesley, 2:605

Halyburton, Thomas (1674–1712), 1:99, 100, 103; 2:445

Haman, Mary, of Bristol, 1:213

Hamilton, Mr T., of Bristol, 2:601, 608

Hamilton, Mrs, of London, 1:246
Hampson, John (c. 1732–1795), itinerant, 1:639, 643
Handy, Jonathan, of Templemacateer, 2:518
Handy, Samuel, of Tyrrellspass, 2:518, 521
Hankinson, Mrs, of London, 1:144, 147–48, 154, 157, 161
Hannah, maid in Delamotte home, 1:121
Hannah, maid to Mrs Gibbs, 2:593
Hanney, Mary, of Bristol, 1:208
Hanson, Mary, of London, 1:162
Harding, Dr, physician, of Donington, 2:424
Harding, Suky, of Bristol, 1:315
Hardwick, Joseph, of Leeds, 2:619
Hardwick, Thomas, of London, 2:562, 564, 577, 605
Hardy, Miss, of London, 2:603
Harley, Lord Edward (1689–1741), 2nd Earl of Oxford and Mortimer, 1:84
Harley, Lady Henrietta Cavendish (1693–1755), 1:84
Harper, Mrs, of Islington, 1:130
Harris, Howell (1714–1773) (Charles spells first name "Howel"), 1:171, 174, 252, 255, 257, 263, 265, 284–86, 288–89, 291, 314–17; 2:371, 427, 441, 501, 503, 556
Harris, Jephthah, of London, 1:131, 143
Harris, Rev Richard (d. 1766), vicar of Lantrisant, 1:288
Harrison, Mr, of Cork, 2:536
Haskins, Mr, of Bristol, 1:314
Hastings, Lady Elizabeth ("Betty," 1683–1739), 1:83
Hastings, Lady Elizabeth (1731–1808), daughter of Lady Huntingdon, 2:608
Hastings, Lady Margaret (1700–1768), sister-in-law of Lady Huntingdon, 2:631
Hastings, Lady Selina (1737–1763), daughter of Lady Huntingdon, 1:608

Haughton, John (d. 1781), itinerant, 2:526, 643–44
Hawkins, Mrs Beata, of Frederica, Georgia, 1:2, 4–9, 12, 15–16, 19, 21–25, 27, 40–41, 69
Hawkins, Elisabeth, of Bristol, 1:215
Hawkins, Thomas, surgeon, of Frederica, Georgia, 1:7, 11, 69
Hawks, Mr, of Bristol, 1:296
Hawley, Jacob, of Leeds, 2:618
Hawthorn, Mr and Mrs, of London, 1:238
Hay, Thomas (1710–1797), Viscount Dupplin, and later 9th Earl of Kinnoull, 1:84
Haydon, Mr, of Frederica, Georgia, 1:7
Haynes, Mr, of Wick, 2:598
Heally, John (fl. 1740–1750), itinerant (Charles spells "Healey"), 2:389, 393, 518–19, 552, 574, 577–78
Heather, Mr, of London, 1:127
Hermsdorf, Captain, serving in Frederica, Georgia, 1:5–6, 13–14, 21, 29–31, 33, 37, 40
Hervey, James (1714–1758), of Weston Favell, 2:559, 599, 628
Hervey, Mr and Mrs, of Hereford, 2:575
Hewish, Mr Jo., of Bradford-on-Avon, 2:608
Hiam, Mr (a Quaker), near London, 2:373
Hide, Mr, of Plymouth, 2:473
Hill, Mr, dancing master, Charleston, 1:47
Hilland, John (d. 1749), of London (Charles spells "Hiland"), 1:235
Hilland, Mrs Martha (d. 1767), of London (Charles spells "Hiland"), 1:235
Hillingworth, John, of Leeds, 2:618
Hind, Mrs, of London, 1:136, 142, 151, 157
Hinsom, "Sister," of London, 1:238
Hird, Mrs Grace, of Frederica, Georgia, 1:18–19
Hird, Thomas, constable of Frederica, Georgia, 1:7–8, 13, 28

Hitchens, James, of Gwennap (father of Samuel and Thomas) (Charles spells "Hitchins"), 2:474, 476

Hitchens, Samuel (1722?–1746), of Gwennap (Charles spells "Hitchins"), 2:474

Hitchens, Thomas (1723–1746), of Gwennap (Charles spells "Hitchins"), 2:476

Hoare, Joseph (1709–1802?), of Jesus College, Oxford, 1:155

Hoblyn, Rev William (1723–1759), curate of St Ives, Towednack, Zennor (Charles spells "Hoblin"), 2:358, 360, 363, 365, 410, 514

Hodges, Anne (d. 1740), of Bristol, 1:278

Hodges, Rev John (c. 1702–1777), rector of Wenvoe, 1:285, 319, 327; 2:379, 406, 444, 446, 459, 569

Hodges, Joseph (1710–1778), of London, 1:173

Hodges, Walter, Vice-Chancellor of Oxford (1741–1744), 2:420

Hoffman, "Sister," of London, 2:502

Hogg, Thomas (d. 1750), of London, 2:596

Hogg, Mrs Thomas, of London, 2:596

Holland, William (1711–1761), of London, 1:103; 2:563

Hollis, Isaac, of High Wycombe, 1:156

Holloway, Samuel, of London, 2:406

Holmes, Elizabeth, of London, 1:252

Holt, Mr, of Bearfield, 1:213

Hooper, Mrs Elizabeth, of Bristol, 1:196, 276, 306

Hooper, John, of Bristol, 1:219

Hooper, William, of Bristol, 1:270, 308, 312, 316, 331

Hopper, Christopher (1722–1802), itinerant, 2:643

Hopson, Elizabeth ("Betty"), of London, 1:169

Hopson, Esther Sutton ("Hester," 1714–1794), of London, 1:156, 158–59

Horne, Rev Thomas (b. 1708), of Christ Church, and vicar at Spelsbury, 1:79, 91

Horton, William, of Frederica, Georgia, 1:16, 21, 29–32, 86

How (Howe, Howes), John, of Nottingham, 2:344

Howard, Mr, of London, 1:158

Hoy, Mr, of London, 2:574, 590

Hud, Edward, of Bristol, 1:213

Hud, Francis, of Bristol, 1:210

Hudson, Mr, in Newgate prison, 1:137, 139

Hunting, "Sister," of London, 1:262

Huntingdon, Countess Selina Hastings (1707–1791), 1:xxii, 295; 2:344, 424, 432, 434, 440, 499–500, 528, 532, 548, 607–10, 631

Huntington, Sally, of Bristol, 2:567

Hurst, Sarah, of Oxford, 1:161

Hutchings, John (b. 1716), of Pembroke College, Oxford (Charles spells "Hutchins"), 1:91, 145–46, 148–50, 158, 177, 183–84

Hutchinson, John (d. 1754), of Leeds, 2:605, 616

Hutchinson, Mr, of London, 1:45

Hutchinson, Sally (mother of John), of Leeds, 2:605, 615

Hutton, James (1715–1795), of London, 1:67, 85, 91, 95–96, 98, 100, 112, 134, 137, 142, 146–47, 156, 165, 233, 249, 252, 257, 263; 2:515

Hutton, Rev John (1676–1750), College Street, Westminster, 1:67, 69, 86, 93, 154

Hyfield, Catherine, of Bristol, 1:280

I'Anson, Sir Thomas (c. 1701–1764), 2:604, 623–24

Ibison, Sir Henry, of Leeds, 2:619

Ibison, Mr, of London, 1:247, 249

Indivine, Captain, of ship that took Charles from Charleston to Boston, 1:52, 59, 67, 71

Ingham, Rev Benjamin (1712–1772), of Aberford, 1:xix, 1, 8–13, 15–16, 34,

68, 70, 86, 88, 114, 122, 158, 261–64, 267; 2:628, 631, 636
Ingham, Ignatius, of Aberford, 2:631
Ingham, Lady Margaret (*née* Hastings, 1700–1768), of Aberford, 2:631
Inkersley, Joseph, of Leeds, 2:619
Innys, Rev, curate of Devizes, 1:58, 132, 216; 2:490, 492
Isham, Euseby (d. 1755), rector of Lincoln College, Oxford (1731–1755), 1:80

J., E., of London, 2:435
J., J., "the drummer," of Newcastle Upon Tyne, 2:620
Jackson, Jane, of London, 1:234, 237
Jackson, Mr, of Birr, 2:551
James, Captain John, of Bristol, 2:557, 579
James, Thomas, an attorney of Brecon, 2:560, 569–70
Jameson, Mr, near Athlone, 2:519
Jeffreys, Miss, of Bristol, 1:216
Jenkins, Herbert (1721–1772), of Monmouthshire, 2:444, 473
Johnson, Miss Kitty, of Cheshunt, 1:83
Johnson, Mr, of Barley Hall, 2:347
Johnson, Mr, of Manchester, 2:639
Johnson, Mr, of Wakefield, 2:615
Johnson, Mr, of York, 2:644
Johnson, Mrs, of Barley Hall, 2:614
Johnson, Mrs, of Cheshunt, 1:83
Jones, Catherine ("Kitty," 1736–1768), daughter of Robert and Mary, 2:530
Jones, James (d. 1783), itinerant, 2:355, 382–83, 477, 577, 580, 583, 649
Jones, John, 2:548
Jones, Mrs John, of Bandon, 2:548
Jones, Jonathan, of Darlaston, 2:489
Jones, Mary (1733–1781), daughter of Robert and Mary, 1:321
Jones, Mrs Mary (*née* Forrest, 1712–1788), of Fonmon Castle, 2:416, 421
Jones, Mr (d. 1744), of Bristol, 2:562
Jones, Mrs (widow in 1739), of Bristol, 2:447, 449, 607

Jones, Mrs, of Fonmon, 2:607
Jones, Robert (1706–1742), of Fonmon Castle, 1:319–22, 327, 612, 642
Jones, William (1718–1781), of Caernarfon (Trefollwyn Blas), 2:526–27
Joy, Mr, of London, 1:76
Judge, Anne, of London, 1:260

Keech, Mr (d. 1751), of Evesham, 1:229
Keech, Mrs, of Evesham, 2:594
Keech, Patty, of Evesham, 2:477
Keen, Mr, of London (son of Thomas), 2:381
Keen, Thomas, of London (a Quaker), 1:183, 263; 2:433
Keith, Jane, 2:583
Keith, John, 2:595
Keith, Mary (*née* Erskine), of London, 2:595
Kempthorn, "Sister," of London, 2:575
Kendrick, William (Charles spells "Kindrick"), 2:397–98
Kent, Hannah, of London, 1:242
Kinchin, Rev Charles (1711–1742), rector of Dummer, Hampshire, 1:78–79, 80, 86, 91, 99, 145–46, 155, 158
Kinchin, Miss Molly, sister of Charles Kinchin, 1:177
King, Rev James (d. 1759), Prebendary of Tipper at St Patricks, Dublin, 2:514
King, "Sister," of London, 2:528
Kinsman, Andrew (1724–1793), of Tavistock, 2:462, 473
Kirkham, Bernard ("Banny," b. 1718), of Stanton, 1:80
Kirkham, Mrs Demaris, mother of Robert and Bernard, 1:189
Kirkham, Rev Robert (c. 1708–1767), rector of Stanton, 1:79, 80; 2:532
Kirkham, Sarah ("Sally"), 1:82
Kitchinor, Eleanor, of Bristol, 1:209
Knight, Anne (*née* Robinson), 2:532–33; 2:609
Knight, Titus (1719–1793), itinerant, 2:635

Knowls, Lionel, of Birstal, 2:397

L., Mr, near Morvah, Cornwall, 2:411

L., Mrs B., 2:559

Laba, Mr, of London, 1:84

Labbé, Mr, of Bristol (Charles spells "Labu"), 1:200

Labbé, Mrs, of Bristol (Charles spells "Labu"), 1:200

Lambert, Mrs Anne ("Nancy," née Wesley, 1701–?), 1:140

Lambert, John, brother-in-law of Charles Wesley, 1:83, 86, 94, 140

Lambert, John, Jr, nephew of Charles Wesley, 1:269

Lamberto, Don Pedro de, Commander of Spanish cavalry, St Augustine, Florida, 1:35, 37

Lampe, John Frederick (1703–1751), 2:456, 499, 553

Larwood, Samuel, itinerant, 2:405

Lascelles, Henry, Jr, of Frederica, Georgia (Charles spells "Lassel"), 1:19

Laserre, Mr, of Charleston, South Carolina, 1:47

Lavington, George (1684–1762), Bishop of Exeter (1746–1762), 2:548

Lavington, Mary, prophetess, 1:176, 236

Law, William (1686–1761), of Putney, 1:58, 87, 216

Lawley, Mrs Anne, of Frederica, Georgia, 1:13

Lawley, Richard, of Frederica, Georgia, 1:11, 12

Lee, William (b. 1726), son of Sir William Lee (1688–1754), 2:582

Legg, Mrs, of London, 1:71

Leigh, Theophilus (1693–1784), of Oxford, 1:181

Leslie, Charles (1650–1722), 1:95

Lewis, John, of Bristol, 1:181, 200

Lewis, "Sister," of London, 2:590

Lewis, Timothy, printer, of London, 1:263

Leyshon, Molly (d. 1750), of Garth and Ludlow (cousin of Sarah Gwynne) (Charles spells "Leyson"), 2:560, 593

Lillington, Mrs (d. May 1741), of Bristol, 1:306–307, 309

Lincoln, Mrs, of London, 2:476

Linford, Mrs, of Bristol, 1:220

Litchfield, Mary, of London, 1:264

Lloyd, Mr, of Islington, 1:158, 169

Lloyd, Mrs, of Islington, 1:158

Lloyd, Rev Richard (1699–1775), rector of Rathcormack, 2:540

Lloyd, Samuel, of London, 2:568, 605–606

Lovybond, Mr, itinerant, 2:605

Low, Counsellor, of Tyrrellspass, 2:520

Loyola, Ignatius (1491–1556), 1:258, 268

Lucas, Richard, itinerant, 2:643

Lundy, Miss, of London, 2:604

Lunell, Mrs Anne (née Gratton, d. 1748), of Dublin, 2:535

Lunell, Benjamin, of Dublin, son of William and Anne, 2:535

Lunell, William (1699–1774), of Dublin, 2:535, 553

Luther, Martin (1483–1546), 1:103–104, 115, 120, 234, 268; 2:496, 509

Lynch, Colonel, serving in Georgia, 1:47

Lynn, Mr, of London, 1:71, 142

M—, Mrs, of Chelsea, 2:499

M., Mrs, of Dublin, 2:512, 516

Mackintosh, John Mohr, Captain of Highlanders, Georgia, 1:27–28

Macune, Mrs, of London, 1:246–47

Maddern, John, of Zennor and itinerant (Charles spells "Madern"), 2:466

Manaton, Dr Pierce (1704–1743), physician, of Oxford, 1:98–99

Manning, Rev Charles (1715–1799), vicar of Hayes, 2:597, 601

Marcus Aurelius, Emperor of Rome (121–180), 2:604

Marsh, Elizabeth (d. 1744), of London, 2:422

Martin, Charles, of Bristol, 1:281

Martin, Josiah, of Gloucester, 1:189

Martin, Margaret, of London, 1:265

Mary, maid in Delamotte home, 1:120

Maskew, Jonathan (1718–1793), itinerant, 2:618

Mason, Mr, of London, 1:174, 246

Mather, Dr Cotton (1663–1728), 2:592

Maw, John (c. 1667–1753), of Epworth, 2:354, 389

Maw, Mrs, of Epworth, 2:392

Maxfield, Thomas (d. 1784), itinerant, 1:222, 227, 229, 231, 233–39, 261, 265, 269, 294; 2:444, 463, 610

Meriton, Rev John (1698–1753), itinerant, 2:356, 404, 406–10, 413–16, 419–20, 460, 468, 490, 493, 494, 496, 561

Metcalf, Charles (1716–1779), of London, 1:137, 142, 152, 159–60, 171–72

Metcalf, Mrs (mother of Charles), of London, 1:147, 149

Micklethwait, Alderman, of Leeds, 2:619

Middleton, Dr John (d. 1760), of Bristol, 1:277; 2:407, 573, 577, 584, 587

Middleton, Sarah, of London, 1:295

Milbourne, Mr (d. 1743), of London, 2:338–39

Millar, Rev, of Dublin, 2:509, 515

Miller, Rev Ebenezer (d. 1763), rector of Christ Church, Braintree, Massachusetts (Charles spells "Millar"), 1:56, 58

Mills, Elisabeth, of Bristol, 1:218

Milner, Dr, physician, of Leeds (Woodhouse), 2:616

Milsom, Susanna, of Bristol, 1:204–205

Mitchel, Mr, of Bristol, 1:281

Mitchel, Mr, of St Ives, 2:365

Molther, Philipp Heinrich (1714–1780), Moravian, 1:232–33, 236, 239–40, 246–47, 249, 258–59, 263, 265–66

Montagu, Lady Mary Wortley (1689–1762), 1:84; 2:582

Montagu-Dunk, George, 2nd Earl of Halifax (1716–1771), 2:582

Moore, Francis, of Frederica, Georgia, 1:29

Moore, Lieutenant, of the *Hawk* man-of-war, 1:32

Morgan, Mrs, of Westcote and Idbury, 1:226–27, 230–31

Morgan, Rev, vicar of Westcote and Idbury, 1:226–27, 231

Morgan, Richard (1714–1785), of Oxford, 1:86

Morgan, William, 1:86

Morison, Elisabeth, of London, 1:242

Morris, Anne, of London, 1:295

Morris, Daniel, of Bristol, 1:202

Moss, Thomas, Fellow of Collegiate Church, Manchester, 2:647

Motte, Mrs, of Bristol, 2:607

Motte, Rev, rector of Newington, 1:180

Mountstevins, Joseph, of Bristol, 1:204

Mouse, Mrs Lucy, of Skidaway Island, Georgia, 1:34

Munchin, Mr, of Darlaston, 2:377

Muncy, Jane, of London (Charles spells "Munsy"), 1:234

Müntzer, Thomas (1489–1525), 1:268

Murgatroyd, Rev John (c. 1703–1768), curate of St. John's Chapel, Leeds, 2:388, 619

Murray, Grace (1716–1803), of Bristol, 1:251; 2:394, 568, 579–80, 583. *See also* Bennet, Grace

Murray, Sarah ("Sally," d. 1739), of Bristol, 1:201

Murray, William (1705–1793), of London, 1:84

Musgrave, Miss Molly, a cousin of Sally Gwynne, 2:569

Musgrave, Mrs, of London, 1:87, 106, 108, 144

N., Mrs, of Cork, 2:542

N., Rev, of Dublin, 2:514

Nance, John (c. 1717–1785), church warden of St Ives, 2:357, 364, 409

Naylor, Joseph, of Leeds, 2:619

Naylor, Mrs Mary (d. 1757), of Bath, 2:450, 490, 494, 496, 530–31, 609

Naylor, Stephen, of Freshford, 2:588

Neal, Mrs, of Oxford, 2:532, 594

Nelson, John (1707–1774), of Birstall

and itinerant, 2:370, 377, 389, 400, 404–406, 423, 425, 431, 479, 615–16

Nelson, W., of Portland, 2:461

Newington, Mr, in Newgate prison, 1:137–39

Newton, Dr, of London, 1:86, 159; 2:452

Newton, Misses (three daughters of Dr Newton), 1:159

Nichols, Charles, of Bristol, 1:204

Nichols, Dr, of Wormley, 1:86

Nichols, Joanna, of Bristol, 1:218

Nichols, Mrs, of Bristol, 1:192

Nichols, Mrs, of London, 1:142

Nichols, Prudence, of Bristol, 1:200

Nitschmann, David (1696–1772), bishop of Moravian Church, 1:78

Norman, Mrs Mary (1695–1779), of Bristol, 1:196

Norton, Miss, of Leeds, 2:616, 618, 622, 626, 630, 634

Norton, Sarah, of Bristol, 1:196, 209

Nowers, Edward, of London, 1:170

Ockershausen, John, of London and itinerant (Charles spells "Oberhausen"), 2:397

Oglethorpe, James Edward (1696–1785), 1:xiii, xviii, xxii, xxvi, 1–5, 8–13, 15–33, 35, 39–45, 48–50, 54, 58, 64–65, 67, 71, 73, 74–78, 80, 83–84, 86, 94, 96, 99

Okely, Francis (1719–1794) (Charles spells "Oakley"), 1:168, 169, 182, 191, 194, 200

Okely, John (1721–1792) (Charles spells "Oakley"), 1:168, 169, 181–82, 194, 200

Oldham, Adam, of Manchester, 2:640, 648

Oldham, Mrs Adam, of Manchester, 2:648

Oldmixon, John (1673–1742), 2:592

Ord, Mr and Mrs, of Hexham, 2:622

Osborn, Sir Danvers (1715–1753), 3rd baronet, of Chicksands, 2:582

Owen, Esther, of London, 1:257

Oxlee, William, of London (Charles spells "Oxley"), 1:237, 253, 255, 262

P., Justice, of Passage, 2:539

P., Miss, of Evesham, 1:187

P., Mr, of Shepton Mallet, 2:445–46

Page, Henry, of Bristol, 1:197

Page, Mrs Henry, of Bristol, 2:600

Paine, Mrs, of East Grinstead, 1:169

Parker, Anne, of London, 1:242

Parker, Henry, of Savannah, Georgia, 1:43

Parker, Jane, of Bristol, 1:218

Parker, Mr, of Epworth, 2:354, 371

Parker, Mr, of London, 2:247

Parker, Samuel, 2:432

Parkinson, Rev Dr, rector of Kinsale, 2:548–49

Parnel, Mrs, of Bristol, 1:304

Parsons, Mrs Elisabeth (d. 1740), of Bristol, 1:202, 206, 218, 292

Pascal, Blaise (1623–1662), 1:57

Paterson, Mr, of Dublin, 2:508

Patrick, Mrs, of Cornwall, 2:473

Peacock, Rachel, of Bristol, 1:325

Pearce, Mrs, of London, 2:531

Pearce, Richard, of Bradford-on-Avon, 2:608

Pearce, Sarah, of Bristol, 1:206

Peck, Mary, of London, 1:264

Pendarves, Mrs Mary (née Granville; later Delany; 1700–1788), of London, 1:69, 77, 81

Pepusch, Dr John Christopher (1667–1752), 2:529

Perkins, Mrs, of Frederica, Georgia, 1:8–9

Perrin, Sarah (1721–1787), of Bristol, 2:404, 499, 559, 579, 586, 608–11, 613, 616, 618, 622

Perronet, Charles (c. 1720–1776), of Shoreham and itinerant, 2:475, 499–501, 503, 513, 516, 566, 608, 640, 644

Perronet, Edward ("Ned" or "Ted," 1721–1792), of Shoreham and itinerant, 2:475–76, 478–79, 481, 485, 487, 578, 583–86, 588–89, 602, 644

Perronet, Miss Elizabeth, of Shoreham, 2:566

Perronet, Rev Vincent (1693–1785), vicar of Shoreham, 2:475, 528–29, 531, 560, 563–68, 574, 578

Peters, Sarah, of London, 2:559

Philipps, Sir John (c. 1666–1737), 4th baronet, of Picton (Charles spells "Philips"), 1:67

Philips, Captain, of Cardiff, 1:284, 289, 291; 2:446

Phillips, Rev Edward (1701–1777), rector at Maesmynis, Wales (Charles spells "Philips"), 2:448, 503, 505, 527, 534, 557–58, 561–62, 572

Philips, Mr, of Manchester, 2:638, 641, 648

Philips, Mrs, of Cardiff, 1:290

Philips, Mrs, of Devizes, 2:490–92

Piers, Lady Comelia Gertrude (née Pigott), 2:602

Piers, Mrs Henry, of Bexley, 1:121

Piers, Rev Henry (1695–1770), vicar of Bexley, 1:96, 100, 117–21, 123, 125–26, 141, 146, 152, 178–79, 265; 2:339, 371, 372, 406, 420

Piesch, Georg (1700–1753), German Moravian, 1:158

Piesch, Rosina (née Münster, 1703–1779), German Moravian, 1:158

Pike, Mr (d. 1749), of London, 2:578

Pike, "Sister" (d. 1743), of London, 2:338

Pindar, Mr, 2:431

Piriam, Mr, of London, 1:174

Plasted, Mr, of Boston, 1:57

Platt, Mrs, of London, 1:145, 148

Pocock, "Sister" (d. 1751), of London, 2:605

Polier, Rev, visiting from Switzerland, 2:616

Pope, Alexander (1688–1744), 1:78, 147

Poppleston, "Sister," of Plymouth, 2:473

Potter, John (c. 1674–1747), Bishop of Oxford (1715–1737), Archbishop of Canterbury (1737–1747), 1:77, 83, 87, 171, 178

Powel, Mr, of London, 1:83; 2:511

Powell, Samuel (d. 1772), printer, of Dublin (Charles spells "Powel"), 2:509

Powell, Mrs., 2:511

Pr., Rev, of Evesham, 1:223

Pratt, Mrs, of London, 1:110

Preston, "Sister" (d. 1748), of Dublin, 2:526

Price, Rev John, vicar of All Saints church and St Lawrence's church, Evesham, 1:225

Price, Mr, of Youghal, 2:549

Price, Mrs Roger, of Boston, 1:56

Price, Rev Roger (1696–1762), commissary and rector of King's Chapel, Boston, 1:55–59

Price, Thomas (1712–1783), of Watford, 1:287

Priestly, Matthew, of Leeds, 2:619

Prior, Matthew (1664–1721), 1:78; 2:540, 647

Purdy, John, of Bristol, 1:265

Purnell, Mrs (d. 1740), of Bristol, 1:280–82

Putnam, Sarah, of Bristol, 1:207

Quick, John, of Bristol, 1:202

R., Mr, of Athlone, 2:552

Ramsay, Andrew Michael (1686–1743), 1:95

Rapin de Thoyras, Paul (1661–1725), 2:598

Rawlins, Mrs, of Bristol, 1:316

Raymond, Miss Dinah (d. 1756), of London, 1:170–71, 173–74

Read, Mr, in Newgate prison, 1:139

Redford, Sarah, of London, 1:256, 264

Reed, "Sister," of Bristol, 1:325

Reed, Thomas, of Bristol, 1:313

Reed, Will, of Frederica, Georgia, 1:17, 20

Reeves, Jonathan (d. 1787), itinerant, 2:413, 541, 621–22

Reeves, Miss, of London, 1:152, 157–58

Rhodes, Mrs, of London, 1:69

Ricard, Mrs, of London, 1:256

Rich, John (1692–1761), of London, 2:451

Rich, Priscilla (*née* Wilford, c. 1713–1783), of London, 2:451

Richards, Rev John, vicar of Porthkerry (1728–1757), 1:320–22

Richards, Major, serving in Georgia, 1:21, 29–32

Richards, Michael, of Cardiff, 2:446

Richards, Mr (d. 1751), of Reading, 2:503, 606

Richardson, Hannah, of Bristol, 1:298–99, 311, 314, 417

Richardson, Mrs (d. 1746), of London (wife of cousin of Charles Wesley), 2:456

Richardson, Nathaniel, 2:456

Rider, Mr, of Bristol, 1:215

Rider, "Sister," of Manchester, 2:638

Ridgworth, James and Elizabeth, of Manchester, 2:647

Ridley, Richard, of London, 1:249, 255, 260, 262

Rigby, Mrs, of London, 1:177

Rivington, Charles (1688–1742), publisher in London, 1:6–68, 88, 131, 141

Roberts, Anne, of London, 1:258

Roberts, Squire, of Hexham, 2:482

Robertson, "Sister," of Bristol, 2:532, 608

Robin, servant of Benjamin Seward, 1:187–88

Robinson, Matthew (c. 1713–1745), of Oxford, 1:85

Robinson, Mrs, of Frederica, Georgia, 1:18

Robinson, Rev Richard (1709–1794), rector of Elton, Yorkshire, 2:533

Robinson, Sarah, of London, 2:502

Robinson, William, 2:532

Robson, John (b. 1715), 1:157, 272; 2:355, 371

Rock, Mr, of Newnham Hill, 1:89

Rogers, Mr, of Devizes, 2:490

Rogers, Mr, of London, 1:170–71, 174

Rogers, Mr, of Nottingham, 2:374

Rogers, "Sister" (d. 1745), of Bristol, 2:438, 443

Rolt, Mr, of Cork, 2:550

Romley, Rev John (1711–1751), of Epworth, 2:354, 485

Rouquet, James (1730–1776), of St John's College, Oxford, 2:531

Rowell, Jacob (d. 1784), itinerant, 2:644

Rowley, Mrs John, of Darlaston, 2:489

Rowley, Rev John (d. 1756), vicar of Darlaston, 2:376

Rudd, John, of Aberglassney, 2:570

Rudd, Lady Elizabeth (c. 1706–1802), sister-in-law of Sally Gwynne, 2:570

Rudd, Sayer, of Snowsfields, 2:370

Russel, Mary, of London, 1:264

Rutter, Benjamin, of Bristol, 1:191, 194, 200; 2:532

Rutter, Sarah, of Bristol, 1:204

S., Benjamin, in Leeds, 2:626

S., N., of Bristol (female), 2:579

Salmon, Thomas (1679–1767), 2:592

Salthouse, Nicholas, servant for Charles Wesley, 2:424, 428, 431

Sant, Daniel, of Nottingham, 2:401

Sarney, John (d. 1773), of Oxford, 1:79–80, 82, 85, 88–91, 97, 148

Sarney, Mrs John, of Oxford, 1:90

Savage, Abigail, of Bristol, 1:216

Savage, Mr, of London, 1:137

Sawyer, Alderman, of Leeds, 2:619

Scions, Mr, of Islington, 1:172

Scott, Mr, of Islington, 1:172, 175

Scougal, Henry (1650–1678), 1:88, 90

Searle, Mr, of Bexley (Charles spells "Searl"), 1:122–23

Searle, Mrs, of Bexley (Charles spells "Searl"), 1:120–23, 125

Seaton, Mrs, of London, 1:239, 245, 258

Selby, Mrs, of Bradford-on-Avon, 2:608

Sellers, Mrs Lydia, of London, 1:176

Seward, Benjamin (b. 1705), of Badsey/Evesham, 1:152, 154, 158, 160, 178, 183–88, 221, 229–30

Seward, Mrs Benjamin, of Badsey/Evesham, 1:188, 230

Seward, Henry, of Badsey/Evesham, 1:222–25, 228, 230

Seward, William (1711–1740), of Badsey/Evesham and London, 1:231, 234, 279, 283–84

Sharp, John (1645–1714), Archbishop of York (1691–1714), 1:125

Sharp, Richard, of Leeds, 2:619

Shaw, John, of London, 1:170–71, 176, 178, 194

Shaw, Samuel (1635–1796), 1:92

Sheep, Jane, of Bristol, 1:319

Shent, William (1715–1787), of Leeds, 2:348, 405, 583, 618, 624–26, 630, 633–34

Shepherd, William, itinerant, 2:357, 366, 369, 421

Shirdock, Elisabeth, of Bristol, 1:200

Shrievely, Mary, of London, 1:258

Silvester, Mr, of Islington, 1:158

Simpson, Rev John (b. 1709–1710), evangelist, 1:232, 235, 237, 239, 242–43, 246, 248, 254, 258, 262–63, 269

Skelton, Charles (c. 1725–1798), itinerant, 2:633

Skinner, Hannah, of Bristol, 2:598

Skinner, Mrs, of Bristol, 1:195

Slocombe, John (d. 1776), itinerant (Charles spells "Slocum"), 2:407

Smith, Alderman, of Leeds, 2:619

Smith, Edward, of Epworth, 2:354

Smith, John, 1:223

Smith, Lucretia, of Bristol, 1:193, 198

Smith, Mr, of Congleton, 2:478

Smith, Richard (b. 1714?), of Christ Church, Oxford, 1:80, 85

Smith, "Sister," of London, 2:564

Smith, "Sister" E. (d. 1741), of Bristol, 1:302

Soane, Mrs Martha, of London (Charles spells "Soan"), 1:250; 2:355

Somerset, Mr (d. April 1750), of London, 2:592

Somerset, Mrs Martha (d. 1749), of London, 2:501

South, Robert (1634–1716), 1:98

Spangenberg, August Gottlieb (1704–1792), Moravian, 1:43; 2:370

Spanin, Anne, of Bristol, 1:206, 218

Sparks, Mr, of London, 1:117, 131, 133, 135, 137–39, 149, 151, 155, 158

Sparrow, Mrs Jane (d. 1748), of Lewisham, 1:182, 247, 269; 2:401, 451, 529, 559

Spenser, Averel, of Bristol, 1:211

Spenser, Edmund (1552?–1599), 1:98

Spenser, William (d. 1779), of Bristol, 1:209

Spittle, Mrs, of Wednesbury, 2:649

Spring, Lucy, of London, 1:253

Stanley, Lady, of London, 1:69

Stanley, Mr, of Bristol, 1:297, 325

Staples, Abraham, of Bristol, 1:206

Star, Mr, of Charleston, South Carolina, 1:47

Star, Mr, of Way Wick, 2:422

Stephens, John, mayor of St Ives, 2:357

Stephens, Mrs, of Plymouth, 2:473

Stevens, Sarah (b. 1666), of Bristol, 1:210, 212

Stockdale, John, of Cork, 2:540

Stone, William, of Shepton Mallet, 2:461

Stonehouse, Rev George (1714–1793), vicar of Islington, 1:140–42, 144–45, 148–50, 152, 154, 156–62, 164, 167–75, 178–79, 215, 233–34, 248, 262, 265

Stonehouse, Mrs Mary (née Crispe, 1722–1751), of Islington, 1:159, 175

Stonehouse, Miss (sister of George), in Bath, 2:575

Storer, Mrs, of London, 1:134

Stotesbury, Mrs Mary (d. 1759), of Newington Green, 2:595

Stratten, Mary, of Bristol, 1:312

Streat, Mr, at Islington, 1:172

Street, Justice, of Devizes, 2:493

Stuart, Prince Charles Edward (1720–1788), the "Young Pretender," 2:392, 449

Stuart, James Edward (1688–1766), the "Pretender," 1:207

Sutherland, Mrs, of London, 1:243, 261

Sutton, Mr, of Devizes, 2:492, 495

Swindells, Robert (d. 1783), itinerant, 2:477, 551

Symonds, Rev William (c. 1684–1776), vicar of St Ives, Towednack, Zennor, 2:360, 363, 365, 411

Syms, John (1714–1757), of London (Charles spells "Sims"), 1:115, 127, 129–30, 136, 142, 146–47, 149, 152, 162, 164

Syms, Joseph, 1:116

Syms, Mrs, of London (Charles spells "Sims"), 1:115–16, 134, 154

Syms, Peter (1716–1790), of London (Charles spells "Sims"), 1:115–16

Syms, Robert, 1:116

Syms, Thomas, 1:116

Syms, William, 1:116

Syrus, Ephraem (c. 306–373), 2:432

T—, Miss, of York, 2:627

T., Rev, of Athlone, 2:552

T., H., of London (woman who brought charge against Thomas Broughton), 1:164–65, 168

T., J., of Bristol (converted prostitute), 1:202

Tackner, Ambrose, of Frederica, Georgia, 1:3

Taylor, David (1715–1783), itinerant, 2:344, 346–47, 394, 400

Taylor, Jeremy (1613–1667), Bishop of Down and Connor, 1661–1667, 1:133

Taylor, Mary, of Bristol, 1:213

Taylor, Mrs, of Bradford-on-Avon, 2:438

Taylor, Mrs Samuel, of Quinton, 2:342

Taylor, Rev Samuel (1711–1772), vicar of Quinton, 2:342, 406, 459

Taylor, Thomas, of Manchester, 2:488

Thomas, Margaret (d. 1740), of Bristol, 1:280

Thomas, Mrs Mary (1690–1745), of Bristol, 1:215

Thomas, Rev Philip (c. 1710–1781),

curate of Gelligaer and Wenvoe, 1:286, 332; 2:446

Thomas, Richard, 2:498

Thomas à Kempis (1380–1471), 2:509, 618

Thomasin, Miss, maid of George Stonehouse, 1:144

Thomson, Rev George (1698–1782), vicar of St Gennys (Charles fluctuates in spelling "Tomson" or "Tompson"), 2:408, 414–16, 422–23, 472, 474, 574

Thorold, John (1703–1775), of Windsor (later Sir John Thorold, 8th baronet), 1:88, 90, 158

Tillotson, John (1630–1694), Archbishop of Canterbury (1691–1694), 1:154

Töltschig, Rev Johann (1703–1764), Moravian (Charles spells "Tilcheg"and "Telchig"), 1:122, 264

Tomochichi, Indian chief, Georgia (Charles spells "Tomo-chachi"), 1:37

Topping, Mrs, of Oxford, 1:79

Tower, Thomas, trustee of the Georgia Colony (Charles spells "Towers"), 1:26

Townsend, Mr, of Bristol, 1:280

Townsend, Mr, official at Newgate prison, Dublin, 1:280; 2:338–39

Townsend, Mrs, of Oxford, 1:155

Townsend, Sarah, of Bristol, 1:210

Trapman, Susanna, of Bristol, 1:206

Trapp, Rev Dr Joseph (1679–1747), 1:78

Trathen, David, itinerant, 2:583

Trembath, John (d. 1793), of St Gennys and itinerant, 2:474

Trounce, Captain, of Tolcarn, 2:467

Tubbs, Eleanor, of London, 1:258

Tucker, Joseph, itinerant, 2:631, 639, 643

Tucker, Josiah (1712–1799), 1:283

Tucker, Thomas, of Bristol, 1:200

Tucker, William ("Billy"), itinerant, 2:570

Turner, Mr, of Westerham, 2:595

Turner, Mrs, of London (sister of John Bray), 1:101, 104–106, 128, 133, 141, 271, 274

Upton, Mr W., of Leeds, 2:619

Vaughan, Mrs, of Islington, 1:156–57, 159, 164, 169, 171, 226
Vazeille, Mrs Mary (*née* Goldhawk, 1710–1781), of London (later Mrs John Wesley), 1:578, 594, 602
Veel, "Sister," of Plymouth, 2:473
Venn, Rev Richard (1691–1739), rector of St Antholin's church, London, 1:157
Verding, Joseph, of London, 1:115–16
Verelst, Harman, accountant for Georgia Colony Trust (Charles spells "Virelst"), 1:70, 83
Vernon, Rev Edward (1695–1761), rector of St George's church, Bloomsbury, 1:261
Vernon, James, trustee of Georgia Colony, 1:26, 45, 67, 96
Vigor, Mrs Elizabeth (*née* Stafford, d. 1775), of Bristol (a Quaker), 1:317; 2:558–59, 576, 580, 586
Vigor, Francis, of Bristol, son of Elizabeth (a Quaker), 1:317; 2:558, 575, 580, 606
Viney, Richard, of London, 1:227, 232, 252, 272; 2:425

W—n, Mr, in Bristol, 1:197–98
Wade, Mr, of Aughrim, 2:551–52
Wade, Mrs (b. 1651), of Tyrrellspass (mother of Mr Wade), 2:521
Waite, Thomas, prisoner at Oxford, 1:79
Wake, William, 1:77
Walcam, Elizabeth (b. 1733), of Bristol, 2:601
Walcam, John, of Bristol, 2:601
Walker, B., of Bristol (female), 1:303
Walker, Francis, itinerant, 2:610–11
Walker, Rev Samuel (1714–1761), rector of Truro, 2:639
Walker, W., of Birstall, 2:397
Waller, James (d. 1802), of London, 2:456, 460, 464, 467, 560, 582, 594–95, 599–602

Waller, Misses (three sisters of James), 2:599, 602
Waller, Mrs, of Westerham (mother of James), 2:595
Walpole, Sir Robert (1676–1745), 1st earl of Oxford, 1:26
Wane, Mr, of Conham, 1:277, 279; 2:437, 443
Wane, Mrs, of Conham, 2:443
Warburton, Thomas, of Cork, 2:550
Ward, Francis (1707–1782), of Wednesbury, 2:376, 648
Wardrobe, Rev Thomas (d. 1756), minister of Hexham Presbyterian church, 2:482–83
Washington, Henry (b. 1717), of Queen's College, Oxford, 1:101, 136, 138, 142
Wathen, Dr Samuel (d. 1777), surgeon, of Bristol and London, 2:599, 603
Watkins, Mr, of London, 2:372, 475, 580
Watson, Ann, of Newcastle, 2:390
Watson, J., of Evesham, 2:623
Watson, Margaret, of Newcastle, 2:390
Watson, Mr (d. 1752), of Newcastle, 2:390, 392
Watson, Robert (b. 1711), of Queens College, Oxford, 1:145; 2:594
Watts, Isaac, 1:124, 148, 297; 2:443
Watts, Mr, of Walbridge, 2:622
Webb, John, itinerant, 2:382–83, 385–86
Webb, "Sister" (d. 1746) of London, 2:454
Webster, Eleazer, itinerant, 2:617
Welch, Mrs Anne, of Frederica, Georgia, 1:xxvi, 2–4, 7–9, 15, 21–25, 27, 33, 40–42, 69
Welch, James, 1:156
Welch, John, of Frederica, Georgia, 1:7
Wells, Mr Christopher (b. 1706), of Jesus College, Oxford, 1:89–90, 98, 114, 146, 148, 155, 284–89; 2:420
Wells, Miss, of Bristol, 2:503
Wells, Rev Nathaniel (b. c. 1697), rector of St. Andrew's, 1:284, 319–20, 322, 329, 332

Wesley, Anne ("Nancy," 1701–?), sister of Charles, 1:140. *See also* Lambert, Mrs John

Wesley, Rev John (1703–1791), brother of Charles, 1:xviii, xx, xxii, xxx, 4, 56, 140, 144, 147, 151, 164, 190–92, 222–23, 232, 251, 260, 269, 281, 287, 295, 323, 329–30; 2:337, 345, 347, 355, 370, 390, 392, 394, 422, 425, 443, 449, 452, 467, 472, 474–76, 485, 498, 515, 532, 570, 595, 601, 622, 628, 637–38

Wesley, Kezia ("Kezzy," 1710–1741), sister of Charles, 1:68, 85, 98, 146, 160

Wesley, Martha ("Patty," 1706–1791), sister of Charles (see Mrs Westley Hall), 2:370, 598, 605

Wesley, Mrs Mary (formerly Vazeille), wife of John, 2:578, 594, 602, 606

Wesley, Matthew (1667–1737), uncle of Charles, 1:41

Wesley, Mehetabal ("Hetty," 1697–1750), sister of Charles, 1:94; 2:455, 589. *See also* Wright, Mrs Mehetabal

Wesley, Phill (1727–1790?), daughter of Samuel Jr and Ursula (later Mrs Earle, in Barnstaple), 1:81

Wesley, Rev Samuel, Jr (1690–1739), brother of Charles, 1:44, 81, 219, 221; 2:476, 562

Wesley, Rev Samuel, Sr (1662–1735), father of Charles, 1:68, 138; 2:354, 408, 510, 572

Wesley, Mrs Sarah ("Sally," *née* Gwynne, 1726–1822), wife of Charles, 1:xxiii, 198; 2:527, 570, 572, 575–77, 579, 580–81, 583, 588, 593–95, 597–603, 605–10, 616, 618, 622. *See also* Gwynne, Sarah

Wesley, Mrs Susanna (1669–1742), mother of Charles, 1:73, 81, 85, 94, 124, 134, 160, 233; 2:408, 431, 543, 575

Wesley, Mrs Ursula (*née* Berry, d. 1742), wife of Samuel Jr, 1:81, 95

West, Mrs John, of London, 1:245, 261

West, John, Jr, (1717–1798), of London (marries Esther Hopson in 1741), 1:149

Westell, Thomas (c. 1719–1794), itinerant (Charles spells "Westal"), 2:392–93

Wheatley, James (d. 1775), itinerant, 2:576, 578, 608–10, 646

Wheatly, Mrs, of Stoke, 2:463

Wheeler, Mrs Anne, of London, 1:161

Whetman, Virtuous, of Bristol, 1:202

Whitchurch, Mr, near Bristol, 1:333; 2:378

Whitcomb, Mrs, of London, 1:159

White, Alexander (d. 1748), of London, 2:563–64

White, Lydia, of London, 2:589

White, Mr, of Roscrea, 2:551

Whitefield, Rev George (1714–1770), 1:xix, 71, 87, 92–93, 142, 155–58, 162–63, 171–76, 178–86, 188, 190, 192, 202–203, 221, 223, 226, 234, 236, 245, 263, 283, 303; 2:427, 462–63, 528, 567, 579, 611, 614, 625, 632, 642

Whitford, John, itinerant, 2:635, 637, 646

Whitting, Rev, of Dudley, 2:382

Wigginton, Mr, of Bristol (Quaker), 1:197–98, 217, 219

Wigginton, Mrs Anne (d. 1757), of Bristol, 1:198

Wild, Mr, of Islington, 1:158, 248, 265

Wildboar, Jonathan, of Bristol, 1:276

Wilder, John (1680–1742), rector of St Aldate's, Oxford, 1:203

William, gentleman servant of Robert Jones, 1:335

Williams, Betty, of Garth, 2:560, 570

Williams, Rev Edward, vicar of Llansbyddyd, 2:569

Williams, Mrs Judith, of Bristol, 1:206, 209

Williams, Mr, of Boston, 1:58

Williams, Mr, of Kidderminster, 1:213

Williams, Mr and Mrs, of London, 1:260

Williams, Rev Rice (1704–1784), vicar at Llansantffraed-yn-Elfael, 2:504, 556

Williams, Stephen, of Cork, 2:550

Williams, Thomas, Jr (c. 1720–1787), itinerant, 2:357, 403–405, 416, 419, 423–24, 427, 475, 638, 646

Williams, Thomas, Sr (c. 1697–1783), of Llanishen, 1:284

Williamson, Rev William (d. 1758), vicar of St Mary Bishophill Junior, York, 2:628–29, 642

Willis, Thomas, of Hanham (Bristol), 1:199, 204, 278–79

Willy, Mr, of Devizes, 2:492, 495

Wilson, J., of Newcastle, 2:430

Wilson, Mrs, of London (second cousin of Charles Wesley), 2:456

Wilson, Richard, Esq., of Leeds, 2:619

Windsor, Robert (1704–1790), of London, 2:574

Winstone, Mrs, of London, 1:170

Wise, Mr, consort of Mary Lavington, 1:176–77

Witham, Mrs Elizabeth ("Hannah," d. 1747) of London, 1:256; 2:441, 498, 515

Witham, Mr (d. 1743), of London, 2:380

Witham, Miss Sally, of London, 2:564

Withers, Justice, of London, 2:574

Wolfe, Shepherd, of London, 1:178

Woods, Joseph, of Birstall, 2:396–97, 399

Woods, Mr, of Abingdon, 1:80

Worlock, Jane ("Jenny"), of Bristol, 1:282

Wormill, Mr W., of Leeds, 2:619

Wotlen, Mary, of London, 1:261

Wren, Mrs, of London, 1:154

Wright, Mrs Mehetabal ("Hetty," née Wesley, 1697–1750), 2:455, 589–90

Wright, William, brother-in-law of Charles Wesley, 1:94; 2:455, 589–90

Wynn, Mr, of Painswick, 1:324, 329, 341

Wynn, Mrs, of Painswick, 1:221

Wynn, Sir Rowland, of Nostell Priory, 2:395

Yapp, Mr (d. 1747), of Bath, 2:501

Young, Anne, of London, 1:237

Young, Dr, of London, 2:576, 578

Young, Edward (1683–1765), 2:554

Young, Mrs, of Dublin, 2:508

Young, Susan, of Cardiff, 1:286

Zinzendorf, Erdmuth Dorothea Gräfin von (1700–1756), wife of Nikolaus, 1:78

Zinzendorf, Nikolaus Ludwig Graf von, leader of Moravians (1700–1760), 1:77, 122, 170, 260, 330; 2:515

Zisca, John (d. 1424), 1:267–68

Zouberbuhler, Sebastian (c. 1710–1773), 1:47, 51, 59, 61, 63–64, 66–67, 71–72, 75

Zouch, Rev Charles (d. 1754), vicar of Sandal, 2:395–96, 399–400

# INDEX OF PLACES

Note: distances from London are calculated to the center of the old City of London.

Aberford, Yorkshire, 3 miles northeast of Garforth, 2:631

Abergavenny, Monmouthshire, 2:533, 572

Aber Menai ferry crossing, Caernarfonshire (Charles spells "Bar-Myni"), 2:505

Aberthaw, Glamorgan, 14 miles west of Cardiff, 1:331; 2:416

Acomb, Yorkshire, 2 miles west of York city center, 2:485, 629

Adwalton, Yorkshire, 2 miles west of Morley, 2:388

Anglesey Island, Wales (Charles spells "Anglesea"), 2:505, 555

Armley, Yorkshire, 1 mile west of Leeds (Charles spells "Armsly"), 2:348, 388

Ashby de la Zouch, Leicestershire, 16 miles northwest of Leicester, 2:623

Athlone, Co. Westmeath, 2:518–19, 542, 551

Aughrim, Co. Galway, 2:551

Avon, Wiltshire, 4 miles northeast of Chippenham, 2:437

Axminster, Devon, 5 miles northwest of Lyme Regis, 2:462

Badsey, Worcestershire, 2 miles east of Evesham, 1:228

Ballyboy, Co. Offaly, 11 miles southeast of Tullamore (Charles spells "Balliboy"), 2:536

Banbury, Oxfordshire, 22 miles north of Oxford, 1:91

Bandon, Co. Cork, 2:544, 547–48, 556

Baptist Mills, Gloucestershire, village half a mile northeast of Bristol on the River Frome, 1:197–98, 201–203, 208, 217–19, 298, 316, 330, 333; 2:437, 453, 458–60

Barley Hall, farmhouse near Thorpe Hesley, 2:347, 388, 401, 614, 625

Barnstaple, Devon, 2:416

Bath, Somerset, 2:497, 501, 530, 532, 562, 575, 577, 582

Beachy Head, Sussex, 3 miles southwest of Eastbourne, 1:66

Bearfield, Wiltshire, village just outside Bradford-on-Avon, 1:213; 2:450, 453, 460, 588, 610

Bedminster, Somerset, 2 miles south of Bristol, 1:221

Bengeworth, Worcestershire, village just southeast of Evesham (now incorporated into same), 1:185, 221

Berkswell, Warwickshire, 6 miles west of Coventry, 1:91

Bexley, Kent, about 12 miles southeast of London, 1:88, 94, 96, 117, 122, 131, 141, 146, 149, 152, 159, 163, 173, 265; 2:337, 371, 381, 451

Biddick, Co. Durham (now a district of the city of Washington, southeast of city center. Charles spells "Biddicks," but in one instance "South Biddicks"), 2:351, 391, 426, 428–29, 480–81, 485

Birmingham, Warwickshire, 2:343, 355, 375, 377, 382, 384, 477, 580, 613, 623, 649

Birr, Co. Offaly, 2:551

Birstall, Yorkshire, 1 mile northwest of Batley (Charles spells "Birstal"), 2:348–49, 388, 393, 396–97, 400, 425–26, 431–32, 479, 487, 615–16, 633–35

Blackheath, Kent, 7 miles southeast of London, 1:173, 176, 178, 257, 262, 264

Blandford Forum, Dorset, 2:370

Blendon Hall, home of the Delamotte family, near Bexley, Kent, 1:88

Blenheim Palace, Woodstock, Oxford, 2:594

Bodmin, Cornwall, 2:357

Bolton, Lancashire, 10 miles northwest of Manchester, 2:637, 643

Bol-y-don ferry, Caernarfonshire (Charles spells "Baladon"), 2:525, 555

Boston, Massachusetts, 1:56–58, 60, 64, 74–75

Castle Island, 1:55

Christ Church, 1:55

King's Chapel, 1:55, 57

Long Wharf, 1:55

Bradford, Yorkshire, 2:425, 635

Bradford-on-Avon, Wiltshire, 5 miles southeast of Bath, 1:197, 205, 214, 216; 2:438, 458, 608

Braintree, Massachusetts, 10 miles southeast of Boston, 1:56–57

Bramley, Yorkshire, 3 miles west of Leeds, 2:636

Brecon, Brecknockshire, 2:560, 569

Brentford, Middlesex, about 10 miles west of London, 2:337, 441, 455, 474, 499, 562, 605

Bridport, Dorset, 14 miles west of Dorchester, 2:369

Brinsworthy, Devon, near Barnstaple, 2:416

Bristol, Gloucestershire, 1:62, 76, 169, 185, 190–92, 197–98, 212, 214, 218, 238–39, 249, 264, 269, 272–76, 278, 283, 291, 293, 294–95, 297, 301, 306, 310, 313–14, 316–18, 320, 324, 330, 333, 335, 357, 378, 403–404, 407, 418, 420, 423, 428, 437–38, 441–42, 444, 446, 463, 474, 490, 497–99, 503–504, 529–30, 532–33, 557, 559–60, 562, 567–68, 573, 575, 579–80, 585, 587, 593, 597, 600, 606–609, 614, 622, 642, 644, 649

All Saints church, 1:293

Bowling Green, 1:192, 195, 198–99, 202, 204, 211–12, 218; 2:310, 462

Brick-yard, 1:193, 196, 200, 205, 213, 215, 220

Bridewell labor prison, 1:313

Bristol Cathedral, 2:587

Downs, 1:278

Gloucester Lane, 1:192–93, 197, 200, 203, 210–11

Horsefair, 1:191, 271, 279; 2:379, 423, 456, 503, 532, 586

Malt-room/Malt-house, 1:270

Newgate prison, 1:75, 77, 133, 136–37, 147, 149, 152, 161, 164, 166, 182, 331; 2:338, 340, 506, 509, 512, 522–23, 525, 574

New Room, preaching house, 2:533, 589, 616

Old Orchard, Quakers Friars, 2:503

Poynt's Pool (Charles spells "Points Pool"), 2:608

Rose Green, 1:192, 196, 270–71, 273, 275–76

St James's church, 1:204, 333

St Nicholas's church, 1:192

St Philip's priory, 1:212

Stokes Croft, just north of the Horsefair, 2:579

Temple church, 1:191, 275, 297

Weavers' Hall, 1:192–94, 198, 200, 204, 220, 270; 2:453, 457

Broadoaks Manor, just northwest of Thaxted, Essex, 1:174

Bromwich Heath, open common in West Bromwich, Staffordshire, 4 miles northwest of Birmingham (Charles spells "Bromidge Heath"), 2:612

Builth Wells, Brecknockshire, 14 miles north of Brecon, 2:503

Bull's Head Inn, in Llangefni, Anglesey, 7 miles west of Menai, 2:555

Burnopfield, Co. Durham, 3 miles northwest of Stanley (Charles spells "Burnup-Field"), 2:428, 430, 481, 483

Bwlch, Brecknockshire, 5 miles northwest of Crickhowell, 2:557

Caernarfon, Caernarfonshire (Charles spells "Caernarvon"), 2:505, 526–27, 534, 555

Caldicot, Monmouthshire, about 12 miles east of Newport, 1:331

Calne, Wiltshire, 5 miles east of Chippenham, 2:562, 606

Camborne, Cornwall, 5 miles west of Redruth, 2:367

Cambridge, Cambridgeshire, 1:87–88, 124; 2:592

Cambridge, Gloucestershire, 4 miles north of Dursley, 2:597, 649

Cambridge, Massachusetts, 1:56–57

Canterbury, Kent, 1:67, 77, 83, 154, 178; 2:433

Cape Cornwall, 2:413

Cardiff, Glamorgan, 1:284–86, 318–20, 322–23, 327–28, 331–33, 345, 378–79, 416–17, 446, 448, 530, 560, 569

Carmarthen, Carmarthenshire, 1:311; 2:572

Cashel, Co. Tipperary, 2:536, 551

Charleston, South Carolina (Charles spells "Charlestown"), 1:39, 44, 46–47, 54, 56, 64, 76

Charlestown, Massachusetts, 1:59

Chelsea, Middlesex, 3.5 miles southwest of London, 2:499

Cheltenham, Gloucestershire, 2:623

Chertsey, Surrey, 3 miles south of Staines, 2:528, 595

Cheshunt, Hertfordshire, 6 miles south of Hertford, 1:83–84

Chester, Cheshire, 2:526

Chilcompton, Somerset, 2 miles southwest of Midsomer, 2:438

Chinley, Derbyshire, 2 miles northwest of Chapel-en-le-Frith, 2:400

Chowdene, Co. Durham, about 2 miles south of Gateshead (now a district in Low Fell), 2:350–51

Christ Church, Cork, 2:536

Churchill, Somerset, 3 miles south of Congresbury, 2:421–22

Cirencester, Gloucestershire, 2:377, 380, 419, 443, 532, 568, 573

Clerkenwell, Middlesex, immediately south of Islington, 1:144
  St John's church, 1:144

Clifton, Gloucestershire, 2 miles west of Bristol, 2:607

Cogges, Oxfordshire, 10 miles west of Oxford (now part of Witney, just across River Windrush from town center), 1:155

Coleford, Somerset, 6 miles west of Frome, 2:438, 460, 558, 576

Coleorton, Leicestershire, 3 miles northwest of Coalville, 2:344

Congleton, Cheshire, 11 miles north of Stoke-on-Trent, 2:478

Conham, Gloucestershire, 3 miles east of Bristol; now a western neighborhood in Hanham, 2:437, 443, 456–57, 459, 472, 573

Cork, Ireland, 2:532, 535–36, 539, 544, 546, 549, 556, 575, 577, 643
  Hammond's Marsh, 2:536
  St Fin Barre's cathedral, 2:544
  St Peter's church, 2:547

Cowbridge, Glamorgan, 12 miles west of Cardiff, 2:418, 449, 530

Cowley, Middlesex, on the River Colne, half a mile south of Uxbridge, 2:529

Cowley, Oxfordshire, 3 miles southeast of Oxford, 1:85, 161

Crowan, Cornwall, 3 miles south of Cambourne, 2:409

Croydon, Surrey, 10 miles south of London, 2:595

Darien, Georgia, 1:37

Darlaston, Staffordshire, about 13 miles northwest of Birmingham, 2:374–76, 489, 613

Darlington, Co. Durham, 2:389, 392

Dartford, Kent, 2:451

Davyhulme, Lancashire, about 5 miles southwest of Manchester, 2:488, 644

Deal, Kent, 8 miles northeast of Dover, 1:66

Deptford, Kent, 4 miles southeast of London, 1:246, 295; 2:370, 453, 566, 590

Derby, Derbyshire, 2:400

Devizes, Wiltshire, 15 miles east of Bath, 2:495

Dewsbury, Yorkshire, 8 miles southwest of Leeds, 2:479, 634

Dinas Powys, Glamorgan, about 4 miles south of Cardiff (Charles spells it "Dennis-Powis"), 1:333

Dolgellau, Merionethshire, about 12 miles north of Machynlleth, 2:505, 556

Dolphin's Barn, Co. Dublin, about 2 miles south of central Dublin, 2:512–13, 516

Donington Park, near Castle Donington, Leicestershire, 7 miles northwest of Loughborough, 2:344, 424, 428, 624

Dorchester, Oxfordshire, about 10 miles southeast of Oxford, 1:90, 95

Downend, Gloucestershire, 5 miles northeast of Bristol (Charles spells "Downing"), 1:299, 303, 306

Downs, anchorage in the English Channel, 1:65–66

Dublin, Ireland, 2:506, 508, 513, 516, 521–22, 535, 546–47, 553, 628, 638

Dublin Bay, 2:535
   Hanbury Lane, 2:514
   Marylebone Lane, 2:511–12
   Newgate prison, 2:512, 522–23, 525, 574
   Oxmantown Green, 2:507
   St Patrick's cathedral, 2:507, 512–15, 535
   Ship Street, 2:525

Dudley, Worcestershire, 2:382–83, 612

Duffield, Derbyshire, 5 miles north of Derby, 2:614

Durham, Co. Durham, 2:351–52, 391, 618, 622

Durham Abbey, 2:622

East Grinstead, Sussex, 8 miles east of Crawley, 1:169

Ebley, Gloucestershire, 2 miles west of Stroud (Charles spells "Ebly"), 1:190–91

Eltham, Kent, 8 miles southeast of London, 1:88, 117, 122, 173, 267, 269
   King John's chapel, 1:269

Epping, Essex, 19 miles northeast of London, 1:86

Epworth, Lincolnshire, 9 miles north of Gainsborough, 1:70, 134; 2:354, 389, 392–93, 425, 431, 485, 487

Eton, Berkshire, on north bank of River Thames opposite Windsor (Charles spells "Eaton"), 2:337

Evesham, Worcestershire, 1:165, 190, 225, 227–28; 2:342, 377, 380, 443, 477, 580, 589, 594, 680, 623

Ewood, Lancashire, about 1 mile south of Blackburn, 2:637

Exeter, Devon, 2:357, 369, 462, 547–48, 584

Falmouth, Cornwall, about 9 miles southeast of Redruth, 2:414

Ferryhill, Co. Durham, 6 miles south of Durham, 2:485

Fishponds, Gloucestershire, 2 miles northeast of Bristol, 1:192, 208, 217, 279; 2:532

Fonmon Castle, in Rhoose, Glamorgan, 3 miles west of Barry, 2:319, 331–33, 416, 447–48, 460, 530, 560, 569, 607, 641

Fort St Andrew, north end of Cumberland Island, Georgia, 1:30, 37

Fort St George, on northern bank of the mouth of St Johns River in northern Florida, 1:35–36

Framilode, Gloucestershire, on bank of River Severn, 7 miles southwest of Gloucester (Charles spells "Frommelow"), 2:597

Frederica, Georgia, on west side of St Simons Island, about 6 miles north of southern tip, 1:11, 17, 20, 34–35, 37, 40–41, 44

Frenchay, Gloucestershire, about 6 miles northeast of Bristol, 1:217

Freshford, Wiltshire, 4 miles southeast of Bath, 1:191; 2:588, 609

Garth, Brecknockshire, 6 miles west of Builth Wells, 2:444, 447, 504–505, 527, 533, 556–57, 560–61, 563, 566, 568–70, 572

Gateshead, Co. Durham, directly across the River Tyne from Newcastle, 2:485

Gaulksholme, house 1 mile southwest of Todmorden, Lancashire, 2:637

Gerrard's Cross, Buckinghamshire, 4 miles northwest of Uxbridge, 1:269

Glan Bran, Carmarthenshire, about 1 mile southwest of Cynghordy, 2:572

Gloucester, Gloucestershire, 1:83, 188–90, 221; 2:472, 503

Gotherington, Gloucestershire, 5 miles north of Cheltenham (Charles spells it "Gutherton"), 2:377, 380

Green Man's Inn, top of Blackheath Hill, Blackheath, Kent, 1:178, 212

Grimsby, Lincolnshire, about 30 miles east of Epworth, 2:342, 354, 485–86

Gulval, Cornwall, just north of Penzance, 2:412

Gwennap, Cornwall, 3 miles southeast of Redruth, 2:362, 368, 408–409, 414–15, 464–65, 470–71, 474

Hainton, Lincolnshire, 15 miles northeast of Lincoln, 2:487

Halifax, Yorkshire, 7 miles southwest of Bradford, 2:582, 635

Hampton Court, Hampton, Middlesex, 1:87

Hanham, Gloucestershire, 3 miles east of Bristol, 1:204, 207, 209, 212–13

Hatfield Heath (or Hatfield Broad Oak), Essex, about 5 miles southeast of Bishop's Stortford, 1:83

Haworth, Yorkshire, 2 miles southwest of Keighley, 2:479, 487, 587, 633, 636

Hayes, Middlesex, 3 miles southeast of Uxbridge, 2:597, 601

Hayfield, Derbyshire, 4 miles south of Glossop, 2:641

Helston, Cornwall, about 15 miles east of Penzance, 2:359, 465, 467

Heptonstall, Yorkshire, 1 mile northwest of Hebden Bridge, 2:636

Hereford, Herefordshire, 2:575, 579–80

Herrnhut, Saxony, 1:122, 147

Hexham, Northumberland, 20 miles west of Newcastle, 2:482, 484, 622

Holborn, Middlesex, 1 mile west of London, 2:441

Holborn Circus, 2:436

Holyhead, on Holy Island, Anglesey, 2:505, 526, 534, 554

Honiton, Devon, 16 miles northeast of Exeter, 1:95

Horsley, Northumberland, about 10 miles west of Newcastle, 2:391, 428, 622

Hotwells, Somerset, about 1 mile west of Bristol, 2:533, 607

Hounslow Heath, Middlesex, 11 miles southwest of London, 2:579, 585

Hungerford, Berkshire, about 35 miles south of Oxford, 2:357, 499, 562

Hunslet, Yorkshire, now a district of Leeds, 1 mile south of city center, 2:625, 631

Huntley, Gloucestershire, 7 miles west of Gloucester, 2:503

Idbury, Oxfordshire, 5 miles southeast of Stow-on-the-Wold, 1:227, 231

Islington, Middlesex, 1 mile north of London, 1:115, 140, 142–44, 147, 149, 154, 156–57, 160–62, 164, 169–72, 174–75, 186, 248, 250, 254, 262, 265; 2:440, 476, 599

Keighley, Yorkshire, 13 miles northwest of Bradford, 2:479, 635

Kendleshire, Gloucestershire, hamlet about 2 miles southwest of Chipping Sodbury (Charles spells "Kendalshire"), 1:296, 298, 306, 316

Kenneggy Downs, Cornwall, 5 miles south of St Ives (Charles spells "Cannegy Downs"), 2:359, 363, 367

Kennington Common, Surrey, about 1 mile south of London, across the River Thames, 1:175, 178, 180–81, 183, 190, 237, 247, 256

Kensington, Middlesex, 1:269; 2:566

Kidderminster, Worcestershire, 1:213

Kingswood, Gloucestershire, 4 miles east of Bristol, 1:193, 210, 220, 270–72, 275, 277, 284, 292–93, 297, 300–303, 306, 308–10, 314, 319, 322, 324, 329–30, 333; 2:338, 403, 419–20, 423, 437, 443, 449, 453, 456, 463, 497, 530, 532–33, 558, 568, 573, 575–76, 579, 581–82, 585, 587–88, 598, 606, 609

Kingswood school, 1:193, 270, 298, 300, 326; 2:634

Kinsale, Co. Cork, about 10 miles south of Cork, 2:545–48

Laneast, Cornwall, 7 miles east of Launceston, 2:408, 474

Lawrence Hill, Gloucestershire, 2 miles east of Bristol, 1:278; 2:579

Leeds, Yorkshire, 2:348, 388, 394, 425–26, 431, 479, 487, 585, 605, 615–16, 618–19, 625–26, 630, 632–33, 645

Leominster, Herefordshire, 12 miles north of Hereford, 2:576, 580, 593, 597

Lewisham, Kent, about 6 miles southeast of London, 1:214; 2:401, 531, 605

Lichfield, Staffordshire, 15 miles north of Birmingham, 2:387

Lizard Point, Cornwall, most southerly point of mainland England, 1:65

Llandaff, Glamorgan, 2 miles northwest of Cardiff, 1:285

Llandrindod Wells, Radnorshire, about 8 miles north of Builth Wells, 2:504, 534

Llanidloes, Montgomeryshire, 11 miles southwest of Newtown, 2:505, 527, 534, 556

Llanishen, Glamorgan, 3 miles north of Cardiff (Charles spells "Lanissan"), 1:284, 286, 320

Llanmaes, Glamorgan, 1 mile north of Llantwit Major (Charles spells "Lanmase"), 1:321; 2:530

Llansantffraed-yn-Elfael, Radnorshire, 4 miles northwest of Builth Wells (Charles spells "Llansaintfraid"), 2:556

Llantrisant, Glamorgan, 8 miles northwest of Cardiff (Charles spells "Lantrissent"), 1:288, 332

London, 1:xxiii, 6, 45, 57, 59, 67–69, 72, 75, 78, 80–83, 86–88, 90, 92–93, 95–96, 98, 100, 109, 115–17, 122, 124, 130, 137–38, 141–42, 146–47, 149–51, 153, 156, 158, 160–63, 165, 168, 174–75, 178–79, 181, 183, 190, 192, 213, 227, 232, 236, 239, 245, 258, 261, 263, 270, 277, 292, 294–95, 297, 335; 2:337–38, 355, 369–70, 373, 395–99, 403–405, 412, 450, 454, 467, 475–76, 490, 495, 498, 528–30, 562–63, 567, 573, 575, 580, 585, 588–91, 594, 599, 603, 644

All Hallows' church, London Wall, 1:130

All Hallows' church, Thames Street, 1:41

Beech Lane, short alley off Beech Street, just east of intersection with Aldersgate Street, 1:160, 163–64

Bishopsgate, 1:93, 154, 164

Dowgate Hill. On the north bank of the River Thames, just west of London Bridge, 1:166

Downing Street, 2:440

Drury Lane, 1:6
Fetter Lane Society, 1:232
Fleet prison, 1:161, 182
Foundery, the Wesleys' meetinghouse in Moorfields, 1:67, 232, 234–35, 237, 239, 246–48, 250–52, 255–56, 261–63, 294; 2:337, 355, 357, 370–73, 380, 397, 401–402, 407, 432, 434–35, 438, 440, 444, 450, 455, 463, 476, 497, 499, 503, 510, 528, 530–31, 559, 562, 573, 585, 591, 595, 601–603, 605
Fresh Wharf, on River Thames just east of London Bridge, 1:92–93
Hick's Hall, 1:263; 2:574
Ironmongers' Almshouses, corner of Cheapside and Ironmonger Lane, 1:151
Lambeth Palace, 1:178
Ludgate prison, 1:87
Marshalsea prison, 1:160–62, 168, 172–73, 182, 247
Minories, 1:151, 164
Moorfields, just outside London Wall at Moorgate, 1:175, 178, 180–82, 232; 2:345, 503, 577
Newgate prison, 1:75, 77, 133, 136–37, 147, 149, 152, 161, 164, 166, 182, 331; 2:338, 340, 506, 509, 512, 522–23, 525, 574
Queen Street chapel, 1:147
Rag Fair, 1:258
Saffron Hill, just east of Holborn Circus, 2:436
St Alban's church, 1:152; 2:432, 599
St Alphage church, London Wall, 1:130
St Antholin's church, Budge Row, 1:93, 149–50, 152, 157
St Bartholomew-the-Great church, 2:498, 501–502
St Benet's church, Gracechurch Street, 1:147
St Botolph's church, Aldersgate, 1:146–47
St Botolph's church, Bishopsgate, 1:154
St Clement Danes church, Eastcheap, 1:151
St George's church, Bloomsbury, 1:151, 261
St. George, in central Manchester, 2:643
St George the Martyr's church, Queen's Square, 1:137
St Helen's church, Bishopsgate, 1:93–94, 135, 156, 256
St James's palace, 1:87
St John Zachary's church, 1:145
St Katherine's church (Charles spells "St Catherine"), 1:164
St Lawrence Jewry church, corner of Gresham Street and King Street, 1:149
St Luke's church, Old Street, 2:340
St Margaret's church, Westminster, 1:149
St Martin-in-the-Fields church, northeast corner of Trafalgar Square, 1:78
St Michael's church, Bassishaw, 1:90
St Michael's church, Crooked Lane, 1:90
St Olave Jewry church, 1:93
St Paul's cathedral, Ludgate Hill, 1:67, 174, 180, 182, 243, 255; 2:338
St Sepulchre's church, Newgate Street, 1:133
St Vedast's church, Forster Lane (now Foster Lane), 1:92
Short's Gardens, 2:373, 433–34, 455
Sir George Wheler's chapel, Spitalfields (Charles spells "Wheeler's" chapel), 1:146, 151
Snowsfields, on south side of the River Thames, just below London Bridge, 1:262; 2:370, 382, 590
Snowsfields chapel, 2:370
Spitalfields, 2:596–97
Spitalfields chapel, 2:596, 601
Westminster Abbey, 1:146; 2:622
West Street chapel, at intersection of West Street and St Martin's Lane, 2:423

Long Compton, Warwickshire, 4 miles northwest of Chipping Norton, 1:82

Ludgvan (or Ludjan), Cornwall, 2.5 miles northeast of Penzance (Charles spells "Lidgeon"), 2:411, 465, 469

Ludlow, Shropshire, 2:575–76, 579–80, 589, 593–94, 597, 599–600, 609–10

Machynlleth, Montgomeryshire, 16 miles northeast of Aberystwyth, 2:534, 556

Maesmynis, Brecknockshire, 3 miles southwest of Builth Wells, 2:448, 504, 534, 557, 561, 566, 572

Maidenhead, Berkshire, 2:562

Malmesbury, Wiltshire, 14 miles west of Swindon, 1:270, 272; 2:423

Manchester, Lancashire, 1:99; 2:400, 489, 638–40, 642–45

St Ann's church, 2:640, 648

St Mary, St Denys, and St George collegiate church (now Manchester Cathedral), 2:643

Mapledurham, Berkshire, about 3 miles northwest of Reading, 1:89–90

Markfield, Leicestershire, about 7 miles northwest of Leicester, 2:373, 424

Marlborough, Wiltshire, 10 miles south of Swindon, 1:80–81, 85; 2:506, 514, 577

Marylebone, Middlesex, 2 miles northwest of London (Charles spells "Marybone"), 1:183, 263–64; 2:511–12

Melbourne, Derbyshire, 7 miles south of Derby, 2:344

Michaelston le-pit, Glamorgan, 3 miles southwest of Cardiff (Charles spells "Michelston Lepit"), 1:287

Mickleton, Gloucestershire, 8 miles east of Evesham, 1:81

Middleton (or Midleton), Co. Cork, about 13 miles east of Cork, 2:547, 549

Middlezoy, Somerset, about 6 miles southeast of Bridgewater (Charles spells "Middlesea"), 2:407

Minehead, Somerset, 2:416

Mitchell, Cornwall, 5 miles southeast of Newquay, 2:357, 369, 415

Moate, Co. Westmeath, 2 miles east of Ballymahon (Charles spells "Moat"), 2:520

Moreton in Marsh, Gloucestershire, 8 miles northwest of Chipping Norton, 2:599

Morley, Yorkshire, 4 miles southwest of Leeds, 2:432

Morvah, Cornwall, 3 miles northeast of St Just (Charles spells "Morva"), 2:360, 366–67, 411–13, 466, 476

Mountmellick, Co. Laois, about 5 miles north of Portlaoise, 2:551

Musselburgh, Midlothian, 6 miles east of Edinburgh, 2:615, 618

Newbury, Berkshire, 16 miles west of Reading, 2:437, 562, 601, 606

Newcastle Upon Tyne, Northumberland, 1:59; 2:349–52, 357, 370, 382, 389–92, 426–30, 440, 476, 479, 483, 538, 607, 618, 620–22, 644

Orphan House, 1:93; 2:621

Ouse Burn (Charles spells "Ewe's Bourn"), 2:620

Stotes Hall, 2:351

Newington, Surrey, 1 mile south of London, across the River Thames, 1:180

Newington Green, between Islington and Stoke Newington, Middlesex, 2:476, 595, 599

Newlands, Co. Durham, tiny hamlet half a mile west of Ebchester (Charles spells "Newlings"), 2:481

Newnham, Gloucestershire, 1:89; 2:588

Newnham Passage, 2:588

Newnham Hill, Oxfordshire, about 12 miles southeast of Oxford, 1:89

North Shields, Northumberland, directly across the River Tyne from South Shields, 2:362

Northampton, Northamptonshire, 2:401

Norwich, Norfolk, 2:610

Nottingham, Nottinghamshire, 2:344, 355, 373–74, 385, 392–93, 401, 425, 432, 624

Nuneham Courtenay, Oxfordshire, 3 miles northwest of Dorchester, 1:90

Oakhill, Somerset, 3 miles north of Shepton Mallet, 2:445–46

Okehampton, Devon, about 23 miles west of Exeter, 2:369

Osmotherley, Yorkshire, 6 miles northeast of Northallerton, 2:485

Owston Ferry, Lincolnshire, 2 miles southeast of Epworth, 2:425

Oxford, Oxfordshire, 1:xix, xxix, 8, 26, 67, 77–79, 81, 84–92, 97–98, 109, 135, 140, 145, 148, 155–56, 158, 161, 163, 171, 180–81, 185, 189, 203, 219, 227, 231, 269, 272, 323; 2:337, 355, 364, 419–20, 432, 503, 531, 568, 573, 568, 573, 580, 589, 592, 594, 597–99, 602–603, 629

  Bocardo prison, 1:156

  Castle prison, 1:79, 89, 145, 155–56

  Christ Church Cathedral, 1:189

  Christ Church College, 2:399, 416, 419, 533, 592

  Queen's College, 1:92, 136

  St Mary's church, 1:123, 189; 2:420

Painswick, Gloucestershire, 3 miles northeast of Stroud, 1:189, 221, 224; 2:241

Passage West, Co. Cork, 5 miles southeast of Cork, 2:539

Paulton, Somerset, 2 miles northwest of Midsomer Norton, 2:558

Peak, forest area in Derbyshire, between Sheffield and Manchester, 2:400

Pelton, Co. Durham, 2 miles northwest of Chester le Street, 2:349, 485

Penkridge, Staffordshire, 6 miles south of Stafford (Charles spells "Pencrage"), 2:477, 489

Penryn, Cornwall, about 10 miles southeast of Redruth, 2:414

Penzance, last town of any size in southwest Cornwall, 2:411, 413

Phillipstown (now known as Daingean), Co. Offaly, about 8 miles east of Tullamore, 2:521

Plaistow, Essex, 6 miles east of London, 1:183

Plessy, township in present parish of Stannington, Northumberland, 4 miles south of Morpeth, 2:351, 391, 429, 481

Plymouth, Devon, 2:462–63, 473

Pool, Cornwall, 2 miles northeast of Camborne, 2:359, 364, 367

Porthkerry, Glamorgan, 2 miles west of Barry, 1:327–28, 331–32

Portland, Dorset, 2:461

Publow, Somerset, 8 miles southeast of Bristol, 1:194; 2:460

Putney, Surrey, about 6 miles southwest of London, 1:87

Quinton, Gloucestershire, 4 miles south of Stratford Upon Avon, 2:342, 377, 380, 477

Randwick, Gloucestershire, just north of Ebley (Charles spells "Runwick"), 1:190

Rathcormack, Co. Cork, 14 miles northeast of Cork (Charles spells "Rathcormuck"), 2:540

Reading, Berkshire, 1:80; 2:503, 531, 606

Redruth, Cornwall, 2:357, 362, 369, 415, 465, 467, 471

Rhayader, Radnorshire, 11 miles north of Builth Wells (Charles spells "Raydor"), 2:505, 556

Ripley, Yorkshire, 3 miles north of Harrogate, 2:349

Riverstown, Co. Cork, about 4 miles northeast of Cork, 2:539

Rode, Somerset, 4 miles north of Frome (Charles spells "Road"), 2:449

Roscrea, Co. Tipperary, 2:536, 551

Ross-on-Wye, Herefordshire, 9 miles northeast of Monmouth, 2:597

Rotherham, Yorkshire, 6 miles northeast of Sheffield, 2:346, 401, 488, 614, 624

Rotherhithe, Surrey, 3 miles southeast of London, on the south bank of the Thames, 1:246

Rothwell, Yorkshire, 5 miles southeast of Leeds, 2:632

Ryton, Co. Durham, 6 miles west of Newcastle (Charles spells "Righton"), 2:483

St Albans, Hertfordshire, 17 miles northwest of London, 2:432, 599

St Andrews Major, Glamorgan, a hamlet adjoining Dinas Powys, 1:284

St Anne's (Hill), wooded area near Chertsey, Surrey, 3 miles south of Staines, 2:595, 594–95, 597, 606

St Augustine, Florida, site of a Spanish fort, 1:21, 29, 31–32, 35–39

St Bride's-super-Ely, Glamorgan, about 6 miles northwest of Cardiff, 1:288

St Gennys, Cornwall, on the Atlantic coast 7 miles southwest of Bude, 2:408, 416, 474

St George's Point, on northern bank of the mouth of St Johns River in northern Florida, 1:29–37, 39

St Hilary, Cornwall, 5 miles east of Penzance, 2:365

St Ives, Cornwall, 2:357–63, 365–68, 392, 409, 412–14, 465–67, 470–71

St Just, Cornwall, 4 miles north of Land's End, 2:366–67, 410–13, 466–70

St Nicholas, Glamorgan, 6 miles west of Cardiff, 1:192, 285

St Simons Island, Georgia, 1:1, 35

St Tudy, Cornwall, 5 miles northeast of Wadebridge (Charles spells "St Eudy"), 1:472

Salisbury, Wiltshire, 1:94–95; 2:370, 441, 592

Saltford, Somerset, midway between Bath and Bristol (Charles spells "Sawford"), 1:318, 326

Salt Hill, Berkshire, now a district of Slough, 21 miles west of London, 2:577

Sandgate, Newcastle Upon Tyne, 2:620

Sandhutton, Yorkshire, 3 miles west of Thirsk, 2:353, 618

Savannah, Georgia, 1:26, 31, 33–34, 44, 46, 64, 142

Seacroft, Yorkshire, 4 miles northeast of Leeds, 2:630–31

Seend, Wiltshire, 3 miles east of Devizes (Charles spells "Seen"), 2:485, 497, 577

Selby, Yorkshire, 13 miles south of York, 2:354, 389

Sennen, Cornwall, at the tip of Land's End (Charles spells "Zunning"), 2:366

Sevenoaks, Kent, 19 miles southeast of London, 2:475

Sheep Hill, Co. Durham, 4 miles south of Blaydon, 2:621

Sheffield, Yorkshire, 2:344–45, 347, 349, 361, 387, 400, 425, 432, 488–90, 614–15, 624

Shepton Mallet, Somerset, 18 miles south of Bristol, 2:445, 461

Sherborne, Dorset, 5 miles east of Yeovil (Charles spells "Sherburn"), 2:461

Shoreham, Kent, 4 miles north of Sevenoaks, 2:475, 498, 501, 528, 531, 563–64, 567, 578

Shoreham-by-Sea, Sussex, 6 miles west of Brighton, 1:65

Siston, Gloucestershire, 7 miles east of Bristol (Charles spells "Sison"), 1:314

Sithney, Cornwall, 2 miles west of Helston, 2:465, 467, 471, 570

Sittingbourne, Kent, 8 miles east of Chatham (Charles spells "Sittenburn"), 1:67

Skidaway Island, Georgia, 10 miles south of Savannah, 1:34

South Leigh, Oxfordshire, 7 miles west of Oxford, 1:90–91, 272

South Shields, Co. Durham, on south bank of the River Tyne, 7 miles east of Gateshead, 2:352

Southwell, Dorset, 2:461

South Wraxall, Wiltshire, 2 miles north of Bradford-on-Avon (Charles calls "Wrexal"), 2:438, 453, 497

Spelsbury, Oxfordshire, 5 miles south of Chipping Norton (Charles spells "Spilsbury"), 1:79, 82, 91

Spen (High Spen), Co. Durham, 3 miles south of Ryton, 2:391, 428–29, 484

Stanley Borough (King's Stanley), Gloucestershire, 1.5 miles west of Stroud, 1:190

Stanton, Gloucestershire, 6 miles southeast of Evesham, 1:82

Stanton Harcourt, Oxfordshire, 3 miles southwest of Eynsham, 1:85, 88–90, 97, 145, 272

Sticklepath, Devon, 4 miles east of Okehampton, 2:408

Stithians, Cornwall, 3 miles northwest of Penryn, 2:464–65

Stockport, Derbyshire, 2:400

Stoke, Devon, 1 mile northwest of Plymouth, 2:463

Stoke Newington, 4 miles north of London, 2:476

Stokes Croft, 2:579

Stone, Staffordshire, 7 miles north of Stafford, 2:648

Stroud, Gloucestershire, 8 miles south of Gloucester, 2:342

Studley, Warwickshire, 4 miles southeast of Redditch, 2:477, 623

Sunderland, Co. Durham, 11 miles southeast of Newcastle, 2:552, 428, 619–20

Swalwell, Co. Durham, 3 miles west of Gateshead, 2:353, 481, 484

Sykehouse, Yorkshire, 10 miles northeast of Doncaster (Charles spells "Sikehouse"), 2:389, 425, 431, 487

Tadcaster, Yorkshire, 9 miles northwest of York, 2:630

Tanfield, Co. Durham, 2 miles north of Stanley, 2:350–51, 390, 426, 428

Tan-y-Bwlch, Merionethshire, about 16 miles north of Dolgellau, 2:505, 556

Taunton, Somerset, 1:95

Tavistock, Devon, 13 miles north of Plymouth, 2:462, 472, 474

Templemacateer, a manor house 4 miles northwest of Kilbeggan, Co. Westmeath (Charles spells "Temple-Macqueteer"), 2:518

Templemore, Co. Tipperary, 6 miles north of Thurles, 2:551

Thaxted, Essex, 6 miles southeast of Saffron Walden (Charles spells "Thackstead"), 1:174–75

Thirsk, Yorkshire, 8 miles southeast of Northallerton, 2:622, 627

Thornbury, Gloucestershire, 12 miles north of Bristol, 2:580

Thorpe (Thorpe Hesley), Yorkshire, 5 miles north of Sheffield, 2:347, 387

Thunderbolt, Georgia, fort and settlement 5 miles southeast of Savannah, 1:34

Tilsworth, Bedfordshire, 3 miles northwest of Dunstable, 2:477

Tipton Green, Staffordshire, 1 mile north of Dudley (Charles spells "Tippen"), 2:383, 477, 612

Tiverton, Devon, 12 miles north of Exeter, 1:80–81, 83–85, 94–95, 98–99, 112, 131

Topcliffe, Yorkshire, 4 miles southwest of Thirsk, 2:618

Towednack, Cornwall, 2 miles southwest of St Ives (Charles calls it "Wednock"), 2:358, 360, 362

Tresmeer, Cornwall, 6 miles west of Launceston, 2:408, 415, 464, 472, 474

Trewellard, Cornwall, 2 miles north of St Just (Charles spells "Trewallard"), 2:467, 469, 471

Trewint, Cornwall, 2:408

Tullamore, Co. Offaly, 2:521

Twickenham, Middlesex, 10 miles southwest of London, 1:78

Tyburn, Middlesex, 1:138

Tyrrellspass, Co. Westmeath, about 12 miles northeast of Tullamore (Charles spells "Tyril's Pass"), 2:516–18, 520, 536, 552

Usk, Monmouthshire, 10 miles northeast of Newport, 2:557, 562, 567

Uxbridge, Middlesex, 15 miles west of London, 2:476

Velling-Varine, Cornwall, 2:368

Wakefield, Yorkshire, 8 miles south of Leeds, 2:388, 394–97, 400, 615, 634

Wallbridge, a crossing of the River Frome next to Stroud, Gloucestershire (Charles spells "Walbridge"), 2:622

Walsall, Staffordshire, 8 miles northwest of Birmingham, 2:343, 345, 374–76, 384–85

Wapping, Middlesex, 2.5 miles east of London, on north bank of the Thames, 1:172, 179, 234, 242, 246, 250, 268, 454, 501

Watford, Glamorgan (now a suburb of Caerphilly), 6 miles north of Cardiff, 1:287

Way Wick, Somerset, 3 miles west of Churchill, 2:422

Wednesbury, Staffordshire, 6 miles northwest of Birmingham (Charles spells "Wensbury"), 1:xx; 2:342, 344, 355, 361, 374–75, 383–85, 400, 402, 421, 433, 477, 489, 612–13, 648

Welling, Kent, 10 miles southeast of London, 1:173; 2:381

Wellington, Somerset, 6 miles west of Taunton, 1:81

Wendron, Cornwall, 2 miles north of Helston, 2:465–66

Wenvoe, Glamorgan, 3 miles north of Barry. Charles spells "Wenvo," 1:285–86, 319, 327–28, 331–32; 2:379, 417, 446, 448

Westcote, Oxfordshire, 4 miles southeast of Stow-on-the-Wold (Charles spells "Westcott"), 1:227

Westerham, Kent, 5 miles west of Sevenoaks (Charles uses common shorter name "Westram"), 2:595

Whickham, Co. Durham, 3 miles west of Gateshead (Charles spells "Wickham"), 2:391, 423, 427–29, 480–81, 484

Whitchurch, Glamorgan, 3 miles northwest of Cardiff, 1:333; 2:378

Whitechapel, Middlesex, just east of Aldgate in London, 1:246

Whitecote Hill, in northwest Leeds (Charles spells "Whitecoat Hill"), 2:618

Wick, Gloucestershire, 7 miles east of Bath, 2:460, 506, 598, 607, 609

Wilmington, Kent, 1 mile south of Dartford, 2:381

Windsor, Berkshire, 21 miles west of London, 1:88, 90; 2:531

Wood, the forested area around Kingswood, Gloucestershire, 1:298

Woodhouse, Yorkshire, a district of Leeds 1 mile north of city center, 2:400, 616

Woodley, Cheshire, 3 miles northeast of Stockport, 2:478

Woodstock, Oxfordshire, 8 miles northwest of Oxford, 1:227; 2:594

Woolhampton, Berkshire, 6 miles east of Newbury, 2:562

Wootton Rivers, Wiltshire, 4 miles south of Marlborough, 1:68, 81, 85

Worcester, Worcestershire, 2:594, 597, 600, 611, 649

Wormley, Hertfordshire, 7 miles southeast of Hertford, 1:83, 86

Wycombe (High Wycombe), Buckinghamshire, 28 miles northwest of London, 1:156, 180, 185, 269

York, Yorkshire, 2:404, 485, 625–29, 644
Cathedral Church of St Peter's (or, the "Minster"), 2:627, 629

Youghal, Co. Cork, about 30 miles east of Cork, 2:547, 549

Zennor, Cornwall, on north coast 4 miles west of St Ives (Charles spells "Zunnor"), 2:360, 367, 411, 413, 466, 469

# INDEX OF TOPICS

Arminians, 1:311

Articles of Religion, 1:104, 162, 217

Assurance, 1:125, 131, 135, 141, 146, 150, 156, 206, 209, 238, 249, 274, 279, 296, 321; 2:378, 389, 400, 474

Atonement, 1:101, 105, 114, 134, 138, 150, 152, 154, 172, 195–96, 253, 307; 2:343, 374, 422, 439, 512, 523, 532, 541, 618–19

Calvinist, 2:427, 500, 628

Christ, crucified, 1:108, 156, 238, 264, 298, 302, 330–32; 2:349, 438, 459, 463, 465, 471, 478, 483, 487, 504, 507, 516, 546, 642

Colony, 1:xviii, 10–13, 30, 40, 45, 58, 70, 72, 74, 96

Communion, Holy, 1:223; 2:388, 536 of the Church of England, 2:623, 640, 644. *See also* Ordinances *and* Sacraments

Conference, 2:406, 444, 459

Conversion, 1:27, 89, 92, 100–101, 109, 117–18, 158, 162, 178, 191, 264, 302, 316; 2:462, 493, 503, 533, 596, 614, 624

Death, 1:xxii–xxiv, xxix, 23, 26, 28, 38, 42, 44, 46, 58, 64, 68–69, 73, 75, 86, 98–99, 105, 114, 120–23, 133, 136–37, 139, 144, 161, 174, 189, 193–94, 198, 200–203, 206, 220, 245, 251, 255–56, 277, 281–83, 293, 296–99, 301, 303–307, 311–15, 318–19, 323, 325, 328–29, 331–32, 337; 2:338–39, 341, 356, 367, 371–72, 375, 377, 381, 390–91, 394–95, 419–20, 422, 427, 429, 433–34, 438, 442–45, 450, 454–55, 473–76, 479–80, 487, 500, 507–508, 513–15, 520–21, 528, 531, 549–50, 554, 558, 560, 563–64, 567, 572, 579, 589–90, 592, 596, 599, 601, 604–605, 613, 616, 621, 622, 640, 649

Deism, 2:595, 604

Deist(s), 1:95, 173

Dissenter(s), 1:150, 153, 205–206, 213–14, 231, 265, 294; 2:343, 382, 446, 477, 489, 492, 523–24, 549–50, 612, 624, 628, 635, 638–39, 644, 647–48

Doctrine, 1:xix, 13, 15, 100–101, 104, 116, 125, 136, 140, 147, 162, 171, 188, 204, 207, 243, 255, 262–63, 265, 270, 274, 288–89, 292, 295, 298, 301, 304; 2:365, 394, 406, 411, 414, 420, 434, 446, 479, 520, 539, 613, 617, 627, 640

Education, 1:46, 54; 2:598

Enthusiasm (of Methodists), 1:162, 203, 257, 268; 2:408, 548

Examination, 2:464

Experience, 1:103, 111, 113, 115, 141, 147–49, 169, 183, 192, 202, 211, 218, 254, 275, 293, 316; 2:340, 418, 460, 553, 558, 630, 641

Faith, finding, 2:436, 461

(Faith-*continued*.)

having, 1:118, 129, 152, 234, 236, 245, 249, 326; 2:351, 521, 642

in Christ, 1:101, 112, 117, 124, 136–37, 141, 148–49, 213, 259, 332; 2:368

in God, 1:118, 325

justifying, 1:151

practical, 2:638

received, 1:137, 141, 144, 150, 170, 190, 211, 244, 296; 2:377, 553, 568

Fast, 1:xx, xxi, 192, 194, 217, 233, 250, 254; 2:402, 440, 448, 486, 612

Fasting, 1:3, 49, 314; 2:374, 425, 466, 470, 521, 632

Field-preaching. *See* Preaching, field

Freewillers, 1:311

Georgia Colony, 1:xviii, 10–13, 30, 40, 45, 58, 70, 72, 74, 96

Grace, 1:5, 10, 104, 117, 121, 124, 126, 133–34, 148, 158, 169, 178, 188–89, 202, 212, 244, 246–49, 262, 265, 270, 273, 275, 279, 293, 299, 308, 311, 312, 316–17, 319, 321–22, 331, 335; 2:343–44, 349, 356, 365, 367, 378–79, 382, 384, 387, 407, 410, 413–14, 419, 431, 437, 439, 442, 444, 450–51, 453, 465, 468, 470, 472, 473, 481, 490, 502, 521–22, 534, 543, 545, 550, 553, 570–73, 577, 582, 589, 613–14, 623, 627, 629, 639, 641, 645, 647

means of, 1:5, 172, 191, 226, 232, 246, 248–49, 251, 256, 259; 2:573, 636

preventing, 1:235

sanctifying, 2:558

Holiness, 1:8, 93, 104, 132, 217, 231, 279–81, 304, 330; 2:354, 372, 380, 425, 466, 541, 627, 643–44

Holy Ghost, 1:3, 106, 109, 119, 121, 135, 141, 156, 159, 173, 175, 184, 189–90, 193, 195, 203, 216, 232, 245, 248, 250, 252–53, 257, 263, 275, 279, 290, 293, 300, 304, 317, 334; 2:344, 372, 377–78, 389, 458, 477, 490, 513, 533, 537. *See also* Holy Spirit

Holy living, 1:80, 133, 295

Holy Spirit, 1:30, 112, 129. *See also* Holy Ghost

Homilies, 1:104, 142, 145, 162, 217

Hymn(s), 1:xvii, 103, 106, 109, 110–11, 121, 124–25, 131, 134–35, 139–40, 142, 148–49, 159, 161–62, 181, 198, 210, 222, 224, 229, 236, 245–46, 248, 251, 257–58, 275, 276, 284, 288, 294, 305–306, 325, 333; 2:343, 349, 356, 377, 394–96, 400, 420, 450, 454, 456, 469–70, 479, 497, 517, 520, 529, 531, 533, 540, 544, 555, 560, 563–64, 570, 581, 582, 591, 593, 596, 599, 604–605, 608, 628, 633

Indians, 1:4, 31, 36–39, 44, 49, 70, 76, 78

Inspiration, 1:13, 156, 176

Itinerant, 1:xviii, xx; 2:394, 424, 466, 620

Jacobite(s), 1:xxii, 207; 2:347, 393, 449–50, 458, 476

Justification by faith, 1:104, 132, 142, 150, 152, 159, 162–63, 181, 183, 194, 204; 2:365

Knowledge, 2:370, 374, 427

of the Lord Jesus Christ, 2:379

of salvation, 2:340, 360

Lesson(s) (scriptural), 1:1–2, 8, 15, 22–24, 46, 60, 99, 117, 119, 120, 123–24, 129, 134, 168, 177, 180, 190, 223, 225, 230, 287, 292, 321; 2:360, 365, 466, 604, 679

Morning, 1:14, 118, 186

Evening, 1:8, 10, 13, 20

Love,

of Christ, 1:102, 104–105, 108, 110, 127, 131, 134, 137–38, 144, 146, 156, 201, 208, 213, 238, 244, 260, 264, 297–98, 300, 302–303, 305; 2:341, 378, 427, 458, 465, 471, 474, 478, 483, 504, 509, 546, 564, 632, 640, 642

of the church, 2:632

of God, 1:89, 94, 114–15, 137, 178, 195, 201, 224, 251, 253, 255–56, 285, 296–97, 305; 2:352, 372, 431,

460, 476, 481, 513, 526, 543, 563, 639
of others, 1:194–95, 198, 202, 207,
209, 272, 296, 307; 2:419, 431, 463,
540, 550, 567, 623, 625, 630, 638, 648
perfect, 2:571
Spirit of, 1:252, 287, 334; 2:414, 599,
607, 633
universal, 1:179, 195, 296, 307, 310,
316
Love-feast, 1:180, 193, 238, 243, 249,
261, 271, 273, 276, 280, 293; 2:338–39,
353, 371, 406, 413, 423, 426, 437, 439,
446, 474, 484, 487, 530, 533, 587, 599,
609, 621, 635

Methodist(s), 1:68, 79, 86, 94, 98, 131,
140–41, 145, 157, 161, 167, 181, 184,
186, 191, 196, 224, 283, 284; 2:342,
376, 383–84, 388, 392, 396–98, 401,
406, 410–11, 423, 427, 466, 536, 540,
548, 560, 592, 596, 605, 611–12, 616,
619, 621–22, 628–29, 631, 634,
637–39, 641–44, 647
Moravians, 1:78–79, 147–48, 234, 243,
258, 271, 295, 330; 2:352, 369–70, 397,
420, 425, 432, 593, 639
Music(al), 2:385, 456, 529

Native Americans. See Indians
New birth, 1:87–88, 90, 94–95, 145, 174,
216, 221, 242, 253, 266; 2:630

Ordained, 1:80, 117; 2:399, 406, 475, 556,
634
Ordinance(s), 1:124, 217, 226–27,
233–37, 239–43, 248–50, 254–58,
260–62, 264–68, 270, 324; 2:356, 370,
374, 414, 420, 569, 629, 633, 637, 639,
641, 645, 648. See also Communion
and Sacraments

Papists, 1:166–67, 204, 207, 311, 329;
2:382, 404, 413, 467, 482, 487, 506–10,
519, 536–37, 540, 544, 548, 550, 639
Parliament, 2:347, 393, 403, 422
Perfection, 1:47, 176, 236, 270, 279–80,
294, 301, 304, 318–19, 322, 324; 2:475

Persecution, 1:xviii, 13, 69, 90, 140, 162,
169, 207, 223, 297; 2:342, 355, 360,
367, 375, 378, 383, 387, 389, 393, 397,
400–401, 421, 458, 464, 466–67, 469,
506, 512, 550, 575, 612, 628
Poor, 1:83, 96, 120, 123, 127, 130, 136,
138, 146, 160, 163, 176, 192–93, 196,
198, 215, 235, 238, 250, 256, 269, 274,
322, 327, 334; 2:344, 349–51, 353, 358,
360, 364, 366, 391, 401, 404, 412, 421,
426, 438, 440, 445, 460, 464, 478, 483,
509, 520–21, 534, 542, 545, 548, 588,
591, 611–12, 616, 624, 630
Prayer(s),
family, 1:120, 226; 2:388, 425, 535,
581–82, 602, 629, 632–34, 636–37,
645
formal, 1:14
public, 1:60, 112–15, 117, 123, 134, 163,
233, 291; 2:629, 632–33, 635–36, 645
Preachers, 1:xix; 2:384, 408, 419, 483,
503, 514, 516, 529, 536, 578, 585, 605,
610, 616–17, 629, 634, 637, 639–40,
642–43
lay, 2:406, 533
Preaching, 2:363, 365, 377, 381, 385–86,
398, 408, 412, 428–30, 433, 440, 447,
450, 454, 458–59, 467–71, 473, 475,
477, 479–80, 482–83, 490–91, 495,
500, 502, 504, 508, 510–16, 524–25,
528, 529–30, 532–33, 535, 539, 542,
544, 546–47, 552, 556–58, 560, 567,
580, 584, 588, 593, 598, 608, 610,
614–15, 618, 621, 623, 625–31, 633,
640, 644
field, 1:180, 183, 204; 2:366
open-air, 2:362
Predestination, 1:147, 179, 285, 288,
292–93, 297–98, 308–309, 311–12,
329; 2:374
Presbyterians, 1:19, 56–57; 2:397, 546
Prisoners, 1:9, 11, 30, 79, 92, 134, 138,
145, 147, 156, 286, 319, 332; 2:379,
418, 425, 439, 446, 491, 547, 619
Prison(s), 1:75, 78–79, 87, 156, 160–62,
167, 178, 217, 313, 328, 330–32; 2:377,
393, 408, 547, 621

Providence, 1:5, 63, 93, 124, 151, 198, 219, 269, 305, 311, 318; 2:390, 394–95, 431, 497, 514, 519, 534, 555–56, 563, 589–90, 621

Repentance, 1:xxi, 133, 149, 183, 194, 272, 283, 309, 316; 2:360, 367, 414, 433, 447, 449–50, 462, 472, 475, 477, 479, 481–82, 484–86, 488, 504, 509, 540, 548, 588, 606, 612, 616, 620–22
Revival, 1:xxx, 140, 181; 2:500, 613, 624
Righteousness, 1:3–4, 8, 13, 31, 90, 102, 104, 106, 110, 112–13, 116–20, 122, 126, 131, 138, 142–43, 148, 155, 160, 170, 178, 181, 185–86, 195–96, 201, 211–12, 215, 218, 230, 232, 252, 276, 279, 284, 287–88, 293, 298–99, 331; 2:350, 358–59, 367, 369, 377, 391, 444, 450, 459–60, 487, 521, 526, 558, 602, 615, 635, 648
Riot Act, 2:347, 493
Riots (rioters, rioting), 1:186, 188, 194, 215, 225, 279; 2:359, 365, 368, 376, 384–85, 392, 401, 411, 430, 467, 475, 482, 486, 488–89, 491–93, 496–97, 506, 508, 574, 576, 611
Roman Catholic (Roman Catholicism), 1:41; 2:392, 440, 508, 544

Sacrament(s), 2:609. See also Communion and Ordinances
Salvation, 1:5, 46, 61, 66, 102, 116–17, 119, 123–24, 126, 130, 143, 145–46, 150, 156, 166, 188–89, 206, 213, 227, 240, 259, 274, 277, 282, 287–88, 303, 308, 311–12, 319, 323, 324, 333; 2:340, 343, 348, 353–54, 360–61, 379, 386, 435, 455–57, 471, 475, 478, 540–41, 548, 552, 576, 589, 620, 625, 628–29, 631
    by faith, 1:104, 123, 128, 139, 146, 148; 2:396, 408
    by grace, 1:121, 148
    of God, 1:136, 189, 312, 361, 417, 455, 492, 514, 520
Scripture(s), 1:xxx, 12–13, 17, 20, 42, 87, 102–103, 108, 117, 124, 126–28, 132, 134–35, 142, 144–45, 150, 155, 159, 175, 179–80, 193, 195, 203–204, 206, 224, 226, 228, 234, 247, 249, 255, 258–59, 262–63, 267, 272, 275, 280, 285, 305, 315, 317; 2:348, 374, 384, 399, 413, 423, 486, 517, 521, 569, 596, 617, 639, 642, 645, 646
Self-denial, 1:194; 2:425
Sin(s),
    dead in, 1:202, 244, 253
    forgiveness of, 1:127, 130, 132, 146, 210, 214, 255–56, 317; 2:373, 460, 537, 550
Singing, 1:13, 93, 96, 100, 103, 110, 112, 114–15, 120, 122, 124–25, 127, 130, 134–35, 140, 144, 157, 169, 174, 176, 178, 181, 186–87, 190, 210, 218, 222, 225, 229, 233, 242–43, 248, 258, 264, 273, 278, 282, 285, 305, 307, 310, 316, 319, 331–33; 2:350, 384, 394, 400, 410, 416, 418, 443–46, 477, 487, 497, 503, 512, 518, 521, 526–27, 530, 533, 545, 560, 570, 582, 585, 588, 595, 602, 604, 606–607, 611–12, 628
Slaves, 1:47
Stillness, 1:227, 233, 236, 239, 240, 243, 246–48, 257, 259, 265, 267–68, 270–71, 295, 324, 329; 2:344, 374

Trinity, 1:83, 112, 216, 224, 317; 2:517

Women, 1:2, 19, 30, 64, 78, 110, 144, 160, 164, 177, 187, 194–95, 198, 207, 211, 234, 236, 238, 243, 246, 249, 255, 263, 276, 287, 290, 297; 2:356, 361, 364, 378, 395, 404, 412, 415, 427, 432–33, 435, 453, 457, 467, 492, 506, 508, 510–11, 545, 609–10, 613, 617
Workhouse, 1:334
Works (not literary), 1:117, 124, 132, 142, 150, 157, 195, 201, 211, 223, 239, 252, 255, 259, 266, 277, 314, 335; 2:354, 372, 374, 425, 440, 463, 484, 497, 523, 526, 535, 542, 565, 586
    good, 1:104, 117, 124, 132, 150, 152, 157, 239, 255, 259; 2:354, 440, 463, 526, 535

first works, 1:xx, xxi; 2:605, 612, 623
of faith and love, 1:299
of grace, 2:571
of the Lord, 2:372, 636
by love, 1:104, 280; 2:511

of righteousness, 1:126
Worship, 1:142, 242
family, 2:645
places of, 2:509, 536
public, 2:535, 645

# INDEX OF SERMON TEXTS

## OLD TESTAMENT

**GENESIS**

3 . . . . . . . . . . . . . 1:273
22:18 . . . . . . . . . . 2:498, 500
32:24-31 . . . . . . . 1:310, 320; 2:373, 406, 517, 525, 529

**EXODUS**

33:12–34:9 . . . . . . 2:577

**NUMBERS**

14 . . . . . . . . . . . . 1:301, 302
16:26 . . . . . . . . . . 1:317

**JOSHUA**

6 . . . . . . . . . . . . 1:314, 328
10:12 . . . . . . . . . . 2:438

**1 SAMUEL**

7:12 . . . . . . . . . . . 2:407

**1 KINGS**

19:1-8 . . . . . . . . . 2:441
19:12 . . . . . . . . . . 1:306

**2 CHRONICLES**

20:17 . . . . . . . . . . 1:323
30:18-19 . . . . . . . 2:500

## JOB
3:17 . . . . . . . . . . 1:56
5:18 . . . . . . . . . . 1:226
19:25 . . . . . . . . . 1:229
22:21 . . . . . . . . . 2:561
23. . . . . . . . . . . . 2:453
23:8-10 . . . . . . . 1:264

## PSALMS
4:6 . . . . . . . . . . . 2:529
16:12 (BCP) . . . . 2:573
37:37 . . . . . . . . . 1:19
46. . . . . . . . . . . . 2:451, 590, 648
46:8-9 . . . . . . . . 2:636
110:1 . . . . . . . . . 2:427
126. . . . . . . . . . . 2:453
126:7 (BCP) . . . . 1:26, 57
130. . . . . . . . . . . 1:272

## PROVERBS
1:20 . . . . . . . . . . 2:458
3. . . . . . . . . . . . . 2:381, 572
8:17 . . . . . . . . . . 2:573

## ISAIAH
1. . . . . . . . . . . . . 1:192, 238; 2:402
1:9 . . . . . . . . . . . 2:480, 488
1:16 . . . . . . . . . . 2:390, 391, 401, 414, 449, 462, 488, 504
1:18 . . . . . . . . . . 2:372
2:10 . . . . . . . . . . 2:392
2:21 . . . . . . . . . . 2:417
3. . . . . . . . . . . . . 1:194
4 . . . . . . . . . . . . 1:196
6:20 . . . . . . . . . . 2:648
9:6 . . . . . . . . . . . 1:294; 2:587
11:6 . . . . . . . . . . 1:224
24. . . . . . . . . . . . 2:682
26:8 . . . . . . . . . . 2:393
26:9 . . . . . . . . . . 2:635
26:11 . . . . . . . . . 2:480
29. . . . . . . . . . . . 1:204
30. . . . . . . . . . . . 1:205
30:13 . . . . . . . . . 2:395
30:18 . . . . . . . . . 1:296

35. . . . . . . . . . . . . 1:193, 209; 2:413, 422, 430, 437, 453, 465, 479, 523, 541, 552, 559
40. . . . . . . . . . . . . 1:221
40:1 . . . . . . . . . . 1:275; 2:361, 365, 379, 408, 501, 504, 506, 596
40:9 . . . . . . . . . . 1:294
40:31 . . . . . . . . . . 2:446
42:1 . . . . . . . . . . 1:220
43. . . . . . . . . . . . . 2:212
43:10 . . . . . . . . . . 2:532
43:25 . . . . . . . . . . 2:543
44:22 . . . . . . . . . . 2:380
45:8 . . . . . . . . . . 1:218, 276
45:15 . . . . . . . . . . 1:251
45:22 . . . . . . . . . . 2:380
50. . . . . . . . . . . . . 1:215
50:10 . . . . . . . . . . 1:260
51. . . . . . . . . . . . . 2:432
51:9 . . . . . . . . . . 2:385, 430, 434
51:11 . . . . . . . . . . 2:444, 532
52:1 . . . . . . . . . . 1:319
52:7 . . . . . . . . . . 2:432
52:8 . . . . . . . . . . 2:498
53. . . . . . . . . . . . . 1:209, 216, 233, 260, 328; 2:362, 525
53:1 . . . . . . . . . . 1:221
53:6 . . . . . . . . . . 2:366
54. . . . . . . . . . . . . 1:261, 281
54:3-17 . . . . . . . . 2:362
54:17 . . . . . . . . . . 2:384
55:1 . . . . . . . . . . 1:205, 237, 269, 284; 2:348, 400, 410, 422, 438, 465, 505, 510, 520, 576
57. . . . . . . . . . . . . 1:262
57:15 . . . . . . . . . . 1:217; 2:436
57:20 . . . . . . . . . . 1:262
58. . . . . . . . . . . . . 1:217, 264
59. . . . . . . . . . . . . 1:218
60. . . . . . . . . . . . . 1:288
60:20 . . . . . . . . . . 2:437, 591, 603
61. . . . . . . . . . . . . 2:580
61:1 . . . . . . . . . . 1:204; 2:549
63:1 . . . . . . . . . . 1:276, 287; 2:363
64:5 . . . . . . . . . . 1:323; 2:629, 632, 636, 647

## JEREMIAH

3. . . . . . . . . . . . . 2:450
8:22 . . . . . . . . . . 2:436
20:7-10 . . . . . . . 2:423

(Jeremiah—*continued.*)
31 . . . . . . . . . . . . 2:481
31:1 . . . . . . . . . . . 2:442
31:34 . . . . . . . . . . 2:481
50:20 . . . . . . . . . 2:461

**LAMENTATIONS**

1:12 . . . . . . . . . . 2:378, 388, 413, 429, 461, 483, 501, 504, 507, 522, 529,
546, 551, 576, 642
3:22 . . . . . . . . . . 2:373, 453

**EZEKIEL**

9 . . . . . . . . . . . . 2:440, 637
14:20 . . . . . . . . . 2:440
16 . . . . . . . . . . . 1:270, 271
18 . . . . . . . . . . . 1:310
33:1-6 . . . . . . . . 2:623, 624, 632, 635
36:24-30 . . . . . . 1:271, 291
37:4 . . . . . . . . . . 1:256, 328; 2:573
37:7 . . . . . . . . . . 1:195

**DANIEL**

9 . . . . . . . . . . . . 2:339
9:9 . . . . . . . . . . . 2:503
9:24 . . . . . . . . . . 1:298

**HOSEA**

2:14 . . . . . . . . . . 2:405, 598
6:1 . . . . . . . . . . . 2:459
11:8 . . . . . . . . . . 1:319; 2:476, 480
13:9 . . . . . . . . . . 2:352, 521, 578
14:4 . . . . . . . . . . 1:306

**JOEL**

2 . . . . . . . . . . . . 2:440
2:1 . . . . . . . . . . . 1:224
2:13 . . . . . . . . . . 2:477
2:31 . . . . . . . . . . 2:429, 448

**MICAH**

7:2-5 . . . . . . . . . 1:247
7:8 . . . . . . . . . . . 2:530

7:18 . . . . . . . . . . 2:402

**HABAKKUK**

3:2 . . . . . . . . . . . 2:626, 635
3:17 . . . . . . . . . . 2:567

**ZEPHANIAH**

1:2 . . . . . . . . . . . 2:440
2 . . . . . . . . . . . . 2:451

**ZECHARIAH**

4:7 . . . . . . . . . . . 1:319; 2:444
4:9 . . . . . . . . . . . 2:615
9:9 . . . . . . . . . . . 2:382
9:11 . . . . . . . . . . 2:425
12:10 . . . . . . . . . 2:517, 534
13:6 . . . . . . . . . . 2:463, 471
13:7-9 . . . . . . . . 2:464, 618, 624, 625, 628, 633, 634, 648, 649

**MALACHI**

4:2 . . . . . . . . . . . 2:487

# NEW TESTAMENT

**MATTHEW**

1:21 . . . . . . . . . . 1:175, 181, 192, 288, 326, 333; 2:357, 432
3:2 . . . . . . . . . . . 1:174
3:3 . . . . . . . . . . . 1:140
3:17 . . . . . . . . . . 2:563, 594
5:1-12 . . . . . . . . 1:224, 229; 2:365, 386
5:3 . . . . . . . . . . . 1:182
5:10 . . . . . . . . . . 1:212
5:13 . . . . . . . . . . 2:616
6:10 . . . . . . . . . . 2:625
6:22-23 . . . . . . . . 1:4; 2:455
7:7 . . . . . . . . . . . 2:354, 474
9:6 . . . . . . . . . . . 1:201

(Matthew—*continued.*)
9:12 . . . . . . . . . . . 2:341
9:20-22 . . . . . . . . 1:220, 321, 333; 2:552
10:7 . . . . . . . . . . . 1:252
10:22 . . . . . . . . . . 2:364, 391, 402, 407, 635
11:5 . . . . . . . . . . . 1:192, 215, 224, 331; 2:366, 367, 373, 480, 504
11:28 . . . . . . . . . . 1:180, 190, 200, 285; 2:407, 462, 465, 478, 509, 556, 602
11:29 . . . . . . . . . . 2:477
13:3-23 . . . . . . . . 1:220; 2:382, 413
13:31-33 . . . . . . . 1:265
15:22-28 . . . . . . . 1:221, 265, 291, 328; 2:343, 404, 413, 420, 436
15:29-39 . . . . . . . 2:407
21:9 . . . . . . . . . . . 2:456
21:22 . . . . . . . . . . 2:430
21:28-31 . . . . . . . 2:367
21:44 . . . . . . . . . . 1:262
22:1-6 . . . . . . . . . 2:470
24 . . . . . . . . . . . . 1:311
24:13 . . . . . . . . . . 2:426, 453
25 . . . . . . . . . . . . 2:439
25:1-13 . . . . . . . . 1:333; 2:645
25:31 . . . . . . . . . . 2:477
27:25 . . . . . . . . . . 2:455, 477, 626
28:18 . . . . . . . . . . 2:373

## MARK

1:15 . . . . . . . . . . . 1:180, 183, 186, 188, 191, 197, 286; 2:342, 360, 416, 430,
472, 511, 576, 629
2:10 . . . . . . . . . . . 1:237
2:17 . . . . . . . . . . . 2:472, 473
7:26-30 . . . . . . . . 1:210
10:23 . . . . . . . . . . 1:94
10: 46-52 . . . . . . . 1:160, 187, 199, 235, 272, 279; 2:356, 408, 538
11:22 . . . . . . . . . . 1:326
13:13 . . . . . . . . . . 2:390
13:37 . . . . . . . . . . 2:531

## LUKE

1:68 . . . . . . . . . . . 2:337, 348
2:14 . . . . . . . . . . . 2:381
2:25-32 . . . . . . . . 1:303, 306; 2:367, 461, 576
4:18 . . . . . . . . . . . 1:231; 2:371, 400
7:22 . . . . . . . . . . . 2:521
7:36-50 . . . . . . . . 1:161, 162, 163, 246; 2:404, 504, 523

7:41-43 . . . . . . . . 2:353

10:29-37 . . . . . . . 1:170, 184, 186, 189, 199, 205, 231, 272, 286, 322; 2:360, 371, 403, 415, 463, 467, 504, 520, 522, 533, 540

10:42 . . . . . . . . . 1:93, 149, 151, 324; 2:392, 533, 537, 572, 642

11:2 . . . . . . . . . . 2:625

11:21 . . . . . . . . . 1:217

11:28 . . . . . . . . . 2:413

12:20 . . . . . . . . . 2:593

12:32 . . . . . . . . . 2:388, 408, 409

13:6-9 . . . . . . . . 2:337, 382

13:8 . . . . . . . . . . 2:453

13:11-17 . . . . . . . 2:470, 474

14:15-24 . . . . . . . 1:210; 2:342, 349, 351, 354, 434, 471, 501, 503, 521, 525, 545

15:4-7 . . . . . . . . 1:330; 2:558

15:11-32 . . . . . . . 1:173, 200, 214; 2:355, 436, 462, 464, 502, 504, 517, 521, 544, 545, 549

16:13 . . . . . . . . . 2:465

18:9-14 . . . . . . . . 2:370, 529

18:22 . . . . . . . . . 1:314

19:10 . . . . . . . . . 2:379, 380

21:26 . . . . . . . . . 2:632

21:28 . . . . . . . . . 2:626, 632, 633, 638

21:34 . . . . . . . . . 2:390, 391, 401, 414, 444, 631

21:36 . . . . . . . . . 2:622, 623

24:46 . . . . . . . . . 2:536

## JOHN

1 . . . . . . . . . . . . 1:214, 241; 2:433

1:12 . . . . . . . . . . 1:208; 2:515

1:29 . . . . . . . . . . 1:232; 2:350, 369, 377, 383, 411, 421, 428, 438, 446, 478, 503, 505, 518, 536, 545, 551, 576, 602, 615, 619, 622, 624, 629, 630, 637

3 . . . . . . . . . . . . 1:164, 174, 207, 229, 252

3:14 . . . . . . . . . . 2:409

3:16 . . . . . . . . . . 1:190, 192, 194, 320, 332; 2:479

4 . . . . . . . . . . . . 1:161, 164, 191, 198, 260

5:1-15 . . . . . . . . 1:325, 327; 2:341, 346, 412

5:14 . . . . . . . . . . 2:627

6:37 . . . . . . . . . . 2:455, 479, 483, 501

6:67 . . . . . . . . . . 2:353, 466

8:1-11 . . . . . . . . 1:162, 170, 209

9 . . . . . . . . . . . . 1:210

9:7 . . . . . . . . . . . 1:242

10:9 . . . . . . . . . . 2:458

(John—*continued.*)
10:10 . . . . . . . . . 2:388, 458, 505, 557
11 . . . . . . . . . . . 1:169, 183, 187, 198, 211, 247, 320
11:40 . . . . . . . . . 2:379, 587
12:32 . . . . . . . . . 1:305; 2:597
13 . . . . . . . . . . . 1:215
14:1 . . . . . . . . . . 2:410
14:6 . . . . . . . . . . 2:599
14:13 . . . . . . . . . 2:342
14:15 . . . . . . . . . 2:463
14:16 . . . . . . . . . 1:183
14:27 . . . . . . . . . 2:407
16:7-11 . . . . . . . 1:185, 186, 189, 195, 275
16:33 . . . . . . . . . 2:429, 605, 606
17 . . . . . . . . . . . 1:220, 309; 2:453, 573
17:24 . . . . . . . . . 2:443
19:30 . . . . . . . . . 1:302; 2:429, 524
19:34 . . . . . . . . . 2:428
20:28 . . . . . . . . . 2:563

## ACTS

1:4 . . . . . . . . . . . 1:209
1:4-5 . . . . . . . . . 2:574
2 . . . . . . . . . . . . 1:261
2:34 . . . . . . . . . . 2:427
2:37-39 . . . . . . . 1:186, 189, 192
2:40 . . . . . . . . . . 2:461
2:42 . . . . . . . . . . 1:270; 2:414, 489, 550, 613
3 . . . . . . . . . . . . 1:331; 2:426
3:19 . . . . . . . . . . 2:349, 415, 483, 537, 642
3:26 . . . . . . . . . . 2:505, 608
7 . . . . . . . . . . . . 1:275
9:4 . . . . . . . . . . . 2:469
13:38 . . . . . . . . . 1:247; 2:373
14:22 . . . . . . . . . 2:344, 347
16:30 . . . . . . . . . 1:227, 264, 319; 2:352, 547
16:31 . . . . . . . . . 1:331
19:2 . . . . . . . . . . 2:344
20 . . . . . . . . . . . 2:431
20:21 . . . . . . . . . 2:484, 540, 622
20:24 . . . . . . . . . 2:343
20:32 . . . . . . . . . 1:293; 2:368, 472, 552, 623, 636
24:25 . . . . . . . . . 2:460
26:18 . . . . . . . . . 2:452, 467, 545
27 . . . . . . . . . . . 2:423

## Romans

1 . . . . . . . . . . . . . . 1:192
2 . . . . . . . . . . . . 1:146, 193
2:29 . . . . . . . . . . 1:94
3:23-24 . . . . . . . . 1:159, 163, 164, 180, 188, 194, 204, 285
4 . . . . . . . . . . . . 1:195
5 . . . . . . . . . . . . 1:196; 2:356
6 . . . . . . . . . . . . 1:198
6:22 . . . . . . . . . . 2:627, 644
7 . . . . . . . . . . . . 1:198, 231, 270, 285
8 . . . . . . . . . . . . 1:173, 198, 200
8:18 . . . . . . . . . . 2:531
8:22 . . . . . . . . . . 2:402
8:31-32 . . . . . . . . 1:213, 222, 287; 2:346, 468
8:32 . . . . . . . . . . 2:348, 349, 354, 568
8:33-34 . . . . . . . 1:258
9 . . . . . . . . . . . . 1:202, 276
11 . . . . . . . . . . . 1:204
12 . . . . . . . . . . . 1:205, 207
12:1 . . . . . . . . . . 2:581
13 . . . . . . . . . . . 1:208
14:17 . . . . . . . . . 1:232

## 1 Corinthians

1:30 . . . . . . . . . . 1:181, 232, 287
1:31 . . . . . . . . . . 2:458
2:1 . . . . . . . . . . . 2:342
3:11 . . . . . . . . . . 1:327
6:9 . . . . . . . . . . . 1:193, 260
6:11 . . . . . . . . . . 1:184; 2:327
6:19 . . . . . . . . . . 1:159
9:16 . . . . . . . . . . 1:160
10 . . . . . . . . . . . 1:319, 330
10:12 . . . . . . . . . 2:412
15 . . . . . . . . . . . 1:282
15:1 . . . . . . . . . . 2:454
15:57 . . . . . . . . . 2:606
16:13 . . . . . . . . . 2:377, 426

## 2 Corinthians

5:17 . . . . . . . . . . 1:212, 217
5:19 . . . . . . . . . . 1:182, 189, 204, 213, 217
5:20 . . . . . . . . . . 1:379
13:11 . . . . . . . . . 2:426

**GALATIANS**

2:20 . . . . . . . . . . 1:187, 204
3:13 . . . . . . . . . . 1:332; 2:621
3:22 . . . . . . . . . . 1:144, 145, 147, 149, 156, 175

**EPHESIANS**

1 . . . . . . . . . . . . 1:147
1:17 . . . . . . . . . . 1:257
2:8 . . . . . . . . . . . 1:123, 130, 133, 134, 141, 146
3:18-19 . . . . . . . . 2:427
6:11-17 . . . . . . . . 1:301; 2:493, 640, 641

**PHILIPPIANS**

1:25 . . . . . . . . . . 1:238
1:27 . . . . . . . . . . 2:616, 641
2:12-13 . . . . . . . . 2:576
3:9-10 . . . . . . . . 1:234
3:10 . . . . . . . . . . 2:425

**COLOSSIANS**

3:1 . . . . . . . . . . . 2:456, 568

**1 THESSALONIANS**

1:5 . . . . . . . . . . . 2:378, 389
4:16 . . . . . . . . . . 2:511
5:23 . . . . . . . . . . 2:368

**1 TIMOTHY**

1:15 . . . . . . . . . . 1:298; 2:520, 537
4:9-10 . . . . . . . . 2:344
6:12 . . . . . . . . . . 1:219

**2 TIMOTHY**

1:7 . . . . . . . . . . . 1:227
2:15 . . . . . . . . . . 1:247
4:7 . . . . . . . . . . . 2:418, 557, 564

## TITUS

2:10 . . . . . . . . . . 2:437
2:11 . . . . . . . . . . 1:284, 319; 2:629, 638
3:8 . . . . . . . . . . . 1:152, 157, 164

## PHILEMON

Philemon . . . . . . 1:230

## HEBREWS

4:10 . . . . . . . . . . 2:466
4:12 . . . . . . . . . . 2:391
4:16 . . . . . . . . . . 2:481, 609, 613
6 . . . . . . . . . . . . 1:292
6:12 . . . . . . . . . . 2:417
9:12 . . . . . . . . . . 2:456
10:38 . . . . . . . . . 2:608
11:1 . . . . . . . . . . 1:208
12:1 . . . . . . . . . . 2:446, 613
12:2 . . . . . . . . . . 2:337
12:12 . . . . . . . . . 2:437
12:18 . . . . . . . . . 1:251
12:22 . . . . . . . . . 2:387
12:24 . . . . . . . . . 2:536
13:8 . . . . . . . . . . 2:414, 483, 577

## JAMES

1:12 . . . . . . . . . . 2:589

## 1 PETER

1:5 . . . . . . . . . . . 2:631
2:12 . . . . . . . . . . 2:440, 608
2:17 . . . . . . . . . . 2:449
2:21 . . . . . . . . . . 2:430
4:7 . . . . . . . . . . . 2:445, 572, 573

## 2 PETER

1:4 . . . . . . . . . . . 1:273
2:9 . . . . . . . . . . . 1:283
3:9 . . . . . . . . . . . 1:283

(2 Peter—*continued.*)
3:12 . . . . . . . . . . 2:502
3:14 . . . . . . . . . . 2:448

## 1 John

1 . . . . . . . . . . . . 1:285
2:1 . . . . . . . . . . . 1:285; 2:407
2:12 . . . . . . . . . . 1:255
3:14 . . . . . . . . . . 1:137, 143, 145, 146, 147, 149, 151, 152, 154, 155, 159
5:6 . . . . . . . . . . . 2:425, 439

## Jude

1:24 . . . . . . . . . . 2:483

## Revelation

1:7 . . . . . . . . . . . 2:614
2:1-7 . . . . . . . . . 2:390
2:10 . . . . . . . . . . 1:217; 2:367, 377, 572
2:24 . . . . . . . . . . 1:295
2:25 . . . . . . . . . . 2:353, 438
3:2-3 . . . . . . . . . 2:457
3:3 . . . . . . . . . . . 2:612
3:10 . . . . . . . . . . 2:449
3:14-22 . . . . . . . . 1:333; 2:373
3:20 . . . . . . . . . . 2:459, 552, 577
4 . . . . . . . . . . . . 2:502
7:14 . . . . . . . . . . 2:416, 423, 426, 428, 431, 434, 471, 514, 572, 596
14:13 . . . . . . . . . 2:454
16:15 . . . . . . . . . 2:626
21 . . . . . . . . . . . 2:434, 437, 476
22:17 . . . . . . . . . 2:371, 378, 418, 452, 471, 525

# INDEX OF SCRIPTURE REFERENCES AND ALLUSIONS

## OLD TESTAMENT

### GENESIS

1:3 . . . . . . . . . . . . 1:115
3 . . . . . . . . . . . . . 1:273
3:15 . . . . . . . . . . . 2:439
13:12-13 . . . . . . . 2:346
19:4 . . . . . . . . . . . 2:490
22:18 . . . . . . . . . . 2:498, 500
32:24-31 . . . . . . . 1:310, 320; 2:373, 406, 517, 525, 529
32:26 . . . . . . . . . . 2:438
39 . . . . . . . . . . . . 1:15

---

### EXODUS

3:2 . . . . . . . . . . . . 2:468
14:13 . . . . . . . . . . 2:361, 492
14:15 . . . . . . . . . . 1:323
14:24-25 . . . . . . . 2:363
17:6 . . . . . . . . . . . 1:191
17:8-13 . . . . . . . 2:644
22:28 . . . . . . . . . . 1:22
24:36 . . . . . . . . . . 2:584
40:34 . . . . . . . . . . 1:310

---

### NUMBERS

9:11 . . . . . . . . . . . 2:635
9:15 . . . . . . . . . . . 2:457
13:30 . . . . . . . . . . 1:301
13:31 . . . . . . . . . . 1:301
14 . . . . . . . . . . . . 1:302
14:17 . . . . . . . . . . 1:301

(Numbers—*continued.*)
16:26 . . . . . . . . . 1:317
22 . . . . . . . . . . . 2:427, 620
23:10 . . . . . . . . . 2:590
23:21 . . . . . . . . . 1:169, 224, 290, 312, 315; 2:441, 628

**DEUTERONOMY**

32:26 . . . . . . . . . 1:335
33:27 . . . . . . . . . 2:428, 491
34:1-4 . . . . . . . . . 2:531

**JOSHUA**

6 . . . . . . . . . . . . 1:328
8:30 . . . . . . . . . . 2:415
10:12 . . . . . . . . . 2:438

**JUDGES**

5:7 . . . . . . . . . . . 2:355
5:28 . . . . . . . . . . 2:380
6:5 . . . . . . . . . . . 2:615
6:30 . . . . . . . . . . 1:225
7:18, 20 . . . . . . . . 1:27
15:14 . . . . . . . . . 2:427
16:9 . . . . . . . . . . 2:359
17:6 . . . . . . . . . . 2:383
19:22 . . . . . . . . . 2:478

**RUTH**

1:16-17 . . . . . . . . 2:427

**1 SAMUEL**

2:12 . . . . . . . . . . 1:215, 247, 290; 2:346, 611
7:12 . . . . . . . . . . 2:407
10:9 . . . . . . . . . . 1:1
14:45 . . . . . . . . . 2:395

**2 SAMUEL**

12:7 . . . . . . . . . . 2:389
14–15 . . . . . . . . . 2:404

16:5-6 . . . . . . . . 2:364, 383, 577
18:13 . . . . . . . . . 2:419
23:15 . . . . . . . . . 1:220

## 1 Kings

10:7 . . . . . . . . . . 1:272
18:21 . . . . . . . . . 1:235
18:37-38 . . . . . . . 1:255
18:38 . . . . . . . . . 1:300
19:1-8 . . . . . . . . 2:441
19:12 . . . . . . . . . 1:306
19:17 . . . . . . . . . 2:614
21. . . . . . . . . . . . 1:313

## 2 Kings

5:1-27 . . . . . . . . 1:134
6:16 . . . . . . . . . . 1:33
6:17 . . . . . . . . . . 1:33, 334
6:31 . . . . . . . . . . 1:165
9:15 . . . . . . . . . . 1:117
9:25-26 . . . . . . . 1:167
10:5 . . . . . . . . . . 2:345
20:2 . . . . . . . . . . 2:442, 516

## 2 Chronicles

20:17 . . . . . . . . . 1:323
30:18-19 . . . . . . 2:500
32:8 . . . . . . . . . . 1:334

## Nehemiah

1:5 . . . . . . . . . . . 1:296
4:1-3 . . . . . . . . . 2:646
6:11 . . . . . . . . . . 1:225

## Job

1:21 . . . . . . . . . . 2:384
3:17 . . . . . . . . . . 1:56
5:18 . . . . . . . . . . 1:226
18:14 . . . . . . . . . 1:296, 306; 2:380
19:25 . . . . . . . . . 1:240, 299; 2:380

(Job—*continued.*)
22:21 . . . . . . . . . . 2:561
23. . . . . . . . . . . . . 2:453
28:8-10 . . . . . . . . 1:264
38:11 . . . . . . . . . . 2:361

---

PSALMS

4:6 . . . . . . . . . . . . 2:529
4:9 (BCP) . . . . . . 1:291; 2:410
8:2 . . . . . . . . . . . 1:107
16:12 (BCP) . . . . 2:573
23:4 . . . . . . . . . . 1:306, 314; 2:433
24:1 . . . . . . . . . . 2:483
31:10 (BCP) . . . . 1:298
32:2 (BCP) . . . . . 1:107
35:1-3 (BCP). . . . 2:386
36:3 (BCP) . . . . . 1:325
37. . . . . . . . . . . . 1:9
37:37 . . . . . . . . . 1:19
39:8 (BCP) . . . . . 1:108
40:1 . . . . . . . . . . 1:108
40:3-4 (BCP). . . . 1:108
40:10 (BCP) . . . . 1:110
41:3 . . . . . . . . . . 1:277
42:4 . . . . . . . . . . 2:625
42:4-5 . . . . . . . . 1:322
46. . . . . . . . . . . . 2:451, 590, 648
46:1 . . . . . . . . . . 2:433
46:8-9 . . . . . . . . 2:636
47:8 . . . . . . . . . . 2:428
52:1 (BCP) . . . . . 1:109
52:1-4 (BCP). . . . 1:20
56:1-5 (BCP). . . . 1:20
56:8 . . . . . . . . . . 1:322
57:1-7 (BCP). . . . 1:21
63:1 . . . . . . . . . . 1:148
63:5 . . . . . . . . . . 1:336; 2:377
65:3-5 . . . . . . . . 1:119
66:20 . . . . . . . . . 1:126
68:30 . . . . . . . . . 2:347
76:10 . . . . . . . . . 1:291
78:20 . . . . . . . . . 2:483, 537
79:1 . . . . . . . . . . 1:287
86:17 (BCP) . . . . 1:322
88:6 . . . . . . . . . . 1:126

91 . . . . . . . . . . . 1:92
91:1 . . . . . . . . . . 1:60
91:1 (BCP) . . . . . 1:225
91:3 . . . . . . . . . . 1:205, 311
93:3 . . . . . . . . . . 2:343, 379, 485
96:8 (BCP) . . . . . 1:252
100 . . . . . . . . . . 2:358
102 . . . . . . . . . . 1:103
107 . . . . . . . . . . 1:108
110:1 . . . . . . . . . 2:427
115:1 . . . . . . . . . 1:109, 127; 2:416
118:16 . . . . . . . . 2:363
118:21 (BCP) . . . 1:5
118:23 . . . . . . . . 2:495
118:24 . . . . . . . . 2:457
118:26 . . . . . . . . 1:296
119:71 (BCP) . . . 2:433
119:109 (BCP) . . 1:13
122:1 . . . . . . . . . 2:625
122:6 . . . . . . . . . 2:374
124:5-6 (BCP) . . 2:365
126:5 . . . . . . . . . 1:322
126:7 (BCP) . . . . 1:26
127:2 . . . . . . . . . 2:500
130 . . . . . . . . . . 1:272
133:1 (BCP) . . . . 2:421
144 . . . . . . . . . . 2:427

## PROVERBS

1:7 . . . . . . . . . . . 1:253
1:20 . . . . . . . . . . 2:458
3 . . . . . . . . . . . . 2:381
7:22 . . . . . . . . . . 1:261
8:17 . . . . . . . . . . 2:573
20:8 . . . . . . . . . . 2:368
20:15 . . . . . . . . . 2:370
25:22 . . . . . . . . . 1:281, 310
26:5 . . . . . . . . . . 1:230
26:16 . . . . . . . . . 2:631

## ECCLESIASTES

1:2 . . . . . . . . . . . 1:267
11:1 . . . . . . . . . . 2:438

## Isaiah

1:9 . . . . . . . . . . 1:265; 2:480, 487, 489
1:16 . . . . . . . . . 2:390, 391, 401, 414, 449, 488, 504
1:16-17 . . . . . . . 2:462, 547
1:18 . . . . . . . . . 2:372
2:10 . . . . . . . . . 2:392
2:21 . . . . . . . . . 2:417
3 . . . . . . . . . . . 1:194
4 . . . . . . . . . . . 1:196
6:7 . . . . . . . . . . 2:365, 366
6:20 . . . . . . . . . 2:648
8:18 . . . . . . . . . 2:378
9:3 . . . . . . . . . . 1:164
9:6 . . . . . . . . . . 1:294; 2:587
11:6 . . . . . . . . . 1:224, 278; 2:359, 477, 494
24 . . . . . . . . . . 2:590
25:6 . . . . . . . . . 1:169
26:8 . . . . . . . . . 2:393
26:9 . . . . . . . . . 2:635
26:11 . . . . . . . . 2:480
26:13 . . . . . . . . 1:204
28:11 . . . . . . . . 1:161
29 . . . . . . . . . . 1:204
30 . . . . . . . . . . 1:205
30:10 . . . . . . . . 2:369
30:13 . . . . . . . . 2:395
30:18 . . . . . . . . 1:296
30:18-19 . . . . . . 1:113
30:25 . . . . . . . . 2:507
30:32 . . . . . . . . 1:297
35 . . . . . . . . . . 1:209; 2:413, 422, 430, 437, 453, 465, 479, 523, 541, 552, 559
35:1 . . . . . . . . . 1:193
35:5-6 . . . . . . . . 2:616
35:6 . . . . . . . . . 1:193
35:10 . . . . . . . . 2:407
40 . . . . . . . . . . 1:221
40:1 . . . . . . . . . 1:275; 2:361, 365, 379, 408, 504, 506, 596
40:9 . . . . . . . . . 1:294
40:31 . . . . . . . . 1:278; 2:379, 418, 446
42:1 . . . . . . . . . 1:220
43 . . . . . . . . . . 1:212
43:1-3 . . . . . . . . 1:108, 111
43:10 . . . . . . . . 2:532
43:25 . . . . . . . . 2:543

44:4 . . . . . . . . . . 1:206
44:22 . . . . . . . . . 2:380
44:23 . . . . . . . . . 1:191
45:8 . . . . . . . . . . 1:218, 276
45:15 . . . . . . . . . 1:251
45:22 . . . . . . . . . 1:299; 2:475
45:22-23 . . . . . . . 1:116
45:24 . . . . . . . . . 1:116; 2:359
48:9 . . . . . . . . . . 1:62
49:15 . . . . . . . . . 2:419
49:16 . . . . . . . . . 1:219
50 . . . . . . . . . . . 1:215
50:2 . . . . . . . . . . 1:254, 329
50:2-9 . . . . . . . . 1:17
50:10 . . . . . . . . . 1:253
51:1-13 . . . . . . . 1:16
51:9 . . . . . . . . . . 2:385, 430, 434
51:11 . . . . . . . . . 2:444, 532
52:1 . . . . . . . . . . 1:319
52:2 . . . . . . . . . . 2:375
52:7 . . . . . . . . . . 2:432
52:8 . . . . . . . . . . 2:420, 498
52:9 . . . . . . . . . . 1:316
52:10 . . . . . . . . . 1:241, 305; 2:346, 495, 509
53 . . . . . . . . . . . 1:209, 216, 233, 260, 328; 2:362, 525
53:1 . . . . . . . . . . 1:221
53:6 . . . . . . . . . . 2:366
54 . . . . . . . . . . . 1:281
54:3-17 . . . . . . . . 2:362
54:7 . . . . . . . . . . 1:199, 261
54:17 . . . . . . . . . 2:384
55 . . . . . . . . . . . 1:205
55:1 . . . . . . . . . . 1:269, 237, 284; 2:348, 400, 410, 422, 438, 465, 505, 510,
                        520
55:11 . . . . . . . . . 1:144, 222; 2:472, 542
57 . . . . . . . . . . . 1:262
57:15 . . . . . . . . . 1:217; 2:436
57:20 . . . . . . . . . 1:263
58 . . . . . . . . . . . 1:264
59 . . . . . . . . . . . 1:218
59:1 . . . . . . . . . . 1:254, 329
59:18-19 . . . . . . . 1:218
60 . . . . . . . . . . . 1:288
60:20 . . . . . . . . . 2:437, 591, 603
61:1 . . . . . . . . . . 1:204; 2:549
61:3 . . . . . . . . . . 2:346

(Isaiah—*continued.*)
63:1 . . . . . . . . . . 1:276, 287; 2:363
63:5 . . . . . . . . . . 2:445
63:12 . . . . . . . . . 2:494
64:5 . . . . . . . . . . 1:323; 2:629, 632, 636, 645, 647
64:6 . . . . . . . . . . 2:413
66:10 . . . . . . . . . 2:646

## JEREMIAH

1:6-19 . . . . . . . . 1:321
1:10 . . . . . . . . . . 1:324
1:18 . . . . . . . . . . 2:462, 468
2:24 . . . . . . . . . . 2:465
4:7 . . . . . . . . . . . 2:448
5:1 . . . . . . . . . . . 2:348
7:1-28 . . . . . . . . 2:360
8:22 . . . . . . . . . . 2:436
13:16 . . . . . . . . . 1:309
15:18 . . . . . . . . . 2:355
17:9 . . . . . . . . . . 1:282
20:7-10 . . . . . . . 2:423
23:29 . . . . . . . . . 1:199, 229, 239, 264, 311; 2:422, 450, 461
31 . . . . . . . . . . . 2:481
31:1 . . . . . . . . . . 2:442
31:34 . . . . . . . . . 2:481
33:25-26 . . . . . . . 2:569
44:16-17 . . . . . . . 1:9
50:20 . . . . . . . . . 2:461
51:20 . . . . . . . . . 1:212

## LAMENTATIONS

1:12 . . . . . . . . . . 2:378, 388, 413, 429, 461, 483, 501, 504, 507, 522, 529,
546, 551, 576, 642
3:22 . . . . . . . . . . 2:373, 453

## EZEKIEL

2:6 . . . . . . . . . . . 2:417
9 . . . . . . . . . . . . 2:440, 637
9:4 . . . . . . . . . . . 2:440
14:20 . . . . . . . . . 2:440
16 . . . . . . . . . . . 1:270, 271
16:6 . . . . . . . . . . 1:270
16:62 . . . . . . . . . 1:329
24:16 . . . . . . . . . 2:535

33:1-6 . . . . . . . . . 2:623, 624, 632, 635
33:5 . . . . . . . . . . . 2:402
33:6 . . . . . . . . . . . 2:390
36:24-30 . . . . . . 1:271, 291
37:1-14 . . . . . . . 1:211, 221, 281; 2:512
37:4ff. . . . . . . . . . 1:256, 328; 2:502, 573
37:7 . . . . . . . . . . . 1:195
38–39 . . . . . . . . . 1:16

## DANIEL

3 . . . . . . . . . . . . 1:34
6:22 . . . . . . . . . . 2:359
9 . . . . . . . . . . . . 2:339
9:9 . . . . . . . . . . . 2:503
9:24 . . . . . . . . . . 1:298
12:13 . . . . . . . . . 2:588

## HOSEA

2:14 . . . . . . . . . . 2:405, 598
2:23 . . . . . . . . . . 1:193; 2:359
6:1 . . . . . . . . . . . 2:459
11:8 . . . . . . . . . . 1:319; 2:476, 480
13:9 . . . . . . . . . . 2:352, 521, 578
14:4 . . . . . . . . . . 1:306

## JOEL

2:1 . . . . . . . . . . . 1:224
2:13 . . . . . . . . . . 2:477
2:31 . . . . . . . . . . 2:429, 448

## AMOS

4:12 . . . . . . . . . . 1:126

## MICAH

6:9 . . . . . . . . . . . 1:331
7:2-5 . . . . . . . . . 1:247
7:8 . . . . . . . . . . . 2:530
7:18 . . . . . . . . . . 2:402

## HABAKKUK

3 . . . . . . . . . . . . . 2:628
3:2 . . . . . . . . . . . 2:626, 635

(Habakkuk—*continued.*)
3:17 . . . . . . . . . . 2:567

ZEPHANIAH

2 . . . . . . . . . . . . . 2:451

ZECHARIAH

3:2 . . . . . . . . . . . 1:173
4:7 . . . . . . . . . . . 1:319; 2:444
4:9 . . . . . . . . . . . 2:615
4:10 . . . . . . . . . . 2:539
9:9 . . . . . . . . . . . 2:382
9:11 . . . . . . . . . . 2:425
12:10 . . . . . . . . . 1:302; 2:388, 439, 517, 534, 572
13:6 . . . . . . . . . . 2:463, 471
13:7 . . . . . . . . . . 1:265
13:7-9 . . . . . . . . 2:464
13:9 . . . . . . . . . . 2:530, 606, 618, 624, 625, 628, 633, 634, 647, 648, 649

MALACHI

3:1 . . . . . . . . . . . 1:124
3:7 . . . . . . . . . . . 2:617
3:13-14 . . . . . . . 1:124
3:16 . . . . . . . . . . 1:327
4:2 . . . . . . . . . . . 1:196, 2:487

# INTERTESTAMENTAL

WISDOM (ECCLESIASTICUS)

5 . . . . . . . . . . . . . 2:635

# NEW TESTAMENT

MATTHEW

1:21 . . . . . . . . . . 1:175, 181, 192, 288, 326, 333; 2:357, 432
2:23 . . . . . . . . . . 2:480

3:2 . . . . . . . . . . . 1:174
3:3 . . . . . . . . . . . 1:140
3:7 . . . . . . . . . . . 2:635
3:9 . . . . . . . . . . . 2:349
3:17 . . . . . . . . . . 2:563, 594
4:6 . . . . . . . . . . . 2:375
4:11 . . . . . . . . . . 2:374
5 . . . . . . . . . . . . 1:229
5:1-12 . . . . . . . . 2:365, 386
5:3 . . . . . . . . . . . 1:182
5:6 . . . . . . . . . . . 1:230
5:10 . . . . . . . . . . 1:212, 224; 2:377
5:13 . . . . . . . . . . 2:616, 638
5:16 . . . . . . . . . . 1:259
5:19 . . . . . . . . . . 1:259
5:20 . . . . . . . . . . 2:358
5:39-40 . . . . . . . . 2:385
5:41 . . . . . . . . . . 1:279
6:5ff. . . . . . . . . . 1:21
6:10 . . . . . . . . . . 2:625
6:22-23 . . . . . . . 1:4; 2:455
7:6 . . . . . . . . . . . 1:264
7:7 . . . . . . . . . . . 2:354, 474, 544
7:14 . . . . . . . . . . 1:85
7:15 . . . . . . . . . . 1:223; 2:358
7:20 . . . . . . . . . . 2:351
7:22 . . . . . . . . . . 1:314
7:24-27 . . . . . . . 2:634
7:27 . . . . . . . . . . 2:428
8:20 . . . . . . . . . . 1:17
8:26 . . . . . . . . . . 2:494
8:28 . . . . . . . . . . 1:199; 2:346
9:1-8 . . . . . . . . . 1:105, 123
9:2 . . . . . . . . . . . 1:208, 210
9:6 . . . . . . . . . . . 1:201
9:12 . . . . . . . . . . 2:341
9:20-22 . . . . . . . 1:128, 220
10:7 . . . . . . . . . . 1:252
10:14 . . . . . . . . . 2:358, 440
10:16-26 . . . . . . 1:33
10:16 . . . . . . . . . 1:69
10:18 . . . . . . . . . 1:11
10:22 . . . . . . . . . 2:364, 391, 402, 407, 635
10:23 . . . . . . . . . 2:495
10:30 . . . . . . . . . 2:395, 451, 555
10:37 . . . . . . . . . 1:219

(Matthew—*continued.*)

11:5 . . . . . . . . . . 1:192, 215, 224, 331; 2:366, 367, 373, 480, 504
11:12 . . . . . . . . . . 1:259; 2:545
11:25 . . . . . . . . . . 1:134
11:28 . . . . . . . . . . 1:180, 190, 200, 227, 285; 2:407, 462, 465, 509, 556, 602
11:28-30 . . . . . . . 2:541
11:29 . . . . . . . . . . 2:477
12:29 . . . . . . . . . . 1:229, 255
12:34 . . . . . . . . . . 2:612
13:3-23 . . . . . . . . 1:220; 2:382, 413
13:20 . . . . . . . . . . 2:416
13:25 . . . . . . . . . . 1:179, 284; 2:624, 627, 632
13:31-33 . . . . . . . 1:265
13:46 . . . . . . . . . . 2:543
14:27 . . . . . . . . . . 2:379
14:36 . . . . . . . . . . 1:119
15:22-28 . . . . . . . 1:211, 265, 291, 328; 2:343, 404, 413, 420, 436, 453
15:25 . . . . . . . . . . 2:420
15:26 . . . . . . . . . . 1:262
15:29-39 . . . . . . . 2:407
15:32 . . . . . . . . . . 2:437, 528, 582, 635
16:23 . . . . . . . . . . 2:649
17:4 . . . . . . . . . . 1:192, 272; 2:558
18:3 . . . . . . . . . . 1:270
18:6 . . . . . . . . . . 1:217
18:6-7 . . . . . . . . 1:241
18:7 . . . . . . . . . . 1:217, 241, 630
18:32-33 . . . . . . . 2:405
19:30 . . . . . . . . . . 1:230
20:6 . . . . . . . . . . 2:370
20:12 . . . . . . . . . . 2:360
20:16 . . . . . . . . . . 2:648, 649
21:1[ff] . . . . . . . . 2:470
21:9 . . . . . . . . . . 1:271, 323; 2:456
21:22 . . . . . . . . . . 2:430
21:28-31 . . . . . . . 2:367
21:31 . . . . . . . . . . 1:202
21:31-32 . . . . . . . 2:366
21:42 . . . . . . . . . . 2:495
21:44 . . . . . . . . . . 1:262
22:6 . . . . . . . . . . 2:470
23:2-3 . . . . . . . . 1:259
23:8 . . . . . . . . . . 1:240, 245
24 . . . . . . . . . . . 1:311
24:13 . . . . . . . . . . 2:426, 453
25 . . . . . . . . . . . 2:439
25:1-13 . . . . . . . . 1:220, 333; 2:645

25:6 . . . . . . . . . . 1:242, 301
25:31 . . . . . . . . . 2:478
25:32-33 . . . . . . . 2:415
26:24 . . . . . . . . . 1:241
26:31 . . . . . . . . . 1:265
26:39 . . . . . . . . . 1:12
27:25 . . . . . . . . . 2:455, 477, 626
28:18 . . . . . . . . . 2:373
28:20 . . . . . . . . . 1:150, 227, 259, 302; 2:598

## MARK

1:3 . . . . . . . . . . . 1:140
1:15 . . . . . . . . . . 1:180, 183, 186, 188, 191, 197, 286; 2:342, 360, 416, 430,
          472, 511, 629
1:22 . . . . . . . . . . 1:321
2:10 . . . . . . . . . . 1:237
2:12 . . . . . . . . . . 1:300
2:17 . . . . . . . . . . 1:205; 2:472, 473
3:17 . . . . . . . . . . 1:252
3:27 . . . . . . . . . . 1:318
4:39 . . . . . . . . . . 1:61; 2:494
5:2 . . . . . . . . . . . 2:357
5:9 . . . . . . . . . . . 1:319; 2:403
5:25-34 . . . . . . . . 1:220; 2:524
5:34 . . . . . . . . . . 1:220
6:50 . . . . . . . . . . 2:379
7:1 . . . . . . . . . . . 1:115
7:26-30 . . . . . . . . 1:210
8:1-10 . . . . . . . . . 2:407
8:3 . . . . . . . . . . . 2:437, 528, 582, 635
8:33 . . . . . . . . . . 2:649
8:34 . . . . . . . . . . 1:314
9:2 . . . . . . . . . . . 1:187
9:24 . . . . . . . . . . 1:112, 133
9:25 . . . . . . . . . . 1:156
10:31 . . . . . . . . . 2:648, 649
10:45 . . . . . . . . . 1:296
10:46-52 . . . . . . . 1:117, 160, 187, 199, 235, 272, 279; 2:359, 408, 538
11:9 . . . . . . . . . . 1:205
11:22 . . . . . . . . . 1:326
11:23-24 . . . . . . . 1:118
12:11 . . . . . . . . . 2:495
12:34 . . . . . . . . . 1:102; 2:521
13:9 . . . . . . . . . . 1:11
13:13 . . . . . . . . . 2:390
13:37 . . . . . . . . . 2:531, 633

LUKE

1:13 . . . . . . . . . . 1:110
1:35 . . . . . . . . . . 1:173; 2:454, 551
1:47 . . . . . . . . . . 1:212
1:53 . . . . . . . . . . 1:212
1:68 . . . . . . . . . . 2:337, 348
2:11 . . . . . . . . . . 2:563
2:14 . . . . . . . . . . 2:381
2:22-32 . . . . . . . 1:102
2:25-32 . . . . . . . 2:367, 461
2:25 . . . . . . . . . . 1:208; 2:367, 638
2:29 . . . . . . . . . . 1:213, 303, 306
2:37 . . . . . . . . . . 2:521
3:3 . . . . . . . . . . 1:140
3:7 . . . . . . . . . . 2:635
3:9 . . . . . . . . . . 2:454
3:12 . . . . . . . . . . 1:180
4:8 . . . . . . . . . . 2:649
4:18 . . . . . . . . . . 1:209, 231, 293; 2:371
5:9 . . . . . . . . . . 1:127, 130
5:20 . . . . . . . . . . 1:118
5:23-26 . . . . . . . 1:118, 119
6:40 . . . . . . . . . . 1:315
7:22 . . . . . . . . . . 2:521
7:36-50 . . . . . . . . 1:161, 162, 163, 246; 2:404, 504, 523
7:41-43 . . . . . . . 2:353
7:44 . . . . . . . . . . 2:404
7:47 . . . . . . . . . . 1:126
8:13 . . . . . . . . . . 2:416
8:14 . . . . . . . . . . 1:322
8:30 . . . . . . . . . . 1:319
8:37 . . . . . . . . . . 1:113
8:40-56 . . . . . . . 1:220; 2:524
9:5 . . . . . . . . . . 1:172; 2:440
9:58 . . . . . . . . . . 1:17
10:19 . . . . . . . . . 1:205
10:29-37 . . . . . . . 1:170, 184, 186, 189, 199, 205, 231, 272, 286, 322; 2:360,
                        371, 403, 463, 467, 504, 520, 522, 533, 540
10:42 . . . . . . . . . 1:55, 93, 151, 160, 324; 2:392, 533, 537, 572, 642
11:2 . . . . . . . . . . 2:625
11:21 . . . . . . . . . 1:217
11:28 . . . . . . . . . 2:413
12:4 . . . . . . . . . . 2:361
12:7 . . . . . . . . . . 2:555
12:20 . . . . . . . . . 2:593

12:32 . . . . . . . . . 2:388, 408, 409
12:37 . . . . . . . . . 2:626
12:52 . . . . . . . . . 1:223
13:6-9 . . . . . . . . 2:382
13:8 . . . . . . . . . . 2:453
13:10-13 . . . . . . . 1:130
13:11-17 . . . . . . . 2:470, 474
13:23 . . . . . . . . . 1:83
13:24 . . . . . . . . . 1:259
13:30 . . . . . . . . . 2:648, 649
14. . . . . . . . . . . . 1:210
14:10 . . . . . . . . . 2:348
14:15 . . . . . . . . . 2:503
14:15-24 . . . . . . . 2:349, 351, 471, 521, 525, 548
14:17 . . . . . . . . . 2:342, 354, 434, 501
14:21 . . . . . . . . . 2:545
14:33 . . . . . . . . . 1:212
15:4 . . . . . . . . . . 1:166
15:4-7 . . . . . . . . 1:330
15:6 . . . . . . . . . . 2:558, 635
15:7 . . . . . . . . . . 2:524, 640
15:8 . . . . . . . . . . 1:135
15:11-32 . . . . . . . 1:173, 191, 200, 214; 2:355, 436, 462, 464, 502, 504, 517,
                        521, 544, 545, 549, 576
15:17 . . . . . . . . . 2:410
15:18 . . . . . . . . . 1:214; 2:355
15:22 . . . . . . . . . 2:413
15:24 . . . . . . . . . 1:191
15:32 . . . . . . . . . 2:411
16:13 . . . . . . . . . 2:465
18:3 . . . . . . . . . . 2:481
18:9-14 . . . . . . . . 2:370, 529
18:11 . . . . . . . . . 1:282, 283
18:13 . . . . . . . . . 2:338
18:22 . . . . . . . . . 1:314
19:10 . . . . . . . . . 2:379, 380
21. . . . . . . . . . . . 2:633
21:15 . . . . . . . . . 2:423
21:19 . . . . . . . . . 1:78
21:26 . . . . . . . . . 2:632
21:28 . . . . . . . . . 2:626, 632, 638, 646
21:34 . . . . . . . . . 2:390, 391, 401, 414, 444
21:34-36 . . . . . . . 2:631
21:36 . . . . . . . . . 2:622, 623, 632, 646
22:19 . . . . . . . . . 1:149, 241, 259
22:31 . . . . . . . . . 2:646

(Luke—*continued.*)
22:57 . . . . . . . . . 1:235
22:61 . . . . . . . . . 2:350
23:40-43 . . . . . . . 1:328
23:46 . . . . . . . . . 2:516
24:5 . . . . . . . . . . 2:649
24:35 . . . . . . . . . 2:647
24:36 . . . . . . . . . 2:580
24:46 . . . . . . . . . 2:536
24:47 . . . . . . . . . 2:485

## JOHN

1. . . . . . . . . . . . . . 1:195; 2:433
1:12 . . . . . . . . . . . 1:208; 2:515
1:29 . . . . . . . . . . 1:232; 2:350, 359, 369, 377, 383, 411, 421, 428, 438, 446, 478, 503, 505, 518, 545, 551, 576, 602, 615, 619, 622, 624, 629, 630, 637
2:10 . . . . . . . . . . . 2:487
3. . . . . . . . . . . . . . 1:197, 223, 229, 252
3:1-10 . . . . . . . . . 1:174
3:5 . . . . . . . . . . . 1:261
3:8 . . . . . . . . . . . 2:366
3:14 . . . . . . . . . . 1:202, 207; 2:409
3:16 . . . . . . . . . . 1:190, 192, 194, 320, 332; 2:479
3:30 . . . . . . . . . . 1:284
4. . . . . . . . . . . . . . 1:161, 164, 191, 198, 260
4:14 . . . . . . . . . . 1:205
4:26 . . . . . . . . . . 1:260
4:32 . . . . . . . . . . 1:231
4:34 . . . . . . . . . . 2:366
4:35 . . . . . . . . . . 2:636
5. . . . . . . . . . . . . . 1:200, 321
5:1-15 . . . . . . . . . 1:325, 327; 2:340, 341, 346, 412, 478, 525
5:4 . . . . . . . . . . . 2:541
5:14 . . . . . . . . . . 2:627
5:35 . . . . . . . . . . 1:305
6:20 . . . . . . . . . . 2:379
6:37 . . . . . . . . . . 2:455, 479, 483, 501, 582
6:44 . . . . . . . . . . 1:235
6:67 . . . . . . . . . . 2:353, 466
7. . . . . . . . . . . . . . 1:205
7:6 . . . . . . . . . . . 2:362
7:49 . . . . . . . . . . 1:189
7:51 . . . . . . . . . . 1:323
8. . . . . . . . . . . . . . 1:287; 2:360

8:1-11 . . . . . . . . 1:159, 162, 170, 209
8:11 . . . . . . . . . . 2:412
8:31 . . . . . . . . . . 2:634
8:46 . . . . . . . . . . 2:615
9:7 . . . . . . . . . . . 1:242
9:11 . . . . . . . . . . 1:242
10:4-5 . . . . . . . . . 1:236
10:9 . . . . . . . . . . 2:458
10:10 . . . . . . . . 2:388, 458, 505, 557
10:20 . . . . . . . . . 1:211
11. . . . . . . . . . . . 1:169, 183, 187, 211, 247, 320
11:16 . . . . . . . . . 2:455
11:25 . . . . . . . . . 1:211
11:39 . . . . . . . . . 1:247
11:40 . . . . . . . . . 2:379, 496, 587
11:43 . . . . . . . . . 1:198, 206
11:44 . . . . . . . . . 1:247
12:26-28 . . . . . . . 1:10
12:32 . . . . . . . . . 1:305; 2:597
13. . . . . . . . . . . . 1:215
13:36 . . . . . . . . . 1:14, 42
14:1 . . . . . . . . . . 2:410
14:1-27 . . . . . . . . 1:15
14:6 . . . . . . . . . . 1:271; 2:599
14:13 . . . . . . . . . 2:342
14:15 . . . . . . . . . 2:463
14:16 . . . . . . . . . 1:183, 215
14:23-26 . . . . . . . 1:106
14:27 . . . . . . . . . 2:407
14:31 . . . . . . . . . 1:46
15:18-20 . . . . . . . 1:16; 2:365
16:1-33 . . . . . . . . 1:17
16:2 . . . . . . . . . . 1:207; 2:388
16:5-15 . . . . . . . . 2:371
16:7 . . . . . . . . . . 1:275
16:7-11 . . . . . . . . 1:186, 189
16:8 . . . . . . . . . . 1:185, 195
16:33 . . . . . . . . . 2:429, 606
17. . . . . . . . . . . . 2:453, 573
17:9-23 . . . . . . . . 1:309
17:24 . . . . . . . . . 2:443
19:11 . . . . . . . . . 1:314
19:30 . . . . . . . . . 1:282, 302; 2:524
19:34 . . . . . . . . . 2:428
20:27-28 . . . . . . . 1:126
20:28 . . . . . . . . . 2:563

## ACTS

1:4 . . . . . . . . . . . 1:209
1:4-5 . . . . . . . . . 2:574
2. . . . . . . . . . . . . 1:205, 261, 273
2:34 . . . . . . . . . . 2:427
2:37 . . . . . . . . . . 1:186
2:37-39 . . . . . . . . 1:261
2:39 . . . . . . . . . . 1:189, 192, 203; 2:344
2:40 . . . . . . . . . . 1:317; 2:368, 461
2:42 . . . . . . . . . . 2:411, 414, 489, 550, 613
3. . . . . . . . . . . . . 2:426
3:1-11 . . . . . . . . 1:106
3:19 . . . . . . . . . . 2:344, 349, 415, 483, 537, 642
3:26 . . . . . . . . . . 2:505, 608
4:20 . . . . . . . . . . 1:125
4:36 . . . . . . . . . . 1:252
5:34-39 . . . . . . . . 1:179, 335
7. . . . . . . . . . . . . 1:275
8:10 . . . . . . . . . . 2:537
8:39 . . . . . . . . . . 1:142, 258
9:4 . . . . . . . . . . . 2:469
9:18 . . . . . . . . . . 1:318
10:29 . . . . . . . . . 1:128
10:47 . . . . . . . . . 1:206
13:38 . . . . . . . . . 2:373
14:22 . . . . . . . . . 2:344, 347, 387, 490
15:31-33 . . . . . . . 1:11
16:30 . . . . . . . . . 1:227, 264, 319; 2:352, 547
16:31 . . . . . . . . . 1:331
17:3 . . . . . . . . . . 1:179
17:6 . . . . . . . . . . 2:343
17:11 . . . . . . . . . 1:186; 2:521
18:10 . . . . . . . . . 2:355
18:17 . . . . . . . . . 1:272
18:24-25 . . . . . . . 1:152
19:2 . . . . . . . . . . 2:344
19:38 . . . . . . . . . 1:230
20:10 . . . . . . . . . 1:267
20:21 . . . . . . . . . 2:414, 484, 540, 622
20:24 . . . . . . . . . 2:343
20:32 . . . . . . . . . 1:293; 2:368, 431, 472, 552, 623, 636
22:4 . . . . . . . . . . 1:268
22:16 . . . . . . . . . 1:28
23:5 . . . . . . . . . . 1:22
24:25 . . . . . . . . . 2:460

26:18 . . . . . . . . . 2:452, 467, 518, 521, 540, 545
27. . . . . . . . . . . . 2:423
27:44 . . . . . . . . . 2:353

**ROMANS**

1:16 . . . . . . . . . . 1:121
2. . . . . . . . . . . . . 1:146, 194
3. . . . . . . . . . . . . 1:147, 150, 188
3:23 . . . . . . . . . . 1:180, 285
3:23-25 . . . . . . . . 1:159, 163, 164, 180, 194, 204
3:28 . . . . . . . . . . 1:124
4. . . . . . . . . . . . . 1:195
4:18 . . . . . . . . . . 1:293; 2:590
5. . . . . . . . . . . . . 1:196, 204; 2:356
5:5 . . . . . . . . . . . 1:256; 2:526
6:6 . . . . . . . . . . . 1:239
6:22 . . . . . . . . . . 2:627, 644
7. . . . . . . . . . . . . 1:198, 231, 285, 294
7:4 . . . . . . . . . . . 2:367
8. . . . . . . . . . . . . 1:198, 200
8:18 . . . . . . . . . . 2:531
8:21 . . . . . . . . . . 1:305, 312
8:22 . . . . . . . . . . 2:402
8:26 . . . . . . . . . . 1:119, 313, 317; 2:646
8:31 . . . . . . . . . . 1:20
8:31-32 . . . . . . . . 1:213, 222, 287; 2:346, 468
8:32 . . . . . . . . . . 2:348, 349, 354, 568
8:33-34 . . . . . . . . 1:258
8:37 . . . . . . . . . . 1:110
8:38 . . . . . . . . . . 2:473
9. . . . . . . . . . . . . 1:202, 276, 292
9:21 . . . . . . . . . . 1:324
9:28 . . . . . . . . . . 1:104
10:3 . . . . . . . . . . 2:391
10:9 . . . . . . . . . . 1:276
10:10 . . . . . . . . . 1:102
10:11 . . . . . . . . . 1:92
11. . . . . . . . . . . . 1:204
11:20 . . . . . . . . . 1:206
12. . . . . . . . . . . . 1:205, 207
12:1 . . . . . . . . . . 2:581
12:15 . . . . . . . . . 1:303; 2:450, 591
12:18 . . . . . . . . . 2:630
12:20 . . . . . . . . . 1:281, 310
13. . . . . . . . . . . . 1:208

(Romans—*continued.*)
13:1 . . . . . . . . . . 1:223
14:17 . . . . . . . . . 1:232

## 1 CORINTHIANS

1:12 . . . . . . . . . . 1:237, 259
1:17 . . . . . . . . . . 1:272
1:21 . . . . . . . . . . 1:288
1:23 . . . . . . . . . . 1:264
1:30 . . . . . . . . . . 1:178, 181, 232, 287
1:31 . . . . . . . . . . 2:458
2:1 . . . . . . . . . . . 2:342
2:2 . . . . . . . . . . . 2:459
2:4 . . . . . . . . . . . 1:93
2:15 . . . . . . . . . . 2:419
3:7 . . . . . . . . . . . 2:629
3:11 . . . . . . . . . . 1:266, 327; 2:511
4:11 . . . . . . . . . . 1:17
4:13 . . . . . . . . . . 2:418
6:9 . . . . . . . . . . . 1:193, 260
6:11 . . . . . . . . . . 1:184, 327
6:19 . . . . . . . . . . 1:159, 304; 2:372, 513
7:16 . . . . . . . . . . 1:314
9:16 . . . . . . . . . . 1:160
9:17 . . . . . . . . . . 1:179
10. . . . . . . . . . . . 1:330
10:12 . . . . . . . . . 2:412
11:1 . . . . . . . . . . 1:298
12:10 . . . . . . . . . 2:405
13:6-7 . . . . . . . . . 2:626
13:12 . . . . . . . . . 1:314; 2:441
14:40 . . . . . . . . . 2:502
15. . . . . . . . . . . . 1:282
15:1 . . . . . . . . . . 2:454
15:32 . . . . . . . . . 2:343
15:36 . . . . . . . . . 1:248
15:52 . . . . . . . . . 2:460
15:55-56 . . . . . . . 1:189, 200
15:57 . . . . . . . . . 2:520, 606
16:13 . . . . . . . . . 2:377, 426
16:13-14 . . . . . . . 2:646
16:14 . . . . . . . . . 2:633

## 2 CORINTHIANS

2:11 . . . . . . . . . . 2:641
3:3 . . . . . . . . . . . 1:295

4:7 . . . . . . . . . . . 1:240
4:16 . . . . . . . . . . 1:303
5. . . . . . . . . . . . . 1:204
5:1 . . . . . . . . . . . 2:346
5:14 . . . . . . . . . . 1:260
5:15 . . . . . . . . . . 1:316
5:17 . . . . . . . . . . 1:113, 212, 217
5:18-21 . . . . . . . . 1:113
5:19 . . . . . . . . . . 1:182, 189, 213
5:20 . . . . . . . . . . 2:379
5:21 . . . . . . . . . . 1:120, 122
6:2 . . . . . . . . . . . 1:117
6:3-10 . . . . . . . . 1:3
6:9 . . . . . . . . . . . 1:245
6:12 . . . . . . . . . . 2:427
8:9 . . . . . . . . . . . 1:270
10:17 . . . . . . . . . 2:458
11:13 . . . . . . . . . 2:388
11:14 . . . . . . . . . 1:240
11:29 . . . . . . . . . 1:246
12:2 . . . . . . . . . . 1:175, 315
12:7 . . . . . . . . . . 1:128
12:9 . . . . . . . . . . 1:220; 2:545, 636
12:10 . . . . . . . . . 1:200
13:11 . . . . . . . . . 2:426

## GALATIANS

1:6 . . . . . . . . . . . 1:236
1:6-7 . . . . . . . . . 1:104, 104
1:8-9 . . . . . . . . . 1:304, 312
1:23 . . . . . . . . . . 2:381
2:20 . . . . . . . . . . 1:108, 187, 204
3:1 . . . . . . . . . . . 1:201, 235, 243, 287
3:2-5 . . . . . . . . . 1:120
3:13 . . . . . . . . . . 1:332; 2:621
3:22 . . . . . . . . . . 1:142, 144, 145, 175, 245, 251
3:24 . . . . . . . . . . 1:184, 264, 283
4:14 . . . . . . . . . . 2:537
4:15 . . . . . . . . . . 2:353, 464
4:17 . . . . . . . . . . 1:248
4:29 . . . . . . . . . . 1:223
5:1 . . . . . . . . . . . 1:113
5:6 . . . . . . . . . . . 1:280
5:12 . . . . . . . . . . 1:234
6:17 . . . . . . . . . . 2:486

## EPHESIANS

1 . . . . . . . . . . . . . 1:147
1:17 . . . . . . . . . . 1:257
2:2 . . . . . . . . . . . 1:190
3:18-19 . . . . . . . . 2:427
3:20 . . . . . . . . . . 1:111
4:22-24 . . . . . . . . 1:3
4:32 . . . . . . . . . . 2:366
5:14 . . . . . . . . . . 1:333
5:19 . . . . . . . . . . 1:333
6:10 . . . . . . . . . . 1:303
6:11-17 . . . . . . . . 1:301; 2:593, 640, 641
6:16 . . . . . . . . . . 2:635
6:16-17 . . . . . . . . 2:645
6:17 . . . . . . . . . . 1:182, 211, 262, 288; 2:389, 437, 595

## PHILIPPIANS

1:23 . . . . . . . . . . 1:207, 306; 2:417
1:25 . . . . . . . . . . 1:238
1:27 . . . . . . . . . . 2:342, 558, 616, 641
2:5 . . . . . . . . . . . 1:213
2:12 . . . . . . . . . . 1:207, 259
2:12-13 . . . . . . . . 2:576
2:16 . . . . . . . . . . 1:272; 2:434
2:24 . . . . . . . . . . 1:117
3:8 . . . . . . . . . . . 2:613
3:8-9 . . . . . . . . . 2:521
3:9 . . . . . . . . . . . 2:391
3:9-10 . . . . . . . . 1:234
3:10 . . . . . . . . . . 2:425
3:14 . . . . . . . . . . 1:298
4:13 . . . . . . . . . . 1:10
4:32 . . . . . . . . . . 2:366

## COLOSSIANS

1:26-27 . . . . . . . . 1:114
2:4 . . . . . . . . . . . 1:240
3:1 . . . . . . . . . . . 2:456, 568
3:16 . . . . . . . . . . 2:420
4:2-17 . . . . . . . . 1:2

## 1 THESSALONIANS

1:5 . . . . . . . . . . . 1:141; 2:378, 389
1:6 . . . . . . . . . . . 2:377

4:1 . . . . . . . . . . . 2:627
4:16 . . . . . . . . . . 2:511
4:17 . . . . . . . . . . 2:410, 428
5:22 . . . . . . . . . . 2:499
5:23 . . . . . . . . . . 2:368

## 2 THESSALONIANS

1:11-12 . . . . . . . . 1:126
2:7 . . . . . . . . . . . 1:211
2:12 . . . . . . . . . . 1:308

## 1 TIMOTHY

1:15 . . . . . . . . . . 1:298, 314; 2:520, 537
2:5 . . . . . . . . . . . 1:330
2:12 . . . . . . . . . . 2:342
4:9-10 . . . . . . . . . 2:344
4:10 . . . . . . . . . . 1:323
5:6 . . . . . . . . . . . 1:328
5:19 . . . . . . . . . . 1:151
6:11-12 . . . . . . . . 1:8
6:12 . . . . . . . . . . 1:219

## 2 TIMOTHY

1:7 . . . . . . . . . . . 1:227; 2:457
1:7-12 . . . . . . . . . 1:9
2:1-12 . . . . . . . . . 1:10
2:9 . . . . . . . . . . . 1:17
2:15 . . . . . . . . . . 1:247
2:24 . . . . . . . . . . 1:172
3:1-16 . . . . . . . . . 1:13
3:5 . . . . . . . . . . . 1:14, 239, 265
4:1-18 . . . . . . . . . 1:15
4:2 . . . . . . . . . . . 2:356
4:3 . . . . . . . . . . . 2:638
4:7 . . . . . . . . . . . 2:418, 557, 564
4:10 . . . . . . . . . . 2:553
4:17 . . . . . . . . . . 1:12

## TITUS

2:10 . . . . . . . . . . 2:437
2:11 . . . . . . . . . . 1:284, 319; 2:629, 638
2:14 . . . . . . . . . . 1:137

(Titus—*continued.*)
3:5 . . . . . . . . . . . 1:126
3:8 . . . . . . . . . . . 1:152, 164

## PHILEMON

1 . . . . . . . . . . . . . 1:230

## HEBREWS

4:1 . . . . . . . . . . . 1:270
4:10 . . . . . . . . . . 2:466, 466
4:11 . . . . . . . . . . 1:305
4:12 . . . . . . . . . . 1:196, 312; 2:370, 391, 469, 489, 637, 642
4:16 . . . . . . . . . . 2:609, 613
6 . . . . . . . . . . . . . 1:292
6:5 . . . . . . . . . . . 2:412, 471
6:12 . . . . . . . . . . 2:417
9:12 . . . . . . . . . . 2:456
10:24 . . . . . . . . . 2:583
11 . . . . . . . . . . . . 1:8
11:1 . . . . . . . . . . 1:208
11:4 . . . . . . . . . . 1:299
11:6 . . . . . . . . . . 1:259
11:7 . . . . . . . . . . 2:486
11:34 . . . . . . . . . 1:136
11:38 . . . . . . . . . 1:20; 2:608
12:1 . . . . . . . . . . 2:446, 613
12:2 . . . . . . . . . . 2:337
12:12 . . . . . . . . . 2:437
12:15 . . . . . . . . . 2:404
12:18 . . . . . . . . . 1:251
12:22 . . . . . . . . . 2:387
12:24 . . . . . . . . . 2:536
13:8 . . . . . . . . . . 2:414, 483, 577
13:20 . . . . . . . . . 1:250

## JAMES

1:12 . . . . . . . . . . 2:589
2:5 . . . . . . . . . . . 1:123
2:20-26 . . . . . . . . 1:152

## 1 PETER

1:3-5 . . . . . . . . . . 1:116

1:5 . . . . . . . . . . . 2:631
1:8 . . . . . . . . . . . 1:299
2:9 . . . . . . . . . . . 1:256
2:12 . . . . . . . . . . 2:440, 454, 608
2:17 . . . . . . . . . . 2:449
2:21 . . . . . . . . . . 2:430
3:9 . . . . . . . . . . . 1:24
3:16 . . . . . . . . . . 1:167
4:3 . . . . . . . . . . . 1:328
4:7 . . . . . . . . . . . 2:445, 572, 573
5:8 . . . . . . . . . . . 1:200

## 2 PETER

1:1 . . . . . . . . . . . 1:185
1:4 . . . . . . . . . . . 1:273
2:2 . . . . . . . . . . . 2:486
2:9 . . . . . . . . . . 1:283
3:9 . . . . . . . . . . . 1:283
3:12 . . . . . . . . . . 2:502
3:14 . . . . . . . . . . 2:448

## 1 JOHN

1:3 . . . . . . . . . . . 2:421
1:9 . . . . . . . . . . . 1:247
2:1 . . . . . . . . . . . 1:285; 2:407, 523
3:14 . . . . . . . . . . 1:112, 137, 143, 145, 146, 147, 149, 151, 152, 154, 155,
                        159, 169
4:1 . . . . . . . . . . . 1:174, 257; 2:641
4:4 . . . . . . . . . . . 2:482
5:6 . . . . . . . . . . . 2:425, 439
5:6-8 . . . . . . . . . 2:593
5:16 . . . . . . . . . . 2:419

## JUDE

1:24 . . . . . . . . . . 2:483

## REVELATION

1:7 . . . . . . . . . . . 2:614
2:1-7 . . . . . . . . . 2:390
2:4 . . . . . . . . . . . 2:468
2:5 . . . . . . . . . . . 2:623
2:6 . . . . . . . . . . . 2:649

(Revelation—*continued.*)
2:9 . . . . . . . . . . . . 2:433
2:10 . . . . . . . . . . 1:217; 2:367, 377, 572, 613
2:13 . . . . . . . . . . 2:413
2:24 . . . . . . . . . . 1:295
2:25 . . . . . . . . . . 2:353, 438
3:2, 3 . . . . . . . . . 2:457
3:3 . . . . . . . . . . . 1:xx; 2:612
3:8 . . . . . . . . . . . 2:369
3:9 . . . . . . . . . . . 2:433
3:10 . . . . . . . . . . 2:449
3:14-22 . . . . . . . 1:333; 2:373
3:20 . . . . . . . . . . 1:107; 2:459, 552, 577, 612
4. . . . . . . . . . . . . 2:502
4:1 . . . . . . . . . . . 1:281; 2:417
6:9 . . . . . . . . . . . 2:374
7:9 . . . . . . . . . . . 2:472
7:14 . . . . . . . . . . 2:416, 423, 426, 428, 434, 471, 514, 572, 596
7:17 . . . . . . . . . . 2:417
10:7 . . . . . . . . . . 2:588
12:9 . . . . . . . . . . 2:493
12:10 . . . . . . . . . 2:610
14:13 . . . . . . . . . 2:454
16:15 . . . . . . . . . 2:626
16:18 . . . . . . . . . 1:299
19:10 . . . . . . . . . 1:300
20:11 . . . . . . . . . 2:525
21. . . . . . . . . . . . 2:434, 437, 476
21:4 . . . . . . . . . . 2:417
22:12 . . . . . . . . . 1:327
22:17 . . . . . . . . . 1:118; 2:371, 378, 418, 452, 471, 525
22:20 . . . . . . . . . 1:305, 312; 2:338, 381

LaVergne, TN USA
07 April 2010
178462LV00003B/72/P